IMAGINING TIBET

IMAGINING TIBET

Perceptions, Projections, & Fantasies

edited by
Thierry Dodin & Heinz Räther

WISDOM PUBLICATIONS • BOSTON

Wisdom Publications, Inc.
199 Elm Street
Somerville MA 02144 USA
www.wisdompubs.org

Most of the essays in this book are based on papers presented at the International Symposium *Mythos Tibet* held in Bonn, Germany, in May 1996.
This symposium was organized by the editors of this book in collaboration
with the Art and Exhibition Hall of the Federal Republic of Germany in Bonn.

Library of Congress Cataloging-in-Publication Data
Imagining Tibet : perceptions, projections, and fantasies /
  edited by Thierry Dodin and Heinz Räther.
     p.   cm.
  Includes bibliographical references and index.
  ISBN 0-86171-191-2 (alk. paper)
  1. Tibet (China)—Congresses. I. Dodin, Thierry.
  II. Räther, Heinz.
  DS785.A1 I45 2001
  951'.5—dc21   2001026030

ISBN 0-86171-192-2
06 05 04 03 02   6   5   4   3   2

Design by: Gopa & Ted2. Set in Sabon 10.25/14.5
Cover painting: Roerich, Nicholas (1874–1947) *Tibet*
© Nicholas Roerich Museum, New York, New York.
Used with permission.

Printed in the United States of America.

CONTENTS

FOREWORD

EVER SINCE European power encroached on the foothills of the Himalayas, Tibet, a hidden kingdom behind snowcapped mountains, has excited the Western imagination. For decades, travelers, explorers, missionaries, soldiers, scholars, and colonial officers have tried to unveil and reveal this hidden land. Tibet became a source of adventure and mystery in a world where there was little magic and mystery. Everything about Tibet came to be seen as esoteric and extraordinary.

This book examines the sources of this fascination in the West and more recently in China, where Tibet is increasingly perceived as an alluring "national minority region." China now promotes Tibet as an exotic holiday destination, appropriating the Shangri-la imagery familiar to Western readers of James Hilton's *Lost Horizon,* Lobsang Rampa's *Third Eye,* and color travelogues on Buddhist hermits and the Tibetan landscape. Hip Chinese stockbrokers go to Lhasa for vacation, young Chinese artists and intellectuals go to Tibet to find inspiration and adventure, to break free of family ties, and to discover themselves in much the same way as the Western hippies who traveled to India in the 1960s.

Compared to Xinjiang, a "national minority" region whose strategic and political significance is equivalent in Beijing's eyes, Tibet receives disporportionately more attention in Western media and popular culture, from comic books to video games, such as *Tomb Raider,* that draw on images of Tibet. The authors in this collection show how

Tibet's religion, art, and political realities are represented by others. This important book should be read by everyone interested in the origin and subtext of such fascination and imagery.

Tsering Shakya
School of Oriental and African Studies
University of London

SCARCELY HAS A REGION captured the imagination as much as Tibet. Even before naming Tibet, the West generated myths about gold-digging ants and amazon nations in the highlands of Inner Asia. Is Tibet, then, a magical land where anything is possible?

With the first concrete reports from the Tibetan plateau, the West learned of a theocracy that—depending on the attitude of the reporter—was either guided by an enlightened priest or held its pagan population in deliberate blindness. One could allegedly find great riches in its rivers, and an overland route from British India to China was to fill the coffers of the British East India Company. Is Tibet a land of undreamed riches?

Tibet and its capital, Lhasa, later became the long-sought Shangri-la of the world's spiritual seekers, a place where one might find the ideal society, a guarantee of eternal happiness, long life, and spiritual well-being. Is Tibet a land of enlightened teachers?

Meanwhile, Chinese Communism fostered opposite images: Corrupt and brutal priests and feudal lords supposedly subjugated Tibet and held the people in a state of constant anxiety and fear. As the story goes, this barbarism came to an end only with the occupation of Tibet by the Chinese People's Liberation Army. Was Tibet a theocratic, feudal tyranny?

The Western image of Tibet changed dramatically with the flight of one hundred thousand Tibetans to India and Nepal under the leadership of the Fourteenth Dalai Lama. Shocked by the violent destruction of an old and venerable culture by a spiritually bereft communism, the world began to offer Tibetans both sympathy and support. At this time, the sudden accessibility of Tibetan Buddhism and its high-ranking representatives fueled the desire for the salvific powers that this rich religious tradition supposedly possessed.

Today, many people all over the world are conscious of Tibet as never before, thanks to numerous books, newspaper stories, and television reports. The images presented in the media, however, seem to echo the images of Tibet formed earlier—even scientific discussions of Tibet have not escaped prejudiced, one-sided projections.

The present volume represents the first comprehensive attempt to explore the various manifestations of our images of Tibet in their aesthetic, political, and intellectual-historical dimensions. This volume emerged to a large extent from a May 1996 symposium that accompanied the opening of the exhibition "Wisdom and Compassion: One Thousand Years of Tibetan Buddhist Art." The symposium was organized by the Art and Exhibition Hall of the Federal Republic of Germany and by the Institute of Central Asian Studies of the University of Bonn. Internationally recognized scholars were invited to present their experiences and research on this topic.

Part One of this book traces the roots and the historical development of images of Tibet. Part Two investigates a number of aspects of these images against the backdrop provided by their social, political, and ideological contexts. The authors in Part Three have taken it upon themselves to comment on various aspects of Tibetan culture in relation to our images of Tibet.

The present book and the symposium upon which it is based would not have been possible without the help of several people and institutions. The editors would like to thank the German Research Council (DFG) for their financial support of the symposium; the Institute of Central Asian Studies at the University of Bonn—especially its director, Professor Michael Weiers—for its support; the Art and Exhibition Hall of the Federal Republic of Germany for making the symposium possible and for ceding the copyrights of many of the contributions to the editors; our friends and colleagues Hanna Schneider, Isrun Engelhardt, John Bray, Toni Huber, and Robert Horres for their valuable help. The

English edition of this book would not have materialized without the manifold efforts of Wisdom Publications, in particular E. Gene Smith and David Kittelstrom. Last but not least, we would like to thank the many authors who have contributed to the present volume and ultimately bore the work's greatest burden.

PART ONE
Missionaries and Scholars

ALPHABETUM

MISSIONUM APOSTOLICARUM
COMMODO EDITUM.

QUA DE VARIO LITTERARUM AC REGIONIS NOMINE , GENTIS ORIGINE
MORIBUS , SUPERSTITIONE , AC MANICHAEISMO FUSE DISSERITUR.

BEAUSOBRII CALUMNIÆ IN SANCTUM AUGUSTINUM,
ALIOSQUE ECCLESIÆ PATRES REFUTANTUR.

STUDIO ET LABORE

EREMITÆ AUGUSTINIANI.

TYPIS SACRÆ CONGREGATIONIS DE PROPAGANDA FIDE.

SUPERIORUM FACULTATE.

Fig. 1 Title page from *Alphabetum Tibetanum* 1762

The Image of Tibet in the West before the Nineteenth Century

Rudolf Kaschewsky

IF WE WISH TO TRACE the beginnings of the myth of Tibet, we need to know exactly what is meant by the "myth of Tibet," so that we can then determine whether and where this phenomenon can be found in earlier times. Since our observations are still young, we are unable to build upon earlier investigations and must attempt to fathom how Tibet occupied the imaginations of people in the past and, above all, their motives for being so occupied.

The oldest evidence often has the most lasting effect upon later developments, despite or perhaps because of the intervening years. Thus, we should not be afraid to venture as far into the past as possible. Many name Herodotus (died 425 B.C.E.)—whose *Histories apodeixis* gave all historical endeavor its documentary method—as the oldest witness to legendary beliefs about Tibet.[1] In the third book of his work he treats the "most extreme lands of the earth" and mentions tribes who live north of the (other) Indians. Near these tribes live strange giant ants that dig up sand containing gold while building their underground homes. Arriving in the morning, gold seekers speedily bag up as much sand as possible before stealing away, since the giant ants can supposedly smell men and pursue them. Here one thinks of the Sanskrit word *pipīlaka*, an adjective whose root means "ant." When this adjective is nominalized, it signifies indeed a special kind of gold. Oral traditions in Tibet tell of similar gold-digging ants, as do both Ladakhi tales and Tibetan chronicles.[2] Is it any wonder that a German monograph that deals with these legends appeared as early as 1873?[3]

Although we find no name that identifies Tibet in Herodotus, the terms *Hai Bautai* and *Ho Bautisos,* respectively the names of a tribe and a river in Tibet, appear in the writings of Klaudios Ptolemaeus (90–180 C.E.). This geographer, who compiled his *Geografike hyphegesis* from older geographies, was authoritative well into the sixteenth century.[4] No less than Erasmus of Rotterdam saw to a new edition of this work in 1533. There is evidence that the name *Bautai* is derived from the Indian *Bhota,* the latter word stemming from *bod,* the proper name of Tibetans from antiquity. The river Bautisos might be the Tsangpo, the main river of Central Tibet. Ptolemy seems to have been familiar with Tibetan customs, although we are yet to determine what cultures and languages mediated such knowledge. He mentions a copper-colored mountain located in the Malaya mountain range, and this mountain corresponds in every detail to Padmasambhava's "copper-colored mountain palace" *(zangs mdog dpal gyi ri).*[5]

Let us turn away from these ancient sources to a somewhat closer past, since a seamless pursuit of our theme across each century is impossible. We will skip over the Mongolian missions of Pope Innocent IV and King Ludwig IX as well as the journeys of the Franciscan monk Odorico de Pordenone and Marco Polo. Each makes passing mention of Lamaism, having had limited contact with Mongols. Odorico, however, did report that the name of the highest lama sounds in Tibetan much like *papa,* the Latin term for *pope (id est papa in lingua sua)!*[6] Presumably he meant the famous 'Phags-pa Lama, who stood in the highest regard in the court of Khubilai Khan during the thirteenth century. Later we will return to this congruence between Christian and Tibetan data.

The Portuguese Jesuit António de Andrade represents a real breakthrough after the rather vague and indirect references of antiquity and the Middle Ages. De Andrade's work *The New Discoveries of the Great Cathay or of the Tibetan Kingdom* appeared in a Portuguese edition in 1626 in Lisbon. De Andrade's report was translated into Spanish (in the same year 1626), Italian, French, and German in 1627. (The last was published in Augsburg). Even Flemish and Polish editions appeared within a short time. A second report from de Andrade appeared in 1628, yet again to be translated numerous times.[7]

De Andrade might rightly be called the first European who ever entered Tibet. Born in 1580, he joined the Jesuits at the age of sixteen and was ordered to Goa when he was twenty. In 1624, he accompanied the Mogul king Jahangir to Delhi, where he joined a caravan heading northwest to an almost completely unknown area where Christian communities were thought to exist. He traveled across Srinagar and Garhwal, through the Alakhnanda Valley, over Badrinath and the 5,450-meter Mana Pass to Tsabrang in western Tibet.

His travel report bears the date of May 16, 1624 and includes fifteen double-sided, closely written folios. Besides typical journal entries, his report contains a short description of western Tibet and its inhabitants. The piety of the Tibetans is emphasized, since they wore small amulets and strictly observed morning and evening prayers. De Andrade mentions the numerous lamas, whom he calls priests, some of whom live in monasteries and others in their own houses. He especially stresses their celibacy, their vows of poverty, and the times of day when they pray. He writes:

> They discharge the largest part of the day with prayer, which they do at least two hours in the morning and just as long in the evening. They sing like us in a quiet tone, just as we sing the cantus firmus.... The lamas seem to me a very gentle people. One scarcely hears a rude word even from a layman.... They even have houses of prayer similar to our own: everything is very clean, and paintings adorn the ceilings and walls....: In Tsabrang, we saw the depiction of a female deity sitting with folded hands, and it was said that she was the mother of God.[8]

The latter was possibly an iconographic representation of Prajñā-pāramitā, the Perfection of Wisdom, who is often understood to be the mother of all buddhas: *dus gsum gyi rgyal ba thams cad skyed pa byed pa'i yum* ("Mother, who has given birth to all buddhas of the three epochs"). De Andrade opines that the Tibetans even had an idea of a son of god who had become human (probably the *nirmāṇakāya*), as well as the notion of the Most Holy Trinity, the Three Jewels *(dkon mchog gsum)*. He mentions the practice of confession and the use of holy water, with which an absolution is undertaken, and which one might consider a sort of baptism. He even describes the expulsion of evil spirits on the first day of the month, although in all likelihood he is referring to the *dgu gtor* ritual, which actually occurs on the twenty-ninth day of the twelfth month.

Are these accounts the beginning of the myth of Tibet? In any case, they were quite sensational and eagerly devoured at the time. When the initial euphoria finally died down and when the representatives of British India initiated contact with Tibet, voices critical of de Andrade were first heard. Steeped in the Enlightenment, the authors of the *Histoire universelle des voyages* of 1749 shrugged off de Andrade's accounts, along with those of Marco Polo and Odorico, as lies and fantastic inventions. De Andrade, who had been in the extreme western part of Tibet, had witnessed rites and customs of the pre-Buddhist Bon religion. These ancient rites were possibly no longer observed in central Tibet, which for its part was increasingly visited by British emissaries who mentioned nothing of the sort.

Hugues Didier, an expert of Romance studies and connoisseur of Portuguese literature, has traced the reception and the continuing effects of de Andrade's accounts in his *Antonio de Andrade à l'origine de la tibétophilie européenne.*[9] Didier refers to the "edifying literature" of this epoch, a genre that often used reports from Tibet. One example is the *Ars moriendi* of Eusebio Nieremberg, which appeared in 1631 in Lyon and used the *sacerdotes Tibetensium* as its paradigm. Having rosaries made of bone and drinking out of bowls made from skullcaps kept death not at bay but constantly before one's eyes. Thus the taste of this-worldliness could be lessened *(ut rerum huius vitae gustum imminuerent)*, and one could apply an antidote to the sins and passions of the flesh *(antidotum...adversus vitia carnisque passiones)*. These practices were not thought barbaric at all, but were instead assumed to be true philosophy *(certe non barbara, sed culta philosophia est)*.

Whenever he speaks of the emerging European "Tibetophilia," Didier makes an important point, when mentioning the newly arising *tibétophilie européenne,* which corresponds to our theme of the myth of Tibet. This tibetophilia is founded, he says, upon two poles: On the one hand, Tibet is the least accessible, most mysterious, and most foreign country of Asia; on the other hand, Tibet is paradoxically the only Asian culture with whom Europeans can identify so much that they seem suprisingly intimate and related—truly a sort of *coincidentia oppositorum!* Didier even goes so far as to see an archetype for the European collective unconscious in this early tibetophilia: the discovery of the "intimate unknown" or the "foreign brother." This impression grows stronger when one compares the sympathy and esteem shown so clearly by de Andrade to Tibetans with his noticeable contempt for both Muslims (whom he calls Mouros) and Hindus. When the Raja of Srinagar threatens to hinder de Andrade's trip to Tibet, the missionary writes in his journal: "Now that we have taken so much sorrow upon ourselves, our hopes are about to be dashed. We shall never see the land which is worth more to us than the promised land *(terra, que pera nós era de mais valia que a de Promissâo)*." *Terra promissionis,* often mistranslated as "praised land," initially signified Palestine, which God had promised to the patriarchs and their descendants, but ultimately refers to the heavenly Jerusalem (Genesis); this conception was later taken up by St. Paul.[10]

Indeed, de Andrade's mission to Tibet was considered a quasi-holy act, following up on the promise made in the eighteenth chapter of the Prophet Isaiah, which describes the conversion of a remote, but powerful, people on Mount Zion at the end of time.[11] Zion was considered traditionally as center of the universe (see e.g., the hymnic description in Isaiah 2.2–5). De Andrade alludes to this sense of familiarity vis-à-vis Tibet in the title of his account: *Novo descobrimento,* the "new discovery of Tibet"; from this Didier concludes that de Andrade saw his trip to Tibet not as a discovery, but as a *re*discovery, the rediscovery of a lost friend or brother, so to speak.[12] This hidden solidarity was strengthened by the antipathy felt by both toward Islam; de Andrade even was suspicious of his Persian (Islamic) translator, because he feared that he, in all cases when similarities between Christianity and Buddhism were mentioned, might have translated incompletely or even in a misleading way.[13]

The faraway and at the same time intimate friend was considered very powerful and influential—perhaps the figure of the legendary "Prester John" played a role, whose empire, if we are correct, was first

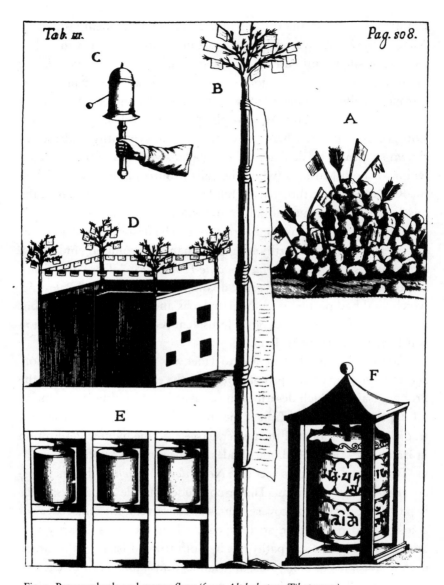

Fig. 2 Prayer wheels and prayer flags (from *Alphabetum Tibetanum*)

mentioned in Occidental literature with Otto von Freisingen around the middle of the twelfth century.[14] In the letters of António de Andrade and also in a contract with the King of Guge (western Tibet), Tibet is always called *Reyno de Potente,* which was translated and taken up in contemporary literature as "The Powerful," "Le Puissant," "Das Mächtige." The relevant commentaries consider the word *potente* a mere distortion of the Indian *bhoṭānta,* which could be "Tibet." But another interpretation might be possible: Quite often Tibetan dignitaries—including the Dalai Lama—are referred to as Gyalwang (Tib. *rgyal dbang)*; it could be that de Andrade understood *rgyal* as *rgyal po* "king" and *dbang* as *dbang po* "powerful," so that the expression *Reyno Potente* could also be interpreted as "Powerful King(dom)."

Whether the similarities between Christian and Buddhist items, which the missionaries like to emphasize so much, are actually based on historic fact is another question. Anyhow, it can be assumed that there was real contact between Tibet and Nestorian Christianity. A letter from the Syrian patriarch Timotheus I from 795 C.E. indicates such contact. In the letter, the patriarch reports that he appointed a metropolitan (archbishop) for the realm of Turkey *(bêth turkayê)* and was about to do the same for Tibet *(bêth tûptayê).* Inscriptions on crosses and references in Tibetan texts from Dunhuang also indicate this connection.[15] The Nestorian patriarch's proclamation is not improbable in so far as the Tibetan empire expanded greatly during the last years of the eighth century and came into direct contact with previously distant neighbors, especially the Turks of Kashgar; the latter doubtless had a Nestorian bishop at that time. De Andrade's belief, already quite widespread at the time, that Tibet had early contact with Christianity is thus not entirely enveloped in myth.

It is not too much to claim that de Andrade and the reception given to his reports in the first third of the seventeenth century are key factors in the further cultivation of the myth of Tibet in Europe. In this context, it is worth mentioning another missionary, the Italian Jesuit Ippolito Desideri (1684–1733), who spent time in Tibet about a century after de Andrade and who left behind extremely valuable records. Desideri's magnum opus, written in the years 1712–33, is his *Relazione e notizie historiche del Thibet e memorie de' viaggi e missioni ivi fatte,* of which the second and third parts ("A Report on Nature, Dress, and Government of Tibet" and "On the False Sect of the Highly Curious Religion Observed in Tibet") are most relevant for our purposes.[16] The conviction that he was dealing ultimately with a "false sect" and a "highly curious religion" did not stop Desideri from striving to produce an appropriate interpretation of Tibetan culture. His explanation of the famous formula *Oṃ maṇi padme huṃ,* for example, is quoted here word for word, since it may mark the memorable beginning of Tibetology in the West.[17] Desideri writes:

> The word *oṃ* is not a meaningful term *(termine significativo)* but instead a sort of decoration at the beginning of a magical formula. The second word *mani* means "jewel," for example, pearl, diamond, or some other sort of gemstone. The third word *peme* is actually composed of two words, namely *pema* and *e. Pema* means a flower that grows in water (in Hindustani *kamal phul*). The word *e* is an invocation *(particola d'appellazione o d'invocazione)* like our "O" and forms a kind of vocative. The last word *hum* is not really a meaningful term either, but is a decorative epithet, the final syllable of this magical formula.

Desideri correctly explains this mantra as an invocation of the bodhisattva Avalokiteśvara. In this context, it is important that *peme* is interpreted as a vocative. More recent research[18] and other writings already cited here have concluded that this is not a locative, as assumed in the majority of translations like "jewel in the lotus," but rather a (formally feminine) vocative.[19] Thus, the first European interpretation of this formula proves to be the correct one. In addition to his studies of relevant texts like the *Bodhicaryāvatāra* and Tsongkhapa's *Lam rim chen mo,* Desideri owes his precise knowledge to long discussions with educated lamas, especially in the sanctuary of Ramoche and in Sera Monastery.

Desideri, who likely had not yet been exposed to Buddhism in India, his first stop, chronicles the development of Buddhism in Tibet precisely, beginning with the mission to Tibet by Urgyan (that is, Padmasambhava) and with its blossoming under the early kings. He also elucidates the doctrine of emptiness, the core concept of Buddhist philosophy. He was quite familiar with the theory of the soul's transmigration and the rebirth of beings in the cycle of existence. He also knew about the difference between Hinayāna and Mahāyāna, and that the latter, the only type of Buddhism in Tibet, believed in bodhisattvas,

Fig. 3 Tibetans und Tibetan deities (from *Alphabetum Tibetanum*)

that is, figures of redemption who have already attained the level of a buddha but who enter again into the cycle of existence on account of their compassion for the beings who are still suffering. Desideri names them *illuminati* (the "illuminated ones"), and *personificazioni della compassione e della misericordia* ("personifications of compassion and mercy"). As the highest of such beings, Desideri counts Avalokiteśvara, whose transcendental aspect embodied in the Panchen Lama of Tashi-lhunpo Monastery is Amitāyus (whose name *Tshe dpag med* he translates well as *vita infinita*).

Desideri sees two primary ways to escape the cycle of suffering, namely the religious-moral path and the speculative-philosophical path, both of which must be combined. In the former, one extinguishes the passions, practices virtue, and takes refuge in the buddhas. In the latter, one gains the higher insight that nothing has its own substance. In light of the similarities Desideri saw with his own religion, such as the highly developed scholasticism and deeply rooted ritualism, one question grew more and more important for him in view of the Tibetans' profound piety: *La mancanza di un fede in Dio.* How is it that their piety has not led them to belief in God? Desideri quickly discovered that the numerous gods are worshiped with complicated rituals had nothing to do with an actual belief in God. He thought that probably the Tibetans consistently rejected all belief in deities with such vehemence because they wanted at all costs to avoid the cult of any sort of anthropomorphic, superficial, or immoral gods, of which there are such a large number in other regions of Asia! So he asked further: Are the Tibetans atheists? Theoretically yes, but practically and implicitly they did indeed venerate God, since they often praised his attributes, such as omniscience and mercy. They also believed in an immortal soul—otherwise how could they believe in rebirth? What also impressed him were the monks' high degree of discipline and the ascetics' nobility, since both lived in constant contemplation and with an extreme lack of life's necessities.

After much reflection, Desideri came up with an answer: It was pleasing to God to let man absorb enlightenment and religious inspiration in a natural state, outside of the range of direct biblical revelation. It is exactly these qualities of enlightenment and inspiration that allow man not only to keep himself from sin, but also to arrive at a love of the good, to an acceptance of virtue, and so forth. Here Desideri sees confirmation of the Holy Ghost's effect as well as of the doctrine of the dispersed seeds of God *(lógos spermatikós)* espoused by the fathers of the Church.

For Desideri, the methods for determining the reincarnation of high lamas were indeed uncanny. He could not help but be amazed when he witnessed the inexplicable wonders at play when a newborn child repeatedly reached for the objects of a deceased lama or used words in a language that he had never learned. He never assumed deceptive manipulations, but he did ask himself whether the Devil *(diabolos)*, that great confuser, could have had a hand in the matter.

Desideri, willing to make sacrifices and possessed with fervor, felt it was his personal duty to lead the Tibetans, already so infused with holiness, to the Christian holy path. He devoted himself to investigating what of Tibetan Buddhism was compatible with Christianity and what was not. He tried to refute instances of the latter with scholastic logic. His profound theological knowledge, especially of the *Summa Theologiae* of St. Thomas Aquinas, was of great use to him, as was his familiarity with Buddhist doctrine and dialectics.

Desideri's investigations and reflections resulted in several works in Tibetan that he composed himself.[20] He knew that he could not simply make edifying didactic remarks, as he had originally planned, and instead saw the necessity of a systematic presentation. In the short time from November 28, 1717 until June 21, 1718, he composed in Tibetan a work with the title *Byung khungs (Concerning the Origin of Things),* which he constructed in the form of a Socratic dialogue. There he writes: "My doctrine is identical with yours when dealing with the nature of things. All things are doubtlessly empty of autonomy, that is, they are all dependent, neither arising nor caused by themselves." And then he continues:

Thus it is logically necessary to assert a first cause, which itself is independent and is the reason for all being. Indeed, from the proposition 'dependent, without having its own substance,' it follows that there must also be a being whom these negative attributes do not touch, since just as it makes sense to speak of something wet only if there is also something dry, one can only speak of something empty, dependent, and determined, if there is also a non-empty, independent being, not determined by anything else. Because all things are empty, dependent, and determined, etc., that other being which is not empty, independent, and not determined must be searched for not within things but outside them.[21]

Further Tibetan writings by Desideri, which bear such ringing titles as *sNying po (The Essence)* and *Tho rangs (The Morning Dawn),* demonstrate Christian doctrine and refute Buddhist teachings. As an author, he names himself *mGo dkar gyi bla ma,* the "lama with the white head."

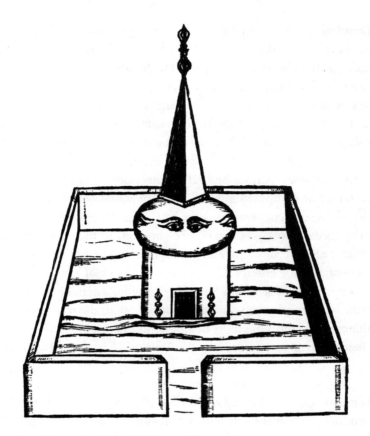

Fig. 4 Stupa illustration (from *Alphabetum Tibetanum*)

Desideri quotes extensively from Buddhist texts, both canonical and noncanonical. He should not simply be seen as the first Tibetologist: He was also the first to single-handedly begin a reasonable debate with Tibetan Buddhism. Today's endeavors of this sort, mostly resorting to platitudes like "both religions are for peace" or "both religions lead to inner contemplation," do not compare.

In noticeable contrast to the high regard earned by de Andrade's accounts after their publication, Desideri's work remained hidden for quite some time. Two of his first letters appeared in 1722 in a French translation (without his consent, he later emphasized).[22] His meaty report, the *Relazione*, was missing for a century and a half and only discovered in 1875 in Pistoia by Carlo Puini, who then saw to publishing the first (incomplete) edition.[23]

We should also mention the monumental *Alphabetum Tibetanum* by the scholarly Augustinian monk Antonius Georgius. This work, appearing in 1763 in Rome, collected facts and myths about Tibet, offering information about its religion and history in over a thousand pages.[24] In the second half of the eighteenth century, a large number of such *alphabeta* were produced by the Pontifical Institute of Missions, the so-called *Propaganda Fide*. The purpose of these encyclopedic texts was to describe various Asiatic languages and writings. In the case of Tibet, however, the linguistic section was supplemented by a much larger and more comprehensive section containing history, myth, and speculation.

After investing a lot of energy into trying to determine the etymology for the name "Tibet," the book investigates the birth of the Buddha *Sha kya thub pa (Xaca Tuba)* according to Tibetan sources. The book considers the names of various Indian gods, and sketches the mythical connections with Manichaeism and earlier Asiatic traditions. One particular chapter (no. 70), for example, is titled *Hopame (Od dpag med) Tibetanorum idem ac Splenditenens Manichaeorum*. It argues various issues such as the mixture of religions *(Commixtio Christianae religionis cum Paganorum superstitione semper monstra gignit)*, and the famous prayer formula *Hommenipemehum (Oṃ maṇi padme huṃ)*. It also asks iconographic questions about the images of Avalokiteśvara, such as *Cenresi (sPyan ras gzigs) album florem Pema in dextera tenet. Cur?* It even discusses the Buddhist notion of emptiness: *Quod nos caelum Vacuum Tibetani appellant* (chap. 71–72) and deals with cosmology (chap. 75ff.)! The Buddhist conception of "sacrifice" *(sacrificii Tibetanorum materies et ritus*, chap. 84) is compared with the Manichaean and Christian conception. It contrasts Buddhist and Manichaean understanding of metempsychosis, with special attention given to the five realms of existence into which one might be reborn: gods, demigods *(lha ma yin, semideorum)*, humans, hungry ghosts *(yi dvags, tantalorum)*, and animals. The cause of all these is the law of karma *(fatum)*, which stems from earlier deeds *(ex demeritis praecedentibus*, chap. 95).

Fig. 5 Procession of monks, probably on the occasion of a new year festival
(from *Alphabetum Tibetanum*)

It names Mañjuśrī *(Giamjang)*, Vajrapāni *(Cihana Torcéh)*, and Avalokiteśvara *(Cenresi)* as the Tibetan trinity. Of further interest are quotes
about the Buddha from Church fathers such as Clement of Alexandria
and Jerome (chap. 125) and some major Tibetan monastic academies
(chapt. 140).

The work's second part, which was later also published separately,
describes the writing and language of Tibet and is more clearly outlined than the first part: (1) The Study of Books and Scripts; (2) Inter-
punctuation; (3) Types of Scripts; (4) Letters; (5) Accents/Phonology;
(6) Letter Sequence; (7) A Comparison with Other Published Tables of
the Tibetan Alphabet; (8) On the Origin of Letters; (9) Additional Signs;
(10) The Subscribed *Va-zur;* (11) Vowels; (12) A Comparison of
Tibetan and Latin Scripts; (13) Ligatures of letters; (14). Syllables with
Two Consonants; (15) Peculiarities of Pronunciation; (16) The Subscribed Letters; (17) Silent Letters; (18) Silent Subscribed Letters; (19)
Syllables with Three and Four Consonants; (20) Homophones; (21)
Magical Scripts; (22) Popular Scripts; and, finally, (23) Numbers. In
the appendices, there are translations of the Our Father, the Hail Mary,
and the Apostle's Creed among other things. In all of this, one sees the
theological depth with which the author conceived his work. For example, he argues that the translation of *rangtrup* (Tib. *rang grub;* Lat.
seipso existens) is "Holy Spirit," which certainly did not deny the send-
ing (Greek *ekpóreusis;* Lat. *processio)* of the Spirit from the Father, but
expressed better "God as the Most High and Truth" *(Verum et Sum-
mum esse Deum)* in Tibetan. The appendices contain additional Tibetan
and Latin documents concerning the permission for the building of
Christian churches by the Capuchins at the beginning of the eighteenth
century. Numerous contemporary illustrations, especially iconograph-
ical, complete the work.

Georgius argues in his magnum opus that Tibet, its religion, and
indeed its entire culture had been influenced by Manichaeism, which
had intermingled with the many traditions already there. The author is
not afraid, for example, of associating ancient Egyptian gods with certain deities of the Lamaist pantheon whose names by chance sound
similar. This view of Tibet as a secret abode of prolific syncretism is an
essential part of the myth of Tibet, which had one of its origins here.

We have arrived at the end of our brief passage through the centuries. In the nineteenth century, the transition to a scientific Tibetology as we now understand the term can be traced. One remarkable example is the Hungarian Csoma de Körös (1784–1842), who went east to search for the original homeland of his people and ended up in Tibet, thus standing firmly in a long line of mystical convergences. But it was this man who in 1834 produced the first grammar and dictionary of Tibetan, one whose scientific standard is still well regarded today.

Csoma de Körös was not the only one to seek his ancestors in Tibet. In Meyer's *Conversations-Lexicon* we read: "According to the theories of many historians, the human race expanded from Tibet and its neighbouring lands, not from Asia proper."[25] Perhaps here lies a key to the beginnings of the myth of Tibet?

NOTES

1 Herodotus, 1959.

2 For the entire argument, please see the third chapter of Lindegger, part 2, 1982.

3 Schiern, 1873.

4 Ptolemy, *Geographie* 6.921. East Iran and Central Asia. Greek text edited by I. Ronca.

5 Kaschewsky, 1983.

6 van den Wyngaert, 1929: 485.

7 Aschoff, 1989.

8 Ibid., 43ff.

9 Didier, 1988–92.

10 Letter to the Hebrews 11.9

11 Isaiah 18.7

12 Didier, 1988–92: 51.

13 Aschoff, 1989: 35.

14 Schmidt and Lammers, 1960: 33.

15 See Uray, 1983.

16 Petech, 1954–56.

17 Ibid., Part VI: 290f.

18 See Miller, 1963: 446–69, esp. 467f.

19 See Martin, 1987: 15. I am indebted to Gregor Verhufen for drawing my attention to this additional confirmation.

20 The Tibetan works of Desideri, long hidden in archives, have been published in recent years by G. Toscano (both in the original version and in Italian translation): 1981ff.

21 Toscano, 1984.

22 Letter from 10 April 1716 in *Lettres édifiantes et curieuses* XV (Paris, 1722). And letter from 13 February 1717 in *Bibliotheca Pistoriensis,* volume 1. (Turin, 1752), 185f.

23 Puini, 1904.

24 Giorgi, 1987.

25 Meyer, 1853: Vol. 12, 713.

Nineteenth- and Early Twentieth-Century Missionary Images of Tibet

John Bray

THE PERIOD FROM 1850 TO 1950 was the heyday of Western missions to Asia, Africa, the Americas, and the Pacific. No mission society was able to establish a lasting base in central Tibet, but several set up stations along Tibet's southern borders in Ladakh, Lahul, Kinnaur, and Kalimpong, and in the Tibetan/Chinese border regions adjoining Kham and Amdo. All these missions saw themselves as part of a missionary advance guard, preparing for the day when Tibet proper would finally be open to them.

That day never came but—perhaps paradoxically—Tibet's closure added to its mystique, implying that the country might have some special significance in the divine plan. In a famous missionary sermon in 1880, the American evangelist W. E. Blackstone speculated that Tibet might be "the last land to be opened to the Gospel…the last land before the Lord returns."[1] Blackstone's sermon was one of the inspirations behind the decision of the U.S.-based Christian and Missionary Alliance (C&MA) to establish its first stations in the northeast Tibetan/Chinese border areas. The C&MA and other missionaries who worked among Tibetans saw themselves as an elite, attempting a uniquely difficult—and perhaps uniquely important—task.

Blackstone belonged to a particular cultural and religious milieu, and there was never any one missionary image of Tibet. Individual missionaries differed in their nationality, educational background, theology, length of time spent in the region, and—above all— personality. Nevertheless, it is possible to identify certain common themes in their writing.

The first is that missionaries developed their own romantic vision of Tibet, particularly in the late nineteenth and early twentieth centuries, that differed from the myth of Shangri-la in that no missionary was prepared to accept Tibet as a serene repository of ancient wisdom. On the contrary, missionary writers emphasized the darker aspects of Tibetan culture because these highlighted the country's need for Christian enlightenment. Romance lay not in the original culture of Tibet but rather in the heroic nature of the missionary struggle in an exotic environment.

The second theme concerns the missionaries' role as interpreters from East to West, as well as from West to East. Robert Ekvall of the C&MA mission in Amdo exemplifies this theme. He was born to missionary parents in Kansu in 1898 and later himself served as a missionary, military interpreter, and anthropologist. Introducing one of his anthropological monographs he wrote:

> From the time when, as a lonely child among my Chinese playmates, I was learning to interpret what I read and treasured of my own culture to others of another, and vastly dissimilar culture, the role of an interpreter has been mine. It has remained a constant throughout most of my life: in the years I spent as a missionary among the Tibetans; when as an army officer my experience took me from the Burma jungles through China to the conference tables of Panmumjom [Korea] and Geneva; and now as one who seeks to interpret Tibet and its subcultures to the Western world before it is too late.[2]

In this article I make no claim to present a comprehensive survey of missionary writing on Tibet; rather, I offer a selection of missionary views illustrating these two themes. I begin with a review of the pioneers who set up mission stations on Tibet's borders in the second half of the nineteenth century. Then I discuss their views of the Buddhist political/religious power structure; their own role as "soldiers of Christ"; their assessments of ordinary Tibetan people; and the beginnings of Christian/Buddhist dialogue. I conclude with an evaluation of missionary literature as a source of information on Tibet in the nineteenth and early twentieth centuries.

The Pioneers

The Tibetan authorities did not allow any foreign missions to establish stations in central Tibet in the nineteenth and twentieth centuries, although Jesuit and Capuchin missionaries had worked in western Tibet and Lhasa during the previous two centuries.[3] The only Western missionaries to reach Lhasa throughout the period under review were two French Lazarist priests, Régis-Évariste Huc and Joseph Gabet, who had been working in Inner Mongolia and entered Tibet from the northeast in 1846.[4] Huc's book, *Souvenirs d'un voyage dans la Tartarie, le Thibet et la Chine*, was first published in Paris in 1850 and became one of the most celebrated nineteenth-century travel accounts of Tibet. It gives a vivid, albeit somewhat idiosyncratic, account of the two priests' adventures on the road to Lhasa and their negotiations with Chinese and Tibetan officials once they arrived. They found an ally in the leader of the Lhasa Muslim community but ultimately were unable to gain permission to stay in Tibet.

In 1846, while Huc and Gabet were still on their travels, the Vatican assigned responsibility for Tibet to the Société des Missions Étrangères (SME) of Paris, and its missionaries made a series of unsuccessful attempts to penetrate into central Tibet from its eastern and southern borders. In 1854, Fr. Charles-Alexis-René Renou established a station in Bonga, just inside Tibet's southeastern border with Yunnan.[5] However, ten years later the SME was forced to withdraw back across the border into China; it continued to work in the Sino-Tibetan frontier areas until 1952, hoping for the day when the border would finally be reopened.

Meanwhile, Moravian missionaries from Germany were making their own attempts to cross Tibet's southwestern borders, and with the same result: August-Wilhelm Heyde and Eduard Pagell tried to cross the Tibetan border from the Indian territories of Ladakh and Spiti in 1855 but were turned back three times. As an interim measure they decided to establish mission stations first in Kyelang (Lahul) in 1856, then Poo (Kinnaur) in 1865, and Leh (Ladakh) in 1885.[6] Moravian missionaries translated the Bible into Tibetan[7] and liberally distributed Tibetan-language tracts both to the inhabitants of the border areas and to travelers from central Tibet, but they were never able to make more than brief forays across the border.

By the late nineteenth century, several other Protestant and Roman Catholic missionary societies were making renewed efforts to enter Tibet from the east and south.

- The Church of Scotland established missions in the Darjeeling and Kalimpong areas opposite Tibet's southern borders from the 1870s onward. Its best-known missionaries were John A. Graham, the founder of "Graham's Homes" in Kalimpong and Tharchin, who had been born in Kinnaur in 1889 and went on to become editor of the *Tibet Mirror* newspaper before being ordained a Church of Scotland Minister in 1952.
- The English Roman Catholic Mill Hill Mission established a station in Leh, Ladakh, from 1888 to 1898.[8]
- In 1895 the U.S.-based Christian and Missionary Alliance estab-

Fig.1 The Moravian missionary August Wilhelm Heyde and members of his Ladakhi/Lahuli congregation in Kyelang (Lahul), ca. 1895.

lished its first contacts with Tibetans from its base in Taochow in Amdo (northeast Tibet). As noted, the best-known C&MA missionary was Robert B. Ekvall.

- In 1892 the English missionary Annie R. Taylor set out from Tachienlu (later known variously as Dartsendo and Kanding) on the Kham/Chinese border. She was turned back near Nagchuka. After returning to Britain in 1893, she formed her own mission known as the Tibetan Pioneer Band and, with a dozen colleagues, set out again for the Darjeeling region the following year.

- The China Inland Mission (CIM) established a mission in Sining (Amdo) in 1885 and subsequently in Tachienlu and Batang (Kham). The best-known CIM missionaries included Theodor Sörensen from Norway, who was based in Tachienlu for most of the period from 1899 until 1922,[9] and the Australian James Huston Edgar, who sailed to China in 1898 and first visited Batang in 1903. Edgar was associated with Kham for the rest of his life, particularly the period from 1922 to 1936 when he and his wife were based in Tachienlu.

Fig. 2 Ladakhi metal workers, ca. 1900. Moravian Mission Collection, Moravian Church House Library, London.

- Two independent missionaries, Petrus Rijnhart and his Canadian
  wife, Susie, settled in the Kumbum area (Amdo) in 1895, and in
  1898 made a heroic but disastrous attempt to travel to Lhasa. As
  Susie Rijnhart describes in her book, *With the Tibetans in Tent and
  Temple* (1902), her husband was killed and their infant son died
  on the journey. They never reached Lhasa, and Susie was forced to
  return alone via Batang.

Thus by the early twentieth century Tibet was surrounded by a
string of missions from various societies on its western, southern, and
northeastern borders. However, the center of the country—and particularly Lhasa—remained closed.

The Power of Buddhism

Throughout this period, missionaries believed that the malign influence of the monasteries was the prime obstacle preventing them from
entering central Tibet. They attributed the monks' opposition to the
fear that they would lose power and influence as soon as ordinary people became aware of a different religious truth. For example, in the
1880s C. H. Desgodins, whose brother served on the Tibetan/Chinese
border with the SME, wrote:

> At present, it is the monasteries that are offering the strongest
> opposition to the opening of commercial and diplomatic rela-
> tions with foreigners, especially Europeans, in the well-founded
> fear of seeing the Tibetan people fall prey to their greed and
> domination.[10]

Monastic rapacity and domination were common themes in missionary writing. In 1910 Edward Amundsen, a Norwegian missionary,
published a novel, *In the Land of the Lamas,* describing the life of a girl
from Batang. One of the protagonists in the novel was sent to the
monastery at an early age. Amundsen's comment on this initially involuntary choice of career was:

Fig. 3 Group photograph of Moravian missionaries and members of their local congregations taken during the visitation of Bishop Benjamin La Trobe in Kyelang (Lahul) in 1902. Bishop La Trobe (bearded with a solar *topi*) is sitting in the upper middle of the picture. Moravian Church House Library, London.

As regards usefulness, he was lost to the world, like so many hundred thousand of the best of the Tibetan nation; yea worse he became from that day a burden to his country, and by degrees a curse to the community.[11]

Similarly, later missionary analysis of Tibetan Buddhism emphasized the power—and at times oppression—of the monasteries. For example, in a history of the C&MA mission, Ekvall writes of one of the largest monasteries in Amdo:

Labrang is more than the greatest visible symbol in the building and organisation of lamaism in north-east Tibet. It is an effective and despotic power of rule controlling not only the worship but the actions and livelihood of thousands...in all things it has well-nigh absolute power over the people of the district.[12]

Ekvall concludes his book by writing rhetorically:

Tibet, where every breeze is freighted with the voiceless suppli-
cation of flapping prayer flags, where streams and rivers turn the
mills of prayer, where prayer wheels spin by pilgrim effort, and
where the matter of an endless petition punctuates all of human
activity—Tibet, the citadel of evil and the land of false prayer,
will only yield as we—missionaries and readers of this urgent
cry—learn truly to pray. Soldiers of Christ pray on.[13]

Soldiers of Christ

Military language was a common feature of missionary writing in
the late nineteenth and early twentieth centuries. In 1902 William Carey
described Tibet as a citadel under siege:

This apparently impregnable Gibraltar of modern missions is
now invested on all sides but one, and the siege is being prose-
cuted with vigour by several societies, working independently
of one another, but directed by a common aim and all cheered
by the not distant hope of scaling the impenetrable walls and
gaining the confidence of the people.[14]

A quarter of a century later two CIM missionaries, Mildred Cable
and Francesca French, were using similar language. Summing up the
recent history of missionary work among Tibetans in the Kansu border
regions and elsewhere, they wrote:

Thus the first skirmish. Now the steady pressure of a besieging
force. Later l'appel and the call to arms, when the hour comes
to capture this fortress.[15]

In describing Tibet as a fortress and themselves as soldiers, these
authors were writing metaphorically. However, the idea that Western governments—backed by real Western armies—might ultimately be instrumental in opening Tibet to the Gospel was common in the late nineteenth

and early twentieth centuries. In the 1880s Desgodins asked rhetorically:

> Two centuries ago, the Chinese government was able to [conquer
> Tibet] with eight hundred soldiers; could not a European gov-
> ernment do the same for good and legitimate reasons?[16]

Referring to the leading arms manufacturers of the day, he gave his
own opinion:

> I am convinced that it will be necessary to call up the all-powerful
> voice of Messers Krupp and Chassepot. Then the Tibetans and
> Chinese will obey, and it will soon be done.[17]

In his view, it would be entirely appropriate if a Western army persuaded Tibet to open up to the forces of Western civilization.

Such ideas came closest to realization in 1903–1904 when the
British expeditionary force led by Colonel Francis Younghusband
fought its way to Lhasa. However, any hopes that British political and
military pressure might make Tibet more open to Western missionaries were doomed to disappointment. The British government in India
established favorable relations with Lhasa, but the main aim of British
policy was to preserve Tibet as a buffer state. The British explicitly dis-
couraged missionaries from entering Tibet for fear that they would
upset the Lhasa authorities.

This policy came as a considerable blow to Annie Taylor. According to one of her biographers:

> Her bitter disappointment at the futility of the Mission to Lhasa
> was the last straw, if anything so heavy as her grief could be
> likened to a thing so light as a straw. She saw clearly that the car-
> rying out of the wish of the government at home must lessen
> British prestige and close Tibet against the Europeans more
> rigidly than it had ever been.[18]

The missionaries therefore remained confined to Tibet's borders.
Partly for this reason, their view of Tibet differed from the Lhasa-centric

view of British officials such as Charles Bell, who formed a close relationship with leading members of the Tibetan elite and favored the creation of a more centralized state dominated by Lhasa.[19] By contrast,
missionaries on the periphery of Tibet tended to emphasize the less
benign activities of the Tibetan political/religious hierarchy. For example, in 1910 Amundsen welcomed the failure of an anti-Chinese rebellion in Kham:

> As a result of the broken power of the lamas, the fertile plains
> of Batang and elsewhere can now be enjoyed in peace by the
> relieved inhabitants—a wonderful change from the days of
> oppression when the bulk of the crops were carried into the
> monastic granaries.[20]

Similarly, in the 1930s CIM missionary J. H. Edgar took the view
that Chinese control over central Tibet would be preferable from the
missionary point of view because it would break the power of the
monasteries and make it possible for missionaries to work in comparative safety:

> It seems impossible as things are now, for Christianity to develop
> in Tibet proper because its antagonist, Lamaism, is a tithe from
> *all* Tibetan families, as well as a local and national form of gov-
> ernment. Hence, the Christian, if banned by his local organisa-
> tion, would become a hopeless outcast, unless he were to
> specialise in hiding his light under a bushel.[21]

By contrast, at the time when Edgar was writing, China provided
the missionaries with the opportunity to operate freely in the border
areas that it controlled in eastern and northeastern Tibet.

"The Romance of Missionary Heroism"

From the missionaries' point of view, Tibet was far from being the
romantic paradise of Shangri-la, but the task of trying to break into it
demanded heroic qualities that carried their own spirit of romance.

Such qualities are highlighted in a collection of foreign missionary adventure stories compiled by John C. Lambert in 1907 and given the appropriate title *The Romance of Missionary Heroism*. In the foreword, the author points out that exciting adventures were an incidental result of missionary activity rather than its main purpose. He nevertheless hoped that the stories he described might lead some of his younger readers to aspire to a missionary vocation when they grew up.

The Tibetan adventures he describes are those of Annie R. Taylor. Much is made of the fact that Taylor had been regarded as a sickly young child but, despite her frailty and her sex, had come closer to the forbidden city of Lhasa than any recent European explorer. Lambert compares her to General C. G. Gordon, the British soldier who in 1885 had died heroically defending Khartoum (Sudan) against Islamist forces led by the Mahdi:

> There is the same shrinking from public notice, the same readiness to be buried from the sight of Europe in some distant and difficult task, the same courage which fears nothing, the same simple, unquestioning trust in the care and guidance of the heavenly father.[22]

Taylor provided inspiration for at least two other authors. These include William Carey, who came across her diary while on a visit to Darjeeling and published it together with a lengthy introduction explaining the background to her travels. The title of his book is characteristic: *Travel and Adventure in Tibet* (1902).

Similarly, Isabel Stuart Robson wrote a book entitled *Two Lady Missionaries in Tibet*. The ladies concerned were Taylor and Susie Rijnhart, who, as noted above, had made a heroic but ultimately tragic journey to central Tibet in 1898–99. Robson's preface begins in typical style:

> Tibet still lies in darkness, its passes more rigidly guarded than ever against foreigners, its people more hostile to intruders; but along the frontiers a cordon of missionaries has been drawn and many lives have been dedicated to the evangelisation of "the great closed land."

As Lambert's foreword indicated, missionary writers were conscious that "romance" was an incidental result of missionary endeavor rather than its prime objective. In the worst case, it might even distract both supporters at home and the missionaries themselves from the main purpose of their work. J. H. Edgar, an Australian CIM missionary who worked in Kham from 1903 to 1936, encountered this criticism early in his career and decided to dedicate his romanticism to divine service. As one obituarist wrote of him:

> Romantic! Before he came away from Australia, a missionary from Palestine asked him if the romance of missions was taking him to China-Tibet, and he decided then and there to consecrate his romantic spirit, and he did it in his own peculiar way—and it no longer gave him thought or worry![23]

Alongside his missionary work, he wrote articles on subjects ranging from geographical reports to anthropological notes on milking customs, sacrifices, convents, and prehistoric remains.[24] Another obituary summed up Edgar's life and philosophy:

> As a Christian missionary Edgar sought to change ancient institutions and hoary rites so as to bring new life and hope to many peoples, but he always thought of his work as romantic, and of life as an enthralling story of thrilling adventure and high romance. Life might bring new channels for its expression, but never could man live in a cold material world. To his friends, and especially to those who had been with him into the highlands of eastern Tibet, James Huston Edgar will always remain the embodiment of all that makes life interesting and romantic.[25]

George Patterson, a Plymouth Brother who was one of the last missionaries to work in Kham, seems to have had a similar view on life. His books on his Tibetan adventures—notably *Tibetan Journey* (1954)—are among the classics of Tibetan travel writing. Patterson describes the swashbuckling lifestyle of the people of Kham with sympathetic approval, while boasting of his own prowess in adapting to it—for example by winning a spectacular horse race. Patterson made a difficult journey from eastern Tibet across to Assam in an unsuccessful attempt to win outside aid for the Khampas in their struggle against the Chinese. His most recent book on the subject, *Requiem for Tibet* (1990), has an elegiac quality, making it clear that he is describing a civilization that has now passed. Patterson always distrusted the Tibetan monkhood far too much to claim Tibet as a Shangri-la, and he regarded many aspects of Tibetan religion as demonic, but his work contributes to old Tibet's image as a romantic land that is now forever out of reach.

Encounters with Ordinary People

Missionary views of the people among whom they worked naturally varied according to the personality of the writer, the nature of his or her experiences, and—to some extent—the period. Nineteenth-century accounts tend to stress what—from the European point of view—ranked as the alien qualities of the Tibetans. These include their lack of hygiene, their strange sexual customs, and at times their hostility. By contrast later twentieth-century missionary accounts show much greater empathy and, in many cases, a deeper cultural understanding reflecting many years of residence in Asia.

Perhaps not surprisingly in view of her experiences, Susie Rijnhart had a grim view of the Tibetans. In her account of her travels across Tibet and the death of her husband, many of the Tibetans she describes come across as harsh and mendacious.[26] She writes of her relief when she had finally escaped Tibet and found herself among Chinese.

Later views are rather cosier. The Moravian medical missionaries A. Reeve and Kathleen Heber, who served in the Himalayas from 1912 to 1926, began their book on Ladakh with the comment that:

> We are not exactly in Looking-glass Land, but we are certainly in some sort of Wonderland, where many things are upside down, topsy-turvy or just the reverse of our notions of correctness, and where the strangest incongruities prevail.[27]

As examples of this topsy-turviness they point out that houses have flower gardens on the roof rather than outside the front door; that the protrusion of the tongue is a polite form of greeting rather than a sign of contempt; that Ladakhis wear their oldest clothes on the outside and the best ones underneath; and even that cows descend the musical scale as they moo whereas Western cows "moo from below upwards." However, they wisely point out:

> In attempting to understand this land and people, we must remember that we are the outsiders and ours are the extraordinary ideas and standards.[28]

Despite its tendency to quaintness, the Hebers' book gives an affectionate view of the various inhabitants of Ladakh in the 1920s. The book tells of encounters with the king of Ladakh as well as with incarnate lamas, describes different parts of Ladakh and their inhabitants, and discusses the problems of practicing Western medicine in a non-Western cultural environment.

Writing from Amdo in the same period, CIM missionary Frank Doggett Learner gave a fairly typical missionary view of the Tibetans' character. He began by pointing out the Tibetans' favorable qualities:

> The Tibetans are a stalwart, frank and fearless people. Taken as a whole, they have many pleasing characteristics. They are good-natured, and have a happy cheerful disposition.[29]

However, in case the reader is in any doubt of the Tibetans' need for salvation, he goes on to add:

> They are comparatively truthful though they are quick at fault-finding. When quarrelling among themselves—and they argue over trifles—they can use very scurrilous language. They live unrestrained lives, and all more or less could be charged with immorality, drunkenness, lubricity and cruelty.[30]

Fig. 4 The CIM missionary Frank
Dogget Learner in Tibetan dress

Criticisms of Tibetan sexual morality were commonplace. Missionaries typically regarded polyandry as a particular scandal. For example, the Moravian missionary Theodor Rechler wrote in 1874:

A remarkable custom unknown among Hindoos, but universal among Tibetans, is the marriage of one woman to several men of one family. The eldest son chooses a wife, who with all her children becomes the property of the other sons of the family. The evils attendant on this custom are probably greater than those which necessarily accompany polygamy, which is also practised in Tibet. It is a sad hindrance in the way of the progress of missionary effort, and will eventually have to be eradicated.[31]

Similarly, A. H. Francke, a later Moravian missionary, commented that:

One of the ugliest customs, morally, of Tibet is the system of poly-andry. It was certainly not introduced by Buddhism, but Buddhism has never raised a finger against it. Before its abolition, there is no hope that the moral condition of the Tibetans can be raised.[32]

Francis Goré, a French SME missionary who worked in the eastern Sino-Tibetan border areas from the 1920s to 1952, took a more meas-ured view, pointing out that economic and social considerations—in particular the paramount need to preserve the family cell—lay behind both polyandry and polygamy. He concludes his discussion with the observation that:

Perhaps some will ask how harmony can reign in households that, according to our conceptions, are so badly arranged. One would have to be Tibetan to know, and in any case, it is neces-sary to take care to avoid judging with our European mentality. Since morals are free, the men and women who are discontented may seek their fortunes elsewhere. The family will intervene in such matters only if its material interests are at stake.[33]

George Patterson was characteristically straightforward on the same topic:

The Tibetans are neither completely polyandrous or completely polygamous: they are completely promiscuous.[34]

With this in mind he took a supply of neo-arsophenamine on his travels so that he could treat patients for syphilis.

Missionary Novels

As the missionaries got to know the Tibetans better, some resorted to fiction as a means of explaining the local lifestyle to an audience in the West. The first example of this genre has already been cited: Edward Amundsen describes the life of a girl from Batang in a book entitled *In the Land of the Lamas: The Story of Trashi Lhamo, a Tibetan Lassie* (1910). The book describes Trashi Lhamo's home and marriage; her capture by robbers; her encounter with Protestant missionaries; the story of a Tibetan rebellion put down by the Chinese general Chao Erfeng; and the heroine's death. It is illustrated with photographs of Batang taken by the American missionary Albert Shelton.

Similarly, Samuel Ribbach, a Moravian missionary who worked in Ladakh and Lahul from 1894 to 1914, wrote a semifictional biography of a Ladakhi farmer in *Drogpa Namgyal: Ein Tibeterleben* (1940).[35] Ribbach's story is set in the village of Khalatse on the river Indus. Although the hero never existed, the descriptions of his village and house are authentic, and missionary records show that many of the minor characters are true to life. Ribbach turned to fiction as a means of making his account more accessible to lay people, but his book also had an academic objective. The foreword by Professor R. F. Merkel of Munich University points out:

> The valuable work that lies before you is proof that—far from the clamor of the day—scientific work is often quickly conducted in the harshest of living conditions.[36]

The book covers Drogpa Namgyal's entire life from birth to death, but the most detailed part of the story is an account of the ritualized negotiations that preceded his marriage and the songs accompanying the wedding itself. Other episodes include accounts of religious festivals and trading journeys to the nomads of the Changthang plateau.

A third example of missionary novel writing comes from the northeast. Robert Ekvall wrote the story of an Amdowa Tibetan nomad, Dorje Rinchen, in *Tents against the Sky* (1954). Dorje Rinchen—known to his family as Doka—becomes a child monk. By the time he reaches adulthood, he seems all set for a prominent career in the monastery but falls in love with Lhamo Mtso, the sister of one of his friends. Leaving the monkhood, he returns to his life as a nomad and achieves a high social standing on account of his skill in animal husbandry and trade, and for leading a raid to steal cattle from a rival nomadic clan. However, his son dies, and Doka becomes obsessed by a sense that he is being punished for past sins. A pilgrimage to Lhasa brings no lasting sense of absolution. He is on the point of abandoning his wife and family for a life of self-abnegation on the fringe of the monastery when he encounters a "yellow head" from another country who points the way to a better spiritual path.

In all three novels, the authors succumb to the temptation to include a missionary message: Each of the three protagonists comes to question his or her religious heritage and leans toward the new religion brought by the strangers from abroad. At the same time, all three accounts give vivid descriptions of life on the borders of Tibet, which make their books much more than simple missionary tracts.

Academic Writing

The missionaries' close contact with the Tibetan border peoples gave them an opportunity for research such as was available to few other Europeans. Research into the language was an obvious necessity, and in this respect the Moravian missionary H. A. Jäschke, whose *Tibetan-English Dictionary* was published in 1881, was one of the most important pioneers. Roman Catholic missionaries in Kham conducted similar pioneering research.[37]

Missionaries had an obvious interest in the history and culture of the societies among which they worked, although in the nineteenth and early twentieth centuries some considered academic study of such topics a diversion from their proper activities of preaching and teaching. The Moravian linguist and historian A. H. Francke initially found it difficult to persuade his superiors of the value of studying Ladakhi folk literature; he argued that such research improved his knowledge of the language, making it easier to communicate the Gospel more effectively.[38]

In 1906 Francke published an article describing his archaeological discoveries during a missionary journey to Zangskar. He began with a kind of disclaimer:

> A mission tour does not provide an opportunity to carry out detailed archaeological research. The missionary penetrates as a pioneer into little-known regions; he sees some new things that in his judgement may be of general interest. So he takes it to be his duty to make notes, and to make these notes available to specially interested circles.[39]

Francke in due course became a full-time scholar, although he continued to work on Tibetan Bible translation from his home in Germany and valued this work as a fulfillment of his original missionary vocation.

Similarly, Ekvall initially combined his missionary work with more academic writing. His first academic treatise, *Cultural Relations on the Kansu-Tibetan Border,* was published by the University of Chicago Press in 1939. His later works include a series of specialist articles and two studies, one entitled *Religious Observations in Tibet: Pattern and Function* (1964) and the other, *Fields on the Hoof* (1968). *Fields on the Hoof* is a detailed anthropological study of the Tibetan nomads among whom Ekvall spent much of his earlier life.

Another scholarly missionary who worked in Amdo was Fr. Matthias Hermanns, a German who served with the Society of the Divine Word (SVD). As Per Kvaerne notes elsewhere in this book, Hermanns was a representative of the Viennese school of ethnology. His works include: *Die Nomaden von Tibet* (1949), *Die Familie der Amdo-Tibetern* (1959), and *Das National-Epos der Tibeter-Gling König Kesar* (1965).

The research of missionaries such as Jäschke, Francke, Ekvall, and Hermanns brought them into contact with a wider circle of scholars and officials. Francke, for example, published articles in publications as diverse as the *Journal of the Asiatic Society of Bengal* (Calcutta), the *Indian Antiquary* (Bombay), the *Mémoires de la Société Finno-Ougrienne* (Helsinki), and the *Zeitschrift der Deutschen Morgenländischen Gesellschaft* (Leipzig), and was in regular contact with academics in many other centers of learning. Despite their physical distance, missionaries were often able to make significant contributions to the academic mainstream.

The Beginnings of Christian/Buddhist Dialogue

As noted above, the early missionaries' view of Tibetan Buddhism was largely negative: They viewed the monasteries as citadels of a malign power that served to obstruct their own efforts to proclaim the Gospel message. Many Tibetans saw the missionaries as agents of outside political forces that aimed at the destruction of their homeland.[40] Power politics on both sides impeded effective communication. Despite this hostile view of the monasteries, however, missionaries frequently established personal friendships with individual Buddhists, both laymen and monks.

An early example was the friendship of Renou of the SME with Lodjrou, an incarnate lama who gave him Tibetan lessons in 1852 in return for the gift of a telescope. Initially, Lodjrou was unaware of his student's identity or objectives, but even when he discovered that Renou was a missionary, he seems to have continued to hold him in high regard.[41]

Particularly in the early stages, language problems served as an additional obstacle to genuine communication. As Jäschke discovered, even apparently straightforward words were open to contrasting interpretations. Writing of the word for "truth" in his dictionary he comments:

> *bdén-pa nyid* seems to be a technical term for truth though the Buddhist understands by it nothing but *stong-pa nyid* [emptiness]. Nevertheless, the possibility of its being misapprehended from this reason ought to be no obstacle to the word being used in its original sense, and re-established in its proper right, the more so as Buddhist philosophy makes but a mockery of truth by identifying it with a negation of reality.[42]

Despite these difficulties, it seems that some meaningful exchanges did take place. Henry Hanlon, an English Roman Catholic priest who worked for the Mill Hill Mission in Ladakh in the 1890s, published summaries of his "Buddhist-Christian Dialogues" in *Illustrated Catholic Missions* and *St. Joseph's Foreign Missionary Advocate*. His accounts are meant to illustrate Buddhist "errors" rather than illustrate a genuinely ecumenical dialogue. Nonetheless, some of the exchanges ring true:

> I remember once in the course of a quiet instruction which I was giving to a Buddhist at Leh, when speaking of the joys of Heaven, being interrupted by him. He calmly told me that our Heaven was but the inferior heaven of the Buddhist, whose supreme happiness is *nirvana* or extinction of all desires. When this stage is reached, there is no more joy or sorrow, heat or cold, hunger or thirst, or any other sensible feeling. They call this state *nyid—stonpa*.[43]

Kurung Tsering, a senior Nyingma lama in the Koko Nor region, is favorably described by several missionaries—notably Frank Doggett Learner and Theodor Sörensen of the CIM. Although there is no evidence that he seriously considered baptism, he read the Christian literature provided by the missionaries and, in a letter to Sörensen, asked serious questions about it:

> According to the Buddhist religion, our place of refuge is the Three Holy Ones, which in essence is the One Supreme or Lama Kon-Chog Chig. According to your Christian religion, there is also one supreme Holy One; what definition do you give of him? If you take refuge in this God, what then is the method for refuge?[44]

He concludes his list of queries with the comment that:

> These ten questions, like a string of precious pearls from a treasury, are presented as a beautiful ornament for the neck of a young, wise and virtuous virgin.[45]

While welcoming such inquiries, missionaries on the Tibetan borders consistently saw themselves as teachers rather than learners: they believed they had little to learn from the practitioners of other religions. An exception was the Scottish missionary J. A. Graham of

Kalimpong, who in 1937 published a pamphlet entitled *Stray Thoughts upon the Possibility of a Universal Religion*. Graham commented that his experience of forty-eight years in India had brought him into direct contact with the adherents of other great religions. These encounters made him long for

> a synthesis of the higher distinctive contributions made towards the realisation of a religion in which the more spiritually minded of all the well known and tenaciously held faiths of the world had found that spiritual fellowship and that inspiration which had linked them in one great brotherhood through a Common Heavenly Father God, whose nature is Love.[46]

The idea of a "synthesis" of religious truth was controversial in missionary circles both then and later. However, in spirit if not in detail, Graham's approach anticipated the more open Christian/Buddhist dialogue that has taken place since the 1960s.

Toward an Evaluation of Missionary Writing on Tibet

Missionaries resembled their contemporaries in that late nineteenth-century views of Tibet tended to be harsh and judgmental. By contrast, as the twentieth century advanced, their accounts tended to become more understanding and—perhaps as a result—more benign.

Throughout the period, two special features of missionary writing stand out. The first is ideological. By the nature of their calling, missionaries were bound to be critical of Tibetan religion, both its philosophical theory and its social and political practice. This viewpoint meant that the missionaries deprecated—or totally misunderstood—much of what they saw. In many cases, their bias weakens their credibility as witnesses. At the same time, the missionaries' critical outlook has an advantage in that it leads them to record aspects of local society that might have been ignored both by official Tibetan or Ladakhi historians and by uncritically sympathetic Western travelers.

The second feature was the length and depth of missionary experience.

Even more than British officials on the frontier—let alone passing travelers—missionaries typically spent years and decades in the regions they served. Long years of residence do not necessarily lead to insight, but they might. As noted above, J. A. Graham's decades in India led him to modify his religious views to adopt a more sympathetic view of other faiths. Ekvall was able to write of the nomads of Amdo that he had "had the rewarding experience of associating with these people on a level of such intimacy that they called me—half in jest and half in earnest—one of themselves."[47] Such qualifications enhance the value of missionary accounts.

From a historian's point of view, missionary literature is often frustrating in that it leaves out many of the questions that one might ask, but this is inevitable given that most published missionary accounts were designed for a specific purpose: to enhance the support of sponsors and supporters at home. As Learner wrote at the beginning of *Rusty Hinges,* his book would

> travel on its way with my eager prayer that God will show each
> one who reads how he or she can share in bringing our glorious
> Gospel to the dark, degraded devil-worshipping people of
> Tibet.[48]

When preparing such literature, the missionaries naturally selected material most likely to appeal to a Western audience. This material tended to highlight the exotic nature of the environment in which the missionaries were working. It often sought to provide a degree of human interest by describing what were seen as the eccentricities of the Tibetans while at the same time stressing their need for spiritual salvation. Missionaries—or more usually their sponsors—emphasized the "romance of missionary heroism" rather than the romance of Shangri-la.

Equally naturally, official accounts tend to gloss over—or ignore completely—the problems that occurred within missions and the strains faced by individual missionaries. Archival sources such as letters and diaries—which are outside the scope of this paper—may provide a corrective, showing the missionaries as less perfect, but also more human, than official versions would have us believe.

But all these sources are partial and incomplete. To borrow a phrase from St. Paul—one of the earliest Christian missionaries—they are "like puzzling reflections in a mirror."[49] In this respect, the search for historical understanding has much in common with the search for religious truth.

NOTES

1 Ekvall, 1938.

2 Ekvall, 1968: vi.

3 For the Roman Catholic missions in the seventeenth and eighteenth centuries, see, *inter alia,* Rudolf Kaschewsky's "The Image of Tibet in the West before the Nineteenth Century" in this volume.

4 For a recent biography of Huc, see Thevenet, 1980.

5 See Bray, 1997b.

6 On the Moravian mission, see Bray, 1983; 1992.

7 Bray, 1991.

8 For the history of this mission, see Bray, 1997a.

9 On Sörensen, see Kvaerne, 1973.

10 Desgodins, 1885: 225 (my translation).

11 Amundsen, 1910.

12 Ekvall, 1938, 170.

13 Ibid., 188.

14 Carey, 1902.

15 Cable and French, 1925.

16 Desgodins, 1885: 428 (my translation).

17 Ibid.

18 Robson, 1910: 111.

19 See Alex McKay's paper in this volume.

20 Amundsen, 1910: 74.

21 Edgar, 1930–31.

22 Lambert, 1907: 118.

23 Dye, 1936.

24 Some seventy-two articles on such subjects are cited in Kuløy and Imaeda, 1986.

25 Anon., 1936.

26 Rijnhart, 1902.

27 Heber and Heber, 1926: 18.

28 Ibid., 21.

29 Learner, 1934.

30 Ibid.

31 Rechler, 1874: 230.

32 Francke, 1907: 172.

33 Goré, 1938: 204 (my translation).

34 Patterson, 1954: 96.

35 See also the English translation: *Culture and Society in Ladakh,* trans. John Bray (New Delhi: Ess Ess Publications, 1986).

36 Ribbach, 1940: 8 (my translation).

37 See, for example, Anon., 1901.

38 Bray, 1999.

39 Francke, 1906: 645–61 (my translation).

40 I discuss this point in greater detail in Bray, 1997b.

41 Ibid.

42 Jäschke, 1881: 271.

43 Hanlon, 1892–93: 430.

44 Kvaerne, 1973: 56.

45 Ibid.

46 Minto, 1974: 193.

47 Ekvall, 1968: ix.

48 Learner, 1934: viii.

49 1 Corinthians 13: 12 (New English Bible).

TIBET IMAGES
AMONG RESEARCHERS ON TIBET

Per Kvaerne

S INCE THE PUBLICATION in 1978 of Edward W. Said's *Orientalism*
(1995 [1978]), it is no longer possible for us in the West to attempt
to understand the "Orient"—broadly speaking, the Middle East, in Said's
sense—without realizing that such an endeavor is beset by innumerable
prejudices, habits of thought, and instinctive attitudes. Looking back on
more than 250 years of Tibetan studies, we can certainly say of Tibet, as
Said did of the Orient, that it "was not (and is not) a free subject of
thought or action" (*Orientalism*, 3). As a small contribution to our common endeavor to elucidate the "myth of Tibet" I shall offer some examples of Tibet images among researchers on Tibet, taking the term
"researcher" in its broadest sense and including also one or two travelers. I make no pretensions at all to completeness; I only hope to show that
the images of Tibet have been influenced by personal ideological incli-
nations as well as the general atmosphere of society as a whole.

I shall deal only with researchers in the West, thus leaving our colleagues in India, China, and Japan aside. I shall in no way attempt to present a historical synopsis of Tibetological research. I shall merely try to
present some aspects of researchers who seem to me, in various ways, to
be typical of their times and to reflect some general attitude or ideology
in Western society at a given moment. Therefore, if I have chosen not to
discuss scholars such as Jacques Bacot, Rolf A. Stein, or David L. Snellgrove, it is simply because their research does not seem to me to reflect in
any readily discernible way values or attitudes extraneous to their research.

By way of introduction, let me mention four trends of the mid- and late nineteenth-century mental landscape of the West, some of which, as we shall see, have remained influential until today: (1) evolutionism—the idea that biological as well as social and intellectual life develops in stages from simple and "primitive" to more complex and sophisticated forms; (2) imperialism—the conviction that the social and intellectual superiority of Western civilization justified the existence of colonies and empires such as the British Empire; (3) romanticism, which, taking the form of the so-called nature-mythology school in the study of religion and mythology, regarded man's instinctive reaction to various natural phenomena as the ultimate source of religious ideas; and, finally, (4) rationalism, the belief that rationality and reason are the only valid source of knowledge.

The aspect of Tibetan culture that most impressed Europeans was the highly visible role of Buddhism and the innumerable monasteries to be found in Tibet and neighboring regions such as Ladakh. Clearly, a society possessing a theocratic system of government could not easily be categorized in terms of elementary and primitive stages of human evolution, but in nineteenth- and early twentieth-century literature one rarely finds a positive evaluation of Tibetan monasticism or indeed any aspect of Tibetan Buddhism.

Western images of Tibet during this period seem to be dominated by two intellectual attitudes: rationalism and the nature-mythology school. From the point of view of Western rationalism, Tibetan Buddhism was regarded as a "fall" from the original, rational doctrine of the Buddha—as a degeneration into a fossilized, despotic aberration. One suspects that the widespread anticlericalism in Western Europe at the time contributed to this image. A colorful, but not atypical example of this attitude was expressed by the French explorer Fernand Grenard (whose real name was Joseph Fernand). His experiences in Tibet, it must be admitted, were not the happiest: his companion Dutreuil de Rhins was killed by Tibetans and Grenard himself barely escaped with his life:

> The Tibetans...build thousands of temples; make tens of thousands of statues; prostrate themselves; mutter endless prayers; grind out an even greater number by water-power or by hand; say their rosaries; celebrate solemn services; make offerings and

give banquets to all the gods and all the devils; wear amulets and relics; write talismans; wave streamers covered with prayers or lucky emblems, which the breath of the wind sends flying through space; pile up numberless heaps of stones with pious inscriptions; ...drink down without compunction the divine nectar *(dudchi)* composed of the ten impurities, such as human flesh and worse; practice exorcism, witchcraft and magic...dance strange and frenzied sarabands to drive out or shatter the devil: and thus is Tibet made to spin distractedly, without rest or truce, in religion's mad round. (Grenard, 1904: 310–11)

The popular religion could more readily be categorized as an early, simple stage of the evolutionistic scheme than could the monastic system; however, scholars were more liable to resort to the nature-romantic notion that Tibetan popular religion was (and is) based on emotions of awe and insignificance caused by the overwhelming grandeur of the Tibetan landscape and the harshness of its climate. In fact, few images of Tibetan religion have turned out to be as tenacious as this particular idea. The following description of how the cult of mountain deities, a fundamental aspect of Tibetan popular religion, arose was written in 1995, but could equally well have been written a century ago:

The mountains of Tibet have always been a place of dreamlike beauty and frightening terror. Avalanches descend daily, and sudden torrents following violent storms devastate entire valleys. A rockslide can bury a village or a herd of yak. Anyone can be killed by a falling rock.... Dangers threaten everywhere.

The light of dawn or of the evening sun throws threatening shadows. The dark outlines of the mountains wander across the fields. In the ghostlike moonlight the mountains are transformed into a silvery, eerie landscape, in which trees and bushes darkly loom. A stone begins to roll, a startled crow swiftly flies up...

In such an environment man is in need of protection. (Nicolazzi, 1995: 59. Translation mine.)

This poetic description evokes a moonlit mountain landscape by Caspar David Friedrich rather than Tibet.

One of the early, Victorian-period travelers on the borders of Tibet was Captain William Henry Knight, an officer in the British army in India. Although he did not penetrate into Tibet itself, he did travel in Ladakh. He has described his adventures in a book entitled *Diary of a Pedestrian in Cashmere and Thibet* (1863). Captain Knight reveals himself as the very prototype of the colonialist military officer, amused and condescending in his attitude toward the local population. In relating an episode from his visit to the monastery of Hemis, he makes no attempt to hide a supercilious sneer prompted by what he clearly regarded as the blind superstition of the Tibetans:

> During the day we had a good opportunity of seeing the Lamas go through their private devotions. The operation appeared simple enough. Each as he entered the court and passed along the rows of wheels, by simply stretching out his arm set the whole of them in motion, at the same time repeating "Om mani panee" in a dolorous voice to himself. Coming then to the large wheel with painted characters, he gave it an extra energetic spin...and having thus expended his energies for the time being, he again disappeared as he had come. One of the smaller wheels I found in a state of neglect and dilapidation...and thinking it a good opportunity to discover something as to the meaning of the system in general and of "Om mani panee" in particular, I quietly abstracted the inner contents, in full assurance that it would never be missed; that the wheel itself would go round as merrily as ever, and that, as far as the prayers were concerned, there were still sufficient left behind...to satisfy the conscience even of the devoutest of Lamas. (p. 200)

Facing the page where these words are found, the modern reader is amazed to discover, neatly mounted in each copy of the book, a piece of the original paper strip with printed prayers that Knight stole at Hemis! Knight also informs us that the prayers were "inclosed in a coarse canvas cover...marked with what was no doubt the official seal of the particular society *for the diffusion of ignorance at Lassa* from which it had originally emanated" (p. 200, italics mine). Speaking of the images of the Buddha, he observes that "[a] certain rotundity of form, however, and appearance of *comfortableness,* rather tend to suggest that the pleasures of the table at least have not quite been renounced among the other pomps and vanities of Buddhist life" (p. 201).

One of the results of European imperialism that was to have profound consequences for Tibetan studies was the discovery, early in this century, of the walled-up library in the Buddhist temple-caves at Dunhuang in northwestern China. Times were such that several European scholars were able to send vast quantities of these texts back to libraries in Paris and London, where they kept several generations of scholars busy and probably will continue to do so for the foreseeable future. Among these texts was a large number of early Tibetan documents, including some that deal with cosmological and ritual questions, apparently without any trace of Buddhist influence. It was therefore natural that once some of these texts had been edited and studied, scholars, above all in France, should turn their attention to what seemed to be the earliest religion of Tibet.

The image projected by scholars of this early Tibetan religion was not always liable to arouse feelings of sympathy. In her book *Les religions du Tibet*, published in 1957, Marcelle Lalou, the foremost expert at the time on these early Tibetan documents, characterized the pre-Buddhist religion of Tibet, known as Bon, in the following words: "If I had to define in two words that which seems to me most characteristic of the milieu of Bon, I would say: blood and poison" (p. 12, translation mine).

Bon is depicted as a ritualistic religion obsessed with bloody sacrificial rites and with administering poison to enemies. But Marcelle Lalou, too, is not without a nature-mythological bent of mind when she states:

> Nor is it impossible that some of the events recounted are renderings by means of imagery of the impressive and dangerous phenomena of the Tibetan climate, and that they for the most part are simply inspired by the characteristics of the seasons that regulate the life of the pastoralists. (p. 10, translation mine)

However, not all scholars wished to (or had the necessary philological competence to) take these documents into account. Another approach to early, pre-Buddhist Tibetan religion was to assume that whatever could be found in the popular religion or in later ritual texts that was not clearly or explicitly Buddhist represented survivals of the ancient, autochthonous religion of Tibet, which, on the basis of such sources, could be reconstructed by the Western scholar. A curious blend of evolutionism and romanticism can be found in some of the work of the German scholar Helmut Hoffmann. Speaking of the "original religion" of Tibet, he places it at an early evolutionary stage of human culture, stating that "Today we are in a position to say with some certainty that the original Bon religion was the national Tibetan form of that old animist-shamanist religion that at one time was widespread not only in Siberia but throughout the whole of Inner Asia, East and West Turkestan, Mongolia, Manchuria, the Tibetan plateaux and even China" (1961: 14–15).

The term "animist-shamanist" consistently used by Hoffmann to describe early as well as popular Tibetan religion was to prove extremely tenacious, and is still found today. This idea was, as mentioned, combined by Hoffmann with the nature-romantic idea of the forces of nature being the wellsprings of religion:

[T]he Tibetans of those days were apparently completely subject to the powerful and formidable nature of their natural surroundings. Their completely nature-rooted and nature-dominated religious ideas revolved reverently and submissively around the powers and forces of their wild highland landscape whose divinities were reflected in the idea of numerous good and evil spirits the Tibetans thought to see all around them. (Ibid., 17)

In the first decades of this century, evolutionism was opposed in the field of ethnology and history of religions by a completely different theory, the so-called Kulturkreislehre. This theory was "developed at the beginning of the twentieth century by German ethnologists in order to provide ethnology with a cultural-historical perspective and thus to secure for ethnology a place in the science of history" (Eliade, 1987:

Vol. 8, 396). It was above all the Viennese linguist and ethnologist Pater Wilhelm Schmidt who developed the model of culture circles into a global system by means of which he claimed to be able to reconstruct the oldest, most primeval type of human culture and the subsequent development of all other types of culture from this source. The oldest culture, styled "primitive culture," was that of hunters and gatherers; from it developed three so-called primary cultures: (1) matrilineal and agricultural; (2) patrilineal and "higher hunting"; and (3) patrilineal and pastoral-nomadic. One important aspect of the Kulturkreislehre was the theory that the religion of the primitive hunters and gatherers was characterized by a simple, monotheistic belief in a high god associated with the sky—in fact, Schmidt spoke in theological terms of an "Ur-Offenbarung," a primeval, original revelation that was only gradually supplanted by belief in magic and polytheism. In other words, Pater Schmidt postulated the opposite process from that taken for granted by the evolutionists, who regarded monotheism (or agnosticism) as the final stage of intellectual evolution. Further, he claimed that among the "primary cultures," only the nomadic pastoralists had preserved the belief in a monotheistic sky god, although not in its pristine purity.

It is perhaps not well known that the ideas of the Kulturkreislehre have been applied to Tibet as well. A representative of the so-called Viennese school of ethnology is, however, to be found in the person of Pater Matthias Hermanns who spent many years in the 1930s and 40s in Amdo, the northeastern part of Tibet, where he intensively studied the culture of the nomads. He not only arrived at the conclusion that Amdo was the cradle of Tibetan civilization, and that the culture of the nomads of Amdo to a large extent perpetuated the most ancient form of Tibetan culture, but he also reconstructed the prehistoric diffusion of pastoral nomadism from the steppes of western Central Asia to northeastern Tibet. Here, among the nomads of Amdo, he claimed to find— entirely in accordance with the postulates of the Kulturkreislehre—the belief in a high god: "numerous customs and practices of their social life clearly show that above the host of spirits and fairies, demons and devils, they believe in a high god." (1959: 311, translation mine).

The historical perspective of Hermanns eventually led him to postulate exact dates for events that most researchers generally assigned to the realm of mythology; thus he claimed that the famous Gesar epic of the Tibetans arose some two thousand years ago: "We regard this period from about 400 B.C. until the fall of the Han Dynasty in 220 A.D. as the heroic epoch of the Tibetans, in which the national epic of the people came into being." (1965: 268).

Likewise Hermanns discovered the reflection of different phases of cultural development in the various myths preserved in oral and written sources (the latter, of course, not exclusively preserved among the nomads of Amdo):

> While the oldest myths indicate the period of the breeders of horned cattle, whose primeval king descended direct from heaven to the earth and, after having fulfilled his mission, returned to heaven without experiencing death, the later myths reflect the conflict with the simple horse breeders. In the following period culture heroes introduce further innovations, in order to develop constantly the hybrid culture of the ruling breeders of horned cattle and the conquered agriculturalists.... Thus the birth throes of a new culture are portrayed. (Ibid.)

Few, if any, scholars today would still utilize Schmidt's Kulturkreislehre as a historical paradigm. The virtue of the Kulturkreislehre, however, was to focus on broad historical trends, and, in the case of Hermanns, to relate Tibet to fundamental historical processes on the Eurasian continent. He also makes use of a second concept, which, as we shall see, has been taken up by other scholars as well: Tibet as a repository of archaic forms of biological and—more importantly— social life. In other words, he created the image of Tibet as a sanctuary:

> Here have been preserved a number of archaic forms of animal and plant life that otherwise have long since died out on our planet. This fact alone would suggest that in this country archaic cultures have likewise been preserved. Cut off from each other by high mountain ranges and deep valleys, the most diverse ethnic groups have survived or else, under the influence of the unique environment, formed a separate and distinctive nation. (1949: xi)

I would like to mention a scholar who has contributed to Tibetan studies an image of Tibet as a sanctuary: Siegbert Hummel, whose originality and erudition are only now slowly gaining the recognition they deserve. Hummel has studied mythological elements in Tibetan, Egyptian, and Etruscan religions, arguing that they show traces of neolithic cultural continuities (although he does of course also point out later, historical contacts) between Central Asia and the Mediterranean world. In the field of linguistics, too, he has attempted to link Tibet with a vast and archaic cultural-linguistic web, styled "proto-altaic." Thus Tibet becomes a precious and unique area for what one might call the "cultural archaeologist."

It is impossible to speak of researchers on Tibet in the past century without mentioning Giuseppe Tucci (1894–1984). Tucci was not only an exceptionally erudite and versatile scholar, whose activities were related to many parts of Asia, but also by all accounts a charismatic personality. His attitude to fascism in Italy until the end of the Second World War was, however, apparently ambivalent; one of his close friends and associates was Giovanni Gentile, Mussolini's minister of education at the beginning of the fascist regime (Benavides, 1995: 174). Tucci's attitude toward Tibet was similarly ambiguous, as has been pointed out by Benavides. Much of his early work was concerned with the philosophical systems of India. Tucci "claims that all forms of Indian and Tibetan thought are based upon an experience that alone gives these forms their content and real value. On the other hand, referring to the actual practice of the Tibetans, Tucci considers "Lamaism" the formalistic mechanization of the rites of an Indian gnosis.... Lamaism in its present state is, for him, the result of an obfuscation, a passing from mystical contemplation to the torpor of the services performed in the monasteries" (Ibid., 165). Such were Tucci's views in the 1930s; in the 1950s, however, he expressed a kind of admiration for Tibetan society, which he regarded—when he last visited Tibet in 1948—as still uncontaminated by the ills besetting the modern world, chief among which were "politics." Tucci now claimed that:

The Tibetans are not far different from us: only they were long ensnared by a religious and magic outlook on life, in which the boundaries between the realms of reality and possibility, of truth and imagination were not clear-cut ones. The intellect in them had not yet reached such a degree of freedom as to stamp out the dreams of the soul. (Tucci, 1956: 98)

He then continues with a passage in which one may perhaps discern a certain nostalgia for the corporatist ideals of fascism, paradoxically combined with romantic longings for the absolute and limitless freedom of the individual:

In Tibet man had not yet disintegrated: he still sank his roots fully into the collective subconscious which knows no difference between past and present. In that uniformity of feelings and thoughts you could hardly expect a full-fledged personality...to strike out for himself, discarding that indistinct background. That would require a self-sufficient, lonely soul having its isolation as its only guide. In Tibet on the contrary greatness had always been measured in function of conformity to tradition. (Ibid., 98)

On the balance, however, he concludes on a positive note: "The medieval aura still enshrouding Tibet...still allowed man a greater mastery than Western ways of life." This was because

The State was not an anonymous tyrant poking his nose everywhere and controlling all you did, you had, you said and, according to some ideologies, even what you thought. In Tibet the State was a few people you could get personally—and humanly—in touch with, and not the shapeless red tape tying up and squeezing everything and threatening to shatter civilization.... Give me a personal master any time rather than an abstraction named State or democracy or what not, in whose hand I should feel hopelessly enslaved. Man has indeed been born under an unlucky star, and only the saint or the poet can somehow struggle free from it. (Ibid., 101)

When, as Tucci probably would have seen it, the twentieth century finally caught up with Tibet in the form of the Chinese invasion and subsequent occupation in 1950–51, it became impossible to travel to Tibet, and he seems to have gradually lost interest in Tibet. His restless spirit eventually led him to other parts of Asia, first to Nepal, and later to Swat and regions even farther to the west.

While Tucci left Tibet for other parts of Asia, a new generation of Tibetologists in the 1960s and 70s turned to the study of Tibet, and especially of Tibetan Buddhism. Most of these scholars were trained in North America, and a few in Europe. The background and motivation of this generation of students have been described with honesty and insight by Donald Lopez as follows:

> The invasion and occupation of Tibet...were to bring...significant shifts in the western construction of Tibetan Buddhism. ...In the 1960s, scholars from European universities...traveled to India to work with refugee Tibetan scholars in the translation of Buddhist texts. Popular interest in the exotic world of Tibetan Buddhism also boomed as Evans-Wentz's 1927 rendering of a Tibetan text he dubbed *The Tibetan Book of the Dead* became part of the LSD canon.... At the same time, the U.S. Library of Congress was sponsoring the publication of thousands of heretofore unknown Tibetan texts.... In this way, the long mysterious Tibetan archive became as if magically manifest in the stacks of American university libraries.... There was constant reference during this period to the present perilous state and how it differed from "pre-1959 Tibet." (Lopez, 1995b: 264–65)

Lopez describes the feeling of extreme urgency that we who were students in that period experienced. He points out that this feeling was intensified by certain fundamental Buddhist ideas:

> Western students of Buddhism imbibed this rhetoric of urgency from the Buddhist texts they studied. ...Unlike with Desideri or Waddell, the aim of study is not to defeat Tibetan Buddhism in ideological battle; instead Buddhist doctrine is sympathetically

regarded as valuable because of its salvific powers in the modern world. (p. 266)

Buddhism in general, specifically Tibetan Buddhism, was now viewed with admiration:

> The view of Tibet as a closed society that had so fascinated and vexed European travelers in the colonial period was now represented as a reason Tibetan Buddhism was more authentic than any other.... Like other Buddhist traditions, the Tibetans based claims to authority largely on lineage.... Now that lineage was in danger of extinction. There was something apocalyptic about it, as if the Tibetans, long conservators of timeless wisdom in a timeless realm, had been brutally thrust from their snowy sanctuary into history.... For the oral tradition not to be lost, locked within the minds of aged and dying refugee lamas, it had to be passed on...the young Tibetans appeared to be losing interest in their religion, seduced by materialism, nationalism, and rock music. There seemed to be only one group ready for the task: American graduate students. (p. 268)

Reading these lines recently for the first time, I was struck by how accurately they described my own state of mind in those days; and I think that most of us who were young in the sixties and seventies have retained something of this sense of urgency and personal involvement. Whether we have also retained the myth, in Lopez's words, of Tibet as "a fragile site of origin and preserve, still regarded from the periphery as a timeless center" (p. 269) must be for others to judge; but Tibetan studies have continued to evolve.

Today the study of Tibet and Tibetan culture in all its aspects is extremely diversified and far-ranging, a fact to which this volume bears eloquent witness. It is probably premature to attempt to distinguish underlying trends and presuppositions of current research, in which we as scholars are ourselves so intimately involved. Nevertheless, I would like to point out one present trend, or, if you prefer, "image" of Tibet that I regard as significant—the effort to insert the study of Tibet into a wider regional or even global historical or social context. Few serious scholars today would regard Tibet as a country somehow outside the rest of the world or as a mere repository of Buddhist culture long since lost in its land of origin. Inward-looking, exclusively text-oriented Tibetology is no longer viable (although some anthropologists occasionally seem to feel a need to flog dead horses). To illustrate my point, I shall briefly present four contemporary scholars, all of them "Tibetologists" in the sense that their research has been, to a large degree, concerned with Tibet: historian Christopher I. Beckwith; social anthropologist Geoffrey Samuel; sociologist Ronald D. Schwartz; and historian of religions Hanna Havnevik.

In 1977 Beckwith published an article that in my opinion is one of the most important in recent decades for the understanding of Tibetan history. Inventing a new term, "florissance" (from French, in the sense of "flourishing" or "flowering"), it is entitled "Tibet and the Early Medieval *Florissance* in Eurasia: A Preliminary Note on the Economic History of the Tibetan Empire" (1977). The original contribution of this article was that it inserted the Tibetan empire, which entered the historical scene in the early seventh century A.D., into a context in which "the Eurasian world was shared by a number of very large states, the most notable of which were the Tibetan, the Turco-Uighur, the Chinese T'ang, the Arabo-Persian, the Greek Byzantine, and the German Frankish empires.... Furthermore, in many aspects of their economic, political, and cultural developments their histories are very closely parallel" (p. 89). Beckwith gives a broad overview of the development of trade, finance, and subsequent urbanization throughout these empires in the seventh to the ninth centuries, a process in which the Tibetan empire, too, participated; and he shows how the "absolutely astonishing economic and cultural growth across Eurasia, from Japan to England" (p. 93) had similar political and social repercussions in all these empires, due not to parallel developments, but resulting from economic interdependence. Beckwith has convincingly established the importance of viewing Tibet in a global context; and, as we shall now see, this perspective has in recent years been extended from the study of history to the social sciences.

In 1993, Samuel published a remarkable book, with the somewhat provocative title *Civilized Shamans: Buddhism in Tibetan Societies* (1993). This book gives a unique and detailed overview of all the different polities—theocratic states, principalities, tribal federations, and stateless regions—that together constitute the vast area of the Tibetan world, reminding us that the centralized theocratic state headed by the Dalai Lama with Lhasa as its capital was only one—albeit the largest— of the Tibetan states. It also gives a brilliant historical account of religion in Tibet, from the time of the early Tibetan kings until today, providing much new information and new insights. On top of this, however, Samuel subjects Tibetan religion, both in its social and doctrinal dimensions, to a systematic analysis using categories that have already been applied to other Buddhist cultures in Asia. In particular, he distinguishes between what he calls "clerical Buddhism" and "shamanic Buddhism." He further distinguishes between two distinct "shamanic complexes" in Tibetan religion: Tibetan folk religion and shamanic Buddhism. By the latter term, he refers to Tantric Buddhism, in that it is "centered around communication with an alternative mode of reality (that of the Tantric deities) via the alternate states of consciousness of Tantric yoga" (Ibid., 8). Having established these categories, he draws the conclusion that—on the level of religious practice—"Lamas in Tibet function as shamans, and they do so through the techniques and practices of Vajrayana Buddhism" (Ibid., 9).

This is not the place to discuss Samuel's use of the term "shamanism." What is of importance, however, is that when taken together with the complementary term "clerical," he is able to provide a coherent theoretical framework within which Tibetan religion and society may be analyzed in terms that are also applicable to other Asian societies, thus inserting Tibet into the larger surrounding world. Only then—and this is an important consequence—is it possible to relate Tibet to serious contemporary issues such as human rights, colonialism, and international law.

Issues of human rights and colonialism are the point of departure for Canadian sociologist Ronald D. Schwartz's recent work relating to Tibet. His research focuses on Tibet as an arena for nation-building and political protest by Tibetans directed against the Chinese state. In this movement of national protest, a crucial role is played by Tibetan monks and nuns whose strategy of nonviolence has successfully defeated the Chinese administration in appropriating symbols of political legality. Schwartz's most significant contribution, however, is to present an image of Tibet in which he perceives the Tibetan movement of national protest as related to similar movements elsewhere in Asia. In other words, he analyzes the Tibetan phenomenon in terms of models with which social scientists are already familiar.

> Buddhism in contemporary Tibet is identified with progressive political ideas such as democracy and human rights, as well as nationalist opposition to Chinese rule. Tibetan Buddhist monks and nuns have played leadership roles both in initiating protest and in disseminating new ideas. Within the last five years, movements for democracy have occurred in other Asian Buddhist societies, including Mongolia, Burma, and Thailand. These countries may have very different social and political histories, but they all represent societies and cultures that have been shaped by Buddhism. Buddhist ideas and leadership figure in much of the recent opposition to military/authoritarian regimes in Asia.
>
> *Protest initiated by monks and nuns in contemporary Tibet should be investigated in the light of comparable developments in other Asian Buddhist societies.* The orientation and political participation of Tibetan monks and nuns may then be understood in terms of structural and institutional features common to Buddhist societies. (Schwartz, 1994a: 728, italics mine)

Schwartz proceeds to a concrete comparison between Tibet and Burma, another Buddhist country previously under colonial rule:

> There are some parallels between the situation of monks and nuns in Tibet and the conditions Tambiah describes for monasteries in Burma during and after British colonial rule, where the "domination by a Western colonial power activated Buddhist monks into a tradition of political action" through a vacillating

and destructive religious policy that led to the "atrophy of any hierarchical authority exerting control over the monks and monasteries." Tambiah concludes that the "weakened, atomistic nature of sangha organization" contributed in turn to the "politicization of monks and their engagement in militant, anticolonial, nationalist politics." (pp. 729–30)

A similar process is seen to be at work in Tibet today.

The most significant contribution Schwartz has made to Tibetan studies is his book, *Circle of Protest: Political Ritual in the Tibetan Uprising* (1994b), a detailed presentation and analysis of demonstrations against the Chinese state by Tibetans in the five years 1987–92. Underlying the entire book is the assumption that "the situation in Tibet under Chinese rule can be compared with political developments in the Theravadin Buddhist countries of Thailand, Burma, and Sri Lanka" (p. 222). Thus while "the demonstrations that have taken place in Lhasa since 1987 are acts of cultural invention" (p. 8), and hence specifically Tibetan, Tibet is presented nevertheless as one aspect of the strife-torn, contemporary world.

A commitment to solidarity with the Tibetan people has, in fact, become an underlying premise for many scholars engaged in Tibetan studies today. This, too, reflects an image of Tibet as an arena for the struggle for universal human values—a vastly different image from that of the superstitious and contemptible natives who were the object of Knight's highhandedness in 1860. One recent scholarly study in which the theme of solidarity is explicitly stated is Norwegian researcher Hanna Havnevik's *Tibetan Buddhist Nuns: History, Cultural Norms and Social Reality* (1989). This book (translated into French as *Combats des nonnes tibétaines* (1995) was provided by the author with the following dedication: "To the brave nuns in Tibet, who fearlessly fight to regain the independence of their country." The French version has an additional section in which the role of nuns in the protest movement against the Chinese state is dealt with in detail; we should also note the author's attempt to understand the role of the nuns by making use of certain theoretical models from social anthropology, elaborated by Anthony F. C. Wallace and others, regarding the phenomenon called "revitalization." Without dwelling on the substance of this term, we once again see that Tibetan studies have been integrated into a wider, ongoing discussion and made relevant to a wider scholarly community.

I embarked upon this investigation by mentioning evolutionism as one of the intellectual products of the nineteenth century. Gradually, evolutionism was left behind, to be supplemented by other intellectual fashions, resulting in other images of Tibet. Having now reached the end of this ramble through more than a hundred years of Tibetology, I wonder whether I may not have fallen into the subtle trap of construing my own variant of evolutionism, seeing in Tibetan studies a hidden entelechy toward ever greater human involvement, ever greater solidarity, and so on. Perhaps the uniqueness and dignity of the individual is compromised not only by focusing on abstractions (favored by the Chinese state) like "progress," "profit," and "stability," but also on "nation," "culture," "religion," and "rights." Who can say how future generations will judge *our* images of Tibet?

PART TWO
The Sight of the "Other"

"Truth," Perception, and Politics

THE BRITISH CONSTRUCTION
OF AN IMAGE OF TIBET[1]

Alex C. McKay

Introduction

WHEN WESTERNERS THINK OF TIBET TODAY, the name conjures up a series of images around terms such as "Dalai Lama," "Roof of the World," and "Shangri-la." These images can be divided into two categories. The first, with which this paper is primarily concerned, comprises the historical image. This set of representations, upon which much of our academic research is based, was largely constructed by the British officials who served in Tibet between 1904 and 1947.

The second category of images is the "mystical," or, as some prefer, the "mythical," whereby Tibet is perceived as a spiritual realm beyond precise empirical understanding. Despite the existence of a historical image of Tibet, this mystical image retains considerable power. For example, Tsering Shakya, a Tibetan historian who grew up in England, likes to tell the story of an academic colleague who told him that "I can never get used to the idea of a Tibetan driving a car."[2]

Although we have created similar mystical images of unknown lands before (such as those of Australia, or the source of the Nile), they faded and disappeared as those lands became known to European science. Yet the mystical image of Tibet survived its encounter with modern science. The answer to the question of how and why that has happened can be found in an examination of the perceptions and political motives involved in the British construction of the historical image of Tibet.

The British Presence in Tibet

The Anglo-Tibetan encounter began in earnest in 1903–1904, when a British mission under the command of the Indian Political Officer Lieutenant-Colonel Francis (later Sir Francis) Younghusband fought its way to the Tibetan capital Lhasa. Younghusband's mission was designed to ensure the security of British India's northern frontier from Russian infiltration. While Russia was always seen as the principal threat to India, at various times China, Japan, and Nazi Germany were also suspected of seeking to subvert British interests in India through this route.

The Younghusband mission brought Tibet within the British sphere of interest as a "buffer state" preventing subversion, or in the most extreme fear, invasion through India's northern frontier. To ensure their control of this "buffer state," the British wanted to post representatives in Tibet, preferably in Lhasa, where, as Younghusband put it, a British officer could "practically run the whole show."[3]

An alternative policy would have been to allow China to control Tibet. There was support for that solution from a number of elements in the British government, particularly the Foreign Office, which tended to take a more pro-Chinese stance than the Government of India. But the Indian view was that if China took over Tibet, the frontier would remain unstable because the Tibetans would resist Chinese rule, and that instability was something they feared Russia could take advantage of. India also considered the Chinese "unpleasant neighbors,"[4] and liable to pose a threat to British influence in other parts of the Himalayas, such as Nepal and Bhutan.

Younghusband's mission established a permanent British presence in Tibet, with British officers stationed in so-called trade agencies at Gyantse in central Tibet, Yatung in southern Tibet, and, after 1936, in Lhasa itself. There was also an agency at Gartok in western Tibet, but this was staffed by provincial government for most of the period, and was of only symbolic political importance.[5]

The British officers posted to these "trade agencies" were selected by the Indian Political Department, which was, in effect, the diplomatic corps of the Government of India. The Political Department served the interests of the Raj, which were not necessarily the same as the interests of the British government in Whitehall. Although called "trade agents," the role of these imperial officers was actually similar to that of the Residents in the Indian princely states: to obtain information concerning local events and personalities and to influence the local authorities to follow policies that benefited British interests.

It should be noted that the trade agents obtained information both through official channels and by the use of what the Government of India itself termed "secret agents," which is not something either the British or the Tibetans have found diplomatic to mention subsequently.[6]

The trade agents stationed in Tibet were under the immediate command of the political officer in Sikkim. That officer was officially recognized as the Government of India's principal advisor on Tibetan affairs. Among those Sikkim political officers were such famous names on the frontier as David Macdonald, Colonel F. M. Bailey, and, most influentially, Sir Charles Bell, who served as political officer in Sikkim for most of the period from 1908 to 1921.

Of the many officers posted to Tibet, only twenty served for long enough to have had any real influence on Anglo-Tibetan relations. For want of a collective term for these men, I refer to them as the "Tibet cadre."

The Tibet cadre followed the usual British Indian strategy of trying to ally with the local rulers in order to influence them to support British policies. In the absence of a single paramount authority in Tibet during the 1904–1912 period, the cadre had little success. But in 1910, when China sent troops into Lhasa in an attempt to establish their authority there, the Thirteenth Dalai Lama (who had only returned to Tibet from exile in Mongolia and China a few months earlier) fled to India.

Although the prevailing British view at the time, both in India and at Whitehall, was that the Dalai Lama was now a figure of no secular importance, Charles Bell understood the opportunity that had presented itself. He deliberately set out to befriend the Dalai Lama and apparently succeeded in gaining his trust.

In 1911, when the Chinese revolution broke out, the Chinese position in Tibet soon collapsed. The Dalai Lama returned to Tibet, with Bell now in the powerful position of being the Tibetan leader's most trusted foreign advisor. Bell established a policy of support for the Dalai Lama that was to remain the fundamental basis of British Indian policy in Tibet until 1947.

Information and Early Images

Although fear of Russian influence had been the immediate cause of the Younghusband mission, an underlying cause was the British desire for more information about their northern neighbor. Prior to the mission, European knowledge of Tibet was very limited. Such knowledge as did exist, from a brief mention in Marco Polo, for example, already emphasized the magic and mystery with which the region had long been associated in Indian sources. While there were reports from eighteenth-century Jesuit and Capuchin missionaries, these had not been widely disseminated, and the basis for European Tibetan scholarship had been established by the works of nineteenth-century pioneers such as Brian Henry Hodgson and Csoma de Körös, who had not actually visited Tibet.

European adventurers and explorers, and Indian *pandits* who had been trained by British intelligence in the arts of mapping, had traveled in Tibet in the nineteenth century. But at that time the Lhasa government was trying to prevent Europeans from entering Tibet, principally because they saw foreigners as a threat to their religion. Tibet was generally successful in keeping Europeans from reaching the main political and cultural centers, and details of Tibet's government and leading personalities thus remained largely unknown to the outside world.

The British could not allow this situation to continue. Their imperial system relied on the use of information, particularly that of strategic and political value, and they made great efforts to ensure that the flow of information from British spheres of interest was not disrupted. This need made the Younghusband mission a logical imperial response to the lack of intelligence about their northern neighbor.

Tibet's policy of isolation had led to considerable public interest in what became known as the "forbidden land." The allure of the unknown meant that not only the government, but also the British public, wanted to know more about Tibet. That demand was temporarily filled by a number of books about the Younghusband mission, written by officers or journalists who accompanied Younghusband. As we might expect, these writers wanted to justify the mission. Thus the Tibetan government and the religious system surrounding it were presented in a negative light, the use of modern weapons against primitively armed irregular forces was defended, and so on.[7]

Their descriptions of Tibet and its people in these accounts were typical of the discourse of war. The *London Times* correspondent, for example, described the Tibetans as a "stunted and dirty little people."[8] Even frontier officers who were later to describe the Tibetans in laudatory terms then joined in condemning them as (to quote a military report to which Bell contributed) "untruthful and faithless, deceitful and insincere." This report also described Tibetan Buddhism as "a disastrous parasitic disease."[9] But this discourse must be seen in context; it was produced by a state of Anglo-Tibetan conflict, and these negative images were, in general, characteristic only of that period.

We are all now familiar with the concept that knowledge is constructed in a form determined by dominant power structures, and with the argument that this construction was used by the imperial powers to denigrate local knowledge, social structures, and power systems, which ultimately prevented an objective understanding of one society by the other. Yet, in the case of Tibet, the images produced, after the initial period of conflict at the time of the Younghusband mission, were largely positive ones. After 1910, the British began to describe Tibetan government and society as decent, virtuous, and of value to the world at large—generally the sort of image that we might have expected if the Tibetans had hired a modern American public relations firm! As we will see, however, there was a sound political motive behind this construction.

"Truth," Perception, and Policy

Three main factors shaped the positive images that emerged from the Anglo-Tibetan imperial encounter: the search for "truth," individual perception, and international politics. We should not overlook the fact that, at least in the case of Tibet (and, I suspect, in other areas of imperial encounter), colonial officials did try to discover the "truth" about their subject—the "truth," that is, as they understood it; and without entering into a deep analysis of that understanding, we may describe it as a belief in empirical and scientifically ascertainable records.

This search for "truth" was seen, in the ethos of the time, as a morally higher purpose behind an imperial official's day-to-day activities. Increasing the existing body of knowledge was considered part of the "civilizing mission" of the imperial nations, and this greater good could be used as a moral justification for less ethical actions. Lord Curzon, the viceroy of India, who was the driving force behind the Younghusband mission, was in no doubt that increasing the body of knowledge was part of the wider function of an Indian official. "It is," he proclaimed, "equally our duty to dig and discover, to classify, reproduce and describe, to copy and decipher, and to cherish and conserve."[10]

Thus, after the initial period of Anglo-Tibetan conflict, cadre officers did intend to find the "truth" about Tibet. There was a personal factor in this. Most cadre officers wanted to serve there. They were interested in Tibet and wanted to learn as much as they could about the country and its people because it attracted them personally. If it did not, it was very easy for them to get a transfer back to India. Those who stayed for a year or more were there because they wanted to be there.

This meant that cadre officers made considerable efforts to establish accurate records of Tibet, and in most cases where their information was unreliable, they said so in their reports. For example, Indo-Tibetan trade figures were given to the government with the warning that most traders actually avoided the trade registration post, in order to avoid paying customs duties.[11]

Yet although cadre officers generally sought to present a true picture of Tibet, their own inherent perceptions naturally affected their reports. These officers had passed through a process of education, training, and selection that produced individuals with a particular character and perspective. Virtually all of them came from families with a tradition of imperial service. They were educated at British public schools, and universities or military colleges, and most had served in the Indian Civil Service or the Indian Army before applying for Political Department service in Tibet. The political officers in Sikkim generally chose the trade agents personally, and they selected successors in their own likeness. This process was deliberately designed to, and generally succeeded in, producing a collective mentality—a group of individuals with a very similar perspective on Tibetan matters.[12]

These perceptions did change with time and varied with the individual. For example, when the Gyantse Trade Agency was opened, the agent there hired a Tibetan Buddhist exorcist, who "kindly expelled all the devils and spirits from the new stables" in a "very interesting" ceremony. Yet another officer, who was clearly equally interested in Tibet, nevertheless described similar religious rites as "dreadful examples of the backwardness of Tibet...[and a]...complete waste of money."[13]

Yet individual variations in perception were largely submerged in a collective approach to, and understanding of, Tibet that was deliberately inculcated in these officers by the imperial training process they had undergone. This process meant that while cadre officers gained a great understanding of Tibet, and made genuine efforts to encourage what they considered improvements there, they never forgot that their first duty was to the Government of India. It should not be forgotten that this training process was not designed to produce detached observers and social scientists. It was designed to produce imperial frontier officers who could be relied on to follow the general trends of Government of India policy, and the result was that the cadre did describe Tibet from the perspective of British imperial frontier officers.

Perhaps the most obvious characteristic of this perspective was its very narrow class base. Just as the British imperial process marginalized indigenous "subaltern" voices, so too were the voices of British "subalterns" marginalized. More than one hundred British clerical, communications, and medical staff served at the trade agencies. This includes the Europeans who spent the longest time in Tibet (two British telegraph sergeants) and the European who spent the longest time in Lhasa (a British radio officer). But all three of these men were what the English call "working class," and their names—Henry Martin, W. H. Luff, and Reginald Fox—have been forgotten by history. As far as I can ascertain, none of them left any record of their experiences or impressions of Tibet, and there are only passing references to them in the cadre officers' memoirs.[14]

No matter how experienced or knowledgeable these support personnel became, they were excluded from the image-making process. The perspectives they gained from their social contacts with the lower levels of Tibetan society were lost. Equally there was little opportunity for the emergence of a British feminist perspective, as only a handful of cadre officers' wives or daughters visited Tibet.

The most obvious affect of the cadre's class-based perceptions was the marginalization of the voice of Tibet's lower classes. Some officers did criticize the conditions that the peasantry endured, but the cadre maintained a positive image of Tibet by attributing misrule to the period of Chinese domination before 1911, and they stressed that conditions were improving under the Dalai Lama's rule. Overwhelmingly, contemporary British sources stressed the happiness and contentment of the peasantry, who "unwashed though they may be...are always smiling." In this discourse even "the slavery was of a very mild type."[15]

When we read their reports, we must also remember that the cadre officers had careers to consider. At least two trade agents who served briefly in Tibet recorded private impressions of the country that were in great contrast to the prevailing image. One recalls "the dominance and brutality of the Lamas and officials towards the serf population."[16] Another officer in the 1940s confided to his diary that "I have serious doubts whether Tibet is at all fit for independence.... As we don't seem to do much developing of Tibet, I question whether the Chinese would not be able to do it to our own mutual advantage."[17] But neither officer appears to have expressed these views officially. They were doubtless aware that expressing views diametrically opposed to those of their superiors was unlikely to advance their careers. This gave them an incentive to self-censorship and helped to ensure that the Tibet cadre spoke with one voice.

The cadre's unified voice was a powerful weapon. They were the main provider of information on Tibetan affairs to the Government of India and they guarded that status very carefully. For example, during their early years there, they went to considerable lengths to get rid of Europeans serving in the China Customs Service post at Yatung, and they also succeeded in getting rid of a China consular post on the eastern Tibetan frontier. The British officers who worked for the Chinese often provided the government with reports contradicting the cadre's view, and their elimination ensured the cadre's control over information from Tibet.[18]

As well as controlling other European official "voices," the cadre was generally able to control the entry of private European travelers to the region. They did this by requiring that travelers wishing to enter Tibet from India obtain a permit from the political officer in Sikkim before being allowed near the border region. The Tibetan government also wanted to keep foreigners out, and so Tibetan and British officials played out an elaborate charade in which each blamed the other for excluding Europeans from Tibet, while in fact allowing in only those whom the cadre wanted to admit. Thus, with some notable exceptions such as Heinrich Harrer and Alexandra David-Néel, who entered Tibet illicitly, only those who were approved of by the Government of India, such as the distinguished Tibetologist Professor Giuseppe Tucci,[19] managed to enter Tibet.

Permits to travel across the Indian frontier as far as Yatung were actually fairly easy to obtain. By the 1940s several hundred visitors a year were allowed to go there, but it was much more difficult to get permission to travel into the Tibetan hinterland.

After an American traveler, William McGovern, published various derogatory comments on the political situation in Tibet in the 1920s, travelers were required to sign a statement agreeing to submit to the Government of India for censorship anything they wrote about their journey.[20] This was designed to ensure that information from Tibet remained within the control of the Tibet cadre and their government, and this regulation largely succeeded in silencing any alternative European perspectives. Those who provided an alternative account, such as McGovern, were criticized in official media using the weight of evidence from those whose travels and writings had been officially approved of.[21]

The cadre's "voice" became the dominant one because it deliberately suppressed alternative perspectives. Thus most of the information concerning Tibet from this time was provided by, or reflects the perspective of, a small group of around twenty men of the British offi-cer class.[22]

Before turning to the question of how the cadre's views were affected by the political requirements of their government, one other factor that affected the cadre officers' accounts of Tibet should be noted. This factor was neither personal nor political, but commercial. Human nature meant, and still means, that the general reading public in the West was interested in the sensational and colorful aspects of that land. As the officers' books were published by commercial pub-lishers and since it became increasingly difficult to market a purely pos-itivist work, officers needed to take account of public taste. Thus when Colonel Bailey submitted draft chapters of a book describing his time in Tibet, the publisher's reader returned it with suggestions on how to make it more interesting for the general public. The reader advised Bailey that

> the general reader wants something more human—a hint of the authors [sic] physical and spiritual reaction to his disappoint-ments and to his successes.... A little description too of the peo-ples...the scenery also...which must be colourful [and have]...a thrill in the telling.[23]

The result of this commercial demand was that cadre officers' books contained the commercially necessary "colorful" and "thrilling" images. They provide numerous descriptions of "sky burials," monas-tic dances, hermit's retreats, aristocratic pageantry, oracle's trances, and so on. Thus, although cadre officers personally had a more balanced view of Tibet, popular demand by the reading public led to this empha-sis on exotic images. This commercial factor has been largely ignored in the debate over Orientalism, which ascribes political motives to the human attraction to, and desire for, "exotic" images.

We should also remember that the deliberate distortion of Tibet's image was not the monopoly of European imperial powers. In the nineteenth century, the Chinese representatives often filed false reports from Lhasa (about the number of men on their payroll, for example), knowing that their central government was unlikely to question the accuracy of reports by their "men on the spot." Official Tibetan correspondence was similarly liable to present a false picture. It was common practice there to send a written communication, while entrusting the messenger with verbal instructions that altered the "official" order.[24]

Politics

Political factors greatly affected the British construction of an image of Tibet. As we have seen, although cadre officers wanted to learn the "truth" about Tibet, their ability to produce a "true" image was affected by their own cultural perceptions, by their tendency to withhold views that were clearly opposed to those of their superiors, and by commercial factors. Most significantly however, the information obtained by the cadre officers was deliberately shaped into an image that served the political interests of British India and the imperial government's allies in Tibet's ruling class.

While the cadre was largely responsible for constructing and promoting this image through their written works, the British Government's refusal to recognize Tibet as independent created a fundamental gap between the cadre's officers' understanding of Tibet and the image that their government allowed to be constructed.

In deference to the Chinese claim that Tibet was part of their territory, Whitehall refused to recognize Tibetan independence for fear of damaging Anglo-Chinese relations, particularly trade ties. As Whitehall acknowledged Tibet as part of China, it didn't want British officers getting involved in Tibetan affairs or offering support to Tibetan independence. Whitehall wanted its trade agents to restrict themselves to dealing with trade. The cadre disagreed with these restrictions, believing that an independent Tibet was in British India's best interests, but as government employees they could not openly oppose Whitehall.

The cadre, however, found that defining Tibet's status was an issue that could be avoided as Tibet developed to the point where its independence would emerge as a fait accompli. But if Tibet was to develop into a recognized independent state, it had to be a strong and clearly defined entity on the modern nation-state model. But while a nation-state has features such as fixed borders and a single central authority,

Tibet defined itself by other (primarily religious) criteria and did not fit the nation-state model.

Charles Bell therefore encouraged the Dalai Lama to transform his territory into a strong and unified modern state. In the decade between 1913 and 1923, following Bell's advice to the Dalai Lama, Tibet adopted most of the symbols and attributes of an independent state. It created its own flag, currency, and stamps, determined its frontiers in agreement with the British, reorganized its economy, bureaucracy, and provincial government, and, with British assistance, strengthened its military forces.

Ideas and images were part of a battle to establish a view of Tibet on the international stage, and the cadre used them as a weapon in their attempts to develop a strong Tibetan "buffer state." They saw "in the case of Tibet...[little or no]...difference between propaganda and policy."[25] In other words, the image they constructed depicted the ideal Tibet that cadre policies were designed to create.

Creating an image of Tibet as a nation-state and friendly neighbor to India involved projecting a distinct Indo-Tibetan identity, separate from that of China. Thus one political officer wrote that "One of our main political aims [was] showing that Tibet had its own art etc and that in some ways Tibet is more closely allied to India than to China [sic]."[26] That meant that the cadre were keen to support travelers such as Professor Tucci, who brought out these aspects of Tibet's historical culture, and whose apparently unbiased findings supported their own.

National unity was essential to a strong Tibet, and Bell clearly stated that "We want a united Tibet."[27] Thus the cadre tried to encourage Tibetan national unity at different social levels. For example, it created a Tibetan football team in designated "Tibetan colors" and played international football matches, Britain versus Tibet. When it started a school in Gyantse in the 1920s, it encouraged the children to wear Tibetan clothing and gave them photos of the Dalai Lama as prizes, rather than money.[28] These were all deliberate actions with the stated aim of "developing the...national consciousness of Tibet."[29]

In order to cement the cadre's alliance with the Dalai Lama and his Lhasa government, Charles Bell and his successors designed this new Tibet to suit both parties. The British got a strong "buffer state"; the

Dalai Lama got British support in modernizing his institutions, strengthening his power, and resisting China. Thus both parties cooperated in presenting and preserving the image of a united and progressive Tibetan state.

This is not to suggest that the Tibetans were mere puppets. They were, as the British later acknowledged, shrewd diplomats, who, in the classic diplomatic maneuver of a small state between large empires, tried to play one power off against the other, and they too had their spies in the other powers' camps.

A "Core" Image

The main point of this historical image of Tibet constructed by the British, what we might call the "core" image, was of Tibet becoming a modern nation-state, united under a single government sovereign within its borders, existing as a friendly, and indeed admirable, neighbor to British India. That core image was most clearly articulated by Charles Bell, who wove the key ingredients together. As Bell described it,

> Modern Tibet…rejects…Chinese suzerainty and claims the status of an independent nation, [one in which]…national sentiment…is now a growing force. The Dalai Lama is determined to free Tibet as far as possible from Chinese rule [and in this he has the support of] the majority of the Tibetan race…[who]…see in him…the only means of attaining their goal. Anglo-Tibetan relations are of cordial friendship as they are both religious peoples, in contrast to the Chinese. Tibet would at length secure recognition of the integrity and autonomy of her territory.[30]

Charles Bell's ultimate aim in constructing this image was to ensure an independent Tibet, but he was a very shrewd and far-seeing diplomat and a master of the art of influencing policy. He stopped short of advocating Tibetan independence, but led policy in a direction that would have eventually made that inevitable, and the Government of India was generally persuaded to support his carefully argued policies and subtle means of getting around Whitehall's restrictions.

The core image Bell articulated was the basis for the historical image of Tibet. Later cadre officers followed his definitions and assumed their readers' familiarity with Bell's works. For example, the secretary to the political officer on his 1936–37 mission to Lhasa, F. Spencer Chapman, suggested that readers might compare an illustration in his book with the same scene in an earlier work of Bell's. Arthur Hopkinson, the last British political officer in Sikkim, lecturing in 1950, stated that "I do not wish to waste your time by repeating facts of ancient history with which you are already familiar from books and articles, such as Sir Charles Bell's."[31]

To uphold this core image, the cadre shaped additional information to support it. For example, the Dalai Lama's supreme authority was certainly undemocratic in Western eyes, but the cadre presented it in positive terms. Spencer Chapman wrote that "Naturally there will always be some who from jealousy or other motives criticize one who has the strength of character to assume such autocratic power."[32] These positive descriptions—the people, for example, were commonly described as "extraordinarily friendly...always cheery"[33]—had a specific purpose: They created an impression of the Tibetans as worthy allies of the British.

Yet it is important to remember that one reason these images have survived is that they were generally opinions genuinely held by the cadre officers, and these opinions have been reiterated by more recent travelers to Tibet. Few Europeans who have encountered the Tibetans would dispute the statement by the last British representative in Lhasa, Hugh Richardson, that visitors of different nationalities "all agree in describing the Tibetans as kind, gentle, honest, open and cheerful."[34] An image may be both "true" and politically valuable.

Censorship

We have seen why a particular image of Tibet was created by the cadre, but the actual process of controlling the image was carried out by the imperial Government of India.

While the government had trained its officers and therefore expected to be able to trust their judgment as to what information could be presented to the public, officials were required, by both civil and military regulations additional to the Official Secrets Act, to submit for censorship anything they wrote for publication. The cadre officers generally accepted the need for this system. For example, when the long-serving trade agent David Macdonald wrote his memoirs, the India Office noted approvingly that he was "anxious that we should strike out anything that is considered objectionable."[35]

One particularly sensitive issue with which the censors were concerned was the fact that India occasionally supplied arms to Tibet, because that implied recognition of Tibet as an independent state, something that provoked great opposition from the Chinese. Hence, Macdonald's references to these arms supplies were removed from his manuscript by the censors. Macdonald was told that it was "most important that nothing should be said which could tend to damage relations with...any other foreign power."[36]

Similarly, when writing his first book, Charles Bell referred to Tibetan troops being "armed with the new rifles," but the next sentence, which explained that the British had supplied these weapons, was removed by the censor[37] (although as is so often the case with censorship, the facts were obvious to everyone involved, including the Chinese).

The government even claimed the power to restrict its officers' private conversations. For example, it did not wish to publicize the existence of goldfields in western Tibet, to avoid encouraging prospectors. A Captain Rawling, who traveled through western Tibet at the conclusion of the Younghusband mission, was instructed to "avoid all reference in conversation to information...regarding the goldfields."[38]

Censorship was not only carried out directly by the government. Organizations such as the Royal Geographical Society and the *London Times* acted as imperial support structures by adding a further level of censorship. These bodies acted in close association with the Government of India and ensured that anything they published would be acceptable to India. In return, their leaders could expect to be given privileged access to information, events, and places, and even direct "subsidies," such as Reuters news agency in India was given.[39]

Arthur Hinks, the long-serving secretary of the Royal Geographical Society, kept in close touch with the Tibet cadre and played an important role in the image-making process. Hinks censored information both before and after it was officially censored. When F. Spencer Chapman submitted a paper to the society concerning his visit to Lhasa in 1936–37, Hinks forwarded it to the India Office for censorship after "cutting out a number of things which I am sure you would not like." There was now, he hoped, "nothing left to which objection could be taken." When the India Office made further changes, Hinks agreed these parts were "very properly removed."[40]

The reason government maintained a close relationship with these knowledge-disseminating bodies was because articles they published carried great authority; they became part of the body of "dominant knowledge." Although the intended audience for the historical image of Tibet was never clearly specified, it certainly included the sort of audience that would read the *Times* and join the Royal Geographical Society. The information these organizations published was understood by its readers to be "true," because it was based on empirical evidence and provided by persons of similar outlook and class. It represented the "official knowledge" of the readers' society.

Thus when the *Royal Geographical Society Journal* heavily criticized the book by the American traveler McGovern and praised those of Bell and Macdonald, readers generally accepted that McGovern's account could not be relied on, while Bell's and Macdonald's books could. These judgments have had a lasting effect. Today Bell's and Macdonald's books are recommended by the Tibetan government-in-exile and are frequently reprinted, whereas McGovern's book gathers dust in specialist libraries.

The Mystical Image

I referred earlier to the mystical image of Tibet whereby Tibet is seen as a sacred land in which the paranormal is commonplace. This mystical image was, and is, the principal competition to the historical image. While this image predates the Tibetan encounter with the West, it has been greatly extended by Western writers, including many who have never visited Tibet, such as James Hilton, whose book *Lost Horizon* provides much of the "Shangri-la" image that is associated with Tibet.[41]

This European mystical discourse was created for other Europeans; certainly much of it bemuses the Tibetans, although they have learned to benefit from it. While it was expressed in the language of myth, not science, it did appear to contradict the more prosaic views of those in regular contact with the Tibetans. This meant that since the cadre officers also appealed to a European audience, they were forced to deal with this apparently contradictory image.

Yet the cadre did not try and destroy Tibet's mystical aura. Instead, they tacitly encouraged it, because the cadre found that "mystic Tibet" could serve as a useful secondary image with which to promote the idea of Tibet as a separate state. The historical and mystical images were separate, and my concern here is not with the construction or content of the mystical image, but with the fact that the cadre used it to promote their own political aims.

The cadre found that the mystical image, which reached a wider audience than its historical construction, could serve British interests. There was no inherent conflict between the two. The mystical image was not a political issue in the sense that neither the Chinese nor the Russians sought to profit politically by emphasizing Tibet's mystical aura. The mystical image was, and indeed is, a weapon against which China has had no effective response.

The mystical image reinforced Tibet's separate identity, but it was also a positive moral weapon, and claiming the moral high ground became of great importance after the Chinese takeover in the 1950s. It was, therefore, an image that assisted the aims of the British Indian officials and their Tibetan allies.

Consequently, as long as travelers avoided referring to political matters, the cadre had no particular objection to the Tibetan journeys of those sincerely interested in Tibet's spiritual culture—travelers such as Alexandra David-Néel, or the German-Bolivian Lama Anagarika Govinda. The cadre took a benign view of even the most eccentric of these visitors as long as they steered clear of political matters. But they prevented a number of renowned scholars of mysticism whom they considered politically unreliable (the Roerichs, for example) from entering Tibet from British India.[42]

Alexandra David-Néel trod a fine line here. While the cadre

objected to her ignoring its frontier travel regulations and commenting on the British policy of excluding travelers from Tibet, her works were immensely popular, and, as they enhanced the idea of Tibet's separate identity, they furthered British Indian interests. The cadre therefore refrained from commenting on her travels.

Mysticism thus added to the positive awareness of Tibet and its unique culture, and the cadre implicitly encouraged it in its writings. For example, in Younghusband's account of his mission to Lhasa he describes Tibet in typically mystical terms as "a mysterious, secluded country in the remote hinterland of the Himalayas."[43]

There was also a personal factor in this. The cadre was not opposed to mystical enquiries per se. While remaining convinced of the need for empirical evidence, many of them were attracted to the mysticism with which Tibet was associated. For example, Younghusband, the cadre's "founding father," and Arthur Hopkinson, the last British political officer of Sikkim, both retired to a spiritual life.[44]

This attraction to Tibet's fundamentally religious character was another factor influencing the predominant mode of expression in British imperial writings on Tibet. It appears to resemble what Lionel Caplan, in discussing the image of the Gurkhas, has called "a pastoral mode" rather than the discourses of power that are associated today with the term "Orientalism." Caplan describes this "pastoral mode" as a discourse in which subordinate peoples in the imperial process are represented in approving terms.[45]

While maintaining a paternal perspective, these works are not primarily concerned with power in the sense usually associated with "Orientalism." The subjects are not exoticized; rather, the shared inherent qualities of both parties are emphasized and the paternal relationship is portrayed as based on mutual respect. Thus Hopkinson wrote that "the Tibetans value their independence as much as you or I do."[46] It is this "pastoral mode" that predominates in the works of cadre officers.

Conclusion

In conclusion, we might ask what was the effect of the image construction process? Ultimately the cadre failed to bring independence to

Tibet, but the restrictions imposed by Whitehall had made that impossible anyway. Yet they left us with an understanding of Tibet that reflects the political realities of the imperial age. In the absence of a viable alternative, the image of Tibet they constructed became the dominant historical image followed by Western academics. Tibetans, who are probably more united now by opposition to the Chinese than they ever were by the British, have adopted this historical image and used it to promote the interests of the Dalai Lama's government-in-exile, which remains the dominant Tibetan voice today.

However, the fact that the cadre was allied with Lhasa's ruling class meant that the British adopted and consequently privileged the Lhasa perspective. Their alliance with the Lhasa ruling class meant that they did not, for example, articulate the interests of those eastern Tibetan principalities, which aspired to autonomy and even to closer ties with China. Thus the historical image is Lhasa-centric.

Yet, as it largely reflected the Dalai Lama's perspective (except in the crucial area of independence), the Tibetan government-in-exile has generally continued to accept this historical image the cadre constructed. For example, they publish a book list that recommends books by Bell and other cadre officers. In particular, they recommend the account of Tibet written by Hugh Richardson, which depicts the history of a united Tibetan state and portrays the British as dispassionate observers of events in Tibet.[47]

The mystical image of Tibet survives today to a large extent because it serves Tibetan interests in that it emphasizes the separate and unique nature of Tibetan civilization. To an extent it compensates for the fact that the Anglo-Tibetan alliance left the exiled Tibetan government to rely on a historical image that Tibetans consider, as the Dalai Lama put it, "incomplete,"[48] particularly in the crucial area of Tibet's political status.

This failure to establish an image of Tibet fully consistent with the Tibetans' self-image was partly due to both the inherently class-based and imperial perceptions of the cadre officers and their alliance with the ruling elite within Tibet. But it was principally the result of Whitehall's refusal to recognize Tibetan independence.

This divergence between the image of Tibet that the British constructed and the Tibetans' self-image also provides the clearest example of the way in which the historical image failed—due to the political requirements of wider British policy—to reflect the "truth" as it was understood by the "men on the spot." By any practical definition, Tibet functioned as an independent state in the period 1913–1950. But it was never formally recognized as such by any power, with the exception of Mongolia, whose own status was then questionable.[49] Yet cadre officers, who dealt with its government on a day-to-day basis, accepted that "Tibet is just as much entitled to her freedom as India."[50]

But as Hugh Richardson recently wrote, while "[i]n all practical matters the Tibetans were independent.... [t]he British Government...sold the Tibetans down the river." He goes on to reveal that "I was profoundly ashamed of the government."[51] But although cadre officers disagreed with Whitehall's Tibetan policy, they were government employees and ultimately had to follow orders. Clear statements of support for Tibetan independence were usually given only after an officer had retired and was able to speak as an individual, rather than as an official.

We are now beginning to reexamine Tibet's historical image. Questions may be asked about such matters as social harmony and the sense of national and religious identity, of various communities outside Tibet's central provinces, and of groups such as the *ragyaba* (the disposers of the dead), whose status appears to have been equated to that of India's "untouchables."

I am not suggesting that we are now liable to create any major revisions of the received historical image of Tibet beyond a more balanced view of the aspirations of marginalized groups in Tibetan society. And the British construction of an image of Tibet perhaps tells us as much about British imperial history as it does about the Tibetans. Historically, Tibet had a distinct identity and culture, which the Tibetans understood in Asian religious, rather than Western political, terms. It is now up to us to understand their terms rather than to continue to accept our own.

NOTES

1 Research for this paper was undertaken with the assistance of the British Academy, the Leverhulme Trust (U.K.), and the International Institute for Asian Studies, Leiden. My thanks are due to Professor Peter Robb of the London University School of Oriental and African Studies for his assistance. Excerpts from this paper, which was originally delivered at the Oosters Genootschap in Nederland (The Netherlands Oriental Society), Leiden, April 1996, also appear in my doctoral thesis (McKay, 1995).

2 Shakya, 1992: 15.

3 French (1994: 243), quoting Oriental and India Office Collection (formerly the India Office Library and Records: hereafter OIOC) MSS Eur F197–177, Younghusband to his wife.

4 Personal papers of Major R. K. M. Battye, courtesy of the Battye family, unpublished report dated 19 August 1935.

5 For details, see McKay, 1992.

6 Ibid.

7 See, for example, Landon (1988), Younghusband (1985).

8 Landon, 1988: 107.

9 National Archives of India (hereafter NAI) Foreign Department 1910, External B, April 12–13, "Military Report on Tibet" by Captain V. E. Gwyer; an attached file note states that this was compiled with Charles Bell's assistance. The report is also in OIOC L/Mil/17/14/92.

10 Anderson, 1992: 179, n.30, quoting a speech by Lord Curzon.

11 OIOC MSS Eur F157–304, Gyantse Agency Diary, 29 April 1909.

12 McKay, 1995: 30–73.

13 NAI Foreign Department 1905, Secret E, March 341–368, Gyantse Agency Diary, 18 December 1904; OIOC L/P&S/12/4201–1863, Lhasa Mission Report, week ending 19 March 1944. This latter report was by Major George Sherriff, the noted botanist who made a number of journeys in Tibet, and only left after failing a medical. While often critical of the Tibetan system, he was clearly attracted to the country and its people.

14 See, McKay, 1995: 214–15.

15 Chapman, 1992: 150; Bell, 1992: 93.

16 OIOC MSS Eur F226–34, IPS Collection, interview with Mr Meredith Worth ICS.

17 Cambridge South Asia Library, Frederick Mainprice Collection, diary entry of 22 July 1944.

18 McKay, 1995: 83–86; also see Lamb, 1989: 101–2, 125–28.

19 Re Tucci, see OIOC L/P&S/12/4247, various correspondence.

20 OIOC L/P&S/10/1011–3605, Government of India to India Office, 5 September 1923.

21 Re McGovern and the affect of his journey, see McKay, 1995: 88–89; see also McGovern, 1924.

22 The cadre included an Anglo-Sikkimese and two men best described as Indian-born Tibetans, but these three individuals had thoroughly absorbed the mentality of the British officer class before being admitted into the cadre ranks.

23 OIOC MSS Eur F157–319, anonymous comments on typescript (unpublished) autobiography by Lieutenant-Colonel F. M. Bailey, original emphasis.

24 Bell, 1992: 87, 139.

25 OIOC L/P&S/12/4605, Government of India to the India Office, 27 July 1942.

26 OIOC L/P&S/12/4247, B. Gould to E. P. Donaldson, undated, February 1946.

27 Bell, 1992: 259.

28 McKay, 1994: 372–86.

29 OIOC L/P&S/12/4197–3864, Lhasa Mission Report by B. Gould, 30 April 1937.

30 Bell, 1992: 5, 126, 139, 140, 213–14, 269.

31 Hopkinson, 1950: 230.

32 Chapman, 1992: 194.

33 Macdonald, 1991: 57.

34 Richardson, 1984:10.

35 OIOC, L/P&S/12/3977–206, undated memo to Mr. Walton (India Office).

36 OIOC L/P&S/12/3977–206, Government of India to D. Macdonald, 3 February 1931.

37 OIOC L/P&S/12/3982, various correspondence; Bell, 1992: 162.

38 NAI, Foreign Department 1906, External B, July 15, anonymous file note, May 1906.

39 Kaminsky, 1986: 176–77.

40 OIOC L/P&S/12/4193–3143, A. Hinks to J. C. Walton (India Office), 3 May 1938 and 12 May 1938.

41 Hilton, 1933; re the construction of Western images of Tibet by European travelers, see Bishop, 1989.

42 McKay, 1995: 86–89, 193. Re Roerichs, see OIOC L/P&S/12/4166–2292, Gyantse Annual Report 1927–28, and MSS Eur F157–245, various correspondence.

43 Younghusband, 1985: 2.

44 While Younghusband's spiritual interests may be described as "mystical," Hopkinson became an Anglican clergyman. Re Younghusband, see French, 1994.

45 See Caplan, 1991: esp. 590–94.

46 Hopkinson, 1950: 233.

47 See Anon. (n.d.)

48 Personal interview with H. H. the Fourteenth Dalai Lama of Tibet, March 1994.

49 For more details on that treaty, see Mehra, 1969.

50 Bell, 1987: 56.

51 Richardson (n.d.).

TIBETAN HORIZON

TIBET AND THE CINEMA IN THE EARLY TWENTIETH CENTURY

Peter H. Hansen

"I WONDER IF JAMES HILTON ever set foot in Tibet," wrote Spencer Chapman in "Tibetan Horizon," a 1937 essay in the journal *Sight and Sound*. "Certainly the producers of the film version of *Lost Horizon* would have benefited if they had been able to visit this remote and inaccessible country. They might have saved themselves even this inconvenience if they had been able to see the photographic results of Mr. B. J. Gould's recent diplomatic mission to Lhasa."[1] Chapman had been responsible for making documentary films in Tibet during Gould's mission, and his article promoted the upcoming screening of his films in London. While the mission was still in Tibet, Chapman had shown many of his Tibetan films to Tibetan audiences along with a variety of Western films that the mission had brought with them to Lhasa.

The parallel between these two events in the early twentieth century—making documentary films in Tibet and showing them to Tibetans—raises two related questions, which I will address in this essay. What was the portrayal of Tibet in these films? And how did Tibetans react to them? To answer these questions, I will examine some of the films made in Tibet in the early twentieth century, especially those taken during the Mount Everest expeditions in the 1920s and the Gould missions to Tibet in the 1930s and 1940s. Since many of the films made in Tibet are still unavailable for viewing, much of what follows is, of necessity, somewhat speculative. Yet I want to suggest that the portrayal of Tibet in these films was shaped by the Tibetan reaction to them. Tibet was represented in documentary films in ambiguous ways that call into question the extent to which Western representations of Tibet, such as the book or film versions of *Lost Horizon,* were merely projections of Western fantasies. While I am unaware of Tibetan reactions to *Lost Horizon* in the 1930s (and there may well have been some), the Tibetan reaction to these documentary films suggests that the relationship between Tibet and the cinema was profoundly intercultural.

Tibetans as well as the British contributed to the construction of cinematic myths of Tibet. British documentaries concentrated on the rituals of Tibetan Buddhism at the expense of depictions of everyday life in Tibet. This was as much the result of Tibetan desires as of Western myths. In the 1920s, Tibetans were so offended by the portrayal of Tibetan life in the Mount Everest films that they canceled future Everest expeditions. Yet in the 1930s, Tibetans watched Western movies and films about Tibet. In consequence, they envisioned a place for the cinema within Buddhism.

These intercultural exchanges and documentary films of the early twentieth century were the product of a unique moment in the history of Tibet and the history of film. The controversies over the Everest films ensured that few people other than British diplomats were allowed to make films in Tibet. In the 1940s, especially during World War II, the British increasingly used the cinema in Tibet as an instrument of British propaganda, a tendency that became even more pronounced in the 1950s after the Chinese invasion and has changed only recently. Since a few articles and film festivals have surveyed the portrayal of Tibet in the cinema since the 1950s, I will not directly discuss these more recent developments.[2] I will, however, close with some brief reflections on the implications of this large archive of documentary films for recent feature films and the politics of Tibetan culture in the present.

Perhaps the earliest films ever made in Tibet were shot during the British attempts to climb Mount Everest. In the face of Chinese military threats in the early 1920s, Tibet had given the British permission to ascend Everest in exchange for British weapons. Cinematographer Captain John Noel made two silent films on these expeditions: *Climbing*

Mount Everest (U.K., 1922) and *The Epic of Everest* (U.K., 1924). In addition, his film company brought a group of Tibetan monks from Gyantse to London without the permission of the Tibetan government to perform on stage before screenings of *The Epic of Everest* in 1924. The Tibetan government was so offended by the performances of the "dancing lamas," and by certain scenes in the film, that it withdrew permission for future Everest expeditions by the British, until Chinese military threats reappeared in the early 1930s.[3] In addition, the controversy over the "dancing lamas" tipped the balance of power within Tibet from the military to the monasteries in the mid-1920s, and affected the way British and Tibetans viewed future films about Tibet.

Both Everest films incorporated extended anthropological travelogues of Tibetan life. *Climbing Mount Everest* showed Tibetan dances, weaving, headdresses, monasteries, sports, and so on. The following intertitle is representative: "Visiting the towns of Kamba, Shekar and the Monastery of Rongbuk, we gained many interesting glimpses into the life, manners, and customs of the strange people of Tibet." Like other ethnographic surveys of Tibetan life, these films recorded ceremonies and classified a variety of Tibetan "types." Even the porters were so classified through film. One of the longest, and by far the most interesting, sequences in the film shows General C. G. Bruce, leader of the Everest expedition in 1922, meeting Zatul Rinpoche, the head lama of the Rongbuk Monastery, followed by dances of the other monks at the monastery. Noel's second film, *The Epic of Everest*, also developed the contrast between the extroverted, aggressive, and manly British climbers with the introverted, passive, and squalid but mystical Tibetans. The film shows the British climbers walking confidently into the mountains that Tibetan legends claimed were inhabited by deities. The film concluded by invoking the powers of the Rongbuk lama, as a mystical explanation for the expedition's failure to reach the summit.[4]

The London performances of the "dancing lamas," which continued a well-developed practice of putting "natives" on display, generated widespread interest in Britain. By studying its ancient texts, nineteenth-century scholars had aimed to recover the "essence" of Buddhism that preceded its "decline" into "Lamaism," but the dancing lamas, as the word made flesh, now questioned British assumptions that Buddhism was a textual object under their control. But their performances and certain scenes in the film upset the Tibetans. In the most controversial scene, a Tibetan man appeared to pick lice out of a boy's hair and then eat the lice. (The scene does not appear in current viewing copies of the film.) F. M. Bailey, the political officer of Sikkim, warned the filmmakers that the "lice-eating" scene had caused offense when the film had been shown in India. "The Tibetans say that this is not typical and will give the world the wrong impression."[5]

By the spring of 1925, these events led to the cancellation of future expeditions to Everest. The prime minister of Tibet complained to Bailey that "they have enticed and taken away to England four or five monks, whose photos as dancers have appeared recently in the newspapers. We regard this action on the part of the Sahibs as very unbecoming. For the future, we cannot give them permission to go to Tibet." The prime minister also demanded "the immediate return to Tibet and handing over of the monks, who have been taken away deceitfully." After Leslie Weir visited Lhasa as political officer of Sikkim in 1930, he reported that the Dalai Lama had seen pictures of the "dancing lamas" in the weekly picture papers and looked "on the whole affair as a direct affront to the religion of which he is the head." In addition, the maharaja of Sikkim and an agent of the maharaja of Bhutan had seen the film in Darjeeling and found the "lice-eating" scene "extremely repugnant."[6]

The controversy over the dancing lamas also intervened in the internal politics of Tibet. Conflicts between the monasteries, the police, and the army had split "traditionalists" and "modernists" in Tibet in 1924. A possible coup attempt by Tsarong Shape, the Tibetan commander-in-chief, and Laden La, a Sikkimese official in Lhasa to train the police force, has remained the subject of much speculation. In the event, the Dalai Lama demoted Tsarong and other military officers immediately after the performances of the dancing lamas and at the same time refused permission for another Everest expedition in April 1925. Since Tibetan permission for Everest had been given in the context of Sino-Tibetan military hostilities and in exchange for British weapons, the fate of the Everest expeditions was inextricably linked to the political fortunes of Tsarong and the military in Tibet. After earlier offenses, the controversy over the dancing lamas as well as other events in Lhasa weakened the positions of Tsarong and the Everest expeditions.[7]

The global reach of early twentieth-century cinema expanded the audience for the Everest films to include even the Tibetans themselves. The Dalai Lama saw pictures of the dancing lamas in the London papers, and officials from Tibet, Sikkim, and Bhutan watched the Everest films in India. These media enabled the Tibetans to see themselves as they were seen by others, and the Tibetans responded by vigorously challenging what they saw. Tibetans recognized that they were part of a global media environment when they objected to the "lice-eating" scene because it would "give the world the wrong impression." Tibet also banned film crews from later Everest expeditions because access by the media—the right to make representations—had itself become one of the bargaining chips of diplomacy.

As a result of these controversies, few people were allowed to make films in Tibet in the late 1920s and early 1930s. William McGovern apparently made a film during his secret trip to Tibet in the early 1920s, but over the next decade a number of travelers were explicitly denied permission to enter Tibet because they intended to make films there.[8] Yet at the same time these travelers were being turned away, British diplomats and officials (among them F. M. Bailey, Charles Bell, Leslie Weir, and Frederick Williamson—British political officers in Sikkim) made their own films in Tibet. During the height of the controversy over the dancing lamas in 1925, Bailey filmed the monks at the Gyantse Monastery preforming their "devil dances." One of Bailey's films, *Tibet, circa 1928* (U.K., c. 1928), shows porters drinking tea, farmers harvesting wheat, a man spinning a prayer wheel, a shepherd herding his flock with a slingshot, a man plowing with a yak, and a caravan of yaks loaded with wool.[9] A few foreign scientists obtained permission to film in Tibet. Wilhelm Filchner, a German geophysicist and polar explorer, filmed dances at the Kumbum monastery in northeast Tibet beginning in 1926, and later journeys in Tibet and Nepal added footage for a film entitled *Dancing Lamas and Soldiers* (in the Buddhist Kingdom), (Germany, c. 1937).[10] Charles Suydam Cutting, an American ethnologist and botanist, made films recording spinning at Gyantse, yak caravans, the monasteries at Shigatse and Lhasa, and animal-skin boats on the Tsangpo River.[11] As far as I am aware, however, the films by these British diplomats or foreign scientists received only limited circulation.

Tibetan and British fears about the representation of Tibet on film may well have been realized by the few commercial films about Tibet. A short film entitled *Tibet: Land of Isolation* (U.S., 1934), made by American James A. FitzPatrick as part of his well-known series of travelogues is a good example. Although it is unclear where the film was shot, the soundtrack is more Chinese than Tibetan in inspiration. The film provides commentary on everyday life in Tibet, including yaks, butter-making, the role of women, earrings, tongue greetings, river crossings, the possibility of finding gold, local medical practices, and the influence of "Lamaism." FitzPatrick's travelogue is essentially a visual catalogue of many Western myths about Tibet. The film's closing narration is typical: "And so life goes on among the people of Tibet where the progress of civilization is at the mercy of priestcraft and the destinies of men are eternally limited by the impregnable boundaries of superstition, ignorance and fear. And it is with this thought that we say farewell to Tibet, land of isolation."[12]

With such inauspicious precedents, and the Tibetan reluctance to let anyone make films in Tibet, why did British diplomats make their own films in Tibet? Basil Gould, for example, appears to have made filming Tibet a priority during his missions to Lhasa from 1936 into the 1940s. As Gould's private secretary in Tibet from 1936 to 1937, Spencer Chapman made films of Tibet, which he later showed to the Tibetans.[13] These were not the first visual images to be shown in Tibet: Earlier expeditions had brought lantern slides into the Himalayas. As early as 1920–21, Charles Bell watched films in Tsarong's private screening room, and F. M. Bailey showed films there in 1924. In the early 1930s, Frederick Williamson showed the Tibetans Charlie Chaplin and "Fritz the Cat" films. In 1935, Williamson also showed the Tibetans films he had taken in Tibet in 1933, as well as "a little mild propaganda with films of King George V's Silver Jubilee Celebrations and of the Hendon Air Display, as well as others of educational value."[14]

Basil Gould's use of film during his 1936 mission, however, appears to have been the most systematic effort up to that time. While Gould may have been following precedent, in his autobiography he indirectly suggests several other reasons for making films in Tibet. It seems the films gave Gould a positional credibility with his British colleagues and Tibetan contacts. Gould noted that a British government official "was most likely to be helpful if he was interested in the peoples with whom I had to deal. In this connection 'Kodachrome' ciné films of Sikkim, Bhutan and Tibet were of value." Since Gould also showed them to the Tibetans, these films also established the mission's credibility within Tibet. "The sight of themselves on screen was convincing proof to Tibetan audiences that what they saw was real."[15] Gould does not mention a wider context that is more speculative but perhaps more revealing. During the 1920s and 1930s, there was an extensive discussion within the British Empire about the use of the cinema in the education of indigenous peoples. This discussion led to several efforts to use film to record indigenous customs for anthropological research and to disseminate information of an educational nature among "natives." Gould showed the Tibetans films he had taken in Kenya, and his use of film in Lhasa was probably influenced by these wider contemporary debates over the use of the cinema in other parts of the empire.[16]

Whatever Gould's motives, it is clear that both British and Tibetans were influenced by the presence of Gould's film cameras. The mission staged some events for the cameras. When they entered Gyantse, for example, "Chapman went ahead with two cinemas" to shoot their arrival and official reception. At first, Chapman had to capture Tibetans on film before they knew what was happening. Consider Chapman's routine when he set up his cameras in advance and waited for a ceremonial procession: "As soon as they came into view I would 'shoot' them with the 35-mm. telephoto, then take a medium 16 mm. color 'shot,' return to the big camera again and take a near shot, repeat this with the color-camera, meanwhile firing off any still-cameras that I had been able to fix in the right position."[17]

Initially, the Tibetans were suspicious of Chapman's filming, especially since his 35-mm. film camera had a large lens. "But when, by using air mail each way, we were able to get the Kodachrome film back from England in time to show the officials moving photographs of themselves in natural color their enthusiasm knew no bounds and they did all they could to help me." After the mission had been in Lhasa a few months, Chapman filmed a ceremony on the roof of the palace at dawn, and wrote in the mission diary: "Now that most of these officials have seen our films they take the presence of the 'camera man' as a matter of course."[18] Nevertheless, when Gould filmed the installation of the Dalai Lama in 1940, he noted that "this film was all taken more or less from a place of hiding behind a garden wall." Tibetan officials asked Chapman to film them at home, and he considered himself "like a court photographer." During the six months he spent in Lhasa, Chapman took 2,500 still photographs, 13,000 feet of 35-mm. film, 6,000 feet of 16-mm. Kodachrome color film, and 6,000 feet of 16-mm. black and white film.[19]

Even though Chapman took so much raw material, only one reel of Chapman's 16-mm. film survives in the British Film Institute. Chapman's 1936 film shows views of Lhasa and the Potala Palace, making whitewash for the palace, the Dalai Lama's shrine, an abbot, monks in ceremonial robes, the regent and his attendants, a pet fox and panther cub, flowers, geese, several dogs, and an extended sequence showing the regent's retinue traveling outside of Lhasa. Gould's 1940–41 films have survived in greater numbers and contain similar material.[20] Gould records leaving the residency in Sikkim and events en route to Gyantse and Lhasa. The climax of these films is the installation of the Dalai Lama. Afterward, the mission returns to Gangtok and Bhutan. The films provide intimate portraits of the families of the Dalai Lama, the maharajah of Sikkim, and the maharajah of Bhutan. These reels also show a number of official receptions, sporting events, and shots of wild flowers.

These cinematic representations of Tibet in the Chapman and Gould films were the product of a process of mirroring, an intercultural dialogue between British and Tibetans in which each contributed to the cinematic representation of Tibet. With their emphasis on the long journey and the ceremonial places and practices of Buddhism, Gould's films render the journey to Lhasa as a pilgrimage to see the installation of the Dalai Lama. The patterns of Tibetan daily life are almost completely absent. With the exception of the scene showing people making whitewash for the Potala Palace (itself a religious site), Chapman's films depict few Tibetans at work. Tibetan pets appear as often as ordinary Tibetan people. Gould's attention to Tibetan sports and flowers also suggests that this is not a comprehensive ethnographic survey of Tibetan culture. These films incorporated both British projections of their myths about Tibet and Tibetan assumptions about what was worth filming in Tibet. This process of mirroring occurred most directly when the British mission showed their films of Tibet to Tibetans in Lhasa.

While they were in Lhasa, the British mission showed Tibetans their films about Tibet as well as other Western films. Before the Gould mission arrived in Lhasa, they checked their films to identify "those suitable for Tibetan audiences." Spencer Chapman also mentions that he spent much time "cutting out the parts unsuitable for Tibetan audiences."[21] Although no one ever identifies what criteria they used to judge films suitable or unsuitable, it is worth speculating. British diplomats in the 1930s were certainly aware of the Tibetan reaction to the Everest films of the 1920s. They avoided the depictions of ordinary life, such as the infamous "lice-eating" scene that had offended the Tibetans in the 1920s and concentrated instead on the places and practices of Tibetan Buddhism.

Chapman's Lhasa mission diary for 1936–37 describes a "typical" cinema party, when the British showed films to Tibetans. (For an extended extract, see the appendix to this article.) Alongside Chapman's own "florid" descriptions of his guests, he describes a deeply intercultural event. Films of Tibet and the West were shown side by side. "We started, as some of them had never before seen films, with something familiar to them, a film we have taken of the Potala and the Lhasa bazaar. This was followed by Rin-Tin-Tin in *The Night Cry*." The juxtaposition of these two reels is difficult to interpret. What does one make of the popularity of Charlie Chaplin and Rin-Tin-Tin, a dog, in Tibet? Elsewhere, Chapman attributed the popularity of *The Night Cry* to "the simplicity of its theme and because it dealt with a subject—sheep farming—which was familiar to them." In addition, Chapman noted that Charlie Chaplin films depicting "the subtle comedy of dropping ice-creams down old ladies' evening dresses, and hitting unsuspecting people on the head with a mallet, appealed irresistably to the

Tibetan sense of humour." More optimistically, Gould suggested that the Tibetan appreciation of Charlie Chaplin and Rin-Tin-Tin demonstrated that "Tibetans laugh at just the same things and in the same tone, and appreciate beauty in just the same things, as Englishmen."[22] But the process of cross-cultural translation that occurred in these cinema parties was far more complicated and not nearly so transparent.

The Tibetan films that were shown to the Tibetans are even more difficult to interpret since we know so little about what they contained. If his surviving film is any guide, Chapman's films about Tibet consisted primarily of local landmarks, rituals, pets, and dignitaries. After the mission had been in Lhasa some time, Chapman made a point of showing his guests film versions of themselves. Such scenes were apparently very popular. Large numbers of monks and soldiers "gatecrashed" these events. The regent and other officials requested private cinema parties at their own homes. Tsarong received the following letter from his son who was then in school in Darjeeling: "Is there any talking picture in Lhasa? I heard there is talking picture in Lhasa, and every gentleman doesn't work, but go to see picture every night. I have nothing more to say."[23]

Few Tibetans made their own films in this period. On at least one occasion, Tsarong filmed the Anglo-Tibetan soccer matches outside Lhasa, and at other times he showed British visitors his own 8-mm. home movies.[24] A few films made in Tibet in the 1940s by Tsarong and by Jigme Taring have survived in private collections in the U.S. and India. From what I have heard of these films from people who have seen them, they depict the same ceremonies, dances, and so forth that feature so prominently in British films that Tibetans were shown at this time.

The longer-term consequences of the British cinema parties in Lhasa are difficult to assess. Chapman reported that at one of their last cinema parties in February 1937, the audience was about to request another reel of Rin-Tin-Tin when "just then, by a lucky coincidence (we thought), the projector ran a bearing and the performance stopped. Apart from work on former Missions this machine has already projected some 150,000 feet of film since we came to Lhasa, and must have given an incalculable amount of pleasure." Both Gould and Chapman commented on the ability of films to break down cultural barriers with

Tibetans. Chapman put this in the context of the mission's other intercultural endeavors: "Their great need for advice on political questions,
the multifarious efforts of the Doctor, the entertainments provided by
the cinema projector and the wireless loud-speaker had all done their
share in breaking down what few barriers there are between the
Tibetans and ourselves."[25] In his official report of the mission, Gould
wrote of the positive political effects of showing films in Lhasa:

> There is nothing which Tibetans like better than to see them-
> selves and their acquaintances in a frame or on the screen. Invi-
> tations to photograph families and monasteries were numerous,
> and monks were amongst the most ardent of our cinema clien-
> tele. A senior monk official recently suggested that it would
> cause much satisfaction in Lhasa if arrangements could be made
> to take a cinema record of holy Buddhist place[s] in Burma,
> India and Ceylon and to show [them] in Lhasa.[26]

In other words, one consequence of these Lhasa film parties was
that "a senior monk" articulated a positive role for the cinema within
the transnational Buddhist world. He apparently hoped to see the rest
of the Buddhist world on film just as he had been able to see Lhasa's
monasteries and holy ceremonies. This monk may even have seen the
cinema as an agent in the global expansion of Buddhism. The dancing
lamas of Everest in the 1920s may have gone to London out of similar
"missionary" motives. These media enabled such monks to spread their
message to other parts of the world as Buddhist monks had been doing
for hundreds of years within Asia.

These Tibetan reactions and uses of film should warn against any
suggestion that the cinema or other "Western" technologies were necessarily in conflict with Buddhism or Tibetan culture, or that they were
only the medium of transmission for Western representations. Yet this
"senior monk" developed his hopes for the potential of the cinema
from his exposure to *British* films of Tibet. British film parties showed
Tibetans the images of Tibet that the Tibetans wanted to see. Here the
criteria employed by the British mission in selecting films "suitable for
Tibetan audiences" remain undefined but their origins are perhaps

clearer: It was the consequence of the interplay of British assumptions and Tibetan expectations.

The images that Tibetan and British audiences were *not* shown are also significant. They were not shown images of everyday life in Tibet such as those that offended the Tibetans in the Everest film. Even the anodyne scenes of Tibetan farming in F. M. Bailey's films were absent. Consider the description of a scene from the 1930s called the "lama debate," filmed either by Basil Gould or, possibly, by Charles Bell: "The lama debate. Indian and Tibetan monks. Former brings a book to prove his point, becomes over excited, pulls his opponent's hat off and wrestles with him." In another description of a similar scene, two lamas present their disagreement to an arbitrator who rules in favor of the lama who brought a book to support his point of view.[27] The notes also suggest that this scene was cut from versions shown to British audiences.

It is unclear if Tibetans were ever shown films of Buddhist holy places in the rest of the world. It is clear, however, that the British thought the films they showed to Tibetans in the 1940s were examples of British propaganda. During 1942–43, Tibetans were shown newsreels on the Indian war effort, Churchill's visit to Canada and Iceland, *Victory in the Desert*, and other war newsreels of all kinds. In 1943, an official in the India Office recommended for showing in Afghanistan and Tibet a film called *London, 1942* because it "gives the right impression of British power and purpose." He also thought that a film on St. Paul's with its "religious flavour" was particularly suitable for Tibet. Another British mission to Tibet during World War II wrote: "There is no doubt that the cinema at Dekyilinka can be made into the most powerful of all our propaganda weapons. To paraphrase a famous saying 'give me the films, and I will produce the results.'"[28]

During World War II, the British were not the only people to make such films, and the Tibetans were not the only intended audience of such propaganda. A Nazi film, *Geheimnis Tibet* (Germany, 1942), was made from footage taken by Ernst Schäfer in Tibet in 1939. Another film, *The OSS Mission to Tibet* (U.S., 1943), recounted a U.S. diplomatic mission to Tibet to arrange the transport of military supplies. Propaganda about Tibet could also be directed at a variety of international audiences. In 1944, after Gould showed his films on the installation of the Dalai Lama and on Bhutan to an audience in London consisting of officials from the Ministry of Information, the India Office, and the Foreign Office, one of these officials told Gould: "It would do the Americans a lot of good to see the film of Tibet; it should help to convince them that Tibet is not a part of China."[29]

The documentary moment in which Tibetans watched films of Tibet in Lhasa was ending in the late 1940s and had become a distant memory by the early 1950s. The Indian delegation to Tibet, which inherited the British mission in 1947, continued to show Indian and English films in Lhasa. Although Heinrich Harrer, the Austrian mountaineer who took refuge in Tibet during the war, had never before made a film, the young Dalai Lama gave Harrer a camera and asked him to film ice-skating and religious ceremonies and festivals: "As soon as it became known that I was filming and photographing under instructions from His Holiness I was not interrupted." The Dalai Lama also commissioned Harrer to build a cinema at Norbulingka, his summer palace. Harrer opened the cinema in 1950 with a documentary on the capitulation of Japan and his own film of Tibet. The Dalai Lama, who had practiced assembling the projector over the winter, then showed a film he had taken of the landscape of Lhasa, a long-distance shot of a caravan, and a closeup of his cook.[30] These were among the last such cinema shows in Lhasa before the Chinese invasion of Tibet later that year.

The legacy of these documentary films in Tibet from the 1920s to the 1950s is ambiguous. These films could offer visions of Tibet that were very different from prevailing myths in the West. Take, for example, the review in the *London Times* of Gould's 1936–37 Lhasa films:

> The film's great achievement was to present, however ramblingly, a true, vivid, and sufficiently comprehensive picture of life in Lhasa, stripping its cheerful citizency [*sic*] of mumbojumbo and investing them, from the beggar to the Minister of State, with a slightly embarrassed reality, more suggestive than any amount of sensational legend.
>
> It must be admitted that the Potala and the great monastery of Drepeing [*sic*] recalled, even while they transcended, the

architectural wishfulfillments of a Californian realtor which are
to be seen in the film *Lost Horizon*. [31]

Although these films could prompt such criticisms of certain Western myths of Tibet, they could also reinforce others. The same review
in the *Times* said that Gould's film gave the audience "an authentic
glimpse of the nearest thing to Never-never-land extant in the modern
world." Chapman's films of "devil dances" in 1936 may also not have
seemed very different to his Western audiences from the Everest films
and the "dancing lamas" of the 1920s.

Did the "Tibetan horizon" of these films merely become yet another
"lost horizon"? These films did not portray Tibet as the Shangri-la of
James Hilton's or Frank Capra's *Lost Horizon*. As more became known
about Tibet, some qualities formerly associated with Tibet were transferred to "Shangri-la," a placeless utopia.[32] Yet to the extent that these
documentary films have disappeared into the obscurity of film archives,
this "Tibetan horizon" has indeed been lost for the last fifty years.[33]
When Lowell Thomas, Sr., and Lowell Thomas, Jr., released *Out of
This World: A Journey in Forbidden Tibet* (U.S., 1952), a travelogue of
their journey in Tibet in the late 1940s, their commentary mentioned
the Chinese invasion in 1950. When a film version of Heinrich Harrer's
Seven Years in Tibet (U.K., 1956) was made in the mid-1950s, some
reviewers regretted that the producers had not used documentary
footage made by Harrer and others in Tibet, but instead relied on
reconstructions of his adventures in a studio and on location in India.[34]
In later years, documentary footage of the brutality of the invasion or
the experience of exile understandably overshadowed the earlier documentary films made in Tibet.

Yet the "Tibetan horizon" of these documentaries has continued to
influence Hollywood films about Tibet. Both Jean-Jacques Annaud's
Seven Years in Tibet (U.S., 1997), based on Harrer's memoir, and Martin Scorsese's *Kundun* (U.S., 1997), based on the official biography of
the Dalai Lama, reproduce Tibet from the 1930s to the 1950s with
impressive fidelity.[35] While this essay is not the place for an extended
review of these films, it is worth noting that both productions replicate
the visual imagery of these documentaries. Both films reproduce

Gould's cinematic depiction of the ceremonies of the Lhasa year and the procession at the Dalai Lama's installation. They also recreate the Lhasa cinema, with the Dalai Lama viewing newsreels in his screening room. Both films also convey familiar myths. In *Seven Years in Tibet* the people of Lhasa casually offer pearls of wisdom about the harmony of Tibet in comparison to the West, and *Kundun* opens with a prologue extolling thousands of years of Tibetan nonviolence. *Kundun* breaks with certain Hollywood conventions and develops like a mandala from the viewpoint of the young Dalai Lama. But this very perspective ensures that ordinary Tibetans are glimpsed only fleetingly through the Dalai Lama's telescope, and the political intrigues of the regent are rendered incompletely and off-screen, just as such subjects were cut from the documentaries.

Yet *Seven Years in Tibet* and *Kundun* and the earlier documentary films resemble one another in a more profound sense: They are products of the intercultural exchange between Tibetans and Westerners. Many Tibetans served as advisors and appeared in the cast of the Hollywood films. Indeed, the Dalai Lama edited the script for Kundun with screen-writer Melissa Mathieson, who recalled that the Dalai Lama was "very concerned about the way some Tibetan characters and ceremonies might be presented, such as the Dalai Lama's court oracle. He knows how that might appear to Western audiences."[36] If British diplomats edited their documentary films to meet Tibetan expectations in the 1930s, Tibetans were able to influence Hollywood productions much more directly by the 1990s. Throughout the twentieth century, Tibetans have shaped the "virtual Tibet" presented in Western films.[37]

Thus, it would be tempting but misleading to view the large archive of documentary films as the repository of the "real" Tibet that existed before the Chinese invasion of the 1950s. If you want to see what Tibet looked like before 1950, with very few exceptions, you have to watch films made by British diplomats or by a small number of other Western visitors to Tibet. But what do these films represent? Are they Western fantasies or the "real" Tibet? They are neither one nor the other, but a combination of both. These films are examples of the intercultural construction of Tibet by Westerners and Tibetans in conversation with one another. Attempts to use these documentary films to locate an "authentic" Tibet outside this process of dialogue would be misguided. These films represent not a "lost horizon," but a series of celluloid reflections of British and Tibetan images mirroring one another. The "Tibetan horizon" of these documentary films is, in a literal sense, the product of a double vision.

Appendix: Cinema in Lhasa, 1936

[December 4, 1936:] "The Yapshi Kung, with his wife and large family, came to dinner. These dinner parties, preceded and followed by film shows, are now a great feature of our life here.

"Tonight's party was typical.

"Our guests, having been invited for six o'clock, arrived an hour early. Gould and Richardson were drafting telegrams, Nepean and Dagg were engaged with wireless, Chapman was cutting a film and our only sitting room was festooned with innumerable strips of film.

"However, Norbhu held the fort until we were ready. The party consisted of the Duke, a lean, very short-sighted but very charming old aristocrat in his long yellow silk Shappe's robe; his wife, a shy rather florid woman wearing her hair looped up over a coral-studded triangular crown, with immense turquoise earrings, a charm box and a striped brown and red apron over an exquisite dragon-patterned Chinese silk dress; several grown up sons and daughters, one of the former being a favorite of the Regent; and four small children. After drinks—we find Tibetans drink Cinzano, rather reluctantly, or lemonade—we went downstairs for the first part of our performance. Here it was at once apparent that something unusual was afoot. It transpired that Norbhu had told three or four of the Potala monks that we were having a cinema show and that they could come. But about thirty monks, reinforced by as many soldiers from the neighbouring Norbhu Lingka barracks, had 'gatecrashed' the room; and while several monks had already taken the chairs reserved for our guests the rest of the crowd completely blocked all ways of approach. As soon as the monks had been forced to sit on the floor and our guests—though somewhat crowded—had taken their seats we started, as some of them had never before seen films, with something familiar to them, a film we have taken of the Potala and the Lhasa bazaar. This was followed by Rin-Tin-Tin in *The Night Cry*. This film has been a tremendous success in Lhasa; it is simple, moving, and of a subject with which they are familiar, nor does it leap from subject to subject as is the way of modern films. By the end of the fifth reel the women were weeping on each other's shoulders and imploring Rin-Tin-Tin to bite the villain's nose. After a Charlie Chaplin to restore their emotions we went upstairs to dinner while the uninvited monks were ejected.

"At dinner, to make the most of the small room, we sat, backs to the wall, on high Tibetan cushions while a variety of hors d'oeuvres-like dishes were served on the usual low Tibetan tables. Our guests proved less able to accustom themselves to foreign food than ourselves; but when Gould appeared with an armful of crackers the spirit of the party improved, and we were amazed to see a four-year old girl fearlessly holding a firework, while her brother, aged six, who had been told to behave exactly like his father, smoked a cigarette with apparent enjoyment.

"At eight o'clock bedecked with paper hats, we went downstairs to continue our film show. Color films of Tibet, more Charlie Chaplin, the Hendon Air Pageant 1929, color films of Sikkim, yet more reels of Tibet, what would they like for the last reel? After some deliberation perhaps they would like to see a Charlie Chaplin. And so at eleven o'clock the party ended, and after a final drink our guests mounted their ponies and rode home through the clear Tibetan night." (Source: "Lhasa Mission 1936, Diary of Events," Dec. 4, 1936, L/P&S/12/4193, British Library, Oriental and India Office Collections, London.)

The author is grateful to the National Endowment for the Humanities for a fellowship, which made this paper possible, to the Kunst und Austellungshalle der Bundesrepublik Deutschland for its hospitality, and to the other participants in the "Mythos Tibet" Symposium for their comments.

Notes

1 Chapman, 1937: 122.

2 For a useful survey and typology of films about Tibet, which was itself prompted by a film festival, see Scofield, 1993. For other examples of such film festivals, see Harris, 1992; Emmons and Roy, 1992–93; Farrell, 1993.

3 For detailed information about these events, see Hansen, 1996.

4 See *Climbing Mount Everest* (1922) and *The Epic of Everest* (1924) viewing copies at the National Film and Television Archive, British Film Institute, London (hereafter NFTVA). For further discussion of Everest, see Hansen, 1996, and Ortner, 1999. For a discussion of relevant issues for documentary films, see Nichols, 1991; Loizos, 1993; Renov, 1993; Rabinowitz, 1994; Rony, 1996; and MacDougall, 1998.

5 Bailey to Hinks, November 18, 1924, Unsworth, 1991: 150, EE/24/2, Royal Geographical Society Archives, London (hereafter RGS), and L/P&S10/778, Library, Oriental and India Office Collections, London (hereafter OIOC). See also Almond, 1988; Lopez, 1995b, 1998.

6 Prime minister of Tibet to Bailey, April 12, 1925, L/P&S/10/778, OIOC; EE 27/6/13, RGS; and Unsworth, 1991: 51–52. Weir to Hinks, July 26, 1931, EE 44/5, RGS.

7 See Hansen, 1996. On the rumored coup attempt by Laden La in 1924, see McKay, 1997. On this period in general, see Goldstein, 1989 and Lamb, 1989.

8 See the rejected applications to film in Tibet of Lt.-Col. V. A. Haddick, 1930–31, L /P&S/12/4240; Mrs. Edwin Montagu, 1933, L/P&S/12/4271; and André Guibaut, 1935–37, L/P&S/12/4307, OIOC. William Montgomery McGovern's film of his 1922 journey in Tibet, exhibited under the titles of either *Mysterious Tibet* or *To Lhasa in Disguise* (UK, 1924), is now lost. See *Nation and Athenaeum* (12 Jan. 1924) and Low, 1971: 288.

9 See *Tibet, circa 1928*, NFTVA. This is the only one of Bailey's films that has a viewing copy. Charles Bell's films, which he made during trips to Tibet after his retirement, are not yet available for viewing at NFTVA. Weir's films remain in private hands. Williamson's films are in the Cambridge University Museum of Archeology and Anthropology and also have no viewing copies. Shotlists on the reel canisters in Cambridge suggest that Williamson's films contain material that is broadly similar to Gould's films. The Liverpool Museum holds some films of Tibet, but, according to Christina Baird, Curator of Oriental Collections, there is no comprehensive list of them. See also the useful appendix on "British Photographs and Films of Bhutan, 1864–1949," in Aris, 1994: 148–53.

10 I am very grateful to Luc Schaedler for sharing a copy of Filchner's film, *Möche Tänzer und Soldaten (im Reiche des Budda)*. Some short Tibet films by Filchner are also at the Institut für den Wissenschaftlichen Film, Göttingen.

11 See Cutting, 1940 and his films *China and Tibet* (1929) and *To Lhasa and Shigatse* (1935) at the American Museum of Natural History, New York.

12 See *Tibet: Land of Isolation* (U.S., 1934), viewing copy at NFTVA.

13 Since filming was not among Chapman's official duties as enumerated by the India Office, Gould appears to have given Chapman these responsibilities of his own accord. Gould may have supplied Chapman with cameras that he bought in London. See Gould, 1957: 200 and Chapman, 1938b: 262–66.

14 Williamson, 1987: 206; see also 72, 104, 117–18. For an account of lantern slides, see White, 1909; and for an even earlier Tibetan account of seeing a peepshow in Calcutta, see Aris, 1995: 57. See also Bell, 1928: 263. Bailey showed a film of the king opening Parliament (Lhasa Diary, 30 July 1924, Mss Eur. F. 157/214).

15 Gould, 1957: 192, 206.

16 "Some taken by Gould in Kenya were very good, and should prove attractive to local visitors." Lhasa Mission 1936, Diary of Events [hereafter Lhasa Diary], 26 Aug. 1936. L/P&S/12/4193, OIOC. Chapman also showed film he had shot in Greenland. Chapman, 1938a: 250. For an example of the discussion elsewhere, see Orr, 1931: 238–44, 301–6, and the related discussion in Mackenzie, 1986: 68–95.

17 Chapman, 1938a: 247. On entering Gyantse, see Lhasa Diary, 12 Aug. 1936, L/P&S/12/4193, OIOC.

18 Chapman, 1937: 124; Chapman, 1938a: 274. Lhasa Diary, 24 Dec. 1936, L/P&S/12/4193, OIOC.

19 For Gould's comments on the installation, see the transcript of "Tape recording by Sir Basil Gould at a viewing held at the British Film Institute on Wednesday, 10th February, 1954, of his films featuring visits to Lhasa in 1936 and 1940, and to Bhutan in 1940," Related Material 1147, British Film Institute Library, London. On the amounts of film, see Chapman, 1938a, 245–46, and Chapman, 1937, 122.

20 For Chapman, see Sir Basil Gould Collection, Reel 1 (Lhasa: 1936); the other reels in this collection contain Gould's films from the 1940s. See NFTVA viewing copies. The Pitt Rivers Museum, Oxford, holds some film shot by Spencer Chapman. Marina de Alarcón, curatorial assistant at the museum, reports that very little of it is of Tibet and that what exists is in very poor condition.

21 Barker, 1975: 132. See also Chapman, 1938a, 246.

22 Lhasa Mission Diary, 4 Dec. 1936, L/P&S/12/4193, OIOC; compare Chapman, 1938a: 247–52. For other film shows, see Dec. 7, 11, 15, 21, 29, 1936, and Jan. 1, 12, 25, 30, 1937. For assessments of Chaplin's popularity, see Chapman, 1937: 125; and Gould, 1957: 207.

23 Lhasa Diary, 27 Nov. 1936, L/P&S/12/4193, OIOC; and Chapman, 1938a: 252.

24 Lhasa Diary, 14 Sept. 1936, 17 Nov. 1936, L /P&S/12/4193, OIOC.

25 Lhasa Diary, 5 Feb. 1937, L /P&S/12/4193, OIOC, prints the figure 1,50,000, which might be read as 1,500,000 or 150,000; the latter is more likely. Chapman, 1938a: 324.

26 Basil Gould, Report on the Lhasa Mission, 30 April 1937, L/P&S/12/4197, OIOC.

27 See the descriptions of reel 6, and color films "(3). 100" in the annotated notes on Tibet films. These are filed with Basil Gould's notes but probably represent Charles Bell's notes on his films. Most of the annotations recommend cutting out material. See Related Material 1147, British Film Institute Library, London.

28 On war newsreels, see Lhasa Diaries, 20 Sept. 1942, 9 May 1943, and 13 June 1943; for "St. Pauls," see Rolfe to Todd, Film Section, British Council, [1943]; for "give me the films," see Lhasa Diary, 20 Sept. 1942; all in L /P&S/12/4605, OIOC. The British missions stayed at "Dekyilingka" outside Lhasa and showed their films there.

29 R. Peel to Gould, 30 Aug. 1944, L/P&S/12/4180, OIOC. *Geheimnis Tibet,* sometimes called *Enigma of Tibet* or *Secret of Tibet,* was produced for Heinrich Himmler. The *OSS Mission to Tibet* is sometimes catalogued as *Inside Tibet.* See the Motion Picture, Sound, and Video Branch, National Archives, College Park, Maryland.

30 Harrer, 1953: 231, 246, 248–51. According to Hugh Richardson, personal communication, the films Harrer showed the Dalai Lama were given to him by the British, and later Indian, missions.

31 "Colour Film of Tibet. Mr. B. J. Gould's Journey," *Times,* 20 July 1937. See also "Devil Dances in Tibet. A Film in Colour," *Times,* 27 Nov. 1937.

32 See Bishop, 1989, and Lopez, 1998.

33 The NFTVA includes many reels but few viewing copies of films made in Tibet by F. M. Bailey, Charles Bell, James Guthrie, and George Sherriff.

34 For criticisms of the 1950s film of *Seven Years in Tibet,* see *Monthly Film Bulletin,* 24 (1957): 107.

35 Among the perceptive reviews, see Abramson, 1998: 8–12, and Norbu, 1998: 18–23.

36 *New York Times,* 7 Sept. 1997.

37 See Schell, 2000 for a discussion of the recent films and the influence of Buddhism in Hollywood.

OLD TIBET A HELL ON EARTH?

THE MYTH OF TIBET AND TIBETANS IN CHINESE ART AND PROPAGANDA

Thomas Heberer

Introduction

IN THIS PAPER, I will investigate the depiction of Tibetans in Chinese art and official propaganda, focusing on depictions in official journals, in art, and in literature. Although products of individual artists, these depictions reflect stereotypes common in official Chinese stances. Such representations of the "other," the alien, serve, among other things, to legitimate power and rule and are an expression of valuation and subordination, evoking positive or negative sentiments. The very representation of such paradigms and stereotypes is a kind of propaganda, and art and propaganda are thus intertwined.

In examining this phenomenon, I refer repeatedly to other "minorities" besides Tibetans. Today the fundamental ethnic contradiction in China is not between Han Chinese and Tibetans but rather between a mono-ethnic political party—the Communist Party—and a multi-ethnic society. Tibetans, then, are but one ethnic group among many in China, and there is no special depiction of them in Chinese art as distinguished from the depictions of other ethnic groups. My discussion of the representations of Tibetans thus applies equally to all ethnic minorities in China.

China's Ethnic Puzzle

China is a multi-ethnic state in which live fifty-five officially acknowledged "national minorities," that is, non-Chinese (that is, non-

Han) ethnic groups.[1] These groups live alongside the dominant population group, whom Westerners call "Chinese" but who refer to themselves as "Han." According to the 1990 census, national minorities, with 91.2 million people, make up 8.04 percent of China's total population, and that percentage is increasing. The 2000 census counted 106.43 million national minorities, which is 8.4 percent of the population. The "autonomous" Chinese regions in which most minorities live, however, comprise about 64 percent of China's total landmass, though the Han population is still a majority in these regions. The populations of the autonomous regions are the result of a long process in which a great variety of tribal communities intermingled with and were assimilated by the Han. The Sinologist Wolfram Eberhard writes:

> In 1,500 B.C.E., there was neither China nor the Chinese. The area of present-day China was inhabited by a large number of tribes with individual cultures. Indeed, the majority of these tribes belonged to one branch or another of the Mongolian race, but other races were also present. Likewise, there was no great "founding father" of the first Chinese empire. Rather, it formed slowly from assimilation and integration over the course of a century.[2]

One can question the uniformity of Chinese culture—a claim often put forth by the Chinese—even before this date. Historians frequently count as Han groups who exhibit noticeable differences in their language, clothing, lifestyles, mores, and customs, including the Hakka, the Cantonese, and the inhabitants of Fujian. The Communist government continues the practice of earlier rulers by counting various groups as Han and welding them into a fictional, homogeneous unity. The government favors replacing the many local languages with a single language, Putonghua (or Mandarin Chinese), for both academic and everyday settings; replacing local dress with uniform fashions; and reducing local customs to a few common aspects.

China's largest minority, the Zhuang, number around 15.5 million people, while its smallest, the Tibetan Lhoba, number only 2,300. Outside of China, little or nothing is known about the actual situation of most of the smaller nationalities, since they do not have any representatives who might report it. Tibetans are the ninth largest nationality according to the 1990 census, having 4.6 million people (0.4 percent of the total population and 5 percent of the minorities).

The Chinese View of "Barbarians"

One finds ethnocentric images,[3] which favor one's own group and marginalize neighboring peoples, in practically all societies of the world. At the margins begins "the beyond, the mythical realm of shadows, spirits, and fabulous creatures."[4] When contrasted to "us," the mastering of the "other" leads to its "barbarization."[5] Such ideas are not peculiar to China, which has undoubtedly developed an especially refined worldview. These self-images not only constitute a self-contained sense of identity, they serve also as a transethnic cultural consciousness that considers all groups who lie outside the cultural "center" to be, according to such logic, culturally inferior. Because Chinese central power and culture have continued for two thousand years, traditional ethnocentric notions dominate the pattern of behavior toward non-Han people and the expectations of how they should behave toward the central power. Imperial China understood itself as the cultural center of the world and its culture as the culture of all humanity. Accordingly, in traditional perceptions it was acknowledged that numerous other people had settled well-defined areas, but only one people was entrusted with the mandate of ruling humanity. This people inhabited the earth's epicenter, the "Middle Kingdom" (Zhongguo), and its emperor was the Son of Heaven.[6] Therefore, no borders existed: Even the Great Wall was regarded as a rampart of protection only, but not as a border.[7]

The bearers of the ancient Chinese river-culture perceived the surrounding people as "barbarians." They categorized these surrounding barbarians according to: the direction in which their lands lay; their distance from the epicenter of the world, namely, the emperor's court; and the barbarians' purported behavior toward this epicenter. The imperial court expected tribute, and the leaders of other people were thought of as vassals. Generally, such relationships existed only with weaker and culturally inferior peoples, so the Chinese, isolated for centuries on end, could constantly assert their feelings of superiority. From a very early date, the agricultural Han despised the surrounding nomads and hunters who were regarded both culturally and technologically inferior to them. Confucianism, the state ideology for centuries, was the ideological foundation for this Sinocentric contempt for "barbarians." According to Confucian ideas of social hierarchy, no egalitarian concepts existed, because no two things were equal. Between any two people, one was always older, male, or more highly ranked. These notions were duplicated in Chinese relations with outsiders, with the Chinese empire at the top of the hierarchy. The rest of the world was made up of those areas that directly bordered the empire, like Vietnam; those areas along its margins, such as Korea and Japan; and more distant areas inhabited by "outer barbarians." Confucianism also despised barbarians because, according to the great historian of Chinese antiquity, Sima Qian (ca. 186–145 B.C.E.), they "know nothing of *li,* the proper [Confucian] rules of life and *yi,* the duties of life."[8] To be different was by the ancient Chinese interpreted as an expression of ignorance of the social structure of human relations and of the Confucian rites. They concluded that "barbarians" were unable to control their "emotions," that they tended rather to give way to their feelings and would behave "like birds and wild animals."[9] Zhu Fuyuan, a leading Confucianist at the time of the Han emperor Wu Di in the first century B.C.E., stated that the legendary Xia, Yin, and Zhou rulers deemed the barbarians more animal than human.[10] The idea that barbarians are essentially animalistic pervades the entire history of China. It was even claimed in the T'ang Dynasty (618–907) that barbarians were "creatures with human faces but the feelings of beasts and neither our race nor of our kind."[11]

The philosopher and statesman Wang Yangming confirms the persistence of similar ideas during the Ming Dynasty (1386–1644):

> Barbarians are like wild animals. For Han officials to try to govern them through civil administration would be like a man trying to tame a pack of deer in his own living room. They will eventually jump on your altars, walk on your tables, and wildly

destroy everything. If one is in the wilderness, one should use methods befitting its nature. To split up the domains of the various chiefs means to establish zones of restriction and fits into the policy of circumcizing stallions and castrating boars.[12]

Comparisons between non-Chinese peoples and animals do not appear solely in official histories: They appear also in the very names for other people. Up to the founding of the People's Republic of China, the names for ethnic groups were sometimes represented by characters whose radicals had beastlike connotations. In history, for example, the character for the Di, the northern barbarians, contained the radical "dog," the character for southern barbarians, the radical for "worm," and the character for the western Qiang, a radical meaning "sheep."

Categorizations of this sort are in no way peculiar to the Chinese; they are found in many societies.[13] They pervade European intellectual history as well. In this regard the similarity between the ancient Chinese and the ancient Greek writers, such as Herodotus, is quite astounding.[14] Even Plato relegated barbarians to animal realms. Kant and Marx implied the same—to name only two more recent examples. Kant saw the history of humanity as a series of evolutionary stages that ascended from animality through brute humanity to personality.[15] For Marx, humans only differentiated themselves from animals with the production of foodstuffs.[16] Therefore, in the European history of political ideas, wild men who lacked the refinements of civilization were perceived to be closer to the animal realms. The nineteenth-century anthropologist Theodor Waitz asked whether "a portion of humanity should not be assigned to zoology."[17] In the history of the world the definition of what is human has often been applied to members of one's own culture and denied to others.[18] Accordingly, other communities were often relegated to the animal or semihuman sphere because their otherness or their culture was perceived as inferior. One example of the perception of cultural otherness as abnormal, backward, and inhuman from a European perspective can be found in the statement of a European captain who described the Indians of the northwest coast of America in the eighteenth century with the following words: "Since they were naked, possessed not a trifling of European manners, and spoke not a word of

Spanish, we thought them to be totally wild."[19] Much like the Chinese historian Sima Qian, the European captain classified Indians according only to their lack of his own culture and behavioral norms.

Even in ancient China, a group was judged according to its culture and lifestyle. Meal preparing, for example, was one aspect in such judgments. Barbarians were classified according to how they consumed their meals, whether "cooked" *(shou)* or "raw" *(sheng)*. The Confucian classic *Li Ji (Book of Rites)* says accordingly,

> The people who inhabit the far-eastern district, the I, are crafty and wily. Even farther away are people who do not know how to cook. The people who inhabit the far-southern district, the *Man*, are simple and honorable. Even farther away are people who do not know how to cook. The people who inhabit the far-western district, the *Jung,* are tough and strong. Even farther away are people who do not know how to cook. The people who inhabit the far-northern district, the *Di,* are fat and coarse. Even farther away are people who do not know how to cook.[20]

Distinctions of this sort offer clues about whether a community could be integrated into Han culture or not. "Raw" barbarians were wild and unruly, "cooked" ones were compliant and obedient.[21] The latter were thus acknowledged to possess a minimal degree of culture and a capacity for civilization, while the former were not. There are similar distinctions in the West, such as those of ancient Greece. Even here, the typical barbarian was a "raw-flesh eater."[22] For some time, the raw/cooked dichotomy engaged social anthropologists, for whom the use of fire was the dividing line. Lévi-Strauss also claimed that this dichotomy showed the transition from nature to culture.[23]

Confucianism did not intend to destroy these "barbarian" people, it only wanted their subordination to the emperor and their integration into the Chinese empire. Its aim was the "cultivation" of such people through Confucian values, that is, through nonviolent cultural assimilation. Even a barbarian could "become the Chinese emperor, but only by entering the Chinese system and by displaying his worthiness," as the Sinologist Wolfgang Franke writes.[24] This basic sentiment has

彰化縣內山生番

西藏寮納克番人

Figs. 1–5
Various "barbarians,"
source:
Yong & Dong 1751

Fig. 1 From Tibet

Fig. 2 From Lukang

魯康布扎番人

淡水右武乃等社生番

Fig. 3 "Cooked barbarian," Zhanghua County

Fig. 4 "Raw barbarian," Zhanghua County

彰化縣大肚等社熟番

羽民國在海東南崖巚間有人長頰鳥喙赤目
白首生毛羽能飛不能遠似人而卵生

Fig. 5 "Raw barbarian," Danshui County

Fig. 6 "Winged man," source: Goodall 1979

Fig. 7 Dancing Tibetans

changed little since. It is the guiding principle of Chinese national policy, which remains true to its Confucian principles:

> To decide whether a nationality should be recognized or not [by
> the emperor of China], one must determine if it is respectable or
> base. To decide whether a nationality is good or not, one must
> see if it obeys [the Chinese]. To decide whether a nationality is
> to be protected or punished, one must determine if it is pros-
> trate or belligerent.[25]

The traditional Chinese view has waned since the middle of the nineteenth century, largely due to European influence, but its underlying principles persist. Schwartz shows that the traditional view remains strong in the villages.[26] In the People's Republic, traditional Chinese and Marxist ideas were synthesized, as both share the belief that non-Chinese races should be assimilated culturally into the Han, and both agree that implementing Chinese economic policy is the best way to bring this about. Ultimately, this means acculturation, the reduction of difference in relation to the Han by means of the Han vision of cultural and economic "development." This reveals the sinocentric belief that Han culture is superior and the sense of mission that it generates. What once was the Confucian is nowadays the socialist "superior culture." Both Confucianism and socialism envision the ethnic minorities either capitulating to or mimicking the development of the Han and eventually being assimilated into its culture, for non-Han people were always perceived as needing to be upgraded to the level of the Han.

In addition to their sinocentric notion of superiority, the Chinese also idealized barbarian races as pure, natural, and primal.[27] Confucius declared, for example, that he wished "to live among the nine barbarian tribes of the East," since he believed that there he might more easily carry out his philosophical concept.[28] Accordingly, Taoists saw harmony and freedom in the original purity of barbarians, while Buddhist doctrines taught that the Chinese and the barbarians were fundamentally equal.[29] This thought reappears today in Xungen literature, which preaches a return to "roots," to authentic tradition, and to primal culture. These days such primal roots can only be found in ethnic minorities at the margins of China. These ideas also prevail among an increasing number of artists who are discovering the minorities' primordiality and their exoticism.[30] We see the same paradox in European literature, often depicting other races on the one side as primitive (whether "barbarians" or "noble savages") and on the other as exotic (whether deceitful heathens or mysterious royalty).[31] All cultures imagine aliens in terms of both fear and fascination. In China as well as in Europe, the tendency to idealize the "savage" was a consequence of social or cultural crisis, in that those "pure" characteristics ascribed to the "noble savage" were just those that one's own society had lost,

Fig. 8
Dancing Tibetans

whether seemingly or actually.[32] In either culture, this has less to do
with the understanding of the "other" than with overcoming one's own
identity crisis.

The Tibetans in Chinese Art and Literature

The term "alien" evokes several associations: the child, the savage,
or the fool.[33] I would like to focus on three such associations that Tibet
evokes in Chinese art and literature or, to be more precise, that Tibetan
men and women evoke:

1. an exotic-erotic image
2. a patriarchal-pedagogical image
3. a historical-primitive image.[34]

These three dimensions of the depiction of minorities affect the collective unconscious and—as we will see in what follows—express what the German historian Waldenfels calls "pre-forms" or "mistaken forms" of reason.[35] Thus, cultural primitiveness is paired with exoticism and socialist bliss. Mystical, instinctual, and sensual elements dominate such depictions, in which the woman and child repeatedly highlight the special role of the Han as a patriarchal teacher and father figure. The content of such images hides political messages that hint of the system's real hierarchy.

THE EXOTIC-EROTIC IMAGE

The artist's depiction of the exotic expresses unfulfilled wishes and longings. He projects upon the "other" his dissatisfactions with his own society, his existential boredom, and his dreams of fulfillment. He

Fig. 9 Singing Tibetans

Fig. 10 Singing Tibetans

Fig. 11 Erotic fantasies: Wa

Fig. 12 Erotic fantasies: Wa

imaginatively constructs poetic images of sensual fulfillment unhindered by social constraints or necessity, "imaginations of the body, adventure, ecstasy, weirdness, and anarchy."[36]

The French anthropologist Michel Leiris calls exoticism the distortion of the other into the "noble savage" or the "honest guy from the bush" or generally his degradation to an object of protection. The exoticly motivated encounter is not based on the interest to learn something about the other on his own terms, or about oneself. Exoticism is ethnocentric decoration and adventure.[37]

And it is exactly this exoticism that appears to characterize the official public image of "minorities" in China. Most depictions show colorfully dressed minorities dancing, singing, and laughing in palm groves, on mountain tops, or in downright bizarre landscapes. They dance wildly, fires blaze, and mythic images are created[38] that send a shiver down the spine of the Han-Chinese who view them. In facial structure, figure, and movement these depictions correspond to Han ideals of beauty. The official cultural policy also adapts minorities' music, song, and dance according to Chinese forms, since the "backward" originals

Fig. 13 Erotic fantasies: Tibetan Woman

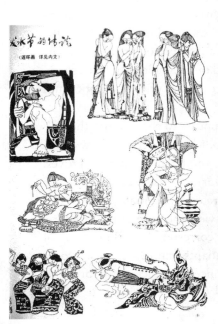

Fig. 14 Erotic fantasies:
Various Minority Women

Fig. 15 Erotic fantasies: Dai

do not meet the Han standards of taste and must be elevated. The other is thus counterfeit (cf. Fig. 7–10).

Eroticism is an important element of the exotic. Historical chronicles describe barbarians as promiscuous *(luan)* and orgiastic. The anthropologist Claudius Müller thus speaks of the "typical anxiety of a high culture when confronted by barbarians' greater sexual potency."[39] China, not surprisingly, repeatedly attempted to impose Confucian sexual morals on barbarians. Such attempts were strongly encouraged after the founding of the People's Republic of China. Anything smacking of liberal sexual relations—such as youth meeting houses, premarital sex between young people, maturation festivals and initiations, or fertility rites—was prohibited, as were non-Han forms of marriage like polyandry, cross-cousin marriage, or levirate, the practice of widows marrying their deceased husband's brother. The People's Republic also persuaded southern Chinese tribes in which both sexes went topless to change their dress customs. At the same time, minorities were (and are) objects of the erotic and, in some cases, sexual imagination. Various publications and artworks connected others' customs repeatedly with imagined sexual practices, often resulting in massive conflicts between ethnic minority groups and Han-Chinese. To name just a few examples:

- At the end of the 1970s, there was a scandal at the opening of the new airport in Peking when a large mosaic at an airport restaurant was unveiled. Though tastefully rendered, it depicted, among other things, naked, bathing Dai woman. In Xishuangbanna it is not uncommon for Dai women to bathe naked in rivers or lakes. But it was asserted by the Chinese authorities that "Dai representatives" had complained about the mosaic's voyeuristic quality. The artwork was veiled for a long time, which caused many Chinese to seek out the airport restaurant in order to peek behind the curtain.

- In 1979, a dispute waged among cultural critics about whether traditional music festivals should be again permitted in southern China, as these festivals encouraged dancing, bawdy songs, and sexual liberty among the young. They had been forbidden during the Cultural Revolution on account of "obscenity" and "debauchery."

- In 1987, a conflict erupted when it was claimed that Tibetans had objected to depictions made in an article in the journal *Renmin Wenxue* on incest, sodomy, and other sexual practices in Tibet.[40] The Tibetans—so the argument ran—thought this insulting and condescending.[41]

- In 1989, riots occurred in Muslim areas when tens of thousands took to the streets to protest a book about Islamic sexual mores and practices. The book interpreted the taboo surrounding pork in sexual terms and characterized the minaret as a phallic symbol.[42]

In these examples Tibetans and Muslims were thus depicted as primitive, uncivilized, and impelled by uncontrollable, animalistic urges. In the aforementioned literary contribution Tibetan women were described as sexual objects, thus allowing Han-Chinese to imagine taboo sexuality through Tibetans. The unconcern toward nakedness characteristic of Tibetans and other minorities is attached to the desire to break out of Han sexual taboos. However, those images of Han are an expression of unconscious desires of wildness, exoticism, promiscuity, sensuality, and sexual desire. The Han-Chinese are able to express relatively freely a patriarchal sexual mythology about minority women that would be taboo as regards their own women (cf. Fig. 11–20). And another phenomenon appears to be at work here, too: Chinese are able to occupy symbolically other cultures in their depictions of their women's bodies. This becomes abundantly clear when one realizes that nakedness is avoided generally in Han society but is thought "typical of barbarians."[43]

And even when such symbols do not directly represent the socio-economic condition of that culture, they still express its inner essential being, its "life juices."[44]

THE PATRIARCHAL-PEDAGOGICAL IMAGE

A patriarchal kinship myth pervades the official Chinese descriptions of the relationship between the Han-Chinese and minorities. Han are described as father figures or elder brothers. Surrounded by members

Fig. 16 Erotic fantasies: Da

of minority groups, they advise, teach, and instruct them; they are teachers and role models. This is expressed by the name "big elder brother" *(lao da ge)*, the name Han have given themselves in relation to minorities. Fathers or older brothers have the task of educating the children and younger siblings—a common Confucian theme that one also finds in other parts of the world. This patriarchal concept finds its ideological expression in the Han idea that the most advanced culture is that of the "father ethnic group," that is, the Han. They thus conceive society as a homogeneous ethnic community, a closed unit like a family, where there exists a division of labor between the superior and the inferior. The head of the family (the Han) has the duty to protect the family, to educate, instruct, and advise its members. The children (minorities) are expected to be loyal and to respect the father and his educational concepts (cf. Fig. 21–28).

Patriarchal notions that treat Tibetans and other "barbarians" like children can be found in historical records, too. In an eighteenth-century chronicle we read:

> It is necessary to discipline the [Tibetans'] habits kindly. Justice should become the foundation of their society. They must learn frugality and compassion. One should also teach them sincerity, reverence, and trustworthiness. Only then could there be hope that such wild barbarians will develop a proper sense of respect and gratitude.[45]

Women also dominate the representation of minorities in art and photography. Hannelore Bublitz sees them as a symbolic representation of the infantile: "Women take over the place both of the exotic and the infantile. The feminine appears to be opposite to culture and progress."[46] This interpretation is also applicable to the Chinese view of minorities. One sees a similar identification of the other with the feminine in the European context. There, the woman is the embodiment of nature—primal, wild, and thus uncivilized.[47] The feminine is symbolically "unveiled," so that the female body becomes a "dark continent" that can be illuminated voyeuristically.[48] And there one also sees a gender-specific dimension where the woman symbolizes "the place of the other where

Fig. 17 Erotic fantasies: Lisu

Fig. 18 Erotic fantasies: Tibetan man

Fig. 19 Tibetan family

Fig. 20 Erotic fantasies: Miao woman

Fig. 21 Cultural festival of minorities

Fig. 22 Cadre of the People's Liberation Army instructs Tibetan militia

Fig. 23 Mao amid the "Nationalities Family"

Fig. 24 Late Chinese Commander-in-Chief Tzhu De teaches late Panchen Lama (modern thangka)

Fig. 25 Han official bringing new political books to Tibetans

Fig. 26 Chinese leaders welcome Tibetan reincarnation

Fig. 27 Uighur child and "father" Deng Xiaoping

Fig. 28 Model Chinese soldier helping Tibetan people

Fig. 29 Dim minority woman   Fig. 30 Wild Tibetan man

the human being = male puts itself in a moral-spiritual relationship, occupying the position of the superior rational subject."[49] The Han thus doubly strengthen their hierarchical status in relation to the femininity of minorities: The Chinese are not merely father figures, but progressive father figures. This patriarchal myth demonstrates that China is not a nation in which nationalities enjoy equal rights in a "voluntary association of free individuals." It rather conceives society as a family in which the Han, as the dominant ethnic group, adopt the father's role.[50] Not only does the Chinese term for state, *guojia*, imply this relationship (as a compound word made of the characters for country and family), the hierarchical ranking of ethnic groups confirms it.

THE HISTORICAL-PRIMITIVE IMAGE

The belief that the other is primitive has a variety of functions: It defines the subject's identity, it legitimizes political claims, and it orders others in terms of one's own hierarchy. Such beliefs appear in all cultures, whether Chinese, socialist, or European. One also finds in historical chronicles the characterization of minorities as backward. In a history of Tibet written by He Ning (1792), for example, we find the following passage:

> The customs of the Tibetans [are] completely abject and despicable. The people all appear unwashed and uncombed. Their figure resembles a dog or a sheep. Both monks and laity are equally greedy. [Tibet] is a place where the old is being preserved and nothing changes.[51]

These traditional marks of "civilizing arrogance" correspond well with historic-materialistic concepts developed, for example, by Joseph Stalin in the 1930s.[52] According to his "doctrine of socio-economic formations," the societies of all nationalities in history can be classified into five categories: primitive, slave, feudal, capitalist, and socialist.

Fig. 31 Poor and backward Tibetans

This concept, which has its origin in the European history of ideas (for example, Turgot),[53] fits well with traditional Chinese hierarchical thinking.[54] In this way every ethnic group had their fixed position in the hierarchy of nationalities and in its relationship with the "most advanced" people, the Han. Under socialism the Han could retain their traditional position and function in relation to non-Han people: As the societies of the national minorities were considered inferior to that of the Han, the culture of the Han remained the highest-ranking one. It was the duty of the Han to civilize and modernize the minority societies. The cultural avant garde, representative and guardian of culture and civilization, was now no longer the emperor's court, his officials, the gentry, and the traditional examination system, but rather the Communist Party with its functionaries and its educational system. The duty of every nationality was to catch up with the Han as quickly as possible and to bring its economy and society into line with that of the Han. The patriarchal state correspondingly had to initiate suitable measures and policies. It decided what was useful for a minority, what was advanced or backward, civilized or uncivilized, and which customs or habits were beneficial or harmful and had accordingly to be abolished or reformed. Even today school students learn that ethnic minorities are economically and culturally more backward than the Han (cf. Fig. 29–35).

The Chinese treatment of minorities confirms this: The Communist Party claims that the immediate responsibility of any ethnic group is to catch up with the big brother so that it may be embraced by (socialist) society. The patriarchal socialist state, however, initiates this process and determines the minority's needs and which of its customs and habits are "healthy" (progressive and reformable) and which are "unhealthy" (primitive and dangerous). The morality of the Han, of course, is the yardstick by which such customs are measured. Many non-Han officials in China have adopted this rhetoric, as when Tibetan cadres repeat catch phrases about the "brutality of serfdom" before 1959. When I asked an official of the Wa (a people who live along the Chinese-Burmese border) about their traditional practice of headhunting, he answered that the Wa "were forced to adopt to this practice by the Guomindang" (the party that ruled China before the founding of the People's Republic), an opinion obviously learned during his study

Vor der Befreiung wurde das arbeitende Volk in Tibet auf grausame Weise unterdrückt und gefoltert:

(1), (2) Schädel sowie Hand- und Armknochen von nieder-gemetzelten Leibeigenen

(3), (5) ·Handblock und Fußschellen — von Leibherren be-nutzte Folterinstrumente

(4) Obdachlose Leibeigene mußten im Freien über-nachten.

(6) Leibeigene wurden gezwungen, ihren Leibherrn zu tragen.

Fig. 32 Evidence of old Tibetan society's cruelty

Text: Before liberation Tibetan laboring people were brutally suppressed and tortured: (1), (2) skull, hand, and arm bones of massacred serfs; (3), (5) hand stocks and feet shackles used for torturing serfs; (4) homeless serfs had to live in the open; (6) serfs were forced to carry their owners.

in the Central School for Nationalities in the second half of the 1970s. Non-Han cadres have only recently begun to question the chracteriza-tion of certain of their histories, societies, and customs as "backward."

Fig. 33 Tibetan woman

Stereotypes like those mentioned above are an obstacle to earnest discourse and debate between the Han and the non-Han people and their cultures. The demystification of the strange and unknown, of the "other," the understanding of exoticistic prejudices and stereotypes remains an important task. The key aspect of such stereotypes is the concept of hierarchization, because it perpetuates and legitimizes inequality and tutelage. The American philosopher Michael Walzer has pointed out that the idea of a cultural hierarchy always poses a threat for the people whose culture is devaluated. Hierarchies, says Walzer, are never "innocent," because they tend toward policies of discrimination.[55] The classification as inferior is thus an obstacle to true autonomy or self-administration, because those nationalities are seen as incapable of successful management and self-government.

But we should not overlook one difference between Confucian and Western ideas about other people. According to the Confucian world-view, people of other ethnicities could equally attend the state's examinations and enter and climb up the government hierarchy if they only possessed the requisite knowledge. Not race but culture justified the feeling of superiority. Unlike the West, which has always in a stronger way associated culture with race, China defined culture behaviorally.[56] A barbarian was such only because he or she was ignorant of Confucian rituals.

The Image of Tibet in Official Propaganda

China justifies its occupation of Tibet in four ways. It appeals to four legitimizing patterns:

1. historical legitimization
2. legitimization of liberation
3. economic development legitimization, and
4. social welfare and care legitimization.[57]

HISTORICAL LEGITIMIZATION

China has justified its rule of Tibet with several different, and sometimes conflicting, appeals to history. Its official propaganda claims that ancestors of the Tibetans enjoyed since ancient times a familial relationship with the Han-Chinese. This relationship was supposedly confirmed during the Tang Dynasty (618–907) with various politically motivated marriages and treaties that developed a relationship of kinship and friendship. The Chinese appeal to two facts to support this claim. First, in the Potala there stands a statue of the Tang princess

Fig. 34 Praying Tibetans

Fig. 35 "Wild" Tibetans

Wencheng, who was married to the king of the Tibetan Tubo Empire in 641.[58] This statue—so the argument goes—is worshiped till today. Second, a memorial of the 823 pact between China and Tibet stands near Jokhang Monastery, which reportedly displays the following inscription:

> In the interest of preserving unity, uncle and nephew agreed to enter into an alliance. In the future, this bond shall remain unbroken. Gods and men witness this event that all future generations will hail.

Close economic and historical contacts, it is argued, also created the preconditions for establishing a unified political entity. Since the (Mongolian) Yuan Dynasty (1271–1368), Tibet was thought subject to the jurisdiction of the "central government," an assumption that remained unchanged up through the Republic of China (1912–49). This is the view still held by the People's Republic. Here we can see a different concept of nation and state in operation. The Chinese government sees all the ethnic minorities as part of the entire race of Chinese people. As a matter of fact, the term used in China for the "Chinese" (Zhongguoren) applies to all inhabitants of China regardless of their ethnic belonging. The "Han" is only one of fifty-six nationalities in China. Unlike Western Europe, where many nationalities formed their own nation-states in the eighteenth and nineteenth centuries (ethnicity being the principal basis of nationality), in China territory is considered to be the basis of nationality. For instance, after Mongolia declared its independence (which later led to the founding of the People's Republic of Mongolia), Sun Yat-sen, the founder of the Republic of China in 1912, wrote that Mongolians were Chinese and will remain so, even if they might have forgotten that for the time being. Thus, according to the Chinese view, China simply had not been able to exercise its legitimate rights over Tibet for a while because of the weakness and division of its territory. This view of Tibet as historically part of China is encouraged even in popular literature. A poem from the Communist Party newspaper reads, for example:

Sun and moon have one mother: light
The Han and Tibetan have one mother as well: China.[59]

A recent book describes belonging to China as the aspiration of most Tibetans:

There is something special in the modern history of Tibet, the submission of its local government to the Motherland's central government. That such a relationship might be a problem is false belief held only by a handful of Tibetans. These people lawlessly wish to divide Tibet from the Motherland only because imperialists have sown dissension in the ranks of such separatists. This belief is incompatible with Chinese national interests and unbearable to Tibetans themselves.[60]

Furthermore, China uses tourism to bolster its claim that Tibet has always been a part of China. While showing palaces, monasteries, and temples, Chinese tour guides point out a number of items intended to prove the official claims: gifts from Chinese emperors, Tibetan paintings made in their honor, tributes paid by Tibetan dignitaries to Chinese rulers, and documentation of various Chinese restoration projects. Chinese tour guides thus emphasize the historic, cultural, and symbolic commonalities shared by Tibetans and Chinese, even as Tibetans themselves highlight the differences and separation.[61]

THE LEGITIMIZATION OF LIBERATION

China claims to have frustrated the attempts of foreign imperialists to divorce Tibet and China since the nineteenth century. It also claims to have liberated Tibetans from serfdom by dissolving Tibetan feudalism and giving its people personal freedom and democratic rights. This liberation, it is said, gave the Tibetan people a fundamental right to safety. In 1974, a Chinese book claimed:

As a consequence of feudal serfdom, Tibet was a model of political corruption, economic stagnation, and cultural backwardness prior to liberation. Its three great feudal lords were the reactionary government, the monasteries, and the nobility, each of which cheated the people out of their last pennies. Serfs were susceptible to the widest possible variety of torture: beating, flogging, flaying, blinding, and the cutting off of tongues. The Tibet of old was a hell on earth![62]

Fig. 36 Modern thangka

Fig. 37 Tremendous changes in Tibet

This "old Tibet" was regularly shown to tourists on official Chinese tours until well into the 1980s. The Lhasa Museum of the Tibetan Revolution displays dried human arms, flutes made from human thighbones, and silver-plated skulls that are alleged to have been taken from victims of torture and human sacrifice.[63] More subtle forms have replaced this clumsy propaganda in the meantime.

Thanks to the Communist Party, Tibet has "changed from a feudal serfdom to a socialist society and has leapt several centuries in a single bound." In its 1992 report on the state of sovereignty and human rights in Tibet, the Press Office of the State Council of the People's Republic of China opened with the following statement:

Tibet was once considered to be a mysterious region. This mystic veil has since been removed, and Tibet presents itself open to the world now. It has undergone tremendous changes from an extremely dark Middle Age into modernity.[64]

Fig. 38 Chinese soldiers bring modernity to Tibet

The Legitimization of Economic Development

China also claims to have helped Tibet develop its agriculture, lay the foundation for its modern industry, create its network of highways, and institute its modern education and health care, all of which have contributed to a higher standard of living. Tibet, China's official propaganda claims, also receives developmental assistance from other Chinese provinces. As proof, China maintains that:

> For every 100 urban households, there are 212 bicycles, 88 color televisions, 84 cassette recorders, 42 washing machines, 24 refrigerators, and 26 cameras.

China even claims to have historical evidence for such aid: Historical accounts from the eighteenth century describe the Qing courts' aid as proof of a favoritism for which the Tibetans could never thank China enough.[65]

The Legitimization of Social Welfare and Care

China has supposedly guaranteed the Tibetans freedom of religion, although this freedom is severely limited:

Fig. 39 Chinese modernity is coming to Tibet

Fig. 40 Serfs have become mining workers

Everyone who violates the law and commits crimes in the name of religion will be punished according to the law. In recent years, several monks and nuns have been punished because they violated the law and committed crimes that deserve to be punished, including rioting, endangering the public safety and order, causing others physical injury, damaging and stealing property, arson, and murder. Not a single one was imprisoned or punished because of the exercise of his or her religion.

Religious movements that do not fall within official boundaries and appear dangerous to the state are harshly persecuted. However, according to the official propaganda, religion itself does not need to be abolished, since it will wither away anyway.[66] Current assessments of religion also reflect traditional notions of religion, for religion was already suspect in ancient China. For one thing, the Chinese themselves did not have a religion of redemption; in the philosophical Confucianist worldview, religion and superstition were seen as two sides of the same coin. Because institutions that threatened the state often emerged from religion, its practices were subject to strict regulation and control. If a religion was loyal to the state, it was tolerated. If not, it could be suppressed when necessary. The Communists continued this tradition in portraying religion as something foreign, something having come from outside, something potentially dangerous to the state, and something that historically has won influence and power only when government was weak. The identification of religion with superstition and with hostility toward the state has been common in the People's Republic, too. Therefore, ethnic minority religions are not only seen as backward, superstitious, and weird, but also threatening. Such religions are thought to have hidden agendas, and the mystical dimensions of Tibetan Buddhism are regarded to be especially alien, dangerous, and treasonous. The fascination with the Dalai Lama (which the Chinese describe as the "Dalai-Lama fad") instead of Peking, the fervent attachment to spirituality instead of modernity, the ritual conspiracy—all this separates Tibet and Han-China and frightens the latter with the thought of hidden national dangers. As regards human rights in Tibet, the Chinese also complain of "international anti-Chinese powers" that manipulate questions about human rights to "realize their dreams and ambitions to divide China, wrench Tibet away, and undermine socialist China."[67]

Conclusion

Representations of Tibetans in Chinese art and literature display a certain ambivalence toward their primitiveness and eroticism. Official Chinese propaganda characterizes Tibetan (and non-Han) society and culture as uncivilized, brutal, oppressive, and man-eating, even if there have been periodic oscillations between harsher and more generous images. Textbooks and other official forms of propaganda present such negative images to both Han and non-Han. The latter see themselves often as "primitives" who need the "bigger, older brother" to guide and enlighten them. Many non-Han people display an obvious inferiority complex as a result. Minorities often begin speeches apologetically with sentences like, "we are a very backward race with little culture or education." Minority religion and traditions are seen as frightening and superstitious, their cuisine barbaric and unpalatable, their clothing colorful but disheveled, their lifestyles primitive. Chinese only reluctantly employ ethnic minorities as labor since they are thought lazy.

Han neither understand nor sympathize when Tibetans demand autonomy or independence. Most Chinese have internalized the idea that Tibet is an inseparable part of China. They think Tibetans ungrateful for being discontent even after the Chinese gave them streets, factories, schools, and hospitals, and liberated them from "feudal serfdom, oppression, torture, and starvation." China subsidizes Tibet to the tune of billions of dollars, and Tibetans "waste it all." A Chinese man who identified himself as a Christian once exclaimed to me, "If the Tibetans wish to force the issue of their independence after all that we've done for them, then we will attempt to stop them with all the power at our disposal! We will rather extinguish them than let Tibet go."

As long as the Chinese cling to their own imagined superiority, consider the Tibetans inferior, and see themselves as the others' teachers, problems will not be solved. The Chinese cannot resolve this conflict peacefully until they change their way of thinking and accept other cultures. Moreover, equality is not just about equality by law or economic equality. Frank Böckelmann makes this point exactly:

For the uncomparable equality is the beginning of the end,[68] as it dissolves differences and respective identities and thereby assimilates others into the dominant group. One must ask if the conflict between Han and non-Han peoples is one of culture or moreover one of power, since the latter is neither the result of cultural struggle nor limitations, but rather about the control of resources and territory.[69]

The number of Chinese who question the official image of Tibet has grown over the last few years. Visits to foreign countries and greater information have generated a discussion about the "question of Tibet," especially among younger intellectuals.[70] The most famous Chinese dissident, Wei Jingsheng, denounced the Chinese policy on Tibet in an open letter to the late Deng Xiaoping in 1992 and called for a reevaluation of the traditional view of Tibetan history, culture, and the Dalai Lama.[71] But still, the number of enlightened Chinese who sympathize with the Dalai Lama is admittedly small, and nothing is going to change in regard to images of Tibet in the near future. Chinese nationalism is growing at present, and it appears that the official position will become stricter. The propaganda about the Dalai Lama and Tibetan "feudal serfdom" has grown more intense lately after several years of more moderate reports. Just to name a few examples: In 1995, Chinese propaganda linked the Dalai Lama to Shoko Asahara, the leader of the Aum Shinrikyo sect responsible for the poison gas attack on the Tokyo subway system.[72] In 1996, a Chinese journalist wrote about a letter that a local Tibetan government supposedly sent to a religious leader in the 1950s. Apparently, the letter read, in part:

NEWS ITEM: CHINA VIOLATES ITS OWN BAN BY PUBLISHING A CARICATURE OF THE DALAI LAMA, ACCOMPANIED BY AN ARTICLE CHARGING HIM WITH HAVING USED HUMAN HEADS, INTESTINES AND SKIN IN SACRIFICIAL OFFERINGS.
Li Zhenming/China Daily

Fig. 41 Caricature of the Dalai Lama, source: *China Daily* (*Far Eastern Economic Review*, 15 August 1996)

> In order to recite sutras for the Dalai Lama and congratulate him on his birthday, all coworkers of the Xiami office are to read prayers aloud. To do so, they will need sacrificial offerings. Thus we urgently need fresh intestines, two skulls, various types of blood, and an entire human skin. Please bring these articles immediately.[73]

By implying that the Dalai Lama condones such things, Chinese propaganda accuses the Dalai Lama of trying to divide the Motherland in the name of religious separatism.[74] Such accusations do not admit of verification, and the information upon which they are based has been torn out of context. Without an understanding of the cultural background of Tibetan religion and ritual, such propaganda seems reasonable, since it appears to denounce violence, brutality, and inhumanity. While we can see through these claims relatively easily, Chinese readers who receive only certain images of Tibet become socially indoctrinated. Tibetan readers rightfully see such images as an attack on their religion, their spiritual leader, and their nation as a whole. Such propaganda intensifies the conflict between Tibetans and Han–Chinese and, at the same time, strengthens anti-Western, nationalist sentiments among the Han. For ethnic Chinese, the West is trying to pry Tibet from the Chinese nation and attempting to reestablish the horrifying serfdom that once oppressed Tibet.

NOTES

1 In this discussion, I will use the terms "Han" and "non-Chinese peoples."

2 Eberhard, 1982: 8.

3 A good overview of ethnocentrism can be found in Antweiler, 1994.

4 Kohl, 1979: 29.

5 Magill, 1989: 41.

6 For this worldview, see Forke (1925) and Fairbank (1974).

7 Li Ge, 1995: 21.

8 De Groot, 1921: 3.

9 Wickert, 1983:10. See also Granet, 1985: 311. An overview of traditional notions of "barbarians" has been conducted by Müller, 1980. See also Li Ge, 1992: 20ff.

10 Franke, 1967: 1.336.

11 Ibid., 2.335.

12 Ibid., 2.356.

13 See also Müller and Luckmann in Antweiler, 1994: 143.

14 See Goodall, 1979: 62ff. I will not discuss here the role that totemistic elements play in these descriptions. See, among others, Li Zehou, 1992: 23ff.

15 Kant, 1970: 11ff. and 85ff.

16 Marx and Engels, 1969: 21.

17 Waitz, 1859: 8.

18 Lévi-Strauss, 1993: 26. See also Berger and Luckmann, 1970: 110. Berger and Luckmann also discuss the connections between animality and caste in India. See also Perrig, 1987: 31ff., and Ritvo, 1995: 481–500.

19 Loiskandl, 1966: 110.

20 Li Ge, 1992: 102.

21 See Dikötter, 1992: 9ff.

22 See Loiskandl, 1966: 95.

23 Lévi-Strauss, 1964.

24 Franke, 1962: 22.

25 A conference on nationalism held in August 1980 concluded that such values are still quite common today. See Ji, 1981: 79.

26 Schwartz, 1974: 284.

27 Dikötter recognizes manifestations of "cultural and racial nationalism" that strive to create a community and integrate it. Dikötter, 1996.

28 Kungfutse, 1985: 101. When asked by a student how he could live with such "raw" people, Confucius replied, "Wherever an educated man lives, nothing raw can happen." For the position of Confucius, see Hsiao, 1979: 137ff.

29 Hsiao, 1979:663ff. Hildebrand, 1987: 44ff.

30 Kojima, 1994: 2ff.

31 See Loiskandl, 1966: 8ff.

32 One might examine whether the ambivalent view of "minority cultures" expresses what Homi Bhabha calls the "ambivalence of colonial discourses." See Bhabha, 1984.

33 See Waldenfels, 1990: 60.

34 Harrell, 1995a: 10ff. Gladney mentions a similar passage (Gladney, 1994). Gladney also investigates similar examples of the exotic-erotic in Chinese films about minorities. See Gladney, 1995.

35 Waldenfels, 1990: 62.

36 Pickerodt, 1987.

37 Leiris, 1979: 40ff.

38 This is not only true of Chinese images: Egyptian, Greek, and Roman images show barbarians to be sexy, uninhibited, and wildly ecstatic, too. (Loiskandl, 1966: 81ff).

39 Müller, 1980: 74.

40 Ma, 1987. German translation in Kojima, 1994: 66ff and 131ff.

41 For more details, see the Hong Kong newspaper *Zhengming (The Contest)* 3 (1987):10–11.

42 See *Guagmin Ribao (The Light Daily)*, May 15–16, 1989.

43 Eberhard, 1983: 202.

44 Magill, 1989: 60.

45 Dabringhaus, 1994: 150. A Chinese description from the Qing era is analyzed by Becker (1976).

46 Bublitz, 1992.

47 See, among others, MacCormack, 1989.

48 See von Braun, 1994: 82ff.

49 Weigel, 1987: 179.

50 See Brown, 1994: 260.

51 Dabringhaus, 1994: 124.

52 Linck, 1995: 269.

53 Kohl, 1979: 121ff.

54 Gudula Linck characterizes this hierarchy of other peoples in traditional thought as a "difference in the degree of the actualization of their humanity (Chinese = cultured people), such that foreigners move fluidly on a scale between wilderness, immorality, animalistic existence on the one hand and civilization, morality, and true humanity on the other." See Linck, 1995: 282.

55 Walzer, 1996: 186.

56 Harrell, 1995a: 19f.

57 See Weggel, 1982, for a similar, but slightly different categorization.

58 Scarcely anyone in China knows that the Tibetan king received Princess
   Wencheng as a wife in order to stop him from attacking Tang-China. Tibet
   had already enjoyed some military victories against China. On these points,
   see Jagchid and Symons, 1989: 155f.

59 Renmin Ribao in the *Far Eastern Economic Review*, 22 June 1995: 11.

60 Ya, 1991: vi.

61 See also Klieger, 1994: 281ff.

62 Anon., 1974: 5. *The Peking Review* declared in its edition from September 28,
   1971, that the Communist Party liberated Tibetans from a "dark, barbaric
   inferno" (16). A report from 1996 shows that this attitude has not changed:
   "Prior...to 1959, feudal serfdom ruled in Tibet, and this system was even
   darker and more horrible than the European Middle Ages. Serfs and slaves
   were but 'speaking tools.'" See "Über die Menschenrechtslage in Tibet" in the
   Beijing Rundschau 35 (1996): 21.

63 These items are really the relics of saints. See Harrer 1984: 90ff.

64 *Renmin Ribao (People's Daily)*, 23 September, 1992. German translation in
   the *Beijing Rundschau* 39 (1992): 5ff. Since this translation is imperfect, we
   are using the Chinese text.

65 See Dabringhaus, 1994: 137.

66 Anon., 1988: 37.

67 *Renmin Ribao*, 23 September 1992.

68 See Beck, 1993: 124.

69 Böckelmann, 1996.

70 See, among others, the contributions in the newspaper of the foreign opposition, *Minzhu Zhongguo (Democratic China)* 8 (1990): 33–50; 12 (1992):
   70–79; 15 (1993): 54–71; Cao and Seymour, 1998.

71 Wei, 1993.

72 See *Beijing Rundschau* 45 (1995): 6 f.

73 Bai, 1996: 126.

74 See Zhou, 1996: 24.

Tibet, Theosophy, and the Psychologization of Buddhism[1]

Poul Pedersen

THE THEOSOPHICAL MOVEMENT has played an interesting role in the relationship between the East and the West. It has influenced Western ideas of the East, but has also affected the way Easterners see themselves and their religious and philosophical traditions. In this article I shall be concerned with some long-term consequences of the Theosophists' promotion of Oriental wisdom and their attraction to Tibet. I shall argue that the Theosophical staging in the late nineteenth century of the mythical Tibetan mahatmas was a dress rehearsal of things to come: the appearance a century later of real Tibetans as spiritual masters on the Western scene.

The Theosophical Society: Foundation and Ideas

The Theosophical Society was founded in New York in 1875. Its purpose was to study magic and occult science, or, as it was stated in its bylaws, "to collect and diffuse knowledge of the laws which govern the universe" (Campbell, 1980: 28).[2] Nothing was mentioned about universal brotherhood of man or Eastern religion and philosophy. These issues were introduced later, in 1878, when the Theosophists, in Olcott's words, established "relations with Asiatics and their religions and social systems" (Olcott, 1895: 120f.). Most prominent among the founders were Helena Petrovna Blavatsky (1831–91), Russian émigré and later naturalized American, and the American lawyer and journalist Henry Steel Olcott (1832–1907). Blavatsky was the imaginative creator of the

Theosophical ideas, whereas Olcott was the clever organizer who turned the small society into an influential, international movement.[3]

Theosophy is derived from a long and motley tradition of occult and spiritual teachings, which in the mid–nineteenth century moved out of its previous underground, marginal existence and entered popular intellectual life (Webb, 1974, 1976). It was an age of secularization and enormous scientific progress—but also of extraordinary religious and spiritual longing. The "age of Auguste Comte and Charles Darwin," says Peter Gay, "was also the age of Cardinal Newman and William James" (Gay, 1984: 59)—and Madame Blavatsky, we should add, if we wish to cover the range of the century's spiritual concerns. Many people were distressed by positivist science and aggressive materialism and had little faith in the ability of Christianity to guard human spirituality and protect its true place in the universe. Theosophy, spiritualism, and other occult or psychic movements were related to what Hughes called "the revolt against positivism" (Hughes, 1974). They were, however, not simply irrational currents in an overly rational civilization. They reflected the "need for guides through the jungle of modernity" (Gay, 1984: 59), and with their universal views on history and the world, they often displayed a surprising affinity with Enlightenment skepticism. Paradoxically, it was as if they were searching for a rational religion (Godwin, 1994: xi).[4] The spiritual mobilization against modernity was deeply marked by modernity itself.

When the Theosophical Society was founded, the Theosophists had only a vague idea of what Theosophy was, but by the end of the 1870s Blavatsky had given it the shape of a complex evolutionary theory linking cosmic evolution to human spiritual growth—a comprehensive psychology, or "science of the soul," as she said in *Isis Unveiled* (Blavatsky 1923, I: xxxiiif.).[5] It was not simply a "religion" or a "science," but both. As such it was a "higher science" guaranteeing true knowledge by bringing science and ancient religious wisdom together. Blavatsky's aim was, on the one hand, to bridge the divide between science and religion, as was clearly expressed in the subtitle of her chef-d'oeuvre, *The Secret Doctrine* (1921), which defined Theosophy as "The Synthesis of Science, Religion, and Philosophy." On the other hand, she attempted to come to terms with religious pluralism by claiming "that all religions were really one" (Gombrich and Obeyesekere, 1988: 222). Theosophy was bluntly anti-Christian and favored Eastern religions, but it also claimed that it was nothing but the essence of the knowledge contained in all ancient and prehistoric religions descending from "Lemurian" and "Atlantean" civilizations. The Theosophists were heirs to this divine wisdom, which—long ago lost to ordinary people—had secretly been preserved by a benevolent brotherhood residing in Tibet (Blavatsky 1921, 1: xx, 730).[6]

From Egypt to India

Soon after its founding in 1875, the society began to decline. Little was done, members dropped out. Blavatsky was working on her first big book, *Isis Unveiled* (1877), and had little time for anything else. Until then she had—like most occultists—considered Egypt the source of all past wisdom, but the writing of *Isis* made her transfer her "allegiance from the Nile to the Ganges" (Godwin, 1994: 328). Optimistically, she said that Master M. of the Indian Brotherhood would help the Theosophists get to India (Meade, 1980: 180f.). By accident they had made contact in 1878 with the Indian Hindu reform movement, the Arya Samaj, and were invited to join its organization.[7] Blavatsky was delighted because she identified the Samaj leader, Swami Dayananda Sarasvati, as an adept of the Indian Brotherhood. Almost at the same time, Olcott established relations with Buddhist dignitaries in Ceylon (Godwin, 1994: 326). In December 1878 Blavatsky and Olcott (who were now both strongly drawn toward Buddhism) and two of the few remaining members of the society left for India, arriving, after a brief stay in England, in February 1879. It was here the Theosophical Society built its fame and influence.

Tibet came to play a significant part in Theosophical imagination and in the society's promotion of Oriental wisdom. "I have been in Tibet," Blavatsky told a journalist just after she came to America in 1873, and later she claimed to be a "Thibetan Buddhist" (Olcott, 1895: 21f.; Meade, 1980: 174). This had much to do with her constant need for self-promotion but also indicated the shift from conventional occult Egyptophilia to a preference for the East and, in particular, Buddhism and Tibet.

Blavatsky's Two Lives

Blavatsky lived an extraordinary life—or, more precisely, two extraordinary lives. One was the life she lived, the other was the life she made up, and Tibet was part of both. Born in Russia in 1831 into the aristocratic Russian-German von Hahn family, she was from childhood intensely curious about occult and psychic phenomena. At seventeen she married Nikifor Blavatsky, but after two months she left him and fled to Constantinople. Here her real life separates from the one she later made up. According to Meade's sound biography (1980),[8] Blavatsky spent the following nine years away from Russia, making her living in often unconventional ways and always pursuing her occult interests wherever she went. In Cairo she learned snake charming and studied with a Coptic magician. In Paris she performed as a medium. Back in Russia in 1858 she impressed people with her strange powers, and her séances with rappings and poltergeist effects were quite successful. Again in Cairo in 1871 she organized (with little success) a *société spirite* based on the ideas of the French occultist Allan Kardec. Returning to Paris in 1873, she moved in the higher spiritualist circles and met with the famous medium Daniel Dunglas Home. She heard that spiritualism was extremely popular in America and decided to travel to New York.

Blavatsky's own account of these years is quite different.[9] After leaving her husband, the story goes, extensive travels in the Middle East and Europe brought her to England in 1851 where she met Master Morya, whom she would later recognize as a mahatma of the Tibetan Brotherhood. Now followed years of touring in North, Central, and South America, and Asia where she made her first (unsuccessful) attempt to enter Tibet from Darjeeling in 1856. She went to Kashmir and tried to reach Tibet via Ladakh and managed to get sixteen miles beyond the border before she was forced to return to India. From there she went to Java in 1857, just before the Indian Mutiny. She then returned to Russia via Burma, America, and Western Europe. In 1867 she was off again, now to Italy where she joined Garibaldi's army and was wounded at the battle of Mentana. During her convalescence in Florence, Master Morya contacted her again and ordered her to Tibet for training in the occult sciences. She stayed for two years with Morya's mahatma colleague Koot Hoomi near the Tashilhunpo Monastery at Shigatse. In 1873 she was again in Paris where she was sought out by a messenger from Morya. He carried instructions for her about an extraordinary mission. She was to leave for New York, where she should work on the mahatmas' great plan, the founding of the Theosophical Society.

The Theosophical Society in India

Such were the major real and imaginary events leading up to Blavatsky's and Olcott's years in India.[10] They arrived at a time when India was witnessing a growing national and cultural self-awareness, and the Theosophists' egalitarian, anti-Christian attitudes and their defense of Oriental religions opened many doors to influential Indians (Jackson, 1981: 162). Within a year of settling in Bombay they established the Theosophical Society of India with a number of local branches and started the publication of the journal *The Theosophist*. During a visit to Ceylon in 1880 Blavatsky and Olcott converted to Buddhism ("took *pansil*") and founded the Buddhist Theosophical Society. Olcott built strong cooperative relationships with leading Buddhists, which, among other things, resulted in the establishment of important Buddhist educational institutions and religious and cultural-cum-political organizations like the Maha Bodhi Society and the Young Men's and Women's Buddhist Associations.[11]

In December 1882 the Theosophical headquarters moved from Bombay to Adyar, south of Madras. The organization expanded in India as well as abroad. After the Theosophists' arrival in India, Blavatsky's relationship with the Indian Brotherhood seems to have faded away. It was replaced by a close association with Master Morya, Koot Hoomi, and their mahatma colleagues of the Tibetan Brotherhood who were—after all—responsible for her present situation. They were the last of her supervising brotherhoods. In her pre-*Isis* days she had taken orders from the wise Egyptians of the Brotherhood of Luxor, who had been replaced by the Indian Brothers, who were eventually superseded by the Tibetan mahatmas. They would come down from their Himalayan quarters[12] and give a helping hand when needed, or would write letters with instructions and encouragement to Blavatsky and others found worthy of their attention.[13] The relationship with the Tibetan Brothers was extremely important to Blavatsky, and not only for the guidance they gave her. Access to the mahatmas provided her with a direct link to the divine wisdom that was the basis of the Theosophical movement and legitimized her claims to undisputed spiritual leadership of the Theosophical Society.

At the same time as Blavatsky developed her admiration for Tibetan Buddhism,[14] Western scholars took a different view. In the 1870s there appeared a distinction between northern and southern Buddhism. As the oldest branch, Southern Hinayāna Buddhism was seen as closest to the Buddha's original teachings, as authentic, pure, and rational, whereas northern (Tibetan) Mahāyāna Buddhism was perceived as degenerate, superstitious, and corrupt (Almond, 1988). Blavatsky loved her Tibetan mahatmas and thought them in possession of the greatest wisdom on Earth, and she extended her reverence to the Tibetan people. No doubt she agreed with Koot Hoomi when he said in a letter to Allan Octavian Hume, who in 1885 would be the first secretary of the Indian National Congress,

> For centuries we have had in Tibet a moral, pure hearted, simple people, unblest with civilization, hence—untainted by its vices. For ages Tibet has been the last corner of the globe not so entirely corrupted as to preclude the mingling together of the two atmospheres—the physical and the spiritual (Koot Hoomi, 1880, in Barker, 1962: 427).[15]

In 1880 Blavatsky had written to a French correspondent that "at Lhasa, in Tibet, another branch is being formed under the direction of initiated Lamas. Within a few years you will see how our Society will be honoured and sought after" (in Meade, 1980: 216). But in 1884 Blavatsky's Tibetan mahatma connection was exposed as a fraud.[16] The mahatmas proved as imaginary as the Theosophical branch in Lhasa. Painful and disgracing as this dishonor was, it did not, however, stop the expansion of the society in India and elsewhere. It was still sought after. New branches were established and membership rose by the thousands until it peaked in the late 1920s at forty-five thousand (Washington, 1993: 139). In spite of a growing sectarian infight after Blavatsky's death in 1891, the Theosophical movement continued the promotion of Oriental thought. It influenced outstanding scholars on Tibet and Buddhism such as Alexandra David-Néel, W. Y. Evans-Wentz, Lama Anagarika Govinda, Edward Conze, and D. T. Suzuki[17] and in a more popular context paved the way for what Donald Lopez has called "New Age Orientalism" (Lopez, 1994).

Considering that Blavatsky claimed to be a *Tibetan* Buddhist, it is striking that only two among the imagined masters were Tibetans and that there were no real Tibetans in the Theosophical movement.[18] It reflects, however, the fact that there were no Tibetans on the global religious and spiritual scene in which the Theosophists were acting. It is symptomatic that no Tibetans attended the World's Parliament of Religions in Chicago 1893 where several Buddhists from other parts of Asia (Japan, Siam, and Ceylon) were present (Barrows, 1893; Seager, 1993: 8).[19] Tibet and the Tibetans were, in the Theosophical teaching, purely imaginary objects, all made up from various sources such as scholarly works on Buddhism, travelogues, and publications on occult and esoteric knowledge (Coleman, 1895). However, if the Tibetans were absent at Blavatsky's time, she was in many ways responsible for their appearance a century later.

Theosophy and the Psychologization of Buddhism

Carl Gustav Jung was probably the first to recognize the importance of the Theosophical movement for introducing Oriental religion and philosophy to the general Western public (Jung, 1969: 529).[20] By the end of the nineteenth century, the Theosophical Society had become a global organization with about five hundred branches in more than forty countries (Olcott, 1895: 482; Olcott in Howell, 1925: 43). It had thousands of members, and its journals, books, and tracts reached a huge number of readers throughout the world. Recently, Richard Noll suggested that Blavatsky was "in many ways, arguably the most influential woman in Europe and America at the time." Referring to the "enormous Theosophical publishing machine," he characterized the Theosophists' work in these words:

> The great philosophies of the East were distilled and marketed en masse to Western civilization to a greater extent than had ever been possible at any previous time in history. (Noll, 1994: 63–68)[21]

Jung and Noll, however, both understate the Theosophists' importance. It was not only that they strengthened Western interest in Eastern religion and philosophy. Perhaps more important was their introduction of Western interpretations of Eastern traditions to the educated Asian elites. Much of this would become part of Eastern national and cultural identity formation and provide intellectual frameworks for political maneuver and cultural assertion.[22] In this sense, the Theosophical movement contributed to the beginning of Western discursive dominance over Oriental religion and philosophy and stimulated a creative cultural exchange between East and West.[23] One significant aspect of this exchange was the increasing psychologization of the East. Here I shall mainly be concerned with Buddhism and Tibet.

In 1975 Francesca Fremantle and Chögyam Trungpa brought out a new English edition of *The Tibetan Book of the Dead* (1975). In her comments on the translation Fremantle said that it

> is noticeable that several of the words which best express the teachings of Buddhism are part of the language of contemporary psychology, for the attitudes of certain schools of Western psychology often come closer to Buddhism than do those of Western philosophy or religion. (Fremantle and Trungpa, 1975: xvi)[24]

Nathan Katz made the related claim that

> it cannot be an accident that Tibetan missionaries in America...find more fruitful dialogue with Western psychologists (especially Gestalt and Jungian) than with Western theologians and religious leaders. (Katz, 1977:37)

Finally, and more daringly, Daniel Goleman suggested that "the greatest psychologist in recorded history was Gautama Buddha" (Goleman, 1976).

In the nineteenth century Western scholars discussed whether Buddhism was a religion or a philosophy (Almond, 1988). It is, a century later, tempting to suggest that Buddhism is more like a psychology. Half a century ago, Jung emphasized, in spite of his attraction to the Oriental spiritual traditions, that the "East has produced nothing equivalent to what we call psychology" (Jung, 1968: xxix)—a reservation not shared by Fremantle, Katz, and Goleman. Their statements suggest, however, that Buddhism has become much more psychologized than it was in Jung's days and that it has increasingly been brought into a discourse that emphasizes mental health rather than salvation. This is a most complex process, and here I can offer only a brief and simplified account. The process can be divided into three partly overlapping phases.

The first phase begins with Blavatsky. Her teaching is, with all its wide-ranging oddities, basically a *Zivilisationskritik,* which exalts an idealized East in order to castigate the West. As we might expect, it has significant parallels to dominant themes of German idealism and Romantic Orientalism. One is the sense of loss, the idea that the East is in possession of a truth or wisdom the West has lost and can regain only by learning from the East.[25] Another is the fundamental assumption that man's nature is spiritual (Halbfass, 1988; Inden, 1990; Schwab, 1984). These are themes that run through all three phases. Blavatsky favored *spiritual psychology* and detested all materialist positions (experimental psychology, for example[26]), which she made very clear in a note in *The Secret Doctrine:*

Let not the word "Psychology" cause the reader, by association of ideas, to carry his thoughts to modern "Psychologists," so-called, whose *Idealism* is another name for uncompromising Materialism, and whose pretended Monism is no better than a mask to conceal the void of final annihilation—even of consciousness. Here *spiritual* Psychology is meant. (Blavatsky 1921, 1: 680; see also 2: 165)

A century ago "psychology" had a wider meaning than it does today and included what we now commonly bracket as "parapsychology." It was widely thought of in these broad terms by people who, like Blavatsky, reacted strongly against scientific naturalism and who refused to be limited in their "exploration of human mental faculties to the formulae and concepts of physical science" (Oppenheim, 1985: 249).[27] As a "science of the soul" Theosophy brought Buddhism, Tibet, and psychology together in one spiritual discourse, which was shared—more or less—by much popular writing about Tibet in the decades before and after the turn of the century (Bishop, 1989; 1993). All this literature was not, of course, written by Theosophists, but with their "enormous publishing machine" they played a crucial role in establishing the spiritually psychological perspective on Tibet.

The second phase began in the mid-1930s with Carl Gustav Jung's writings on the psychology of Eastern religion.[28] As a psychologist with intellectual roots in Romantic *Naturphilosophie* and vitalism, Jung shared many ideas with the Theosophists (Ellenberger, 1970; Noll, 1994). In numerous commentaries, forewords, and introductions he paved the way in the West for a number of highly influential books about Oriental religion including the bestselling Evans-Wentz edition of *The Tibetan Book of the Dead* and Suzuki's popular *Introduction to Zen Buddhism*.[29] He was a frequent and inspiring participant in the famous *Eranos Conferences* at Ascona from 1933 to 1951 where he met with scholars of religion and Oriental culture.[30] Time and again he emphasized that the Oriental religions provide profound insights into the workings of the psyche. Jung's interest in the East was passed on to other psychologists, mainly of analytic and gestalt observation, who reacted to the scientistic currents and the positivist worship of "facts" in contemporary psychology.[31] The professional psychological involvement had two important consequences. One was that ideas of Eastern religion and psychology became more clearly defined in terms of current Western psychological paradigms.[32] The other was that various Eastern religious practices—and in particular meditation—would be seen as techniques for the attainment of mental health or, in other words, as psychotherapy. We find in this second phase a remarkable continuity with the Theosophical (and Romantic Orientalist) ideas of the West as a sick civilization, which must look to the East for cure. Jung often warned against the dangers of being too dependent on culturally alien resources (Jung, 1969a), but the idea that the East could offer potent spiritual healing remedies to the West became a salient feature of the countercultural movement of the 1960s.

The psychologization of the East had developed in its first and second phase without any participation of Tibetan Buddhists, whereas Hindus and Buddhists from other parts of Asia had taken part from the beginning. The third phase started with the Tibetan diaspora of 1959 and the arrival of Tibetan teachers or missionaries in the West. With the diaspora, Tibet ceased to be a remote and inaccessible place. One hundred thousand Tibetans and the government-in-exile established themselves in India, and Tibet became for political reasons a global presence, and so did Tibetan Buddhism. Before, Tibetan Buddhism had played a secondary role in Western Buddhist studies, but the exile made it possible for Western scholars to establish working relationships with refugee Tibetan scholars in India. This did much to improve the quality and prestige of Tibetan studies. The opening of scholarly and other contacts to the Tibetan community coincided with the explosive Western interest in Oriental spirituality (Lopez, 1995b), and around 1970 a number of Tibetans moved to America to explain what Tibetan Buddhism was about.

The first of these were Tarthang Tulku and Chögyam Trungpa.[33] Tarthang Tulku arrived in the United States in 1969. In Berkeley he set up the Tibetan Nyingma Meditation Center. Many of those who attended his meditation courses had a background in humanistic psychology or were mental health professionals. He saw the need for special courses for such people and established the Nyingma Institute with the aim of transmitting the psychological, philosophical, and experiential insights of the Nyingma lineage. The Nyingma Institute offered a human-development training program designed for therapists and psychologists. Chögyam Trungpa offers a parallel example. He appeared in the United States in 1970 and founded various institutions that gave courses in meditation but that also ran experimental therapeutic communities and offered B.A. and M.A. degree programs in psychology.

Conclusion

One of Chögyam Trungpa's books is titled *Cutting through Spiritual Materialism* (1987). On the cover he is presented as a "meditation master." He believed that most of the people who came to study with him did so because of his reputation as "a meditation teacher from exotic Tibet" (Trungpa, 1987: 53). Here Chögyam Trungpa looks very much like one of Blavatsky's mythical Tibetan masters guarding true spirituality against the world's "uncompromising materialism." The similarity is probably unintended, but it still tells us that myths die hard.

In fact, Tarthang Tulku and Chögyam Trungpa were very un-Blavatskian in their ideas of "true knowledge." Where Blavatsky wanted full control over knowledge and its transmission, they had a much more open-ended and historical approach. Trungpa stated it in this way, warning against regarding knowledge as "ancient wisdom":

> As far as the lineage of teachers is concerned, knowledge is not handed down like an antique. Rather, one teacher experiences the truth of the teachings, and he hands it down as inspiration to his student. That inspiration awakens the student, as his teacher was awakened before him. Then the student hands down the teachings to another student and so the process goes. The teachings are always up to date. They are not "ancient wisdom," an old legend. The teachings are not passed along as information, handed down as a grandfather tells traditional folk tales to his grandchildren. It does not work that way. It is real experience. Therefore, *dharma* is applicable to every age, to every person; it has a living quality. (Trungpa, 1987: 17)

The success experienced by Tarthang Tulku, Chögyam Trungpa, and other Tibetan masters in the West owes much to Blavatsky, Jung, and a century of Western spiritual concerns. But it is no less due to their own pragmatic, and subtle, understanding of knowledge transmission.

Misunderstood and humiliated, as if they had been acting in the wrong play, Blavatsky's imaginary, spiritual mahatmas withdrew from the scene in 1884. A century later, with their successful comeback, it seems as if they had only been waiting in the wings for a more sympathetic audience. This might be true at the level of Western imagination where there is a clear continuity in the ideas of by Blavatsky, Jung, or Californian psychotherapists. But we should not focus our attention on continuities, similarities, or parallels because that will make us blind to important differences. After all, the imaginary mahatmas have withdrawn to the imaginary Tibet and have been replaced by real Tibetans in a real world.

NOTES

1 I am grateful to Toni Huber, George Ulrich, Jørn Borup, and Jesper Sørensen for their helpful comments on a draft of this article.

2 The founders' ideas about Theosophy were not very clear at the beginning, and they even had problems finding a name for the society. Olcott recalls that names like the Egyptological, Hermetic, and Rosicrucian were suggested without being accepted. "At last," Olcott reports, "in turning over the leaves of the Dictionary, one of us came across the word 'Theosophy,' whereupon, after discussion, we unanimously agreed that was the best of all; since it both expressed the esoteric truth we wished to reach and covered the ground of...occult scientific research" (Olcott, 1895: 132). The word *theosophy* was probably coined by the neo-Platonist Ammonius Saccas (c. 160–242) and means "Divine wisdom" (Carlson, 1993: 28).

3 This was not Olcott's merit alone. He and Blavatsky had a huge international network of people who shared their occult interests. Many of these joined the society and set up local branches in various countries. For the basis of what we might call the "Theosophical International," see Godwin, 1994, and Johnson, 1994.

4 Campbell (1980) gives a brief, but useful background to Theosophy and related movements. For an excellent contextual history of spiritualism and Theosophy, see Oppenheim, 1985.

5 Blavatsky explained Theosophy in her two major books, *Isis Unveiled* (1923) and *The Secret Doctrine* (1921), and in *The Theosophical Glossary* (1892). She continually wrote articles for the two Theosophical journals, *The Theosophist* and *Lucifer*. For a clear account of Blavatsky's complex—and often not very clearly expressed—ideas, see Campbell, 1980: 40–48. Most of her work can be found in Zirkoff (comp.), 1950–91.

6 This idea was common at the time. One of the early American Buddhists, William Sturgis Bigelow (1850–1926), for example, was "inclined to think

that Thibet is the greatest centre of knowledge...and there, if anywhere, are preserved the facts which the West has lost with the burning of the Alexandrian library and the extinction of the Rosicrucians" (in Tweed, 1992: 75). See also Camp, 1954.

7 This never actually happened. The relationship with the Arya Samaj broke down. See Olcott, 1895: 394–407, for the Theosophical account of this, and Jordens, 1978: 299ff., for the Arya Samaj point of view.

8 Campbell (1980) is also good, though more useful on Blavatsky's ideas than on the incidents of her life.

9 It forms the basis of her official Theosophical biography. Recent works that accept Blavatsky's own account are Barborka's comprehensive treatment of her relationship to Tibet (1974), Cranston (1993), and Fuller (1988). "Classical" biographies of this genre are Neff, 1937 and Sinnett, 1886.

10 Blavatsky stayed in India until 1885 when she moved to England, where she died in 1891. Olcott remained in India until his death in 1907.

11 See Bechert, 1966: 45ff.; Gombrich and Obeyesekere, 1988: 205f.

12 On the locality of this, see Blavatsky 1921, III: 405.

13 For the Mahatma letters, see Barborka, 1973 and Barker, 1962.

14 On Blavatsky's Buddhism, see Spierenburg, 1991.

15 When Giuseppe Tucci traveled in Tibet in 1948, he noticed that "in Tibet man had not yet disintegrated; he still sank his roots fully into that collective subconscious which knows no difference between past and present" (Tucci, 1956: 130; in Lopez, 1995b). It is basically what Koot Hoomi said in 1880, though here phrased in Jungian terminology.

16 The London-based Society for Psychical Research investigated the matter and declared the whole thing to be a fraud. Richard Hodgeson, who was responsible for the investigation, was very precise when he said about Blavatsky: "For our own part, we regard her neither as a mouthpiece of hidden seers, nor as a mere vulgar adventuress; we think that she has achieved a title to permanent remembrance as one of the most accomplished, ingenious, and interesting impostors in history" (in Carlson, 1993: 42).

17 For David-Néel, see Caracostea (1991); for Anagarika Govinda, see Winkler (1990); for Evans-Wentz, see Winkler (1992); for Conze, see Conze (1979) and Eliade (1973); and for Suzuki, see Sharf (1995).

18 The two Tibetans were the Chohan Lama of Shigatse and Ten-dub Ughien. The rest, Morya, Koot Hoomi, Djual Kul, etc., were Indians. Recently there has been some controversy over the "identity" of the mahatmas. Paul Johnson has suggested that Blavatsky modeled the mahatmas on real persons and offers various clues to who they might be; see Johnson (1994) and (1995), and Algeo (1995.) It is, however, irrelevant to my purpose to know the real person behind a mahatma who does not exist when that real person is not a mahatma.

19 It is a little confusing that the book on the World's Parliament of Religions presents a full-page photograph of "A Lama, Thibetan Priest" (Barrows, 1893, 1: 119)—as if he were present at the occasion, which he was not.

20 See Godwin, 1994, and Conze, 1959: 219.

21 "[T]he ubiquitous Theosophical publications...summarized in plain language (but with a Theosophical slant) the ideas of Hinduism, Jainism, Islam, Buddhism, Western European philosophy, astrology, Neoplatonism, Egyptian religion, vegetarianism, the New Testament gospels and apocrypha, astral projection, clairvoyance and telepathy, polytheistic Greco-Roman religions, the Greek magical papyri (including the 'Mithraic Liturgy'), Gnosticism, alchemy, Hermeticism, and the various Hellenistic mystery cults—just to name a few of the many topics covered in these productions" (Noll, 1994: 67). See also Carlson, 1993: 34.

22 See notes 27 and 31.

23 The Theosophists provide a strong case against Edward Said's simplistic argument against Orientalism as a Western repressive mode of representation (Said, 1978). The relationship between the East and the West was (and is) much more complex and politically ambiguous than Said suggests. Scholars have paid too little attention to the ways Orientals have appropriated the Orientalist discourse. Cf. Ahmad, 1992 and Lopez, 1995a.

24 Cf. "Concepts such as conditioning, neurotic patterns of thought, and unconscious influences, seem more appropriate in this book than conventional religious terms. In the commentary, words such as neurosis and paranoia are used to describe not pathological conditions but the natural results of this fundamental state of mind" (Fremantle and Trungpa, 1975: xvi).

25 This idea was taken up by Eastern elites in the late nineteenth century and became a dominant theme in the pan-Asian movement in the early twentieth century. See Hay (1970) and note 24 above.

26 Experimental psychology as established by Wilhelm Wundt comes out of physiology and models the psyche on the body (Danziger [1991], Hacking [1994]).

27 Many Theosophists had a strong interest in psychology in this wide sense. The leading Theosophical journal, *The Theosophist,* regularly carried articles on various aspects of psychology and psychoanalysis. See Mehta, 1968.

28 Zaehner thought that Jung "has done more to interpret Eastern religion to the West than any other man," (in Meckel and Moore, 1992). Perhaps he was right. I think, however, Blavatsky is a serious rival, though she is not a man.

29 Jung's work on Oriental religion and philosophy has been published in his *Collected Works,* vol. 11, 2d. ed. 1969. Princeton: Princeton University Press. Gómez provides a generous *and* critical reading of Jung's writings on the East. He emphasizes the symbiotic relationship between the West and the East. Western psychological interpretations of the East would become part of

Easterners' own interpretations of their religious or philosophical traditions. In a fascinating symbiosis, Jung's psychology rode the wave of Western fascination with the East even as the East rode on the wave of Western interest in psychology, especially on the wave of psychology as the one substitute for religion that believed itself to be scientifically sanctioned (Gómez, 1995: 242f., n. 46). The Jung-Suzuki-Fromm relationship is a case in point. "Fromm's knowledge of Zen derives almost exclusively from the work of D. T. Suzuki who was in turn influenced in his exposition by Jung" (Jones, 1979).

30 Participants included D. T. Suzuki, Heinrich Zimmer, Mircea Eliade, Giuseppe Tucci, Caroline Rhys Davids, Richard Zaehner, and Joseph Campbell—besides the psychologists Gustav Richard Heyer, Erich Neumann, and Sigrid Strauss-Kloebe. Information gleaned from the pages of the *Eranos Yearbook*, 1933ff.

31 For background, see Leichtman, 1979 and Noll, 1994.

32 Cf. Fromm, 1987. Erich Fromm's highly influential *Psychoanalysis and Zen Buddhism* (1987) was the result of a workshop with Suzuki on Zen Buddhism and psychoanalysis at the Department of Psychoanalysis of the Medical School, Autonomous National University of Mexico, in the late 1950s. The workshop was attended by about fifty psychologists and psychiatrists from both Mexico and the USA (Fromm, 1987: ix).

33 At the time there were only a few older Tibetan teachers in the USA, including Deshung Rinpoche and Geshe Wangyal, a Kalmuk Mongolian (Fields, 1992: 289f.). For Tarthang Tulku and Chögyam Trungpa, see Fields, 1992, chap. 14 and 16.

THE ROLE OF TIBET
IN THE NEW AGE MOVEMENT[1]

Frank J. Korom

"I can say that there is one cultural disease in this country,
and that is what I call hypertrophical eclecticism.*"*
(Bharati, 1975: 129)

Prologue

IN THE FALL OF 1995, I walked into my Anthropology of Religion
course on the first day of class and spotted a cheerful female student wearing a peculiar necklace consisting of a delicate gold chain
attached to a small Tibetan *dorje* (thunderbolt). In this age of *phurpa* letter openers (Klieger, 1997), mail-order mysticism (*Pacific Spirit,* 1995),
and Shangri-la pinball machines (Oppitz, 1974), it does not seem unusual
that a young American would be wearing a sacred object as secular orna-
mentation in light of the fact that Tibetan ritual implements have per-
meated the mass media during recent years; they have even made their
way into popular Hollywood films such as *The Shadow,* in which a magical *phurpa* (ritual dagger) in the possession of a villainous character
occasionally comes alive to terrorize the hero of this celluloid adaptation
of the well-known comic strip. What is unique, however, is this student's
explanation for why she wears the dorje. When asked, she stated:

> This thing is an ancient Buddhist object of power that draws in
> cosmic healing forces. When I wear it, it keeps me healthy and
> happy. It grounds me in the center and makes me feel protected
> from all the negative karma in the universe.

So my assumption was wrong! She did not wear the object simply as a fashion statement; rather, she imbued it with a personal and mystical meaning, much in the same way as a Christian wearing a cross might.

Nevertheless, my student's comment has to be taken in the context of the social circles in which she moves. She is not a Buddhist; nor is she an initiate of Tantra. Instead, she is, as she put it, "a seeker looking for the common good in all religions." Her perspective is central to the syncretic nature of the global New Age movement so prevalent today, and echoes the sentiments of the many Western pilgrims who continually travel to Dharamsala, the hub of Tibetan culture in exile, in the hopes of absorbing fragments of Buddhist wisdom to add to their eclectic store of personal knowledge about New Age spirituality. Sitting in the pubs and restaurants of this picturesque Himalayan hamlet, the ethnographer often overhears Westerners engaged in metaphysical conversations liberally drawing not only on Tibetan philosophy but also on G. I. Gurdjieff, Paramahansa Yogananda, Rajneesh, Yogi Bhajan, Satya Sai Baba, and a host of other teachers who have successfully attracted the attention of Western audiences.

The idiosyncratic combination of various—and sometimes contradictory—strands of thought culled from mystics and sages throughout the world is one of the trademarks of the New Age, and is a point to which I shall return. But the main aim of this paper is to explore some of the ways in which Tibet and portions of its religious culture have been appropriated over time by proponents of the New Age for their own purposes. Before proceeding with this task, it will be useful to locate and define the term "New Age."

Precursors to the New Age

While it is true that the New Age movement in all of its splendor and glory crystallized in the 1970s after the heyday of psychedelic drugs (cf. Watts, 1962; Carey, 1968; Webb, 1988: 63–80) and "flower power" in the United States (Prebish, 1979: 28–40), its roots are to be found in Europe during the previous century. As John Lash has stated, "The New Age as it appears today has its immediate roots in the utopian socialist movements of the nineteenth century" (1990: 52). Indeed, the social utopians of Ham Common in England used the term as a name for their homegrown journal as early as 1843. This highly localized usage seems to be the first deliberate coinage of "New Age" to label a form of alternative social and spiritual consciousness not bounded by conventional religion (Lash, 1990: 54). The use of the term in the Ham Common context was, however, vague and open to speculation. But by the turn of the twentieth century, a British journalist named A. R. Orage (1873–1934) founded a liberal periodical titled *The New Age* to deal with the cultural, political, and literary issues of the day. In addition to his many social interests, Orage was also involved with spiritualism and the occult. Later, in 1914, he became a disciple of the aforementioned Gurdjieff, whose own path was an amalgam of teachings drawn from what he termed his "meetings with remarkable men." Orage's commitment to pursuing an alternative, esoteric spiritual path was characterized by the same eclecticism that marks his mentor and later New Age seekers; that is, the quest was not bound by the teachings of any given master, lineage, or even religion (cf. Webb, 1988).

Orage's impact on the later emergence of the movement was not great, but he must be credited for his solid introduction of the term "New Age," which allowed others following him to utilize and play with the concept. Although Tibet did not play a major role in his thought, the year he died, 1934, was the year that the British New Age proponent Alice A. Bailey (1880–1949) began to write down messages she was receiving telepathically from a spirit known simply as "the Tibetan." The Tibetan's first communiqué revealed to Bailey a millenarian vision of the coming of a new age during the cosmic transition from Pisces to Aquarius, at which time the problems of mankind would be collaboratively solved by a group of highly evolved spirits and their earthly agents (Lash, 1990: 56). For the next fifteen years she continued to receive communications from the Tibetan, whose identity was eventually revealed to her as Djwhal Khul, or D. K. for short. Bailey's transcription of D. K.'s messages was eventually published in 1957 as *The Externalisation of the Hierarchy*. For Bailey and for others, as we shall see, Tibet was the place where such spiritual beings resided in substance if not in form.

Now, the progression of New Age thinking from Orage to Bailey was advanced in 1975 by Dane Rudhyar, whose book titled *Occult Preparations for a New Age* consciously elaborated on the ideas propagated by his predecessors but shifted focus from local to global transformation. Rudhyar also advocated a millenarian vision of a new and improved civilization emerging on earth through the guidance of what he terms "avatars," or spiritually developed incarnate beings, during the age of Aquarius. These avatars are collectively known as the "Trans-Himalayan Occult Brotherhood," which Robert Ellwood describes as a group of "human beings developed tremendously beyond the norm and...benign administrators of the invisible government of the world" (1979: 51). This brotherhood is none other than a grouping of the Himalayan "masters" propagated by Madame Helena Petrovna Blavatsky (1831–91), the controversial founder of the Theosophical Society, and it is to her that we ultimately must turn to locate the immediate roots of the contemporary New Age movement.

Madame Blavatsky drew her mystical vision from a number of sources, including Hindu and Buddhist. Yet although she freely borrowed (and some say, plagiarized) from traditions all over the world, her strongest leanings were toward the religions of India, since she firmly believed that the "masters"—that is, her religious teachers—resided in the Himalayas that are north of India. Blavatsky's fascination with India and Tibet predates the formation of the Theosophical Society in 1875. According to Blavatsky's own reckoning, she first became transfixed with Eastern spiritualism in 1851, when her father took her to London to recover from her first failed marriage. While there, she spied a "princely, turbaned man" in a group of Indian and Nepali delegates visiting the British capital (Ellwood, 1979: 108). The man with the turban, whom she would in later letters refer to as "the Sahib," became her master, and is said to have instructed her to make a pilgrimage to South Asia.

According to her own account, which remains unverified, Blavatsky traveled to India and Tibet sometime between 1851 and 1871. Shortly after this long and mysterious period *in absentia,* she resurfaced in America in 1873, where she met Colonel Henry Steel Olcott (1832–1907), whose *Old Diary Leaves* is one of our major sources on

Madame Blavatsky (cf. Prothero, 1996). Together, they formed the Theosophical Society in 1875 as an institution for combining, among other things, Mayan lore, ancient Egyptian mysticism, Tibetan philosophy, and myths about Atlantis into one seemingly coherent whole. Although the image of Tibet and vague references to Tibetan spiritual culture occasionally appear in Blavatsky's voluminous writings, it could be argued that Tibetan thought played a lesser role in her metaphysical system than the many other teachings to which she had better access. For instance, Blavatsky's magnum opus *Isis Unveiled*, first published in 1877, contains very little on Tibet, except for a few possibly plagiarized lines from the travel accounts of Abbé Huc (Ellwood, 1979: 122; Huc, 1928). Nonetheless, Blavatsky's Theosophical lodge in New York was fondly referred to by her followers as "the Lamasery" (Olcott, 1895: 331–32; Ellwood, 1979: 117), a clear attempt to link Theosophy with Tibetan mysticism.

These sorts of intentional "borrowings" may seem insignificant on one level, but they also suggest that the idea of Tibet was, in fact, firmly planted in the imaginations of these early New Age pioneers. Tibet became, for various reasons to be discussed in my conclusion, a trope for New Age practitioners during this seminal phase of development. Characteristic of the transparent usage of Tibet as a convenient image for fragmentary alternative thinking by New Age pioneers was the association of things Tibetan with non-Tibetan things. Perhaps the most understudied and, by the way, bizarre text to exemplify this point is Pilangi Dasa's (alias Herman Vetterling [1849–1931]) *Swedenborg the Buddhist, or The Higher Swedenborgianism Its Secrets and Thibetan Origin,* published by the Buddhistic Swedenborgian Brotherhood in Los Angeles in 1887.

In his foreword, Dasa states that Emanuel Swedenborg (1688–1772), the Swedish philosopher-cum-mystic "is one moment a Christian, another, a Materialist, and a third, a Buddhist. Now and then a mixture of these. In reality, that is, at heart, he is a Buddhist" (Dasa, 1887: 7). He further encourages us to "read, if you have time, patience, and courage, and in the light of Buddhism, esoteric and exoteric, the theological writings of Swedenborg, and you will learn a few facts worth knowing, namely...that hidden under Judaic-Christian names, phrases, and symbols, and scattered throughout dreary, dogmatic, and soporific octavos, are pure precious, blessed truths of Buddhism" (Dasa, 1887: 9–10). The strange thing about this tract is that there are virtually no references to Tibet until the end of the 317-page monograph. Again, as did Blavatsky, the author relies on Huc's accounts of Tibetan Buddhism to develop an alien aura around the Swedish mystic.

Vetterling was one of the first Americans officially to embrace Buddhism. He converted in 1884 and took the name Pilangi Dasa. Thereafter, he somewhat dogmatically propagated Buddhism, without specific reference to Tibet, in the journal he founded in 1888 titled *The Buddhist Ray*. But *Swedenborg the Buddhist* was his most outrageous treatise, creating in a fictional and dreamlike fashion an astrally projected dialogue between Swedenborg, a Brahmin, a Buddhist monk, a Parsee, an Aztec Indian, an Icelander, an anonymous woman, and himself. Due to his eclectic combination of Swedenborgianism, homeopathy, Theosophy, Spiritualism, and whatever else suited his fancy, many scholars during his lifetime questioned his authenticity as a "real" Buddhist. This is ironic, given the fact that Dasa wrote in 1889 of "the hysteric women, weak-minded men, and plagiarists that have formed the 'aryan'-'buddhist'-astrologic cliques of Boston" (Tweed, 1992: 41). Dasa remained adamant about his brand of esoteric and eclectic Buddhism for the duration of his career, insisting that he was part of a spiritual lineage that directly connected him with the teachings of so-called Lamaism. As he wrote in the first issue of *The Buddhist Ray* in 1888, "It will set forth the teachings imparted by the Mongolian Buddhists to Emanuel Swedenborg" (as quoted in Tweed, 1992: 61).

These ideas may seem naive, quaint, and even comical to us now, but Dasa, Blavatsky, and her aforementioned successor Bailey were experimenting with and writing about spirituality during a period when there was not much organized non-Western religion in the United States (Carter, 1971: 202), making it extremely difficult for them to practice or preach the orthodox tenets of any specific Eastern religious tradition. Nonetheless, their attempts to incorporate Buddhism into their idiosyncratic systems of thought suggest a heartfelt desire to utilize the teachings of the Buddha in developing alternative spiritual paths for the West.

All of the early instances recounted above suggest a keen interest in the image of Tibet—imagined or real—among people who can be said to be the forerunners of the New Age movement in America. Yet even though their enthusiasm was great, their actual knowledge about Tibet and its spiritual culture was severely limited. While it is true that academic knowledge of Buddhist philosophy grew after the 1844 publication of Eugène Burnouf's (1801–52) first scholarly introduction to Buddhism in a European language (Burnouf, 1844), much less was known about Tibetan Buddhism during the lifetimes of Blavatsky and her cohorts. Most of what was known about Tibet was culled from travelers' accounts, which literary figures then utilized to further enhance the mysterious and magical nature of that isolated land. It is significant to keep in mind, however, that Tibet was beginning to emerge in the late nineteenth century as a romantic landscape (Bishop, 1989: 97–135) to fuel Western fantasies of a utopian stronghold in the midst of a politicized, colonial vision of Central Asia (Richards, 1992). Moreover, Tibet concurrently became a complex symbol for Eastern mysticism in general and Buddhism as a generic, homogeneous entity in particular.

It is precisely through Buddhism that Tibet made its entry into the American context after the turn of the twentieth century. It is Buddhism also that attracted many Americans into alternative religious practice at this critical juncture, for it provided a distinctive foreign "intellectual landscape" (Tweed, 1992: xxii, 78–110) for the development of a socioreligious critique of American society based on dissent, which later reemerged as a major reason for a return to the East by contemporary New Agers. In fact, Buddhism was, according to Thomas Tweed (1992: 27), the most popular Eastern religion by 1894. We therefore must consider the development of Buddhism in America as an important aspect of the emergence of the modern New Age movement.

Buddhism in America

The precursors to contemporary New Age thought just discussed lived during a critical time in American social history termed the Gilded Age by historians. Paul Carter (1971: 220) has convincingly argued that this period (1865–95) set the stage for a spiritual crisis in the American psyche due to the skepticism, rationalism, and scientism brought about by a clash of faith and science. It was also a time when Protestant missionaries from America branched out into Asia and encountered Buddhism in reality. As a result of their encounters, the missionaries developed an ambiguous, dual sense of compassion and condescension toward Eastern religions, which was similar to attitudes pertaining to Native Americans around the same time (Carter, 1971: 202).

The combined perception of the Other (cf. de Certeau, 1986; Fabian, 1983) as simultaneously inferior and fascinating needed to be related and compared to something "closer to home" in order to make the alien familiar. It is thus not surprising that Buddhism was aligned with Catholicism by many Protestant theologians and intellectuals. More specifically, Tibetan Buddhism was often noted for its parallels with Roman Catholicism. The infallibility of the Pope and the Dalai Lama, tonsured and celibate monks, and the miraculous births of Christ and the Buddha combined with ritualistic dimensions of worship such as the use of rosaries, the veneration of images and relics, the sounding of bells, the burning of incense and sprinkling of holy water in both religions to provide a powerful polemic for Protestants, allowing them to make the case that "the Catholic Church [was] an occidental copy of Eastern Lamaism" (Carter, 1971: 207). The populist Protestant opinion, by the way, was also reinforced by academic Buddhologists writing at approximately the same time (cf. Lopez, 1996: 8ff).

Catholics, of course, were quick to respond by denouncing Buddhism in the same way that Protestants often denounced Catholicism. In 1888 Merwin-Marie Snell wrote, with partial reference to Buddhism, in *The Catholic World:* "It must be premised that all of these systems [the Eastern religions] embody portions of the primitive traditions of the race, and are so far true and similar to the Catholic religion; but…they have two great evils, apart from the crowning one of their very existence outside the church's pale: first, the divine traditions are only partially retained, and are often so distorted and corrupted as to be nearly unrecognizable; and, second, their special claims have little or no logical foundation, and utterly vanish under a rigid application of the laws of evidence" (Snell, 1888: 451).

Such pejorative comparisons for the negation of specific religions later came to serve a completely different function: namely, to allow spiritual seekers the opportunity to legitimize their practice of one or more faiths at the same time. In other words, rather than using comparison to point out difference, comparison came to be used as a tool for demonstrating the commonality of religions. This mystical oneness of all religions later served New Age communities well, as it had its precursors such as the Theosophical Society. In addition to Theosophy's unprecedented influence in the shaping of American attitudes toward the syncretistic nature of mysticism (Tweed, 1992: 30), the event that most shaped the climate of religious tolerance and comparativism in the Gilded Age was the 1893 World's Parliament of Religions (cf. Seager, 1995) in Chicago. Writing about the event a decade later, Shailer Mathews noted that "Whatever else the Parliament may have accomplished, it developed respect for non-Christian religion on the part of intelligent religious persons" (Carter, 1971: 215).

The gathering brought together spokesmen representing many Asian faiths, including a number of Buddhist theologians from both the Mahāyāna (Japan) and Theravāda (Sri Lanka) traditions. Four years after the Parliament, the American chapter of the Maha Bodhi Society was founded for the propagation of Buddhism. These landmark events, along with the continued publication of Dasa's *The Buddhist Ray* and the philosopher of science Paul Carus' (1852–1919) two periodicals, *The Open Court* and *The Monist,* provided an important stimulus for the growth of Buddhism in the United States. In 1904 Carus, a German immigrant, went so far as to state in *The Open Court* that "*Ex oriente lux* is an old famous phrase which states the truth that our civilization and religion came from the East" (Jackson, 1968: 79).

Extreme polemics in favor of Buddhism had the overall effect of temporarily offering Americans the possibility of "turning east" (Cox, 1977) to search for new religious insights to explain the decline of spirituality in Judeo-Christian traditions after the onslaught of science. This initial fervor for the Orient in general and Buddhism in particular grew for approximately a decade after the Parliament (Jackson, 1968: 75; Tweed, 1992: 26) but waned around 1907. One scholar estimates there were two to three thousand Euro-Americans who considered themselves primarily or secondarily Buddhists and tens of thousands more who were sympathizers (Tweed, 1992: 46) during this period, but Tibet and its varieties of Buddhism, were still only a far-off set of images that would not come to real fruition in America until much later.

At the same time that some Americans were embracing Buddhism, many simply grafted certain Buddhist principles to other beliefs and practices, a trend which, as I have already noted, characterizes New Age thinking in general. As Tweed states, "Many Caucasian Buddhist followers combined traditional Buddhist doctrines with beliefs derived from Western sources" (1992: 40). Even before the Parliament, this trend was already becoming quite established. In an editorial titled "The Intermingling of Religions," published in the popular American magazine *Atlantic Monthly* in 1871, Lydia Maria Child discussed what she termed the Eclectic Church, which would be a harmonious amalgam of the world's great religious traditions. As she prophesied, "Old traditions are everywhere relaxing their hold upon the minds of men. From all parts of the world come increasing manifestations of a tendency toward eclecticism. Men find there are gems hidden among all sorts of rubbish. These will be selected and combined in that Church of the Future now in the process of formation" (Child, 1871: 395). This statement foreshadows the blend of religious ideas that would later be propagated by a host of New Age thinkers from the 1960s onward.

The Decline of Buddhism and the Rise of Eclecticism

According to Tweed's (1992: 157–62) recent study on the American encounter with Buddhism, a decrease in active participation in Buddhist practice occurred around 1912 or 1913 due to the demise of Victorian culture's dominance in American life. This is not to say that Buddhism simply disappeared in the American context, and with it, Tibet, for the influential journal *The Eastern Buddhist* began publication in 1921, and the romance with Shangri-la continued in the 1930s with the popularity of James Hilton's novel *Lost Horizon* and its subsequent film adaptation in 1937. During the twenties and the thirties, a gradual institutionalization of various non-Tibetan schools of Buddhism began to occur in the United States. However, the dialogue about Buddhism within Protestant intellectual circles became less important as religious pluralism and religious experimentation gained increasing prominence between 1920 and 1960, when bohemian lifestyles gave way to hippiedom (Fields, 1992: 195–272). So while Buddhism slowly began to acculturate to American life, new forms of alternative religious practices gained ascendency.

The initial decline of interest in Buddhism and other Eastern religions a decade or so after the Parliament led to a continued attempt on the part of alternative spiritualists to combine ideas from numerous paths into what Ellwood has termed "emergent" religion (1979: 5). In addition to being individualistic and eclectic, emergent religion is characterized by certain "key symbols" (Ortner, 1973) culled from Eastern religions such as meditation and monism, as well as an orientation toward distant and exotic cultures (Ellwood, 1979: 21). G. W. F. Hegel (1770–1831), who was himself fascinated by Eastern cultures (cf. Halbfass, 1988: 84–99), had already noted the strong attraction that such "otherness" had on the Western mind when he stated in 1809 that "Inherent in the strange and remote is a powerful interest,…the attractiveness of which is in inverse proportion to its familiarity" (as quoted in Ellwood, 1979: 20).

Alternative thinkers, themselves marginalized and alienated from mainstream religious thought, sought out the remote as a way of connecting with something completely different and beyond the normative worldview of their own culture (Ellwood, 1979: 11). This "difference" applied not only to "imagined" places like Tibet but also to the individuals who identified with it. People like Blavatsky, Olcott, and Bailey certainly perceived themselves as different, exploiting their liminal status to exoticize their eclectic brand of teachings. Alternative seekers looked for difference in their attempts to blend numerous religious paths.

As Asia gradually became more known to the West during the era of the World Wars, and as popular academics such as Carl Gustav Jung (Jung, 1978; cf. also Bishop, 1984; Gómez, 1995) and Mircea Eliade (e.g., Eliade, 1969; cf. also Korom, 1992) furthered the New Age cause by familiarizing the West with the East and propagating the underlying unity of mystical experience in their comparative studies of archetypes, a new era of "imagining" Eastern thought ensued, both on the popular and academic levels. By 1965, when the U.S. Immigration Act abolished the national origins quota system (Tweed, 1992: 158), many varieties of Buddhism were firmly established in America (cf. Prebish, 1979), including, of course, the Tibetan varieties (cf. Greenfield, 1975: 212–33; Prebish, 1979: 121–55). With the arrival of Geshe Wangyal in 1955 (Cutler, 1995: xxvi), Tarthang Tulku in 1968 (Fields, 1992: 304–8, 312–16), Chögyam Trungpa in 1970 (Fields, 1992: 308–12, 316–18) and Lobsang Lhalungpa in 1971 (*Parabola*, 1978: 44), to name just a few well-known teachers, Tibetan Buddhism had permanently arrived in North America, where by the end of the 1980s there were 184 Tibetan centers for learning and meditation (Morreale, 1988: 222–87).

This notwithstanding, one needs to ask to what degree people were seriously practicing Buddhism. Certainly there were those who took their practice to heart. One psychological study suggests that some Americans in the modern period have turned to Asian meditation practices for the most part to enhance religious experience through rigorous practice (Gussner and Berkowitz, 1988) and personalistic ritual (Stone, 1978). But there were also those during the 1960s and 1970s who were floating in what Robert Greenfield (1975) has termed "the spiritual supermarket," shopping for all sorts of alternative religious experiences. Many of the people I interviewed in 1987 as part of a project on conversion to Eastern religions in America during the sixties (cf. Korom, 1987) narrated their diverse experiments with everything ranging from meditation and chanting to ritualistic sex and drug use. Many of them spent a long period—ten years or more—simply picking and choosing those ideas and practices that seemed appropriate to their lifestyle.

The period in question was, of course, a period of social ferment, a time of establishing a counterculture (cf. Roszak, 1969) in opposition to mainstream American thought and practice. Eastern mysticism, combined with Native American spirituality and a whole host of other practices coming together under the general rubric of the New Age, provided an alternative and radical context to suit the emerging needs of New Age thinkers and practitioners. Yet as Antonio Gramsci (1957) and Herbert Marcuse (1964) both predicted, subversive ideologies disseminated by small, marginalized groups are often reincorporated into the dominant culture's contextual framework over time, often repackaged for mass consumption (cf. also Klein, 1972).

Conclusion

Tibet was an essential part of creating a mythical New Age landscape. While Tibet served as a backdrop for many of the major thinkers in the movement, its religious culture remained rather elusive for most of the development of New Age thinking, possibly because of its relatively mysterious nature, which developed partly as a byproduct of Western fantasy, a point made repeatedly by Peter Bishop in his study *The Myth of Shangri-La* (1989). When Tibet came into the public eye in the 1960s as a result of the Tibetan diaspora (cf. Korom, 1997), however, its culture and religion were embraced by more and more Westerners due, in part, to an increasing number of Tibetan teachers settling in Europe and America. Again, many people who embraced Tibetan Buddhism did so seriously, while others experimented with it along with many other paths of knowledge.

Such a tendency to experiment can be devastating, and criticisms similar to the ones made by Buddhologists in the nineteenth century concerning the "authenticity" of American Buddhist practitioners are echoed today. In a 1978 interview in the quasi–New Age magazine *Parabola* the Tibetan scholar Lobsang Lhalungpa noted that many Western students of Tibetan Buddhism do not go deep enough into the tradition. He stated, "I think that people who wish for exciting experiences have a tendency to explore without going deeper into the disciplines. So they never gain any real experiences in the first place, simply because they have not given enough devotion.... I have known quite a few people who thought that by reading certain esoteric books they had sufficient understanding to do these practices on their own; and finally it created serious psychological problems.... We very often say: There is no use giving a child a wild horse if he isn't trained to ride" (*Parabola*, 1978: 47).

Proverbial Tibetan wisdom castigates those who choose not to practice wholeheartedly, but people have continued to dabble in Tibetan

Buddhism into the current decade. Mass media has certainly played a role in simultaneously popularizing and trivializing Tibet. But more importantly, perceived exotic appeal of Tibetan religious traditions even today has allowed contemporary New Age practitioners to partake of Tibet without committing to its rigorous spiritual training. Moreover, the vision of a better world to come crosscuts many religious paths. Sympathetic American scholars and practitioners have repeatedly pointed out that Tibetan Buddhism carries a millenarian message for all mankind in the Kālacakra prophecy of the coming of Śambhala (Jack, 1977: 70; Thurman, 1985). This same idea, as we have already seen, runs deep in the thought of the forerunners of New Age thinking and continues to play a significant role in the way Tibet is marketed today within New Age communities.

In a recent study, Deborah Root (1996) criticized the purposeful commodification and appropriation of "exotic" traditions by West-erners as a "cannibalizing" of indigenous cultures. In one poignant pas-sage she observes that "[p]art of the reason New Age followers have turned to Native beliefs is the way Native people have come to stand for an abstract, stereotypical quality called spirituality, in which con-sumers imagine that they can know in advance what this spirituality would look like" (1996: 92). She goes on to argue that the taking up of a "disarticulated, fragmentary version" (1996: 93) of another cul-ture's traditions fails to allow for any real dialogue between the parties in question. Wearing a dorje necklace or prayer wheel earrings thus allows the individual to be sympathetic to the Tibetan tradition in a postmodern fashion, but also safeguards the wearer against any deeper engagement with the contemporary issues that Tibet, its people, and its culture are facing on a daily basis. As a result, the Tibetan Buddhist Shambhala becomes confused with the Western-inspired Shangri-la.

Agehananda Bharati, in his usually sardonic way, has also criticized the Western perception of Tibet among New Age seekers, calling it a "fictitious Tibet," the "somewhat auto-erotic credo of a large, and unfortunately still growing, crowd of wide-eyed believers in the mys-terious East" (1974: 1). We do not have to go so far as to agree with Bharati that the whole cultural construction of Tibet is fraudulent, but it is important to place the fragmented production and reception of

Tibet in the New Age movement in context. Tibet's role in the New Age movement must be understood not in isolation from other aspects of Eastern culture, but as part of a larger complex of ideas that freely and often loosely circulate within communities looking for alternative epistemologies.

I suggest that Tibet, while historically playing a lesser role than countries such as India, China, or Japan, served as an important metaphysical trope for the construction of alternative spirituality in New Age thought. Its close geographic proximity with India and its philosophical connection with Buddhism placed it at the center of the New Age imagination, yet its misperceived isolation conveniently served to preserve the aura of distance and mystery needed for the location of inaccessible spiritual masters and esoteric teachings. In this capacity, Tibet's role as an essentialized sacred space vaguely located on the mythic New Age landscape can be seen as a functional necessity for the development of New Age thought. But we must also be aware, as Donald Lopez (1994) reminds us, of the "New Age orientalism" inherent in the ongoing production of a fantastic Tibet, for it denies agency to real Tibetans and erases Tibet from any physical map.

In conclusion, let me turn to a contemporary New Age practitioner who told me recently that the need for a real Tibet is secondary to the "astral" Tibet because it is on the ethereal plane that the masters reside. So if we can simply communicate with the masters through "channeling" (mental/spiritual communication), the need for the physical realm is insignificant in the big cosmic picture. I do not wish to suggest, however, that the total New Age involvement with Tibetan culture has been unproductive, for a number of New Age practitioners have been involved in raising awareness about current issues pertaining to the future of modern Tibet. In this sense, New Age thinking and practice can make useful contributions to confronting and possibly solving contemporary social problems (cf. Woodside, 1989). With people on the fringe still advocating the "ethereal" approach to Tibetan culture, however, there remains an ongoing need to distinguish between Shangri-la and Śambhala.

Notes

1 Research for this paper was generously funded by two separate grants from the International Folk Art Foundation in 1994 and 1995. Judy Sellars deserves a special note of gratitude for bibliographical assistance during the early phases of research. I also wish to thank the organizers of the Mythos Tibet symposium, especially Thierry Dodin and Heinz Räther, for their invitation to speak on this topic.

THE IMAGE OF TIBET
OF THE GREAT MYSTIFIERS

Donald S. Lopez, Jr.

THE ORGANIZERS of our symposium invited me to speak on the topic of "The Tibet Image of the Great Mystifiers (Roerich, David-Néel, Govinda, Rampa)." To consider four such formidable figures, each quite different from the other, in one presentation seems too great a challenge. I assumed that by Roerich, the organizers meant Roerich père, Nicholas Roerich, the Russian poet and painter who left the promised Bolshevik utopia and set out in search of Shambhala. Madame Alexandra David-Néel, the intrepid traveler, was once regarded as a fraud; some questioned whether she had ever been in Tibet. Today, she has been vindicated and rehabilitated as a feminist *avant la lettre*, a woman who left the comfort of her husband and her homeland to travel across Asia, accompanied only by her adopted Tibetan son, Lama Yongden. Her claims of having witnessed certain mystic feats, once challenged, have now been confirmed. Lama Govinda was born Ernst Hoffmann and began a career as a promising Pali scholar before traveling to southern Tibet where, in the parlance of the anthropologist, he "went over the hill" to become, at least in his garb, a Tibetan lama. He wrote *The Way of White Clouds,* an inspiration for Peter Mathiessen's *The Snow Leopard,* and later, a more philosophical work entitled *Foundations of Tibetan Mysticism,* despite the fact that he seems never to have learned to read Tibetan.[1]

Regardless of what else these three might have had in common, they are similar in that they each traveled to Tibet and made a contribution to Tibetology, contributions that have retained their value. Nicholas

Roerich fathered George Roerich, a distinguished scholar of Tibetan Buddhism, best known for his translation of the *Blue Annals*. Madame David-Néel provided vignettes of the Thirteenth Dalai Lama and lesser known lamas of the first decades of this century. And Lama Govinda, or at least his wife, Li Gotami, made photographs of temples in western Tibet, photographs that today have important archival value. The same cannot be said, at least in the conventional sense, about the author who wrote under the name of T. Lobsang Rampa. He never went to Tibet and his contributions to Tibetology remain, at best, dubious.

If Rampa does not belong with Roerich, David-Néel, and Govinda for these reasons, he is often listed with them presumably because they were all, in some sense, "mystifiers." The term "mystify," the dictionary tells us, is derived from the Greek *myein,* meaning to close the eyes and lips, a term used to refer to initiation into religious rites. And indeed, in one sense or another, each of these four figures claimed to be an initiate into the secrets of the cults of Tibetan Buddhism. Yet Roerich, David-Néel, Govinda, and Rampa are referred to pejoratively as mystifiers precisely because their eyes were closed to the realities of Tibetan history and culture, because they were, in fact, not initiates of another cult, the cult of Tibetology. They were, instead, mystifiers, in two modern meanings of the term. First, they mystified Tibet, embellishing the realities of Tibet with their own mystical fancies, and, second, they mystified their readers, playing on the credulity of the reading public. This latter sense of mystify has a strong connotation of intentional deceit, a charge that is vehemently denied by Rampa, the man regarded as the greatest hoaxer in the history of Tibetan Studies. For, although Alexandra David-Néel dressed as a Tibetan to hide her true identity and although Lama Govinda dressed as a Tibetan to signal his new identity, the Englishman who wrote under the name of T. Lobsang Rampa claimed to have been possessed by a Tibetan lama, and over the course of seven years, to have become a Tibetan, not just in his dress, but in his molecules.

I would like briefly to consider notions of embodiment and possession in an effort to raise the question of what authorizes the author of a book about Tibet. The occasion for these reflections is provided by three books published under the name of T. Lobsang Rampa, a man who claimed not to have had his eyes closed but to have had a new eye opened, an eye that allowed him, in his words, "to see people as they are and not as they pretend to be."

The Third Eye, first published in Britain in 1956, tells autobiographically the story of Tuesday Lobsang Rampa, the son of one of the leading members of the Dalai Lama's government. He grew up in a fashionable home in Lhasa, under the strict tutelage of one of the "men of Kham," a seven-foot former member of the monk police named Old Tzu. He attended school, where he studied Tibetan, Chinese, arithmetic, and woodcarving (for printing blocks). Among sports, he enjoyed archery, pole-vaulting, stilt-walking, and especially kite-flying, the national sport of Tibet. The kite season began on the first day of autumn, signaled when a single kite rose from the Potala. At the celebration of Tuesday's seventh birthday, the astrologers predicted the boy's future: "A boy of seven to enter a lamasery, after a hard feat of endurance, and there to be trained as a priest-surgeon. To suffer great hardships, to leave the homeland, and go among strange people. To lose all and have to start again, and eventually to succeed."[2]

He thus joined the Chakpori Lamasery, the Temple of Tibetan Medicine, where he began a rigorous course of study, with a strong emphasis on mathematics and on memorization of the Buddhist scriptures. Teachers would shoot questions at the students such as, "You, boy, I want to know the fifth line of the eighteenth page of the seventh volume of the Kan-gyur."[3] Tuesday soon showed himself to be an excellent student and was chosen as one who would receive the esoteric teachings, so that the knowledge could be preserved after Tibet had fallen under an alien cloud. Thus, he began a period of intensive training designed to impart in a few years what a lama normally would learn over the course of an entire lifetime. He was placed under the tutelage of the great lama Mingyar Dondup, who oversaw the performance of a surgical procedure designed to force clairvoyance, whereafter Tuesday could be instructed hypnotically. The operation, performed on Tuesday's eighth birthday, involved drilling a hole in his skull at the point between his eyes to create the third eye, the eye that would allow him to see auras. When he recovered from the surgery, he was summoned to the Potala where he met privately with the Dalai Lama, "the Inmost One," who had investigated both the records of Tuesday's past incarnation and the predictions of his future, and reminded him of the great work that lay before him in preserving the wisdom of Tibet for the world.

Shortly after his twelfth birthday, Tuesday took the examinations that one must pass in order to become a *trappa*, or medical priest. Each student was sealed inside a stone cubicle that was six feet wide, ten feet long, and eight feet high. Once inside, each student was passed written questions to which he composed written answers. They wrote for fourteen hours a day on a single subject, with the entire battery of tests lasting six days. After successfully passing his examinations, Tuesday accompanied Lama Mingyar Dondup on an expedition to collect medicinal herbs. During their travels, they stopped at the monastery of Tra Yerpa, where the monks built box kites large enough to bear the weight of an adult. Tuesday made several flights in such kites and later suggested design modifications to the monastery's Kite Master to improve their airworthiness.

Upon his return to Lhasa, he was called upon by the Dalai Lama to sit in hiding in the audience room of the Norbulinga and use his third eye to observe the aura, and hence learn the intentions, of an English visitor. Occasionally the man would hold a white cloth to his nose and make the sound of a small trumpet, which Tuesday took to be a form of salute to the Dalai Lama. His aura showed him to be in poor health. However, he had a genuine desire to help Tibet but was constrained by the fear that if he were to do so, he would lose his government pension. Tuesday later learned that the man's name was C. A. Bell.

Tuesday later accompanied Lama Mingyar Dondup on an expedition to the Chang thang, where after a perilous journey through frozen wastelands, they came upon an Edenic valley, warm and luxuriant, where they encountered the yeti. Upon his return from Lhasa, at the time of his sixteenth birthday, he once again entered the examination boxes, this time for ten days. When the results came in, Tuesday was at the top of his class, and was promoted from the rank of trappa to the rank of lama, after which he studied anatomy by working side by side with the Body Breakers, the disposers of the dead.

Finally, the Dalai Lama declared that Tuesday must undergo the initiation of an abbot, the Ceremony of the Little Death. Shortly thereafter he was again summoned by the Dalai Lama, who instructed him to leave Tibet immediately and go to China, with the warning, "The ways of foreigners are strange and not to be accounted for. As I told you once before, they believe only that which they can do, only that which can be tested in their Rooms of Science. Yet the greatest Science of all, the Science of the Overself, they leave untouched. That is your Path, the Path you chose before you came to this Life." *The Third Eye* ends with Tuesday Lobsang Rampa departing for China, looking back for the last time at the Potala, where a solitary kite is flying.

Rampa published a sequel in 1959 called *Doctor from Lhasa*. It begins where *The Third Eye* ends, with Tuesday Lobsang Rampa departing from Lhasa for China, where he enrolled in a medical college. When war with Japan broke out, Tuesday went into service flying an air ambulance, eventually being shot down and taken prisoner. Toward the end of the war, the most incorrigible prisoners, including Tuesday, were transferred to a special prison camp in Japan, located in a village near Hiroshima. On the day that the bomb was dropped he escaped from the camp, made his way to the seashore, stole a fishing boat, and drifted into the Sea of Japan and sailed into the unknown. *Doctor from Lhasa* ends there.

The final work in the trilogy, *The Rampa Story*, opens fifteen years later, in 1960. In Tibet, the lamas, through astral exploration, have located a network of caves and tunnels in the most remote region of the country and are busy physically transporting the most sacred and secret artifacts of the faith from Lhasa to this new site, where they can be preserved from the Communists. At that time, Tuesday Lobsang Rampa was living in Windsor, Canada. He was in telepathic communication with the lamas in Tibet. They informed him that his next task was to write a book, "stressing one theme, that one person can take over the body of another, with the latter person's full consent."[4]

He recounts that the Japanese fishing boat eventually ran aground in the Sea of Japan and landed near the Russian lines. Because of his telepathic ability to calm the fiercest Russian mastiff patrol dogs, he was drafted into the Russian army as a dog trainer in Vladivostok, where he was known as "Comrade Priest." Some weeks later, he hid himself on a freight train bound for Moscow, where he was arrested by security police. After being tortured in Lubianka Prison, he was released and deported to Poland. On the way, the Russian truck he was riding in was involved in an accident and he was seriously injured. While in the hospital, he was transported to a world beyond the Astral, "The Land of Golden Light," to recuperate, where he was met by Lama Mingyar Dondup (who had been murdered by the Communists in Tibet). There he also met the Thirteenth Dalai Lama, who urged him to return to earth and continue his work. The problem was that his body was in deplorable condition. The Dalai Lama explained to him: "We have located a body in the land of England, the owner of which is most anxious to leave. His aura has a fundamental harmonic of yours. Later, if conditions necessitate it, you can take over his body."[5] After the transfer was made, it would take seven years for a complete molecular transformation to take place, after which the new body would be the same as the old one, even bearing the same scars. He was warned, however, that "you will return to hardship, misunderstanding, disbelief, and actual hatred, for there is a force of evil which tries to prevent all that is good in connection with human evolution."[6]

After many adventures he arrived in Kalimpong, where he was met by a delegation of disguised lamas, who accompanied him to an isolated lamasery overlooking Lhasa. In the company of an elder lama, he made an astral journey to the Akashic Record to investigate the past of the man whose body he was to inhabit. He learned that the man was married and made surgical fittings for a living. Rampa decided to meet with the man in the Astral. The man hated life in England because of the favoritism, but had always had an interest in Tibet and the Far East. He recounts how he had been approached by a lama one day, after being knocked unconscious falling from a tree while trying to photograph an owl. The lama had said:

> I was drawn to you because your own particular life vibrations are a fundamental harmonic of one for whom I act. So I have come, I have come because I want your body for one who has to continue life in the Western world, for he has a task to do

which brooks no interference.... Would you like the satisfaction of knowing that your Kharma had been wiped away, that you had materially contributed towards a job of utmost benefit to mankind?... Are you not willing to do something to redeem your own mistakes, to put some purpose to your own mediocre life? You will be the gainer. The one for whom I act will take over this hard life of yours.[7]

And so he agreed. Rampa told him that he would return to take over his body. One month later, accompanied by three lamas, he traveled astrally to London. The man was instructed to fall out of a tree again, at which point the operation was performed to sever the man from his Silver Cord and attach Rampa's cord to the man's body. He entered into the Western body with great difficulty, rose to his feet, and was helped inside by the man's wife. He immediately had to seek employment, and took various freelance jobs to support his wife and himself. When inquiring about a job as a ghostwriter, he was encouraged by a literary agent to write his own book. He was reluctant: "*Me* write a book? Crazy! All I wanted was a job providing enough money to keep us alive and a little over so that I could do auric research, and all the offers I had was to write a silly book about myself."[8] But at the insistence of the agent, he undertook the arduous and unpleasant task of writing *The Third Eye*. After completing the book, he suffered a heart attack and moved for health reasons to Ireland, where he wrote *Doctor from Lhasa*.

He was summoned once more by Lama Mingyar Dondup who told him he must go to "the Land of the Red Indians" where he had one final task to accomplish. The lama told him "[B]e not upset by those who would criticize you, for they know not whereof they speak, being blinded by the self-imposed ignorance of the West. When Death shall close their eyes, and they become born to the Great Life, then indeed will they regret the sorrows and troubles they have so needlessly caused."[9] Rampa, his wife, and their two cats, flew to New York and then to Windsor, Canada, but the climate did not suit him, and he decided to move as soon as he finished *The Rampa Story*, a book that ends with the prediction of a Chinese nuclear attack launched from Lhasa.

I have recounted Rampa's story as, perhaps, he would have wanted it to be told, in a seamless chronology. But that is not how it was written or how it was read. Especially in the last two books, the narrative does not proceed smoothly but is interrupted with discussions and instructions on various occult arts, most often on astral travel but also on crystal ball gazing. There are instructions on breath control and accounts of the earth's prehistory, the golden age when extraterrestrial giants visited the earth in flying saucers. There are instructions on ancient Egyptian death practices, and discourses on Kharma [sic], portrayed as an evolutionary system, where existence is a school in which we must learn our lessons before passing on to the next level; people are impoverished or lose their limbs so that they may learn a lesson. He explains that the religion of Tibet is a form of Buddhism, but that "there is no word which can be transliterated." The closest word for naming the religion of Tibet, he says, is Lamaism, which is different from Buddhism: "[O]urs is a religion of hope and a belief in the future. Buddhism, to us, seems negative, a religion of despair." The prayer of Lamaism is "Om mani pad-me Hum!" which literally means "Hail to the Jewel in the Lotus!" although initiates know that its true meaning is "Hail to Man's Overself!"[10]

But perhaps more important than the occult teachings, I have omitted to this point any mention of the prefaces to the first edition and to the second edition of *The Third Eye*, any mention of the persistent claims that everything written in the books is true and derives from his personal experience. I have also not made mention of the reception of the book, the criticisms to which Rampa responded with such vehemence.

One of the first of such criticisms was published in the *Daily Telegraph* and *Morning Post* in London on November 30, 1956, and reads in part:

> A book which plays up to public eagerness to hear about "Mysterious Tibet" has the advantage that few people have the experience to refute it. But anyone who has lived in Tibet will feel after reading a few pages of "The Third Eye" (Secker & Warburg. 18s) that its author, "T. Lobsang Rampa," is certainly not a Tibetan....

The samples of the Tibetan language betray ignorance of both colloquial and literary forms; there is a series of wholly un-Tibetan obsessions with cruelty, fuss and bustle and, strangely, with cats. Moreover, the turn of phrase in the slick colloquial English is quite unconvincing when attributed to a Tibetan writer.

Given that this is the work of a non-Asian mind—and if I am mistaken, I should be happy to make amends to the author in person and in Tibetan—one can regard only as indifferent juvenile fiction the catch-penny accoutrements of magic and mystery: the surgical opening of the "the third eye"; the man-lifting kites; the Abominable Snowman; the Shangri-la valley and eerie goings-on in caverns below the Potala.

The piece was signed by Hugh Richardson. Prior to the publication of the book, the publishing company of Secker and Warburg had sent the manuscript for review to Richardson, Marco Pallis, Heinrich Harrer, and Agehananda Bharati, each of whom had reported back that the book was a fraud. Secker and Warburg proceeded with publication, apparently more concerned with profit than with truth.

When *The Third Eye* was reprinted, it contained "A Statement by the Author," which began, "In the East it is commonly acknowledged that the stronger mind can take possession of another body." It went on to recount that in late 1947, Cyril Hoskin felt strange and irresistible compulsions to adopt Eastern ways of living. Some months later he legally changed his name to Carl KuonSuo (later changed to Carl Ku'an, for ease of pronunciation in England). He was beset by hallucinations. His memories of his own life began to fade as impressions of "an Eastern entity" increased. On June 13, 1949, he sustained a concussion in an accident in his garden, after which he had no memory of his earlier life, but "the *full* memory of a Tibetan from babyhood onwards." His wife gave him enough information about his previous identity to allow him to pretend that he was an Englishman. He also states that "with my Eastern memory I knew where I had papers, and I sent for them to prove my identity. Now I have sent away those papers again because I am not prepared to have them sullied by such doubts as have been caused in this case."[11] He states that the book was written hurriedly, without copying anything from other books. Further, "No two 'experts' have been able to agree on any particular fault," and that should prove the authenticity of the book because "none of them has lived in Tibet as a lama—has entered a lamasery at the age of seven as I have done."[12] He closes by noting that there is much theosophical literature dealing with possession and that his publishers have in their possession a letter from an Indian swami stating that possession is quite common in the East. He closes with, "I state most definitely that my books, *The Third Eye* and *Medical Lama* are true," and signs "T. Lobsang Rampa (C. Ku'an)."

This was not his only response to his critics. In *Doctor from Lhasa* he describes an unpleasant incident during the funeral ceremonies for the Thirteenth Dalai Lama: "A foreigner was there who wanted all consideration for himself. He thought that we were just natives, and that he was lord of all he surveyed. He wanted to be in the front of everything, noticed by all, and because I would not further his selfish aim—he tried to bribe a friend and me with wrist watches!—he has regarded me as an enemy ever since, and has indeed gone out of his way—has gone to extreme lengths—to injure me and mine."[13] This is an apparent reference to Hugh Richardson, Officer-in-Charge of the British Mission in Lhasa, although Richardson did not go to Tibet until 1936, three years after the Thirteenth Dalai Lama's death.

There are a host of questions raised by Rampa's books, questions raised both by their content and their reception. At the most cynical level, they are the works of an unemployed surgical fitter, the son of a plumber, seeking to support himself as a ghostwriter. The first book, as Richardson suggests, could have been drawn from various English language sources, all easily available at the time, supplemented with an admixture of garden variety spiritualism and Theosophy; the books contain discussions of auras, astral travel, prehistoric visits to earth by extraterrestrials, predictions of war, and a belief in the spiritual evolution of humanity. With the unexpected success of the book, the ghostwriter could go on to concoct a story that would allow the ghost to become flesh. The second and third books, indeed, have little to do with life in Tibet, even as described by Rampa. Their purpose, beyond the obvious demands for a sequel placed upon the author of a bestseller, seems to be to account for the period between around 1930 when Rampa left Lhasa and 1956 when *The Third Eye* was published. In a sense, the other two books serve as an extended apologia for the first, attempting to account not only for the time but more importantly for the authorship, explaining how an eyewitness account of life in Tibet in which everything is true could have been written by Cyril Hoskin, who never left England.

If we were to leave it at that, the works of Rampa would seem to have little reason to detain the scholar, who has better things to do than concern himself with works that are clearly the products of an impostor. As Agehananda Bharati described Madame Blavatsky's *Secret Doctrine,* "[It] is such a melee of horrendous hogwash and of fertile inventions of inane esoterica, that any Buddhist and Tibetan scholar is justified to avoid mentioning it in any context."[14] In seeking information from colleagues in the preparation of this essay, I found that, although everyone I spoke to had heard of *The Third Eye,* no one had actually read it. But *The Third Eye* sold over half a million copies in the first few years after its publication and remains in print and widely available in several languages forty years later. How are we to account for this appeal? Its very popularity may be one reason why it has generally been ignored by professional scholars of Tibet.

I recently used *The Third Eye* in a seminar for first-year undergraduates and had them read it without telling them anything of its history. (The "Author's Statement" has been deleted from the current edition.) The students were unanimous in their praise of the book, and despite six previous weeks of lectures and the reading of standard works on Tibetan history and religion, they found it entirely credible and compelling, judging it more realistic than anything they had previously read about Tibet, appreciating the detail about "what Tibet was really like." Many of the things they had read about Tibet seemed strange until then; these things seemed more reasonable when placed within the context of a lama's life. It is not that the things Rampa described were not strange; it was that they were so strange that they could not possibly have been concocted. When I told them about the book's author, they were shocked, but immediately wanted to separate fact from fiction. How much of the book was true?

With the author unmasked, they awakened from their mystified state, and with eyes now opened, turned away from Rampa and to me for authority. Each of their questions began, "Did Tibetans really…?" "Did Tibetans really perform amputations without anesthesia, with the patients using breath control and hypnotism instead? If a monk violated the eightfold path, was he punished by having to lie motionless face-down across the door of the temple for a full day, without food or drink? Are the priests in Tibet vegetarian? Did priests really only ride white horses? Did acolytes really wear white robes? Did cats really guard the temple jewels? And, of course, Did they really perform the operation of the third eye?"

The answer to each of these questions was "No." But by what authority did I confidently make such a pronouncement? I had not lived in old Tibet and so could not contradict Rampa's claims with my own eyewitness testimony. It was, rather, that I had never seen any mention of such things in any books that I had read about Tibet, in English, French, or Tibetan. And because I had read a sufficient number of such books, I was awarded a doctorate some years ago and, with the proper documents in my possession to prove my identity, had been given the power to consecrate and condemn the products of others, and the power to initiate others into this knowledge. This power, the power to speak both with authority and as an authority, that is, the power to bestow value, had been passed on to me by my teachers, who had in turn received it from their teachers. It was this power that was embod-ied in my "no." But this power had come at a price. For by accepting this power I had had to forever disavow any interest in the possible commercial profits that might derive from my work. It was necessary that I renounce any self-interest in the economic profits of my writing, exchanging such capital for something higher and more noble because it was severed from crass material interests. This was symbolic capital, which would, in its own way, provide for my financial security by ensuring that I would never have to offer my services to a publisher as a ghostwriter in order to support myself, as Cyril Hoskin had done.

It is not that Rampa's claims can be dismissed because they are too strange. If his research had extended to include Evans-Wentz's *Tibetan Yoga and Secret Doctrines*, he could have learned about *grong 'jug*, or "forceful entry," one of the six teachings of Naropa, whereby one can transfer one's own consciousness into that of another being (preferably a well-preserved corpse). Or Rampa may have appealed to Tibetan theories of possession. René de Nebesky-Wojkowitz, in his *Oracles and Demons of Tibet* (published in 1956, the same year as *The Third Eye*), describes in detail the manner in which a deity possesses the body of another, descending uninvited into an unsuspecting person who will become its medium, called in Tibetan the "physical foundation" *(sku brten)* of the deity. He details the tests that Tibetans use to determine whether the possessing entity is actually a deity, or whether it is instead the roaming spirit of the dead.

Or Rampa might have made an appeal to one of the oldest and most storied Buddhist techniques of legitimation, the discovery of the text. In Tibet, Padmasambhava is said to have hidden teachings, called "treasures" *(gter ma)* throughout the Tibetan landscape, to be discovered over the centuries (and into the present century) by the future incarnations of his prophesied disciples at the appropriate historical moment, those prophecies generally contained in the rediscovered text itself. Treasure texts could also be discovered not in the earth, but in the mind of the discoverer. These "mind treasures" *(dgongs gter)* are teachings of Padmasambhava that have remained pristine and uncorrupted, concealed in the discoverer's mind, to be revealed first to the discoverer and then, through him, to the world.

Is it possible, then, to see *The Third Eye* as a mind treasure, a *dgongs gter,* discovered unexpectedly in the mind of Cyril Hoskin at a crucial moment, in 1956, soon after the People's Liberation Army had occupied Lhasa and the Dalai Lama had met with Chairman Mao, the book serving the important purpose of bringing the plight of Tibet to a Western audience of hundreds of thousands who otherwise would have been unconcerned, an audience who would have no interest in Tibet without the trappings of astral travel, spiritualism, and the hope of human evolution to a New Age?

With one notable exception, Western scholars of Tibetan Buddhism have been reluctant to directly confront the question of the historical legitimacy of *gter ma,* to consider the rediscovered texts as, in fact, works composed by their discoverers and hidden only to be revealed.

The fact that the pious fiction of authenticity has been tacitly maintained for so long by scholars of Tibet is itself a fascinating topic to be considered with the larger issue of mystification. (Of equal fascination is the compulsion of the scholar to "correct" Rampa, to point out those elements of the authentic Tibetan tradition that are somehow analogous to his fabrications, to suggest how, if he had only been better informed, if he only knew what the scholar knows, he could have made his work into something other than a hoax, or at least made his hoax more credible.)

I would like, however, to consider a more circumscribed question: When Tibetan incarnate lamas are now being identified among Caucasian children born in Europe and America, what is it about *The Third Eye* that so enrages the expert?

The question is one of authority, and how it is established and maintained. The classic exposition of authority is that of Max Weber, who distinguished between charismatic and traditional authority, which together eventually yielded, at least in the West, to legal authority. Weber defined charisma as "an extraordinary quality of a person, regardless of whether this quality is actual, alleged, or presumed" and defined charismatic authority as "a rule over men, whether predominantly external or internal, to which the governed submit because of their belief in the extraordinary quality of the specific *person*."[15] Traditional authority is domination that rests, instead, "on the belief in the everyday as an inviolable norm of conduct," it is a "piety for what actually, allegedly, or presumably has always existed."[16] The distinction between charismatic authority and traditional authority is difficult to discern, much less maintain, in the case of Tibet, where so much authority of both forms rested with religious clerics. Indeed, the entire system of incarnate lamas can be seen, in Weber's terms, as an attempt to transform charisma into tradition, as something to be passed down over generations. Whether or not Rampa possessed charisma is difficult to judge; those who met him invariably noted the remarkable depression in the middle of his forehead, and he claimed traditional authority for himself through the autobiography he composed. But Weber is less helpful on how charisma is lost, and that is perhaps the more interesting question in the case of Rampa.

In his book, *Authority: Construction and Corrosion,* Bruce Lincoln has argued that:

> In practice, the consequentiality of authoritative speech may have relatively little to do with the form or content of what is said.... [I]t is best understood in relational terms as the effect of a posited, perceived, or institutionally ascribed asymmetry between speaker and audience that permits certain speakers to command not just the attention but the confidence, respect, and trust of their audience, or—an important proviso—to make audiences act *as if* this were so.[17]

Although Lincoln's analysis is directed at speech acts, it also pertains to certain cases of textual authority. The asymmetry between Rampa and his audience is established by Rampa's identity as a Tibetan lama. Once Rampa is shown to be nothing more than Cyril Hoskin, that asymmetry dissolves and it is no longer respectable, and thus, possible, for the audience to accept his authority. *Doctor from Lhasa* and *The Rampa Story* thus set out to try to reclaim that authority by showing why Hoskin is Rampa. It is significant that in his various prefaces and author's statements, Rampa makes no attempt to argue for the accuracy of the contents of his books, he simply declares that they are true. What he seeks to do is to reclaim authority by attempting to reestablish the asymmetry to which Lincoln refers, to at least provide his readers with the possibility of regarding him again as if he were a Tibetan lama. This authority is essential to his identity, a point that eluded Agehananda Bharati in his diatribe against "Rampaism" when he wrote, "I never saw why Don Juan must be a Yaqui (which he is not) to teach something important, nor why a Hoskins [*sic*] must be a Tibetan (which he is not) if *he* has something important to teach."[18]

The problem for Rampa, however, is that in the Tibetan tradition, charisma is inextricable from institution. The authority to speak is passed on through a lineage, a lineage that operates regardless of historical gaps and fissures. Hoskin cannot serve as the authorized representative of Lamaism because he does not participate in the authority of any institution certified by Tibetans or Tibetologists. Richardson wrote in his review of *Doctor from Lhasa,* "No one of my acquaintance who has lived in Tibet and knows the Tibetans—including a genuine Tibetan lama to whom I read the book—had any doubt that it was an impudent fake." Like the *skeptron,* the scepter that was passed among the speakers in Agamemnon's assembly, its possession authorizing speech, the institutions of Tibet, whether they be the monastic academy, the descent of a deity, or identification of a tulku, authorize speech. As Pierre Bourdieu notes, "The spokesperson is an impostor endowed with the *skeptron.*"[19] Cyril Hoskin, like Thersites in Book 2 of the *Iliad,* attempted to speak without the scepter being passed to him. And as Odysseus rebuked Thersites and struck him with the scepter, leaving a wound on his back, so Hugh Richardson (and the authorities he spoke for) showed Rampa to be an impostor who had no right to speak of Tibet, leaving one to wonder whether the depression between Hoskin's eyes was not the sign of a more fatal wound, one which brought an end to his short life as an authority on Tibet, but caused him to be reborn into another realm, for the condemnation by a scholar carries with it a kind of consecration.

And so Hoskin, or Ku'an, or Rampa, who wanted only to be a ghostwriter, became a ghost. As he says in *The Rampa Story,* "my lonely Tibetan body [lay] safely stored in a stone coffin, under the unceasing care of three monks." The unlaid ghost was left to wander, from England, to Scotland, to Canada. In the process, he was able to acquire the authority of another institution, that of the vast literature of spiritualism, going on to write a dozen books on such authorized occult topics as interstellar travel, ouija boards, and the lost years of Jesus. Like a ghost he seemed to wander between two worlds, finding a home in neither. The representation of Tibetan Buddhism historically has been and continues to be situated in a domain where the scholarly and the popular commingle, a domain that is neither exclusively one or the other. The confluence of the scholarly and the popular is strikingly evident in *The Third Eye,* where Rampa draws on the accounts of travelers and amateur scholars (themselves sites of the admixture of the popular and scholarly) and combines them with standard occult elements (astral travel, rites from ancient Egypt, etc.) into a work that is neither wholly fact nor wholly fiction. It is evident that by the time

Rampa wrote his "memoir" there was ample material available from scholars, travelers, and Theosophists to enable him to paint a portrait of Tibet in which his own contributions seemed entirely plausible. Furthermore, he was able to represent the Tibet of Western fantasies in such a way that he himself could be embodied within it.

The author of *The Third Eye,* decried as a fraud, is not exactly a fraud, because, if we are to believe the testimony of those who knew him, he really did believe that he was T. Lobsang Rampa. He may have been delusional; he may not have been a huckster. He set out to be a ghostwriter, someone who writes for and in the name of another, receiving payment in exchange for the credit of authorship. But he was not a ghostwriter in this sense, because he came to assume the identity of the one in whose name he wrote. And the book that he produced also confounds the standard literary categories. It may have begun as a bestseller, a book that is marketed for its short-term profitability, but it has, in its own way, also become a classic, a work that sells well over time. The bestseller is authorized by the public and those who serve it: the publishing companies and the popular media. The current edition of *The Third Eye* contains raves from the *Times Literary Supplement,* "It comes near to being a work of art" and the *Miami Herald,* "What fascinates the reader is not only a strange land—and what could be stranger than Tibet?—but [Rampa's] skill in interpreting the philosophy of the East." The classic, on the other hand, is certified by the scholar, who ensures its commercial durability by providing a reliable market for the book in the educational system, as I have done by assigning *The Third Eye* for my class.

It is not simply that the scholar needs the dilettante in order to define his identity. Lobsang Rampa is rather like the *glud,* the ransom (translated by some as "scapegoat") offered to the demons in a Tibetan exorcism ceremony in exchange for the spirit of the possessed. And so Rampa is given to the public, who does not care what scholars say, and he derives his livelihood in the bargain. In return, the scholar, by renouncing the public, receives symbolic capital by disavowing that upon which he is ultimately dependent; it is the continuing fascination of Tibet that brings students to our classrooms and the public to our symposia. The question that remains is that of the persistent confluence

of the two institutions that Rampa wandered between, Tibetology and
Spiritualism, one that cast him out and one that embraced him. Why
is it that this ghost continues to haunt us, as we remain always startled,
in an uncanny moment, to find his books next to ours on the shelf
marked "Occult"?

NOTES

This essay is an earlier version of the chapter on Rampa in Lopez, 1998: 86–113.

1　This supposition is based on the fact that his major work on Tibetan Bud-
　dhism, *Foundations of Tibetan Mysticism,* contains no references to Tibetan
　works that had not been translated into a European language. He did travel
　in western Tibet, however, and states in his foreword to Evan-Wentz's biog-
　raphy that he planned to revise the translation of *The Tibetan Book of the
　Dead* "according to the Tibetan original." See Winkler, 1982: vii.

2　Rampa, 1964: 44.

3　Ibid: 82.

4　Rampa, 1968: 4.

5　Ibid: 71.

6　Ibid.

7　Ibid: 167–69.

8　Ibid: 194.

9　Ibid: 204.

10　Rampa, 1964: 115–16.

11　Ibid: 7–8.

12　Ibid.

13　Rampa, 1990: 107.

14　Bharati, 1974: 3.

15　Weber, 1958: 295.

16　Ibid: 296.

17　Lincoln, 1994: 4.

18　Bharati, 1974: 11.

19　Bourdieu, 1991: 109.

Not Only a Shangri-la

Images of Tibet in Western Literature

Peter Bishop

Glimpses

THE CLOSING SCENE of Alfred Hitchcock's famous 1954 thriller *Rear Window* shows a character played by Grace Kelly lounging in her fiancé's apartment reading a book. If you look very closely, the title can just be made out: *Beyond the High Himalayas*. Her fiancé, played by James Stewart, has spent the whole film housebound and in a wheelchair on account of an injured leg. As an active photojournalist he is frustrated by his immobility and yearns for action. The Grace Kelly character is involved in the world of high fashion and wears expensive gowns but now wants to go with him on his assignments. He constantly avoids the question, convinced she wouldn't be able to take the hardships—or is he afraid of intimate commitment? Housebound, he uses a powerful telephoto lens to observe his close neighbors with a mix of professional interest and voyeurism, eventually convincing both himself and his fiancé that a murder has been committed in the apartment across the courtyard. The closing scene carries a measured irony: The murder mystery has been solved, but the James Stewart character has aggravated his injury, further incapacitating himself. The Grace Kelly character has called his bluff and for the first time appears dressed casually. The title of the book she is reading can only increase his frustration. *Beyond the High Himalayas* can only allude to Tibet, suggesting both geographical position and an imaginative landscape of adventure and mystery.

The word "Tibet" is not mentioned in this film, merely suggested. We don't know if she really intends going there or if this is just a window into reverie. Certainly the glimpse we are offered could be no briefer. The world it invokes is an elusive one—*beyond*. Beyond not just the Himalayas, but the *high* Himalayas. Perhaps Hitchcock, with his meticulous sense of detail and mischievous eye, could envisage no better signpost for a place that, in the modern world of 1954, was still capable of carrying a profound imaginative charge—elusively located in time and space, just beyond the outer edge of the known world, beyond even the heroic challenges of the highest mountains in a rapidly shrinking and increasingly mundane world.

I have chosen this image because it is one of the most ephemeral and elusive, yet nonetheless direct, references to Tibet that I know, so ephemeral that it is merely a suggestion of a fantasy *about* a fantasy. The prime fantasy is that of a fabulous, exotic, remote, and difficult place. Given the context of a murder mystery, there is also the suggestion of underworld associations. It suggests extremes and is also in opposition to normal daily life. Wealthy, sophisticated city woman exchanges high-heels and haute couture for casual slacks and sensible shoes even just to muse over the possibility of going there. This is the fantasy *about* Tibet. This is not a Shangri-la. Nor is it a fantasy of magic and mystery, nor one of imperial rivalries. While perhaps partaking of aspects of such Western dreams, the fantasy belongs more to the burgeoning world of National Geographic and global adventure tourism. It has been stimulated by two decades of striking visual images in various geographic magazines, by sustained media coverage of Himalayan mountaineering exploits, by an upsurge in the popularity of travel writing, and increased global mobility for affluent tourists.

The fantasy *about* such a fantasy refers to the attitude toward this Tibet, the way in which the image is held. The Grace Kelly character is certainly not gripped by a thaumaturgical rapture, a Lobsang Rampa–like identification with occult and parapsychological initiations; nor is she expressing the pious devotion of a prospective pilgrim, nor the blood and guts heroics of exploration, or the ennui and despair of a utopia seeker, or the scholarly earnestness of an ethnographer, or even the hopeful expectation of self-discovery, -healing, and -improvement. This is the jet-set mood with the photojournalist as hero. Outdoor, practical, voyeuristic, and certainly chic, the idea of Tibet is held at a distance, the posture slightly ironic and whimsical. What a great idea! What an adventure!

Of course, this may seem rather a lot to deduce from such a glimpse. But this example does allow me to raise a number of issues. Why should a longer stare, a more sustained reference, such as a whole book, be more revealing or more useful in terms of understanding Western fantasy-making about Tibet? Elusive glimpses and serendipitous associations have been integral to Western fantasies about Tibet, positioned, as it has been, just beyond the very edge of imperial control for much of the past two hundred years. Such brief, almost ephemeral, moments are comments from the margins, which also begin to question what exactly is central. In the postcolonial era not only has the relationship between center and periphery sometimes been reversed, but the very notions have become problematical, even redundant.[1]

The selection of texts is crucial. To confine ourselves only to substantial accounts of Tibet in novels or in short stories would severely restrict our appreciation of the immense influence that Tibet has exerted on the Western imagination. Casting the net wide—for example, we could usefully read the libretto of a new opera on *The Tibetan Book of the Dead* to be performed in the United States this year—allows us access to a rich field of associations (Gordon, 1996). But why stop there? Why not undertake to examine the extraordinary range of references to Tibet found in the daily newspapers or glossy magazines of the world?

There is also the question of finding appropriate ways of gaining access to Western fantasy-making. Such glimpses, for example, are like slips of the tongue or lapses of attention, those extraordinarily brief moments that reveal unsuspected or even unwanted and unacknowledged associations. If fantasies about Tibet are akin to an extraverted dream, then the merest glimpse can perhaps be the most revealing about the unconscious terrain of Western fantasy-making. As a method they are refractive—bending and deflecting our scholarly intentions and expectations, fracturing and fragmenting our gaze, revealing unsuspected associations (Bishop, 1994).

Then there are questions about the limitations of a textual analysis. It is all too easy to attribute fixed meanings to a text, rather than understanding it as being the product of specific cultural contexts as people selectively engage with words and images. The relationship to such a text can vary considerably—the Grace Kelly character's languidly casual flirtation with Tibet is just one attitude among many. Networks of associations and moments of reverie (Bachelard, 1971) can be evoked by a single word, such as Yeti, Potala, Lhasa, or Dalai Lama. The author of an illustrated storybook for young children, *The Lucky Yak,* claims she wrote the book because her four-year-old son simply loved the sound of the word "yak" (Lawson, 1980). Such a serendipitous relationship to Tibet has to be given its due place.

Portraits of Tibet in overt fiction (and, it may be said, in scholarship with its inevitable correlation between knowledge and power) are often exploitative projections, ideological manipulations, within an orientalist milieu. However, we should be careful not to simply paint Tibet as passive victim, as a "silent other" (Said, 1979). For a full understanding we would have to consider the ways in which Tibetans themselves have not only vigorously contested the various Western images of Tibet but have, for better or worse, also participated in their construction. For example, Tibetan resistance to China has utilized the sympathy inherent within the idealization of Shangri-la to elicit support for its cause. Tibetan tourist operators regularly draw upon stereotyped images. Tibetan teachers utilize dominant Western discourses, such as human and civil rights, physics, psychology, personal growth and holism, ostensibly in order to establish communication, but as a consequence of this they participate in Western fantasy-making about their country and culture.

I have included film as well as travel writing, short stories, plays, and novels, for the notion of literature is broad, even problematical in the contemporary era when a case can be made for the inherent fictional nature of any text, including those of the social and physical sciences. This doesn't mean that such texts are simply erroneous or false, but that the notion of fiction, of imagination, is unavoidable.[2] Finally, the glimpse from the Hitchcock movie reminds us that Tibet is, in Foucault's terms, a heterotopia, a plurality of often contradictory, competing, and mutually exclusive places simultaneously positioned on a single geographical location (1986). Tibet has not always been imagined a Shangri-la.

Clearly space and time do not now permit a full exploration of this topic. The vast output of travel writing, for example, could overwhelm other sources, so while the relationship between overt fiction and travel literature is fundamental to this paper, direct references will be brief (Bishop, 1989). The innumerable products of popular culture that refer to Tibet, from bumper stickers to silk scarves or Tin Tin t-shirts, like the fictional aspect of scholarship, similarly fall outside this paper's scope but must nevertheless be kept in mind. Instead I will explore, in the form of a historical sketch, a variety of ways in which various kinds of literature can be approached.

I want to return to the idea of merely glimpsing Tibet, as in the film *Rear Window*, and go back even further, to a novel of 1835, *Old Goriot*, by Honoré de Balzac (1913). At one point criticism is directed at unquestioning subservience toward administrative systems: "a kind of involuntary, mechanical, and instinctive reverence for the *Grand Lama* of every Ministry" (pp. 178–79, my emphasis). This is the novel's only reference to Tibet, but it is probably the earliest in Western fiction.

By using the phrase "the Grand Lama" almost colloquially, as a metaphor for absolute executive power, Balzac suggests that its meaning was well understood among the literate population of cosmopolitan France at the beginning of the nineteenth century. The Grand Lama is a figure demanding "passive obedience," and the "administrative system," writes Balzac, "silences consciences, annihilates the individual, and...he becomes part of the machinery of Government" (pp. 179). I am surprised, not by the fact that Tibet is referred to at this time, nor by its negative connotations, but by the way it is used so casually and colloquially. Querying such a style of address can lead us deep into the very beginnings of the orientalist assumptions that were to underpin so many of the worldviews taken for granted in nineteenth-century Europe and America.

Such a negative image of Tibet could have arrived, for example, into Parisian culture via the accounts by Catholic missionaries of the eighteenth century, or from the secular study of exotic cultures, which had been gaining in popularity. Certainly there is a similarly brief reference to Tibet seventy years earlier, in Rousseau's seminal work of 1762, *The Social Contract*, where he writes about the religion of the "lamas," bracketing it with Roman Catholicism (1973: 272). He is scathingly critical, insisting that such religions create a conflict of loyalty between religion and citizenship.[3]

As the nineteenth century progressed, Tibet's theocratic government, legitimated by mystical doctrines about reincarnation, increasingly came to be viewed, at best, as inefficient, incompetent, and bizarre, and at worst, as tyrannous, corrupt, and oppressive. However, by the middle of the twentieth century this same religious and civic bureaucracy had come to be considered, at least in much travel writing, as an exemplary and enlightened model.

Turn of the Century

At the close of the nineteenth century, with Tibet well established in the popular imagination, three stories were published in Britain. In 1893 Arthur Conan Doyle, increasingly interested in psychic research and weary of his Sherlock Holmes character, ended the popular series by having his hero die. But popular heroes are not so easily disposed of, and, bowing to demand, Conan Doyle had Sherlock Holmes come back to life, as it were, some two years later in the story of *The Empty House*. Holmes then briefly explained to a startled Watson how he had survived and that he had been to Tibet disguised as a Norwegian explorer, even meeting the Dalai Lama—a bold claim given that only three Westerners had actually reached Lhasa in over a century (1980: 569). Only the world's greatest detective, it seems, could unlock the door to Lhasa. Tibet is imagined as a place of heroic aspiration beyond the known world and the reach of Western surveillance. Its remoteness defines Britain's and Europe's centrality. Sherlock Holmes' associations with the criminal underworld at the heart of the empire are transferred to a geographical underworld at its periphery. Also, at precisely this time, Conan Doyle was absorbed in research about life after death (Higham, 1976). Studies on Tibetan beliefs about death and reincarnation had appeared in London as early as 1767, and Western fascination with that facet of Tibetan culture was well established. It seems appropriate therefore, not only that Holmes should be resurrected, but that Tibet should somehow be involved.

In 1887 Rider Haggard had written the adventure mystery *She,* about three European men who discover an immortal, omniscient goddess in the heart of Africa. Disillusioned and barely escaping with their lives, they declare that they "are going away again, this time to Central Asia [and Thibet], where, if anywhere on this earth, wisdom is to be found" (1971: 7–8). Quite clearly we have entered a very different Tibetan terrain to that of Balzac or Rousseau. The Dalai Lama's role as omnipotent head of a vast system of civic and religious government has here become overshadowed by his spiritual presence. Interest in Tibetan occult feats and mystical insights was not merely confined to Madame Blavatsky's circle of Theosophists believing her account of Tibetan spiritual masters communicating with humanity through telepathy. An omnipotent immortal goddess in Africa is replaced by the wisdom of a living god in Lhasa.

Kipling's celebrated novel of 1898, *Kim,* is located at the heart of the Great Game, the imperial rivalry between Britain and Russia around the northern borders of India. While Tibet always remains out of sight, a no man's land just over the horizon, an old lama on pilgrimage to India plays a central role in the story. This delightful Tibetan—earthy but spiritual, wise but not in the ways of the world, kindly but firm— found a congenial home in the British imagination at the turn of the century. In this story, Tibet is mysterious and elusive, albeit benign and nonthreatening.

When the old lama visits a museum, the British curator shows him photographs of his monastery in Tibet (1963: 9–17). While astonished by this display of European magic, the Tibetan's faith stands firm. Here Kipling touches upon a tension between the West's technological supremacy and its religious doubt. So, while each of these fin-de-siècle stories confidently assumes the legitimacy of an imperial presence in and around Tibet, they also simultaneously reveal an imperial uncertainty about its deepest values. Although politically weak, Tibet, by virtue of a dovetailing of imperial and psychological demands, had geo-mystical power.

With *Kim,* as with Blavatsky's earlier speculations about mahatmas, those imagined Himalayan masters influencing and controlling the spiritual destiny of humanity from their awesome mountain heights, fiction becomes real. So, members of the 1904 British military expedition to Lhasa whimsically kept one eye open for any sign both of mahatmas and of "Kim's lama" or at least used this fictional character as a measure for judging any real lamas they met. It was often with great sadness that they reported the failure of reality to live up to expectations (Bishop, 1989). In an almost symbiotic relationship we find that time and again fiction has influenced the expectations of travelers to Tibet, while travelers' tales in turn provide the raw material for fiction.

Between the Wars

As the twentieth century begins we enter a new set of fantasies. James Hilton's classic of 1933, *Lost Horizon,* is the first Western novel to be mainly located in Tibet. With its invention of the word and world of "Shangri-la" it quickly became both bestseller and Hollywood success. A spiritual community lives hidden in a remote, secret valley, where the knowledge and treasures of civilization were being stored until an anticipated Dark Age had passed. Then, after all the expected destruction, Shangri-la would seed a new dawn, a new renaissance.

At this time Western fantasies about Tibet and its religion had achieved their most coherent form (Bishop, 1989). It was imagined as a land outside the grid of regulated space and time that seemed to be engulfing the rest of the globe. Entering Tibet was imagined as an initiation, as going across a threshold into another world, as going backward in time. Tibet was imagined by many as a dream or fairy-tale land outside of history. It was also imagined by many explorers, travelers, mystics, and dreamers, to be an eternal sanctuary, indifferent to time and space, where spiritual values could be protected. Tibet seemed to offer wisdom, guidance, order, and archaic continuity to an increasingly disillusioned West, particularly in the aftermath of the First World War. It is precisely within this stream of fantasy that Hilton's Shangri-la belongs. However, the iconography of Shangri-la undergoes an extraordinary shift from novel to film, in which, despite a proliferation of readily available visual images, any remote connection to Tibetan aesthetics is abandoned for a Sino-modernism—cool, clean-lined, well-ordered, and spacious architecture.[4]

But this complex utopian fantasy was overshadowed by a sense of loss, a belief that traditional Tibet was doomed, that its time was quickly running out. The main threat was imagined as coming from an unstoppable process of globalization, producing a uniform, dreary materialism. In such an imaginative climate the utopian spiritual fantasy could no longer be entrusted to the literal geographical place. The myth of Shangri-la was born, the hidden valley into which the essence of Western fantasies about Tibet was alchemically concentrated and distilled. In a period of environmental and cultural anxiety, Tibet as Shangri-la was a fertile paradise in the midst of a global wilderness; to an era sickened by an increase in life's tempo and complexity, it was a place where time almost stopped and repose was mandatory (Bishop, 1989).

The image of the reincarnated lamas, with the Dalai Lama as the prime example, was crucial. The Dalai Lama was imagined by many as the final embodiment of the divine Royal Father, the last of an ancient lineage of god-kings (Bishop, 1993). In the 1920s, the French poet, actor, and playwright Antonin Artaud wrote an open letter to the Dalai Lama, begging for help, guidance, and instruction: "O Grand Lama, give us, grace us with your illuminations in a language our contaminated European minds can understand, and if need be, transform our Mind, create for us a mind turned entirely toward those perfect summits.... Teach us, O Lama...how we may no longer be earthbound" (1962: 64). This letter marks the imaginative gulf between the Paris of Artaud and that of Balzac, and in conjunction with Hilton's Shangri-la would seem to confirm the increasing disillusionment and desperation felt by many Westerners toward their own civilization and religion. But Tibet was not only being idealized at that time. Travel writing was beginning to reveal the negative impact of tourism and a quest for quick visual delights. Also, the upsurge in psychic research meant that the geographical actuality of Tibet sometimes receded in importance to the mystical landscapes mapped out by spiritual techniques such as the recently revealed *Tibetan Book of the Dead*. But by the same token, decades of familiarity with Tibet on the part of Western, particularly British, diplomats and travelers began to strip it of its mythic associations.

In Rumer Godden's 1939 novel *Black Narcissus*, the references to

Tibet are extremely brief. A group of European nuns attempts to establish a center for prayer, healing, and education in a remote former pleasure palace high in the foothills of the Himalayas. Their faith and calling are tested by this strange milieu, and eventually the attempt is abandoned. Tibetan references hover quietly around the edges: A Tibetan monk occasionally passes by in the distance; prayer flags flutter; yak tails are on sale in the market. The Tibetan images are not flattering: dirty, smelly, noisy, earthy—"a low form of Buddhism, that is in reality animism" (1971: 157). Indeed, spiritual serenity is not portrayed by Tibetan Buddhism, but by an old Hindu yogi.

The mountains, the Himalayas, envelop, surround, and define the drama. And beyond the mountains lies Tibet—never mentioned, only suggested. Certainly it was not a Shangri-la. The wind coming down the valley from the mountains and from Tibet beyond is constantly disturbing and unsettling, offering both promise and threat.

Post-War Images

In 1947 *Black Narcissus* was made into a highly successful film. Significantly, given the paucity of direct references to Tibet in the novel, the film opens with a dramatic image of two six-meter-long Tibetan Buddhist horns, *radongs*, being blown by monks dressed in the full ceremonial attire of Tibetan Buddhism. Later, at a critical point we hear the mournful sound of the horns, mingled with the wind, coming down the valley from the high Himalayas. Ritual sound and the incessant mountain wind tell of Tibet's presence, beyond even the remoteness and austerity of the former palace where the nuns are struggling. The sporadic presence of Tibet in the novel is condensed in the film into a single, striking image. But the film has lost all the negative connotations about Tibet that were to be found in the novel. Tibet is merely a disturbing presence just at the edge of the frame. Around the same time, the novel *Kim* was turned into a Hollywood film with a similar softening of ambivalence whether toward Tibet or the West.

The process of transforming a novel into a film needs to be examined—in terms of any shift in both narrative and iconographic emphasis, of the change of genre and medium, of the way in which the genre and medium were contextualized and understood at the time (Samuel, 1995). For example, we need consider the difference in status at the time between Rumer Godden's story as a philosophical, albeit popular, novel and as a human interest motion picture—the one considered perhaps slightly educational, the other as part of an entertainment industry, as part of mass culture with all its negative connotations. Such considerations tell us not only about the text's production but also about the possibilities of its consumption.

High Valley, written in 1949 by the Australian partnership of Charmian Clift and George Johnston, is set entirely in Tibet and contains no European characters. Johnston had already written about his visit to Tibet three years previously, allowing us a unique opportunity to compare travel account (1947) with novel. As a weary war correspondent, he had taken advantage of a chance opportunity to wander on horseback and live with Tibetan nomads. But, while distrustful of the monks' immense, almost absolute, power, he did not question the veracity of their spiritual claims. This is an important image about Tibet: accepting the spiritual/parapsychological feats but not necessarily liking them or approving of their use. *High Valley* is a romance with echoes of *Romeo and Juliet*, about a displaced young Chinese man and a young Tibetan woman who fall in love with consequences that are both tragic and inspiring. But Tibet was not just a convenient location for a romance. Something about the place was crucial for the story— perhaps the conflict between, on the one hand, the individual's freedom to believe and to love, and, on the other hand, the collective demands of family and state. Although deeply concerned with existential and even spiritual values, this novel has nothing to do with the "magic and mystery" genre, or the adventure yarn.

High Valley is unusual in fiction about Tibet because it contains no grand plot, no world-threatening adventure, and no imperial designs and because it reveals a quiet care for everyday things. Perhaps this is because it was partly written by someone who had spent time traveling in Tibet and hence showed a sensitivity toward the details of daily life that is so often the hallmark of travel writing. Or, perhaps Charmian Clift's coauthorship was crucial. Fantasies about Tibet are acutely gendered. It may be a cliché, but fiction written or cowritten by women, such as *Black Narcissus,* shows concern for personalities, rather than for action adventures or imperial issues. For example, Han Suyin drew on her direct experience of the 1956 coronation of Nepal's king for the novel *The Mountain Is Young* (1958). Set entirely in Kathmandu, it too is a story of the search both for love and spiritual meaning. Tibet is even more remote, more mysterious than her beloved Nepal. Yet there is a strange sophistication about the few Tibetans in this story, a worldly cosmopolitanism that contrasts with the innocence and artistry of the people living in the Kathmandu Valley. So, the first Tibetans we encounter, at Kathmandu's new airport, are carrying cinecameras and an electric fan. Extraordinary symbols of modern consumption in the mid-1950s! Nevertheless, despite Suyin's almost negative attitude toward Tibet, it still partakes of Nepal's primal innocence as contrasted with Western materialism, cynicism, and spiritual weariness.[5] Perhaps to that extent there is a lingering trace of Shangri-la, albeit one without its utopian, global pretensions, or its aversion to the benefits of modern technology. Significantly, tourists make their first clichéd appearance in Tibet-related fiction.[6]

Like *High Valley,* Lionel Davidson's 1962 novel *The Rose of Tibet* presents a complex and ambivalent image of that country. Unlike travel writing of the time, Tibet is presented in both novels as a contradictory world both of sublime wisdom and gross superstition, of great compassion and terrible cruelty. But unlike *High Valley,* it is still a tale of intrigue, of Tibet caught in global imperial struggles. Davidson's work shows evidence of considerable research and skillfully uses internal monastic and political rivalry within Tibet. As in *High Valley,* the monasticism is presented ambivalently—power, worldliness, and greed are mixed with devotion, duty, and wisdom. Both novels, from completely opposite directions, tell of a place in conflict, of struggles over spiritual and secular power, a place where everyday life is interwoven with sexual passion and dark, occult murmurings.

The Rose of Tibet can be seen as the sophisticated heir to numerous adventure books of the immediate postwar period that were set in Tibet. Written primarily for older boys, their descriptions of Tibetan culture are often poor. But they expose a crucial split between themselves and travel writing. I have argued elsewhere that from the 1920s onward, paradox was lost in descriptions of Tibet (Bishop, 1989). In travel writing we increasingly find exemplary images of Tibetan culture: a utopian land without shadow. However, these children's stories all show an ambivalent attitude toward Tibet. Historically this was a time of great unrest and intrigue within Tibet, a state of affairs fully exploited by fiction.

For example, in the story *On the World's Roof,* Hitler escapes at the end of the Second World War and flees to Tibet along with a small group of SS (Duff, 1950). They plan literally to rain atomic bombs down from the unassailable "roof of the world" onto the major cities, bombarding them into submission. A lone English youth, born and raised in Tibet by a missionary doctor, is parachuted into a remote region to link up with Tibetans opposed to Hitler's plans. Most Tibetans oppose Hitler, but others support him. Corruption and lust for power are seen as integral to Tibetan religious government at the highest level, which is also portrayed as being harsh, with torture being used by good and bad alike. This is more akin to late nineteenth-century Western beliefs than mid-twentieth-century ones. Hitler is finally executed by two Tibetan monks—they wanted to do it themselves, quickly and secretly, so as to forestall any excuse for a Western invasion of Tibet.

The novel fits into a narrow hiatus between the end of the Second World War and the beginning of the Cold War. Hitler and the SS will soon be replaced by the Communists in this drama. It recalls the shadow side to the mahatmas and other fantasies about world rulers influencing, even controlling, the destiny of all humanity from Tibet at the high center of the world, its axis mundi, where extremes are concentrated. At that time atomic power was a symbol both of absolute good and evil, having the potential for both unlimited creation and destruction.

In another such novel, *The Lost World of Everest,* three British male mountaineers are attempting to climb Everest (Gray, 1941). Close to the summit they are swept into a mysterious valley, which is hidden from view by a permanent layer of dense cloud and constant turbulent winds. This is no Shangri-la. There seems to be no way out of the high-walled valley, but a route is found that takes them on a descent into the very interior of Mount Everest. At one point while inside a tunnel, they peer down through a hole, which turns out to be in the roof of an immense cavern many miles in length. Thousands of feet below they see a picturesque landscape of villages, of fields and meadows laid out in the style of early nineteenth-century rural England. The people living in this picture-postcard landscape are descendants of British survivors of the Indian Mutiny of 1857 who had fled to take refuge in a cave. But the entrance had been sealed by Indian rebels, forcing the refugees to find their way to the huge cavern that would become their home for the next one hundred years. Here they shaped their world in accordance with the memories of their distant homeland, memories harking back to the pre-Victorian period. The three modern intruders, after many adventures, eventually lead the "people of the lost world" out from their strange prison and into the glare, confusions, and doubts of modernity.

Identities of place are formed through a constant process of negotiation between fantasies of Self and Other, of Home and Away, of Here and There. If Shangri-la was the supreme 1930s embodiment of a utopian English "Otherness," then Little England was the expression of an idealized "Self." They were the extreme polarities of an imperial identity that spanned the entire empire from heartland to its outermost frontier (Bishop, 1993).

Ever since the 1920s Everest had been a prime symbol for Britain, expressing its right to global leadership through courage, technology, and imperial history, as well as being what was called "a symbol of the loftiest spiritual height" (Ruttledge, 1938: 11). By virtue of its position within the British sphere of control and influence, Everest was placed out of bounds to foreign expeditions for many years—a source of much resentment.

While a victorious post–World War Two Britain was imagined to be safe, it was exhausted. Confidence in the empire had been shaken. Bits of British identity could no longer be entrusted to the far-flung landscapes of a disintegrating Empire. With India recently independent and Tibet about to be lost to China, it was clearly time for Britishness to reclaim its mythic fragments, those split-off, even forgotten and lost parts of its identity that had been casually located in the remotest regions of the globe. Hence this microcosm of Little England, while securely located within the very heart of the highest and still unconquered "British" mountain, had to be returned to the imperial heartland. A war-weary Britain sought to reclaim such healing and revitalizing images that lay beyond the mass madness and destruction of industrialization. The heroic spirit expressed in the attempts to conquer Everest now released a pure Little England from its long imprisonment and exile, like a Sleeping Beauty, and returned it to where it truly belonged, to Britain itself.

I am constantly surprised by the willingness and ability of such authors to use topical events. For example, written in 1949, *Stuart in Tibet* is concerned with a struggle over the identification of the new Dalai Lama between a child chosen by Tibetans and one chosen by the Nationalist Chinese (Buckley, 1949). India is independent, but Tibet is presented as being friendly with Britain. Like the previous novel, this story is part of a renegotiation of British imperial boundaries—the postwar contours of empire. However, while British imperialism may be receding, in this novel it is still confident about its ability and right to intervene in the internal affairs of Tibet.

By 1955, when *The Lost Glacier* was written, Tibet was already being absorbed into China (Styles, 1955). An unmapped piece of territory is discovered on the border between Tibet and Nepal, offering a secret passage through the mountains for an aggressive Communist China. This echoes the actual fears of the British in India over one hundred years before, concerned that the Himalayan wall guarding the northern frontier of its Indian Empire might not be as impregnable as hoped due to the discovery of innumerable unmapped passes. A race begins between Britain and China to find this lost valley. Significantly, it is the last home of the yeti, intelligent and resourceful creatures who even side with the British to defeat the Communist Chinese soldiers invading their valley.

This story is a last gasp of the fantasy that placed Tibet at the center of global politics, a vital yet vulnerable place upon which rests the fate of the world. The geo-political imagination had begun to change. This is emphasized in *The Road to Samarkand*. Almost alone among fiction it approaches Tibet from the north, from Central Asia

(O'Brian, 1976). Set in the interwar years and drawing upon accounts of archaeological expeditions by the likes of Aurel Stein and Sven Hedin, the novel portrays Tibet becoming integrated into the turmoil caused by the collapse of imperial Chinese authority along the Silk Road. Tibet's kinship with Mongolia comes to the foreground. The rigors of landscape combine with militant anti-Western lamas to create an atmosphere of intense hardship. Drawn into this unstable geo-political sphere, one is made quite aware of extreme anti-Western sentiments. There is no imperial confidence in the novel, no assumption that the West has any claim to, or even right to enter, this part of the world.

Contemporary Images

By the mid-1960s Tibet had virtually ceased to have global significance for the West. So too, Shangri-la was moribund as a geographical fantasy. We had begun to enter the era of jet aircraft, space satellites, high-tech global communications, and widespread tourism. Much about Tibet had become demystified. The exile of the Dalai Lama along with a considerable section of the monastic elite had become a long-term fact. The coherence of Western fantasies about Tibet had become fragmented, leaving only old traces and new meanings. Hergé's famous comic *Tin Tin in Tibet,* for example, utilizes a full range of Tibetan stereotypes—including the yeti, levitating, and telepathic monks, *and* a Grand Lama—to make fun of Western clichés (Hergé, 1972). We also encounter a new concern about Tibet's plight, revealed, for example, in a book for younger children, *Wombat and Emu Trekking in Tibet.* Written in 1989 by the Australian woman adventurer Sorrel Wilby, who also wrote a book about her solo crossing of Tibet, it is respectful of Tibetan traditional culture.

There is absolutely no hint whatsoever of Tibet in Somerset Maugham's novel *The Razor's Edge,* which was first published in 1944. The protagonist tells instead of his search in the 1930s for meaning and spiritual wisdom while living with a Hindu teacher in India for many years. However, when the novel was turned into a film in 1984, Hinduism is replaced by Tibetan Buddhism, the ashram by a monastery high in the Himalayas. We could speculate about the film's relocation of spirituality. Perhaps the Hindu guru had become a cliché or partly discredited in the West around this time? As in Bertolucci's recent film *The Little Buddha,* all Tibetan monks are kind and wise, conflict and doubt are minimized.[7] The exiled Tibetan lamas, seemingly divorced from the confusions of secular government, have become idealized. In the last third of the twentieth century, Tibetan Buddhism has become an unambiguous symbol of benign spirituality and parapsychological attainments for a considerable number of non-Buddhist Westerners.

However, there are still lingering traces of the concern about absolute power, which, as we have seen, goes back to Balzac and Rousseau. Individual freedom struggling against the two immense systems of Tibetan theocracy and Chinese Communism is explored in a play by Stephen Lowe, first performed in 1981 in London. But such criticisms of monastic power are rare in a milieu that has seen a split between religious and secular power. Tibetan Buddhism is now portrayed, understandably, as victim. It is no longer the absolute authority in Tibetan culture and has apparently been freed of its political shadow.

We also still come across traces of Tibet as a place where impossible creatures can be imagined. There is a reference to wrathful *bardo* visions in Borges' work *The Book of Imaginary Beings,* although it is typical of the second half of the twentieth century that such a reference is very restrained (1974).

In Arthur C. Clarke's 1960s short story *The Nine Billion Names of God,* a Tibetan monastic community in the Himalayas purchases the very latest and most powerful computer to establish all the names of god, following which the world comes to an end (1972). This story points back to the resourceful use in old Tibet of technology to construct prayer machines. But it also points forward to the reimagining of Tibet using the language of technoculture. It is as if the advent of cyberspace has allowed Tibet to reemerge at a center of global apocalyptic concern, albeit only virtually. A recent TV advertisement for IBM personal computers shows a number of meditating monks sitting amid high mountains. Despite confusing iconography there are clear Tibetan overtones. No computer can be seen, but instead we "hear" a telepathic conversation extolling the wonders of their new IBM machines (see also Barglow, 1994: 195–202). Widespread acceptance or credulity toward Tibetan parapsychological feats is used to reinforce the claims made for computer-enhanced communication. Resonances are established between spiritual space-time and that of cyberspace. This advertisement fits into the long tradition going back to Blavatsky involving long-range communication with Tibetan wisdom. One commentator perceptively refers to an "electronic Shangri-la" (Adams, 1995).

This postmodern mix of parallel worlds of space-time, surreality, and occult powers also found expression in David Lynch's television cult classic of the late 1980s, *Twin Peaks*, where a map of Tibet and vaguely Tibetan techniques are used by an FBI agent in a desperate attempt to solve a disturbing murder. Tibet is portrayed as a beacon from whence to take bearings and guidance into the underworld. Such references to Tibet as part of the cyber age point to a complete split with contemporary travel accounts, which are generally indifferent, even hostile, to technological intrusion (for example, Matthiessen, 1980; Wilby, 1989).

Two novels from the 1980s by William Burroughs bring us up to date. In *Cities of the Red Night*, an unknown, deadly virus is coming from Tibet and other such places along the outer margins of Western control. But the novel expresses ambivalence about the power of this virus: Its destructiveness could perhaps be purging and cleansing of Western culture. However, this interpretation would reduce Burroughs' story into a simple morality tale, losing its ambiguity and wit toward both the West and the East. Certainly in the second novel, wit and ambiguity come to the fore. *The Western Lands* is a postmodern meditation on the landscape of death and grief, in which Tibet has a single mention: "The road to the Western Lands," he writes, "is by definition the most dangerous road in the world, for it is a journey beyond Death, beyond...Fear and Danger.... The Egyptians and the Tibetans made this journey after Death, and their Books of the Dead set forth very precise instructions—as precise as they are arbitrary" (1988: 125). Burroughs' remarks resonate with the upsurge of interest in Tibetan reflections on death and dying, but particularly important, from the perspective of a *poetics*, is the novel's ability to sustain paradox and contradiction, especially both belief and incredulity.

To study fantasies about Tibet is to understand often oppressive mystificatory and ideological processes (Lopez, 1995c). Also, through these moments when an image of Tibet is mobilized, a window is opened onto Western fears, hopes, and desires. Such a study is certainly not just a slightly irritating but unfortunately necessary moment of reflection on our way to refining some truth about Tibet, a passing phase of scholarly clarification. Metaphor and fantasy are revealed at every level of any text's construction. Indeed they, and the participation in myth, are inevitable aspects of any attempt to make meaning, to sustain belief and experience, or to organize understanding, irrespective of whether the perspective comes from scholarship, popular culture, or personal experience. The notion of myth-making must be deepened beyond simple notions of right or wrong, as if myth is just an obfuscation, a mystification or defilement of reasoned objectivity. For example, Derrida refers to "the white mythology which reassembles and reflects the culture of the West: the white man [sic] takes his own mythology...for the universal form of that he must still wish to call Reason" (1982: 213). Similarly, the geographer Denis Cosgrove writes: "Scientific discourse has always been metaphorical...but has proclaimed a privileged 'truth' for its metaphors or models in representing reality" (1990: 345). If we begin to give validity to the myth-making process, then through a poetics (Kearney, 1988) we can begin to evaluate it on its own terms and to explore the imaginative implications of various belief systems, whether they be scientific, political, religious, or just idiosyncratically individual. We also begin to understand our own inevitable participation in the myth of Tibet.

Even in glimpses, Tibet has been a vital landscape by which Western authors, either knowingly or unknowingly, have taken bearings on issues crucial for their own cultures and have sought to explore the contours of their own identity. Various forms of overt fictionalizing about Tibet—novel, short story, film, travel writing—seem to follow their own specific, imaginative trajectories. For example, novel and short story have often formed a contrapuntal relationship with travel writing. By no means has Tibet always been portrayed simply as a Shangri-la. More than travel writing, or even film, novels and short stories have, since the 1940s, sustained an ambivalence toward Tibetan culture, generally refusing to characterize it either as a utopia or as a simple answer to Western problems and anxieties.

Notes

1 The terms Western and Eastern are problematic, continuing, as they do, some kind of essential polarization, which is in itself a fundamental characteristic of an orientalist perspective (Said, 1979). They are also problematic in that they fail to differentiate between the many specific cultures whether in Europe, Asia, America, and so on. This paper, for example, while ranging quite broadly for its sources, nevertheless draws mostly on texts from an English-speaking background. Partly this reflects the balance of output historically, but it is also a product of my own experience and social circumstances. Finally, the terms Western and Eastern fail to differentiate within particular cultures in terms of class, gender, age, ethnicity, and so on. Their use in this paper, must therefore be understood only as a form of shorthand as befits a short but broad outline sketch.

2 This paper addresses images of Tibet in Western literature, but for a fuller understanding should also address the way in which the notion of literature and literariness has, through concepts of "text" and "reading" applied almost universally to natural, social, and cultural phenomena, become established at the heart of contemporary Western social sciences. By such a process Tibet can be reduced to just another "text" to be "read." Such a literary metaphoricity should not obscure the crucial visuality of Western fantasies about Tibet, nor reduce the complex, polyvalent fantasy-making process to one derived solely from literary metaphors.

3 Another similar example of the late eighteenth-century common usage of Tibetan imagery that focuses on the absolute authority and respect accorded to the Dalai Lama comes from an account of Captain Cook's first visit to Hawaii in January 1779. Lieutenant James King of HMS Resolution said that one of the most sacred and powerful of the local priests was revered like the Dalai Lama (Windshuttle, 1994: 86–87). (I'm grateful to Barry Jeremson for drawing my attention to this reference.)

4 While most travel accounts of Tibet have extensively used illustrations, both sketches and etchings, for over two hundred years, a new visuality of Tibet occurred in the 1930s. This was aided by the invention of the portable camera and by the widespread adoption of techniques for the quick, cheap reproduction of photographs in magazines, as well as, to a certain extent, advances in color processing. This new visuality can be seen in collections such as R. Jones Tung's *A Portrait of Lost Tibet* (1980), or the photo-essays accompanying various articles in *The Geographical Magazine* (e.g., Greene, 1936; O'Connor, 1937). It is in contrast to the lack of visual fidelity in films of the time such as *Lost Horizon* (1937).

5 It is interesting to consider Han Suyin's 1958 depiction of Tibetans in her account of visiting Tibet in 1975, which is one of the few to actually praise the effects of Chinese occupation (1977).

6 The beginnings of a tourist-traveler type of rhetoric, if not actual tourism itself, in Tibet probably dates from such works as Robert Byron's *First Russia, Then Tibet* of 1933. It is certainly evident in Lowell Thomas Jr.'s 1950 account *Out of this World*.

7 *The Little Buddha* was made with assistance from Tibetan monks. It is worth comparing *The Little Buddha* with a film made in 1974 by Bertolucci's Italian colleague Liliana Cavani. Shortly after making *The Night Porter* with its extraordinarily dark tale of brutal power and unconscious attraction, she made *Milarepa* for Italian television. Located in contemporary Italy, a young student and his professor have a minor accident in their car en route to the airport to catch a flight to Tibet to research Milarepa's travels. Temporarily stranded by the roadside, they begin an imaginary journey through eleventh-century Tibet. The student takes the role of Milarepa, and the professor becomes Marpa. The ensuing fantasy echoes Castanada's mystical relationship with Don Juan (Witcombe, 1982).

THE DEVELOPMENT
IN PERCEPTIONS OF TIBETAN ART

FROM GOLDEN IDOLS TO ULTIMATE REALITY

Heather Stoddard

THIS PAPER IS ABOUT the rich and mystical art of Vajrayāna—the "seamless expression of Tibet's complex culture"[1]—and the evolution of its perception both outside and inside Tibet.

A good starting point is the vision presented to the outside world at the end of the twentieth century in the exhibition *Wisdom and Compassion*, to which this volume ultimately owes its existence. The exhibition presents—one might say, in a positive sense—a vast panorama of the "myth of Tibet," in which both the uninitiated observer and the Buddhist believer may bask, transported by the extraordinary visual feast offered therein.

I shall attempt to analyze the present-day "myth of Tibet" as it surfaces through the exhibition, and then go back in time to observe a few contrasting moments in its evolution. I take this myth to be not a bilateral East-West dialogue, but rather a complex and many-headed, many-armed creature, like great *yidam* "tutelary" or protector deity in tantric art, made up of many influences and qualities, capable of multiple transformations and of transplanting itself to other lands and contexts. Its properties are essentially neutral, being used and directed in positive or negative ways according to the individual or the society that takes hold of and develops it. An essential component, no doubt the essential component, is, as Giuseppe Tucci well described it, the *mysterium magnum*.[2] The art of Tibet is its visual, tangible expression.

Wisdom and Compassion is in fact the most comprehensive overview of the content and meaning of the art of Tibet to be attempted so far.[3] Marilyn Rhie's chapter on "Aesthetics, Chronology and Styles" gives a general overview, but this is fundamentally not a historical study, and is, rather, a "magnificent display," showing that the present-day understanding of Vajrayāna Buddhism (which seems to the author well on its way to becoming a world religion) has gone far beyond Orientalist concepts in which the "East" (here represented by Tibet) is a curious and exotic object of research being carried out by "objective" and "rational" human beings from a dominant Western, Christian, and scientific world. The "West" is no longer so sure about the reliability of its own assumptions and is moving toward a more subtle and shifting understanding of reality. A different kind of dialogue with the "East" is coming to the surface, especially in the fields of the neurosciences and physics. In this way the two fundamentally opposing Jungian "styles" of the "introspective" East and the "extrovert" West,[4] are fading fast, and perhaps in the long run, merging.

The original concept of the exhibition was that of a giant, 3-D maṇḍala, representing the visual or physical aspect of the teachings of the Buddha, being literally the "Body" of the Buddha in the trilogy of the "supports" of his Body, Speech, and Mind, in contrast to the dual concept of reality, divided into mind and matter in the West. In Tibet art and religion are one, and it is scarcely possible to understand and appreciate the visual representations out of their religious context.

Although the 3-D maṇḍala construction was not built, the idea of the maṇḍala was still used in the exhibition as a means of "initiation" into the meaning of Vajrayāna Buddhism, a way of exploring and entering its symbolic world. This particular maṇḍala of *Wisdom and Compassion* is unique, however, since it is not one that can be found in any of the paintings or three-dimensional *blos lang* maṇḍalas produced in Tibet. Instead of a central deity surrounded by his or her main entourage of divine beings distributed throughout the four quarters, here we find the four quarters of the palace and its residents divided up between the four schools of Tibetan Buddhism, showing their lineages and the particular style of representation each one prefers. On the other hand, within the context of Vajrayāna, all these Tibetan lineages

Fig. 1 Dalai Lama, fresco, Samye Monastery

do inhabit and belong fully to the buddha maṇḍala, and in fact there do exist some rare maṇḍalas with human beings inside the inner ring.[5]

The other aspect of the exhibition is the presentation of a distinctive body of fine art, equal in aesthetic value to any other artistic tradition in the world.[6] This is based on the traditional Western understanding of what an exhibition should be, in that it seeks to draw attention to each object as an individual work of art, attributing both aesthetic value and historical context to each one. As such the exhibition falls both inside and outside of the tradition. It is part of a developing "myth" within the Tibetan diaspora. It is a new construct, based on a practical desire to communicate the sublime reality and exquisite aesthetics of a new (to the Western public) and little-known religion.

The presentation of Tibetan Buddhism through the exhibition is a reflection of this newly accessible, comprehensible world image enacted by the Dalai Lama himself. He is no longer the mysterious incarnation of a divine being living far above the mundane world, ruling as an incarnation of Avalokiteśvara, or as a Central Asian "pontif," or "god-king" from the immense solitudes of his Potala Palace. He is, in his own words, "a simple monk," traveling the world, communicating an equally "simple" message of love and peace to all humanity. At the same time, he is incessantly giving, in all corners of the globe, the great and complex initiation into the Kālacakra, the tantric wheel of time, to all beings who wish to attend.

This is a far cry from the mysterious and decadent image of esoteric Buddhism that flowered in the West, especially in the nineteenth and the first half of the twentieth centuries. The exhibition breathes "l'air du temps," and demonstrates an unveiled Vajrayāna, explaining first and foremost the sexual imagery,[7] rendering comprehensible the vast pantheon, and showing the wealth of styles and the different schools as they developed in Tibet.

Dr. Pal's[8] criticism of the exhibition, that over half of the objects do not even come from Tibet, but from elsewhere in Asia, does not detract, but on the contrary, demonstrates the widespread, enduring influence of this tradition beyond the frontiers of the Land of Snows. This adds precisely to its wealth. In this way, the exhibition projects rather the concept of wisdom and compassion as knowing no boundaries, and the "spiritual empire" of Tibet, which is both a historical and present-day "reality." This positive image proclaims that Tibet was not that "dark," closed land described by British imperialists (especially Waddell) a century ago, ruled over by an idolatrous priesthood who jealously guarded the secrets of their degenerate and demoniacal system of belief.[9] We shall come back to this later.

Vajrayāna developed first in India over several centuries before spreading to Kashmir, Nepal, Central Asia, Tibet, China, Japan, Indonesia, and Burma. In its Tibetan form it was vitally present in a whole series of Asian empires: after establishing itself as the religion of the ruling class in sPu rgyal, the Tibetan dynasty of the seventh century, Vajrayāna spread to their Central Asian territories, including Dun-

Fig. 2 Yab-yum representation, bronze

huang, and on into those of the Tangut, Mongol, Ming, and Manchu Empires; it took hold also in Guomindang China (which had undisguised imperial pretensions), and last but not least in the present Chinese Communist empire.[10] At this present moment, Beijing is obliged to acknowledge the living presence of Tibetan Buddhism and to play according to the established set of rules.[11]

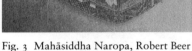

Fig. 3 Mahāsiddha Naropa, Robert Beer   Fig. 4 Gongkar Gyatso: Buddha

Vajrayāna still is the principal religion in Ladakh, northern Nepal, Sikkim, and Bhutan. It is experiencing a revival at present among the Mongolian peoples, in Mongolia and Siberia, and is now spreading through the world at large. A future exhibition might well include examples of Tibetan art from Scotland (by Sherab Palden or Robert Beer), France, or the United States, or even from modern-day Lhasa, where artists like Gongkar Gyatso[12] are experimenting with new styles. A superb *mthong grol* ("liberation on sight") or *gos sku* giant silk appliqué *thangka* was recently made for Tshurphu Monastery in Tibet. The result of a joint international effort, it was designed by an American-Franco-Vietnamese couple, sewn impeccably by six Tibetan women in the Lhasa Tent Factory, and blessed by the Karmapa hierarchy in exile.[13] The "myth of Tibet" and its art is thriving and well.

The globalization of Tibetan Buddhist culture (including its art) has been made possible at the end of the twentieth century by considerable evolution in the diffusion of knowledge of Vajrayāna Buddhism through textual study and practical knowledge gained over the last century, and especially through the prolonged and real exchange between

Tibetans and Westerners, both scholars and Buddhist practitioners, since the 1960s. This process has made the results of research much more reliable and has been instrumental in breaking down the nineteenth- and twentieth-century Orientalist concept of "objective study," which was very much the prevailing dogma in Western universities in the late 1960s, when I began my studies.

The Mid–Twentieth Century: Tibet in Exile and Orientalism in London

If I may be permitted to take my own experience as an example, I believe that the image of Tibetan art in the West has changed significantly over the last thirty years. I left art school in London in 1965 to travel to India and, after a year in Dharamsala, was accepted as a traditional apprentice to Champa-la, *thangka* painter to His Holiness the Dalai Lama. My duties were to wash his paint pots and bring his tea. He

Fig. 5 The thangka painter Champa-la

Fig. 6 Statue of King Songtsen Gampo, in the background bronze of the eleven-headed
Avalokiteśvara, Potala, Lhasa.

also taught me how to stretch and prepare the cotton cloth for painting
and how to make charcoal and brushes. But I would have to wait to
meet Sherab Palden in Samyeling, Scotland, before being allowed to
draw, again and again, the painstaking iconometric image of the Buddha.

At that time, 1966, the full force of the destructive energy of the
Cultural Revolution was lashing out in Tibet. One day there arrived in
Dharamsala two clay masks, so damaged that their original form was
virtually undistinguishable, and yet the entire Tibetan community
there—man, woman, and child, young and old—went to receive blessings from them. I followed the crowd, the only Westerner present, won-
dering at the quiet concentration of that mass of people. As I passed in
front of the battered faces, I knew little of their significance, but could
feel the intense emotion surrounding them and understood that these
two surviving heads belonged to an image that represented the essence
of the identity of a whole people. They belonged to the standing eleven-
headed Avalokiteśvara image in the Jokhang in Lhasa, which was at

the same time the portrait of Srong btsan sgam po, first emperor and unifier of Tibet. This image had been pulled to the ground and destroyed when the temple was desecrated by the Red Guards. The two masks were saved in the scramble and secretly brought out of the country. They are now enshrined as holy relics of the Tibetan community in exile.

The meaning and function of art in Tibetan society, in absolute contrast to "art for art's sake" in the West in the mid–twentieth century, was beginning to dawn on me.[14]

On returning to England in 1967, I became a student in the School of Oriental and African Studies (SOAS), not knowing then that this high seat of learning was created by Lord Curzon as "part of the necessary furniture of empire," because "Oriental studies were no intellectual luxury," but "a great imperial obligation."[15] I discovered and read passionately *Tibetan Painted Scrolls* and *Indo-Tibetica* by Giuseppe Tucci and *Tibetan Paintings* by George Roerich, then looked further. In spite of these richly documented and well-founded studies based on long-term, serious research inside Tibet, the image of Tibetan art in the West was at that time marked by a stereotyped attitude concerning Tibet itself, both inside and outside the university walls. I was discovering Orientalism in England and the structures and presuppositions of the West concerning "objective" study.

Thus in the late 1960s, shortly after the exodus of the Dalai Lama and one hundred thousand refugees, Tibet, the "object" of research under consideration, was only worthy of interest for philologists and students of the northern and eastern branches of Buddhism in China, Japan, and also India, in as much as the original Sanskrit manuscripts had been lost. Tibetan civilization itself was considered anecdotal. It was dead; its language, the "Latin of Central Asia." In SOAS the study of indigenous literature was not permitted (although Dr. Snellgrove himself was studying Bonpo texts with Bonpo scholars).

The art of Tibet was not considered art, but a late and repetitive expression by anonymous artisans who followed fixed patterns handed down by their teachers, without any individual creative leeway except in minor details of composition. It was interesting for its complex iconography and symbolism and as a visual representation of "Northern

Buddhism," but it had very little that was historical—neither dates nor identifiable artists.[16] Furthermore, Tibetan art was considered a hybrid byproduct of two major civilizations, Indian and Chinese, with little or no contribution made by the Tibetans themselves. It was said that they simply juxtaposed, in an admittedly artistic way, various elements borrowed from elsewhere.

It did not seem to occur to anyone that culture in Britain, France, and Germany, was itself hybrid, being the product of the "Christianization" of earlier indigenous systems of belief. Their art, architecture, and philosophy was, one might say, a synthetic hotch-potch, albeit well aligned and elegant, of indigenous elements and classical ones borrowed directly from Greece, Rome, and Egypt. Thus at SOAS in the 1960s, all the elements of nineteenth-century "Orientalism" as described by Edward Said were there: Tibetan culture was ossified; it had "always been the same, unchanging, uniform, and radically peculiar object."[17]

The attitude that was being inculcated (innocently, I might add) was "a kind of intellectual authority over the Orient within Western culture." Our study and research had that detailed, "serious, ponderous style of expertise" born of "objectivity."[18] There was an underlying idea (again in Said's words) "that people, places and experiences can [always] be described by a book, so much so that the book acquires a greater authority and use, even than the actuality it describes."[19] We were, like Renan, studying the "arrested development of our Oriental languages, in comparison to the mature languages and cultures of the Indo-European group." Tibet, the dead civilization, was "totally ossified and incapable of self-regeneration."[20] Anyway, the Chinese Communist Party and the Cultural Revolution had wiped what was left of it off the face of the earth.

But if this was the essentially negative image in the mid–twentieth century following the Chinese occupation of Tibet, it still represented a considerable development from the Shangri-la vision that dominated in the West in the second half of the nineteenth and the first half of the twentieth centuries.

Perhaps it could be said that we were (or at least I was) at that time beginning to move toward present attitudes and becoming (as demonstrated in the exhibition *Wisdom and Compassion*) "modern Orientalists, heroes rescuing the Orient from the obscurity, alienation, and strangeness which we ourselves had properly distinguished"![21]

It was during this period that serious, well-founded "Orientalist" research into Tibetan civilization (and I hasten to say, we in SOAS identified ourselves with this) began to establish roots, as the first

Fig. 7 Arhat Kanakavatsa

Fig. 8 Destroyed statue in Yemar

few individuals managed to stay for lengthy periods in the "Land of the Snows."

Since, in spite of heroic attempts before 1951, the majority of travelers never made it into the heart of Tibetan civilization, the imagination of those who skirted the high plateau or who tried but failed to penetrate its forbidding ramparts was captured by accounts of a land of strange religious practices, of fabulously rich temples filled with golden idols. As P. Hopkirk put it, the "British appetite for gold had first been whetted in 1775 when the Panchen Lama sent Warren Hastings a gift of some gold nuggets and gold dust."[22]

It is well known that there was a traditional taboo on mining in Tibet. However, gold is mentioned in both Tibetan and non-Tibetan sources with such regularity that it might be interesting to monitor the occurences and their context. For Tibetans, gold is the color of the buddhas, and apart from personal adornment, the vast majority of their gold was poured into the art that embellished the monasteries and temples: golden roofs and architectural motifs, books, sculpture, and painting. It is hardly surprising that during the Cultural

Fig. 9 Representation of hells

Revolution gold was scraped or melted off the faces and bodies of images, while the gold reserves kept in the Potala were transported to China.[23]

The mystery of Tibetan Buddhism was without doubt the second main attraction that invited adventurous travelers, from the seventeenth century onward, to climb the inaccessible passes. The fascination took various forms. We do not have time to go through all the descriptions of wonder here, but when Candler finally arrived, "The Potala surpassed the greatest expectations. The golden domes [read roofs] shone in the sun like tongues of fire, and they must strike with awe and veneration the hearts of pilgrims from the barren tablelands."[24]

The squalor of the old city struck many others. Reactions ranged from frank admiration and mystic ecstasy right through to, at the climax in the early twentieth century, revulsion and disdain for what was considered a corrupt religion, a decadent society, and a rigid and repetitive art form. This was a time when the image of Tibet and its society, religion, and art as projected by the outside world reached a paroxysm of magic, mystery, and inaccuracy, in the popular "Orientalist" sense. Images published in books on the subject often had nothing at all to do with Tibet. An approximation from Japan, China, or somewhere else was considered sufficiently appropriate.[25]

The Western world was developing two parallel discourses in relation to Tibet. On the one hand, it was conducting sober, careful research into the language, religion, society, and history. On the other, Tibet had become an object of fantasy, a land of magic and mystery, of talking statues, of levitating yogins and flying monks. The supposed magical or occult powers of the lamas were called (as in Marco Polo's account) the work of the devil, and the lamas were considered idolators, although this last criticism was not specific to Tibet, but rather a vague reflection of the attitude of Christianity toward the rest of the world, since all other religions (with the exception of Islam) quite simply qualified as idolatrous. The worst criticism came no doubt from Waddell who had a gift for lilting phrases and who spoke of "deep-rooted devil-worship and sorcery" and wrote with relish that "the sinister growth of poly-demonist superstition darkly appears."[26]

Evolution of the Outside View of Tibet Especially in Relation to Art

Christendom first heard fleetingly of Tibet through the much-loved and supposedly historical account dictated by Marco Polo in Genova in 1299. This book is at present considered to belong to the category of myth or historical lie, but it is nevertheless the Venetian who first mentioned the land of "Tebet," recently laid waste by the armies of Mongu Khan. Marco Polo speaks of forests, of musk and salt, of gold dust in great quantities, and of its inhabitants who loved to hang corals round the necks of their women and their idols. The best magicians and astrologers in all the provinces (of the Mongol Empire) came from Tibet.[27] These same astrologers and magicians were employed at the court of the Grand Khan Cublay, who is described as "the most powerful man in peoples, lands and treasures who ever lived in the world since Adam." These "wise men" knew so well "the diabolical arts and necromancy that they made sure that no bad weather could pass over the domain" during the three summer months of the year, from June to August, when the lord lived in his two palaces in the prairies. They were

Fig. 10 Monumental sculpture in the Potala

"idolators"—"all they do being the work of the devil, though they make people believe that they do it by holiness and by the work of God."[28]

We may also look at Campicion, described by Marco Polo. He writes,

It is a great and noble city in the Land of Tangut, head and capital of the whole province of Tangut. The people are idolators,

Fig. 11 The Jowo in the Jokhang

Sarrasins, or Christians. The latter have three large and fine churches in the city. The idolators have a multitude of monasteries and abbeys, according to their religion. They have a huge quantity of idols, some so large that they are ten paces high, with other smaller ones, some in wood, some in earth or stone, all covered with gold and very well executed."[29]

Although this last description refers to Tanguts, it is now well established that the Tibetans had a large and thriving Buddhist community in that land, with monasteries and an imperial preceptor at the court, at least until 1227.[30] This same description might also fit well the context in Tibet at that time. The great hall of Sa skya gives us some idea of what the temples must have looked like at that time.

The Eighteenth–Twentieth Centuries

Little more is heard in Western sources until the eighteenth century, and even then, descriptions of images and wall paintings are brief and vague. From time to time a little sympathetic comparison with the Catholic religion is proffered.

In 1716 Ippolito Desideri remarks, for example, when describing a statue of Padmasambhava and one of his mother [sic], a female image (whom he probably took for some form of Mary) that holds a flower and that "[t]hey call God Konciok and seem to have some idea of the Adorable Trinity."[31]

When aesthetic judgment is passed, this is however almost always positive.[32] The Lazarist Huc wrote in 1844–45 at Kumbum,[33]

We were astonished at the vision of the flowers. Never would we have imagined that in the middle of these deserts, among these half savage people, we would meet with artists of such great merit. It was easy to recognise the Buddha, his face, full of nobility and majesty, belonged to the Caucasian type. Conforming to the Buddhist tradition, which pretends that the Buddha, who came from the West, had a face colored white and light red.

The Younghusband expedition (1904) came at the height of the power of the British Empire, and the descriptions of Tibet made by its different members make fascinating reading, adding largely and positively to the creation of the myth. Perceval Landon went to see the Holy

Fig. 12 Naro Kachöma

Fig. 13 Naro Kachöma

of Holies, the Buddha statue known as the Jowo in the Jokhang. He
wrote in awe about what was "beyond question the most famous idol
in the world": "The great glowing mass of the Buddha softly looms
out, ghostlike and shadowless."[34] He also talked of "paradoxical
buddhas," no doubt in reference to the wrathful deities. But it is Waddell, principal medical officer, and collector of Buddhist books and
curios for the British and Indian Museums, who is exemplary in both
his fascination and his revulsion for Tibetan Buddhism. He was so
imbued with his own Aryan superiority that after visiting Tibet for the
first time, he found nothing new to add to his book *The Buddhism of
Tibet or Lamaism,* which, he meekly remarks, "had never been
superceded." All he did in Lhasa was take a few photographs and
acquire some "bulky Buddhist scriptures," the contents of which he
"had already sifted" through in his famous book.[35] I quote a few of his
grosser affirmations, since he set himself up as such an authority, and
indeed he did discover much of great interest, but his influence on the
negative "myth of Tibet" has been enormous.

It is clear that Waddell had a passion for research. He was, in his
own words, "irresistibly attracted to Buddhism, as one of the greatest
living religions in the world," by the "marvellous art" of Ceylon and
Burma. In studying Tibetan civilization, he built a temple in the grounds
of his own residence in Gangtok, Sikkim, and wrote:

VAJRA-BHAIRAVA.
(Tutelary fiend of established church.)

Fig. 14 Yamantaka

In order the more effectively to penetrate the jealous reserve of the Lamas and gain intimate knowledge of their mystic Buddhist ritual and beliefs, I purchased the complete fittings of a Lamaist temple: altars, images, and painted scrolls of the chief Buddhist deities...I prevailed on the officiating Lamas to impart me their hidden mystic rites.

Concerning the art of Tibet and the attitude of Tibetans toward images, he judged: "They have come to be of the most idolatrous kind, for the majority of the Lamas and almost all the laity worship the image as a sort of fetish, holy in itself and not merely as a diagram or symbol of the infinite or unknown." In reference to the pantheon he did admit defeat: "I cannot attempt, at least at present, to give any satisfactory classification of such a disorderly mob." However he did make some attempt and from among the "chaotic crowd of gods, demons, and deified saints" he deigned to classify the tutelary deities as "mostly demonical" (that is, wrathful) and the _ḍākinī_ as "Defenders of the Faith and Witches." He goes on to affirm:

The pictures are mostly paintings...and many of them of considerable artistic merit. The style and technique are clearly of

Chinese origin. The colours are very brilliant and violently contrasted, owing to the free use of crude garish pigments, but the
general colour effect in the deep gloom of the temple, or when
the painting is toned down by age, is often pleasing.[36]

Concerning the sexual imagery, Waddell disguised Naro mKha'
spyod ma by adding a scarf, and Yamāntaka by effacing a telling line.[37]
To explain the existence of this somewhat embarrassing aspect of
Vajrayāna, Waddell explains that "the popular craving for creative
functions in their gods led, in the Tantrik stage, to the allotment of
female energies to these celestial bodhisats."[38]

Following the Younghusband expedition, the situation changed for
the better. Genuine Western mystics began to appear, such as Lama
Anagarika Govinda and Alexandra David-Néel, and each had his or her
individual word to say on art.[39] The French scholarly contingent had
also arrived on the scene, and soon began to contribute fine, sensitive
research work that laid the foundations for the later development of
Tibetan studies in Paris.

In 1909 Jacques Bacot visited the main temple in Lithang, which he
described as "a large light room filled with oriflammes [i.e., thangkas]
hanging close together, from the walls, the beams, the pillars. Over
1000...the multitude vibrates, splattered with slanting rays of brilliant
sunshine of the rising sun. One sees white Chenrasi with multiple heads,
saints in ecstasy in orange halos, blue monsters seated on yellow tigers,
red hells full of fire where devils gallop, devils bent on their torturing,
gods and goddesses enlaced with their thousand arms in furious
embrace...the central idol, his cheekbones and forehead lit up from
below by a butter lamp, like a moon disk, leaving in the shadow his
enigmatic regard, one imagines it to be terrible."[40]

Bacot goes on to give his own particular (French) judgment in terms
quite at odds with what is said elsewhere about the tightly controlled
and uncreative, iconometric art of Tibet: "All Tibetan art is impres-
sionist; even the miniatures are made in relation to the whole, and need
to be observed from a distance. It would be a learned and even psychological process if the criteria were not entirely unconscious. The
Tibetan artist feels, he does not know. Art that is learned can never

produce this maximum effect and harmony which seems always to be the result of hazard."[41] He continues: "Tibetan artists have no sensuality, they are mystics. They are close to our [French] 'primitifs.' In Chinese art sensuality imposes and becomes inspiration. That is the antique civilisation. The difference is profound."[42]

The Question of Aesthetics and Anonymous Artisans

A number of assumptions about Tibetan art have been repeated ad infinitum in Western books on the subject over the last century. These assumptions were based on the Western Romantic view in the nineteenth and twentieth centuries, where "everything was a fit subject for art"[43] and where an artist was in essence supposed to be an individual genius, the creator of new expression, be it in literature, music, sculpture, painting, or architecture. As we have seen, Tibetan art (like the whole of traditional Tibetan civilization) was considered to be unchanging and anonymous. Marco Pallis, a great lover of Tibet who was perhaps the first Westerner to study under a Tibetan artist, Konchok Gyaltsen, in Phiyang Monastery, Ladakh, wrote in 1939 of his aim "to give a picture of an art in being, with the Tradition, which is its life-

Fig. 15 Wrathful deity

blood, still active. The last of the great Traditions of which this can be said unreservedly."[44]

He goes on to say: "A singular consistency of style is observable throughout the vast territories where the Tibetan Buddhist tradition holds sway, in spite of wide climatic and racial diversity. It calls for a trained eye to distinguish whether a certain painting was executed in Lhasa or Mongolia, and whether the photograph of a building refers to Ladakh or to Kham, many miles away to the East."

This observation, which may have been true for the twentieth-century style of painting he was studying, reinforces the concept of the unchanging sameness of tradition. A quick glance at *Wisdom and Compassion* will tell any observer that this is quite untenable. The immense variety of styles and forms is striking, and one may even go so far as to say that no two paintings of the Tibetan tradition are the same.

Furthermore, concerning the anonymity of Tibetan artists, what precisely does this mean? The sculptors *(lha bzo)* and painters *(lha bris)* of Tibet were perfectly well known to the persons who commanded their art. They were far from anonymous during their lifetimes. Many were very well known indeed, and founded schools of art. A significant

Fig. 16 The Thirteenth Dalai Lama's thangka painter, 1937

number of them signed their work with pride.[45] In fact, according to Ernst Fischer's analysis in *The Necessity of Art,* twentieth-century artists in the Western world were more anonymous than any artisan in traditional society: "In the capitalist world the individual faced society alone, without an intermediary, as a stranger among strangers, as a single 'I' opposed to the immense 'not-I.' ...This situation stimulated powerful self-awareness and proud subjectivism, but also a sense of bewilderment and abandon.... The writer's and artist's 'I' was isolated and turned back upon itself, struggling for existence by selling itself in the market place, yet challenging the bourgeois world as a 'genius.'"[46]

The Tibetan artist was, however, known, loved, and respected in society, and had a special status. If he was good, he received many commissions and would begin to train apprentices. Let us finish with a Tibetan viewpoint on the function of art, followed by some excerpts from the earliest account written in English by a Tibetan on the subject.

The Tibetan View: Function and Aesthetics in Art

There is no doubt that the myth of magic and mystery was highly developed in Tibet itself. Teachers, true lamas, were expected to have special powers developed alongside their own spiritual realization. It was they who played an important role in the implantation and spread of Buddhism. It was they whose portraits and mystical visions were painted and sculpted so that others might remember their example and follow them on the path to enlightenment.

According to Buddhism, "Supports of the Body" (of the Buddha), or images, had several different functions, and when a statue is mentioned in a Tibetan text, its function is often clearly indicated as well. They were considered portentous creations. The eleven-headed, thousand-armed Avalokiteśvara, mentioned above, was at the same time a life-size portrait of the first emperor of Tibet. It was invested with sacred power through consecration. The image was inhabited in a special way by the deity, and assured, through its presence, fertile land, timely rain, excellent harvests, healthy cattle, and good fortune for man. It maintained peace and stability in the world and in human society.

Fig. 17 Portrait of an abbot

Fig. 18 Depiction of an abbot

However, the portrait of a lama, made at the time of his death, has another function. It may have been painted especially for his disciples or "sons." They will miss his benevolent, fatherly presence and will need a close likeness of him to remember him and follow him on the path to enlightenment.

The catalogue of the inaugural exhibition of the Tibet House Gallery held in New Delhi, 1965, demonstrated early on a simple, clear Tibetan vision of Tibetan art. We find such a vision again in the exhibition *Wisdom and Compassion*. The Tibet House catalogue is "anonymous," but was written, as everyone who was around at that time knew, by the highly qualified rNying ma pa teacher Sonam Tobgyay Kazi, translator to His Holiness the Dalai Lama and director of Tibet House at that time. He expounded Tibetan art with the structured clarity and depth of one who knows his subject intimately. We shall end with some excerpts from his text:

Fig. 19 Mahāsiddha Māṇibhadra

[Tibetan art] is an art inspired by religion, telling a story, propounding a moral. It is *more than* aesthetics. It personifies the
scriptures and makes the goal of meditation a visual attainment.... Tibetans believe that much of their art is apocalyptical.
The quality of revelation is emphasised. ...Of course there is
room for the imagination of the painter.... The body of the
painting is...assembled according to tradition and training. This
is a product of history. But the life that illuminates the artefact
is gathered from the [painter's] experience of pure vision.
Tibetan art depicts esoteric experiences, gained from the practice

Fig. 20 Sarasvatī

of Tantric Buddhism, and[,] it is claimed, is nothing if...not visionary.

In art one is not concerned with theory but with practice.... The thangkas give you the impression...that the artist has not only projected the colours of the prism of life but that he has also projected the invisible bands of the spectrum that lie on *either* side.

The Tibetan painter creates the...sense of flux in an amazing way. He uses colours which instill a feeling of stillness.... At the same time...the line... has to be energetic, as power—mystical and physical—emanates from the singular figures of the Tibetan pantheon. When the invisible is made visible, as in the manifestations of Vajradhara, or the Wrathful Deities, or through the bliss of those who have experienced Cakrasaṃvara, Hevajra, Kālacakra, and when the transcendental behind nature is manifest, we are made to "see into the life of things." A great veil is lifted and life is forced to take stock of a strange and unique sensation.... The forms in the thangkas remind one of an invocation repeated and lost and repeated again, as prayers must sound to the human ear in the highlands of Tibet.... The prime figures are bathed in light, and they project a quality of effulgence.... All this in a vast and changing world of phenomena.[47]

NOTES

1 Rhie and Thurman, 1991: 12.

2 Tucci, 1974: 33, 44.

3 Béguin, 1977, the earliest major comprehensive exhibition of Tibetan art, took a different stance, presenting a chronological and stylistic analysis. Several other important exhibitions and collections with catalogues have been published since then: Klimberg-Salter, 1982; Essen and Thingo, 1989; Pal, 1990; Béguin, 1990; Pal, 1991. Many other important studies of sites in Tibet have been published, or are in preparation, as are several other exhibitions.

4 Cf. Jung, 1995: 201; and the foreword to Evans-Wentz, *The Tibetan Book of the Great Liberation* (Oxford: Oxford University Press, 1954).

5 For example, an early maṇḍala of Che-mchog Heruka with a family of father, mother, and two sons being initiated into the teachings by Padmasambhava, with all five human beings seated inside one of the inner circles, and identified by inscription.

6 See Rhie and Thurman, 1991: 39.

7 Ibid: 17.

8 Dr. Pratapaditya Pal, well-known historian of Tibetan art, former curator at the Los Angeles County Museum of Art.

9 See Waddell, 1971: 1–2, 326–27. Waddell's abrupt and scathing attitude toward Tibetan Buddhism appears as a symptom of his own personality, as well as of the times. His terminology is often simply inaccurate. In many instances, for example, one should and would today read "wrathful," where

he puts "demoniacal." See p. 348: "the Tantrik forms with [female] energies, mostly demoniacal Buddhas."

10 The government of the PRC invited the Dalai Lama and Panchen Lama to visit China in 1956.

11 Concerning the question of the recognition of the present Panchen Lama.

12 Co-founder of the Sweet Tea House group of modern Tibetan painters, Lhasa, 1985–87, then he went into exile working as graphics designer in the Library of Tibetan Works and Archives in Dharamsala, now lives in London, where he attended the St. Martin's School of Art.

13 The Tshurphu *gos sku* was made by Terris Temple and Leslie Nguyen using 2,000 meters of satin; dimensions: 35 x 23 meters; cost US$44,000. It needs sixty monks to carry it. A Mahākāla appliqué thangka was made in the following year.

14 See Fischer, 1963.

15 Said, 1978: 214.

16 This image has been profoundly modified by serious research. Tucci already showed in *Indo-Tibetica* (1988–89) that artists did sign their names in rGyal rtse sKu 'bum. Many more examples have been found since then. David Jackson's *A History of Tibetan Painting* concentrates on the lives and work of famous Tibetan artists. An earlier "appreciation" reveals the stereotyped vision so prevalent until the 1960s and 1970s. Claude Pascalis (1935) describes objects rescued by P. Pelliot from the Yonghe gong, at the time of the Boxer Rebellion in 1900. On pre-Buddhist Tibetans, who "practiced a sort of animism, Bon," he enquires: "They were rarely sedentary, without intellectual culture, did they have any art? One is tempted to say yes. The character of the Tibetan style, which appears with energy in the artistic production of those who followed on, all formed through foreign influences, reveal nevertheless the original qualities of the people: ingenuity, skill, love of embellishment, taste.... A predilection for the macabre which does not exclude a delicate feeling of harmony and a purity of imagination, manifest especially when the artist expresses himself freely.... Unfortunately, the possibility of giving full expression to his temperament is hardly offered to the Tibetan artist. Tibetan civilisation, essentially Buddhist, is based on the renunciation of the personality, and Tibetan art is almost entirely devoted to religion. It does not waver, in any way, from this fundamental idea. It is the work of lamas, anonymous artists upon which the Buddhist canon imposes its strict rules, forms and unvarying themes."

17 Said, 1978: 98.

18 Ibid: 19.

19 Ibid: 93. Anthropology was presented then as an object of little-disguised scorn by "true" Orientalist scholars.

20 Ibid: 145.

21 Ibid: 121.

22 Hopkirk, 1983: 37.

23 According to reliable sources in Tibet, the late Panchen Lama asked where this gold had gone to, when the Chinese government was declaring its generosity in restoring the Potala. He suggested that the confiscated gold would have covered a far greater restoration of Tibetan cultural heritage.

24 Candler, quoted by Hopkirk, 1983: 184.

25 Braham Norwick has treated this question in several articles (e.g. 1985). See Waddell, 1971: 14, 87, 92, 93, 94, 141, 143, 144, 413, 526, etc. for images taken from other Buddhist traditions in Asia.

26 Waddell, 1971: xl.

27 Polo, 1978: 190–95, 123.

28 Ibid: 123, referring to Tibetans, as well as to magicians of another race called Quesmur(?).

29 Ibid: 96.

30 See Kychanov, 1993.

31 "Ils adorent encore un nommé Urghien…né d'une fleur. Néanmoins leurs statues représentent une femme qui a une fleur à la main et ils disent que c'est la mère d'urghien. Ils adorent plusieurs autres personnes qu'ils regardent comme des saints…les tibétains…il n'y a parmi eux ni sciences ni arts, quoiqu'ils ne manquent pas d'esprit. Ils n'ont point de communication avec les nations étrangères." Jan, 1992: 1117.

32 Georges Bogle (1774–75) writes: "[Ce temple à Tashilhunpo] contenait treize gigantesque personnages qui auraient atteint une hauteur de deux mètres cinquante s'ils avaient été représentés debout; mais à l'exception du dieu de la guerre et d'une autre effigie, ils étaient tous assis en tailleur. Ces collosses, qui étaient en cuivre doré, portaient un pot de fleurs ou une coupe de fruit sur les genoux; ils étaient figurés revêtus d'un manteau, et la tête ceinte d'une couronne ou d'une mitre; tous les détails—notamment les draperies—étaient fort bien exécutées…quand le lama pénétra dans le temple, il se prosterna trois fois en direction de l'autel et de l'effigie de son dieu…il prit la lettre que le dalaï-lama lui avait adressée, conjointement à quatre ou cinq petites statues, de nombreux livres et quelques conques montées dans de l'argent, et plaça le tout sur le trône, juste devant lui." (Ibid: 1137, 1139, and 1141).

33 Ibid: 1334.

34 Landon, quoted in Hopkirk, 1983: 185.

35 Waddell, 1971: xii.

36 Ibid: 326–31.

37 Ibid: 80, see Naro mKha spyod ma with a scarf added to hide her immodestly

leaping lower parts, and p. 363, Yamāntaka in *yab-yum,* with the line on the thigh rubbed out, to confuse the reader, and render illegible the "father-mother" imagery.

38 Ibid: p. 348.

39 See, for example, David-Néel in Kumbum, 1918–19: "I went this morning to see a gigantic cloth over 50 meters long, oh, certainly more than that, representing the Buddha. This dreadful work of art was stretched over the grassy bank of the mountain and an enormous crowd gathered to admire it.... After the festival, I visited the main temples scattered around the mountain, most very rich and decorated with beautiful wall paintings. The ensemble is finer than at Tashilhunpo" (Jan, 1992: 1340).

40 Ibid: 1354.

41 Ibid: 1360.

42 Ibid: 1364.

43 See Fischer, 1963: 53.

44 Pallis, 1939: 345.

45 See Jackson, 1996.

46 Fischer, 1963: 53–54. "Romanticism led out of the well-tended garden of Classicism, into the wilderness of the wide world."

47 Anon., 1965: ii–x, extracts.

PART THREE
Standpoints

Tibetan Monastic Colleges

RATIONALITY VERSUS THE DEMANDS OF ALLEGIANCE

P. Jeffrey Hopkins

Abstract

IN EUROPE AND THE AMERICAS (I am purposely avoiding the seemingly dichotomous division of the world into "East" and "West"), Buddhism and, particularly, certain forms of Tibetan Buddhism are depicted as entirely reason-oriented cultures where allegiance and might do not make right. However, observation of Tibetan monastic colleges reveals that other forces are also at play—noncritical allegiance, disagreement for the sake of gaining economic and social advantage, pretension, opponent-bashing, intolerance of diversity, and so forth—much as in the educational institutions of Europe and the Americas. Nevertheless, a vital system of education is also sustained in these colleges such that they deserve to be called one of the notable achievements of the culture.

Many of us are deeply moved by the Chinese Communist government's oppression and destruction of Tibetan culture and the violent effects on the ecology in an area that serves as the source of the great rivers of Asia. We are stirred by the dire situation of Tibet and its people to the point where we fail to exercise our critical faculties fully out of fear that fault-finding might sabotage the political, moral, and ecological objectives that many of us pursue. I myself have used the facade of speaking through "their own voice" rather than through what could too easily be interpreted as a "privileged" voice. Nevertheless, since the beginning of my five-year residence in a Tibetan and Mongolian

Buddhist monastery in New Jersey in 1963, I have felt that it is necessary to sift through what I have encountered.

Through exposure in my prep school and undergraduate education
to Marxist analysis of social, political, and economic forces, I nurtured
a skepticism and even cynicism about almost everything; an even more
bitter cynicism was behind my earlier teen years as a juvenile rebel.
During my college years I was convinced that everything was corrupt
at the very root; I could spin a story of corrupt motive and practice
with regard to any area of human activity—to the point of boredom.
What has fascinated me since my senior year in college is the possibility of something else—of light cracking through the thick crust of self-
ishness and deceit. Thus I have usually written about the positive
aspects of what I have seen, since the cynical is so well covered by others. Still, it has been imperative for me to keep sifting through the
garbage of pretension and misrepresentation.

For, in order to recognize the possible contributions of Tibet to
world culture, it is necessary to be aware of Tibetan attitudes and practices that do not accord with overblown images. If we are not aware,
our fatuous pretensions—whether driven by calculation or by lack of
close contact with the culture—will, at some point, be drowned by the
force of reality. Then we may become unable to use what is truly helpful; we will be drowned by our own pride, wounded by our original
gullible assessment or by our inability to achieve a more nuanced voice.

Still, I strongly feel that it is not sufficient to engage in destructive
criticism, even if it is clothed in highfalutin terms like "deconstructionism," and even if I recognize in that term the remnants of the Marx-
ism that opened my eyes to perverse forces in society. I do not want to
become satisfied with image blasting, as if the exercise of criticism—
meaning here fault-finding—is sufficient. It is not.

Monastic Colleges

Around Lhasa there are three large Gelugpa[1] monastic universities:
Gan-den,[2] Dre-bung,[3] and Se-ra.[4] Gan-den University, located about an
hour and a half east of Lhasa by land cruiser (approximately forty km),
was founded in 1409 by Tsongkhapa[5] eight years before his death. Gan-

den University is composed of two colleges, Shar-dzay and Jang-dzay, which were founded by two of Tsongkhapa's disciples. The colleges are the primary functioning units of the university, and each has its own administration, its own faculty, and its own textbooks. It would be like having two departments of physics, philosophy, and so forth, with separate administrations, on opposite sides of the lawn at the University of Virginia. Instead of one rotunda at the end of the lawn, each college would have its own rotunda as an assembly hall; thus, there would be three rotundas. Everything else would be in duplicate, with the general University of Virginia being merely a further administrative unit, which, by nature, could not unite the two parts.

The colleges share a curriculum based on Five Great Books of Buddhist India—a program of study that begins around age eighteen and lasts for about twenty-five years—but they use different commentaries on those great books for textbooks. Given that the basic structure of the monastic university is to divide into camps that stimulate intellectual exchange, the main textbooks are subcommentaries written by prominent scholars; these textbooks present the commentaries in a clearer format and attempt to resolve issues unclear or confused in those texts. These commentaries, called the college's "textbook literature,"[6] are the main focus, elevated even to the point where they are the primary objects of concern and allegiance. (Perhaps due to Protestant emphasis on early Christianity, American academics often unwarrantedly assume that the focus of religious systems is on their founder and early history, whereas the focus in this system is actually on the thought of the author of the textbook literature.)

The endeavor at a monastic university is to rediscover (or create) the wholeness of Tsongkhapa's system of meaning without the slightest internal contradiction. This is done with the pretense that the founder's many works themselves are devoid of the slightest internal contradiction, that they fit together in all aspects in complete harmony. The cryptic nature of many of Tsongkhapa's statements leaves room for considerable interpretive creativity that is bounded, to some extent, by his many clear pronouncements. I say "to some extent" because the game allows for positing the founder's actual thought, despite his words, behind what otherwise may seem to be a clear statement. Nothing is left paradoxical; the assumption of consistency dictates the reformulation of the presumed thought behind seemingly incomplete or inconsistent statements.

The framework of the game is transmitted from generation to generation through a teacher's remarking fairly early in a student's training, "It is amazing how there is not the slightest internal contradiction in all of the works of the Foremost Precious One (Tsongkhapa)!" Shortly thereafter, the teacher confronts the student with an apparent inconsistency, as if the student were the origin both of the original proposition that there is no inconsistency and of the apparent self-contradiction. As I see it, a great deal of cultural transmission is accomplished through identification with one's superiors, and, in this case, the identification is forced through the teacher's operating within the presumption of a shared perspective. Sometimes the superior with whom one is identifying is also the aggressor—the teacher makes an outrageous demand that shocks the student and calls forth unacceptable counteraggression, which the student hastens to avoid recognizing by identifying with the teacher and then, when the chance arises, pressing the same outrageous demand on a more junior student. The student thereby becomes the inflicter of his teacher's aggression!

A story from my childhood will suffice to illustrate the process. Out under the elm tree where my puppy was tied, my mother scolded me somewhat vehemently for reasons now not remembered; I immediately turned around and upbraided the little dog unmercifully. (I still remember my mother staring at me awestruck.) This sequence of denying one's own anger and identifying with the hated aggressor, thereby deflecting the aggression away from oneself, creates a psychologically complex bond that is built on the dangerous foundation of anger and separation from oneself. This mechanism of cultural transmission serves to transmit the outrageous demands of many cultural forms with rigidity. As a result, when students of Tsongkhapa's texts find what honestly seem to be inconsistencies and thus fail to find the presumed harmony, they feel guilt at questioning the basic assumption of coherence since it endangers the bond with the teacher. Or they decide that their intellect is inadequate to the task and adopt a superficial, often vehement repetition of the presumption of no inconsistency.

Other students (or even the same students at other times) successfully manage their way through this problem by developing an aesthetic delight in the game of ferreting out inconsistencies and attempting to explain them away. The game is not played individually, but is social, performed in the company of classmates and fellow scholars. The highly satisfying intellectual and aesthetic delight that is shared between students when an artful re-presentation of the founder's thought is put together is the stuff that perpetuates the process; to my sight, it creates an adherence far stronger even than the violent effects of identification with the aggressor. Despite the obvious presence of rigid identification with hated aggressors, such moments of beauty, shared with other participants, are at the heart of the educational system in these monastic universities. As in any university, these are the experiences on which teacher and student thrive. The intense nature of the Tibetan system—built on intimate contact with a teacher and on rigorous debate twice daily—provides many opportunities for such aesthetic epiphanies. Thus, the power of mutually supportive appreciation may explain, in part, the structure of Tibetan universities.

The students identify with the college units to the point where the general monastic university has little significance. (In the reconstructed Gan-den in south India, an alley between these two colleges serves not as a connecting passage but as an invisible wall keeping students from straying into the rival college.) Their members' adherence to these units is so strong that the Chinese Communist government occupying Tibet, despite minor relaxation of religious suppression, has not allowed the colleges to reopen. Fearing the loyalty so successfully inculcated in these units, they have stifled the basic structure that promotes vigorous intellectual interchange.

The lack of easy communication in Tibet and the consequent highly parochial nature of the society are reflected in the monks' intense adherence to these colleges. Factionalism is indeed encouraged, with far more occurring between the Gelugpa colleges than between it and other sects. The Gelugpa sect that formed among Tsongkhapa's followers is, therefore, by no means monolithic in its views, for the basic adherence is to one's college, which is in competition with the other colleges. Students are inculcated with the greatness of the authors of their textbook literature, the authors being viewed, like Tsongkhapa, as incarnations of Mañjuśrī (the deity that is the physical manifestation of the wisdom of all buddhas) or as reincarnations of great figures of Indian Buddhism. One textbook author is considered an incarnation of the Indian scholar Buddhapālita who, in the distant future, will be the chief general of the troops from Śambhala when they come to relieve the world of the scourge of barbarism and inaugurate an age of such great devotion to Buddhism that there will be no other significant religions during that time. Young students are told story after story about the greatness of the author of their textbook literature such that, as one lama said about the years of his early studies, he considered the members of the other colleges as bad off as non-Buddhists!

It is clear that the many doctrinal differences expounded in each college's textbooks are used both for intellectual stimulation and for sociological and economic advantage; they help to establish group identity and a sense of uniqueness that justifies promotion of that group for the receipt of donations. The loyalty generated by such dynamics often obscures straightforward pursuit of knowledge and creates an added tension for knowledge-oriented persons. Still, the situation is multi-sided, for although in a debate between two students the defendant must uphold the position of his college's textbook author, the challenger—usually from the same college—must make this task as difficult as possible, and he easily becomes enamored of the sensibleness of his own attack. (I say "he" because in Tibet women, for the most part, were long excluded from the halls of intellectual pursuit.) Considerable emphasis is placed on winning and losing, and thus students develop elaborate arguments against their own textbook literature. The resolution of this conflict is, for many, a bifurcation of viewpoint—a more public posture that manifests as strong adherence to the textbook author's positions and a more private, highly critical attitude.

The Tibetan scholars with whom I have studied over the last thirty-nine years all seem to have these two viewpoints to varying degrees. One lama, a fine scholar with penetrating insights into larger issues, was so oriented to the public side that on issues of intense disagreement between the monastic textbooks he acted as if there were no disagreement at all. It seemed he wanted me to think that his college's viewpoint was the only one!

Another lama, however, would take me through the positions of three of the main textbook authors, though always within the context of showing the superiority of his own college's view. The variety of opinion with which he was fluent was indeed impressive, often causing me to melt in admiration, but when mentioning the name of the opposing college in the same monastic university, he would suddenly turn his head to the side and spit on the floor! I never ceased to be horrified at this, my disgust magnified, no doubt, by the fact that the floor was covered with a rug. Never mind spit on the floor, but one should never spit on a rug! (My loyalty to my mother easily dominated my new-found loyalty to my lama.) Sitting in hateful conflict at his feet, I was appalled at these not infrequent displays of parochial partisanship directed, of course, at the rival college located just forty paces from his own. He would repeat that the textbook literature of the other, third college—not in his own monastic university—was indeed not so bad, even quite good, but that the textbooks of the rival home-group were pathetic. Pituey! Since we were renting the house, I cautioned him against spitting on the rug, and he got so that he only made the noise of spitting.

Still, he was a grand personality with an incredible capacity to convey the complicated architecture of a worldview, largely through repetition of key issues and positions. Sometimes the repetitions seemed boringly and excruciatingly unnecessary, but when I challenged myself to produce what he was about to say, I would find that I could not quite do it, and thus I would hang on his every word in order to do so. The kindness of his untiring repetitions was considerable. Indeed, one of his intentions was to indoctrinate me such that I would become a follower of his college's textbook literature, but the benefits that I gained from his repetition of focal issues far outweigh the disadvantages.

Nevertheless, particularly insidious was the fact that, despite my wrenching hatred of his partisanship, when I finally began studying that other college's texts I found that I uncontrollably viewed them to be pathetically inadequate even before I had read a word. During my study of their texts I was amazed, over and over again, that scholars of this college could make interesting distinctions. Despite being conscious of my hatred at his partisanship, my identification with my old friend was such that, contrary to my own heartfelt and repeated intentions in pained intensity, I came to be imbued with an attitude toward the other college that was a mental version of spitting on the floor.

That Tibetan scholars and administrators appreciate the power of such indoctrination explains, in part, the busy schedule of a monastic college. When I was in the Shar-dzay College in south India, I fell asleep in the midst of a voice shouting a memorized text, and I would awaken in darkness the next morning to the sound of a congregation of monks praying. With a full schedule of prayers interspersed with classes and debate sessions, the monks are kept busy all day and a good part of the night. Exposed to this unending scenario of activity for two months, my Marxist view of monastics as lazily living off the wealth of the populace was reduced to ash.

A final story will add to the picture. The monastic colleges are further broken down into "house units" associated with the regions from which students come and thus promote another level of parochialism. These, in turn, are broken down into "families." These smaller units provide effective means of addressing the needs of particular students; they are sufficiently small so that students are cared for with concerned attention. Since these units are primarily social and do not have their own textbook literature, they are not the primary units of identification, and thus monks would find it unthinkable to name their house or family unit when asked where their identity lies. In 1972, at a time when I had studied with three scholars from the same house unit (called Ham-dong) of Go-mang College of Dre-bung Monastic University, I was staying in a bungalow on the hill above Dharamsala in north India for several months. One day, I was visited by a scholar who happened upon my place by mistake; after we talked for a while, he remembered having heard of me and, assuming that my allegiance was to Go-mang College, asked, "Are you Go-mang?" Now, although I am a Buddhist, I do not consider myself a Gelugpa, never mind any unit smaller than that. So, thinking of a pithy reply, I answered, "No, I am Ham-dong!" He was stunned, trying to make sense of my identifying with such an unsuitable unit; he did not see that this was exactly what I was suggesting he was doing.

Such centrality of allegiance is reminiscent of a warrior's oath of fealty to his chieftain in Anglo-Saxon England; the warrior's identity was so totally bound to the tribe that if he outlasted his chieftain in battle, such as by being knocked unconscious and taken for dead by the enemy, he was left psychologically homeless, as is depicted in the poem "The Wanderer."[7] Loyalty to one's chieftain was used by Christian missionaries as a model for loyalty to God, the eternal chieftain. The implication in "The Wanderer" is that secular loyalty is to be superseded by religious loyalty to a higher leader. What is so surprising in these Gelugpa universities is that the seemingly higher loyalties are replaced by lower ones—allegiance to Buddha is replaced by allegiance to a college. Indeed, the author of the textbook literature is seen as a buddha of this era, but the form that the allegiance takes, with its biased rejection of other colleges, does not allow it to serve as a valid rationalization. Parochial factionalism in Tibetan Buddhism is deeply at odds with its own professed cardinal doctrine of universal compassion and the call for assuming responsibility for the welfare of all sentient beings, certainly including the members of the neighboring college. No doubt, a good deal of my shock also comes from my own historical position of living at a time when national, ethnic, and religious parochialism is obviously driving the world to its own destruction and from my perception that such factionalism must be overcome for our very survival.

I do not wish to create the impression that such parochial bias completely taints the enterprise of scholarship and spiritual development in these universities, for it does not. Rather, I wish to point out the tension present in a multifaceted situation. Parochial bias is often consciously inculcated to establish a mode of operation, much like a stage facade, that sets a scene in which other activities take place. It brings an energy to study and to debate, a focus for students not yet moved in a universalistic way. The inculcated sense of the unique value of one's college and the awesome responsibility of being a member of this club charges a course of study, during which profound understanding and spiritual progress that run counter to this parochialism may be made.

Thus, it seems to me, the intensity of the elaborate enterprise of Tibetan religious education is fueled in part by the tension created by the demands of biased allegiance that run counter to the core of the central doctrines—universal compassion, universal emptiness, and the experience of all phenomena as manifestations of the mind of clear light. The combative framework of biased allegiance—within which these universalistic attitudes are taught—creates a tension of unresolved energy. That energy, in turn, charges to an even greater height the insistence of the basically opposing postures of blind allegiance and rational inquiry. In a sense, balance is gained not through moderating these two but through intensifying each of them.

Throughout Tibetan culture, there is a dual relationship with and against authority—on the one hand using it to inculcate allegiance and obedience and, on the other hand, putting what seems to be full confidence in reasoning that runs counter to authority. Faced with such a discrepancy, the culture has opted not for one or the other, or a bland mixture of the two, but for a plenitude of both.

Little is done in Tibet in half measures—performing marathon debates in the freezing cold of January such that one's hands crack open and bleed from slapping them together when making a point, drinking forty to sixty cups of tea a day, populating a single temple with literally hundreds of images, claiming an uncountable number of supernatural happenings (many, many speaking statues, images appearing spontaneously out of rock, etc.), and finding not just a few, but scores of reincarnated special beings throughout the country. The immediate ascription of divinity to almost anyone who makes a mark on the culture—ranging from political figures to spiritual geniuses who founded sects or became authors of college textbooks—undermines their own life stories of hard effort over decades of devotion, study, and meditation. The successful are separated from human endeavor. This produces the strange result of denying the efficacy of effort in a religion that by its own description is oriented toward self-development based on inner potential. Claiming divine descent becomes even in this Buddhist society a favored means of attracting attention in order to gain sociological, economic, and political benefits. Separating off the truly holy also excuses ordinary beings from making effort; the culture thereby protects itself from high expectations regarding practice.

The obvious exaggeration involved in many of these claims of divine descent has led to the development of a counterforce, evidenced in monks, nuns, and lay persons who put little stock in the so-called recognized reincarnations, no matter who or what monastic or political institution has put forth the claim. The excessive inflation into divinity conflicts with the internal demands of the religion (1) to assess accurately one's position in an uncontrolled process of cyclic rebirth into pain and (2) to examine carefully the psychological processes that produce one's entrapment. The disparity between inflation and the need for realistic appraisal yields tension, which, in turn, feeds even more energy into the process. Activities with which one has become involved out of uncontrolled identification with the hated can become even more intense.

Within this framework it is very difficult to appreciate the significance of what individual religious figures have accomplished through their scholarship and training. After all, they are incarnations of deities! Would we expect less?! Particularly damaging is the claim that scholars' works are utterly accurate to and thus repetitious of their Indian sources. This perspective prevents noticing the unusual developments that their insights and efforts have wrought for generations of followers throughout the vast realm of the Tibetan cultural region.[8] The claim that the Buddhism of one's own sect is the final word, when put together with the hosts of controversy in the colleges of that very sect would seem to have warranted being drowned out in ridiculous laughter long ago. However, again, both sides of the matter are preserved; on the one hand, the claims to allegiance are insistently pressed, and, on the other hand, intellectual controversies are encouraged to the point where they are almost without limit. Such disavowal of consistency, however disconcerting and exasperating to both insiders and outsiders, has allowed for the flowering of a multitude of aspects in the culture. It also may represent a wise assessment—not explicitly, but through the culture's own dynamics—that life is not so straightforward and simple as to allow for a coherent perspective. The suggestion is that richness is lost when one insists on the drabness of consistency.

One reason why so many persons entered the monastic universities from the seventeenth century onward was to escape the stultifying work and the social rigidity on the estates of noble families. Despite a hierarchy of governmentally recognized lamas privileged from birth, the monastic universities provided opportunities for social and intellectual advancement for persons from the lower classes. Several of my Tibetan teachers testify to the fact that a person from any class could ascend to the top of the intellectual hierarchy through winning debate runoffs—first on the college level, then on the university level, and finally in the interuniversity national competition, emerging as cultural heroes.

Notes

Parts of this paper are drawn from my forthcoming *Reflections on Reality* (2002).

1 *dge lugs pa.* On the transliteration of Tibetan words in these notes, see Wylie, 1959: 261–67.

2 *dga' ldam* (joyous). In Sanskrit, *tuṣita*, which means "sated."

3 *'bras spungs* (rice mound).

4 *se rva* (wild rose).

5 tsong kha pa blo bzang grags pa, 1357–1419.

6 *yig cha.*

7 My translation is available in "The Wanderer," *Virginia Quarterly,* April 1977. Ezra Pound translated the companion poem "The Seafarer."

8 The Tibetan cultural region goes far beyond Tibet; it stretches from Kalmuck Mongolian areas near the Volga River in Europe where the Volga empties into the Caspian Sea, Outer and Inner Mongolia, the Buriat Republic of Siberia, as well as Bhutan, Sikkim, Ladakh, and parts of Nepal. In all of these areas, Buddhist ritual and scholastic studies are conducted in Tibetan. Until the Communist takeovers, youths came from throughout these vast regions to study in Lhasa, usually returning to their lands of origin after completing their studies.

"Violated Specialness"

WESTERN POLITICAL REPRESENTATIONS OF TIBET[1]

Robert Barnett

T IBETANS HAVE NOT ALWAYS accepted foreign representations of
their country without complaint. "I suppose our distant country holds little of interest for your public except for what of the strange
can be written about it, and so you get a strange picture of us. The
most absurd and the most scandalous things are said about us, and...
your writers often contradict each other," wrote Rinchen Lhamo of her
experiences in London at the beginning of the last century.[2] Western
remarks about Tibetans were, in her eyes, often condescending, inaccurate and self-contradictory. Of one official who had described
Tibetans as "a simple people," she commented, "his remark was so
wide of the fact that I could not refrain from laughing.... He knows we
are not so.... He was merely giving utterance to a conventional statement about us put into vogue by the travellers."

Her criticism of the unnamed official provides a fascinating demon-
stration of Tibetan self-definition and self-representation some fifty or
more years before such terms became fashionable; similar comments
can be found in the writings of Tibetan essayists today.[3] Such observations, however, leave unresolved the question as to what relation there
might be between Tibetan and Western sources of representation—
whether, that is, Tibetans are to be regarded as merely passive subjects
in the process whereby views are generated by outsiders about them, or
whether this process is one of the engagement of different voices in
contradiction or competition, or even a concurrence of some sort
between the various parties. In particular, the tolerance by Tibetan officials

and policymakers of such forms of representation raises the possibility that Western condescension toward Tibetans may sometimes be seen as part of a strategy or a political culture among Tibetan leaders according to which the encouragement of de-agentizing views by foreigners was considered expedient or even advantageous.

In this paper I try to map ways in which the Western representation of Tibet that Rinchen Lhamo had so strongly criticized has appeared in political texts in the West since the mid-1980s, and to examine the impact of such representations on the policies of foreign governments. In doing so, I am responding to recent reductionist depictions of Tibetans engaged in the contemporary political and cultural domains as more or less trapped subjects of Western constructions.[4] My study takes a different approach, looking at representations in terms of their functions and intended effects. In particular, I suggest that, rather than merely responding to Western discourses that emerged following the expansion of the Tibetan advocacy movement in late 1987, exile Tibetan policymakers were already by then encouraging this trend as part of an intended and considered strategy. In doing so, they were continuing a tradition of Tibetan political self-representation, using images that were developed in Lhasa long before the Chinese invasion and that they have continued to shape and reconstruct in response to changes in their conditions and objectives.

Political Concepts As Imaginary Representations

Statements produced by political institutions are often viewed in terms of outcome and policy rather than as images, but in this paper I try to look at them initially as if they were literary texts, since it seems to me that they too involve the generation of largely imaginary representations. Political representations differ from literary works in that they include an implicit offer of certain benefits for their supporters if their proponents are able to acquire the power to put them into action, but they share the features of other forms of representation, among which is their tendency to contain contradictions that expose them to weaknesses and instabilities of one kind or another. I have tried to indicate how this process of inherent disintegration is especially marked and significant with regard to political representations, and how it has led Tibetan leaders to seek constantly to adapt and modify the Western circulation of these views.

Treating representations of political status or nationhood as texts of the imagination does not, of course, mean that they have no effect, validity, or plausibility, since clearly this is not the case. They can be seen, in my view, as constituting the collective imagining by a great number of people of a description of their identity and their relations, which is organized around a selected principle or idea to which they ascribe the certainty of fact. This also means that these texts are, albeit in complex ways, authored: They arise because people produce them, not because of some reality that allows only a single interpretation.

I offer this formulation to make it easier to follow the complexities of the political debate over Tibet, since it seems to me that that discussion has been characterized by the collection of facts of different kinds in order to ascribe certainty to one or another of these organizing ideas or imaginary representations. Seen in this way, the debate between China and Western promoters of Tibetan claims is not really a debate—in other words, it is not a process in which arguments either to facts or to interpretations are put forward by each side with the intent that the most persuasive argument wins. It is more the presentation by each side of a strongly held collective imagining that is persuasive only to those who already share that imagining. In the Chinese case, the appeal is often to those who already share the envisaging of China as an integrated nation-state with its borders delineated in some ancient, loosely defined but inviolable historical past.[5] In the case of the foreign supporters of the Tibetan case, their appeals are often based on a notion or principle that is held to be preexistent or overriding—such as the right of a nation to independence or the right of a people to cultural or religious freedom—and which in the Tibetan case is seen to have been violated. In both cases primordiality is the driving force of the argument: On the one hand, China has existed as a unified state including Tibet for centuries, and on the other, Tibetan culture, identity, or society has existed independently for millennia.

Focusing, as I do here, on the views or strategies of Western politicians does not mean that these are crucial or even particularly influential in the

situation in Tibet—among the views held by outsiders, it is the attitudes of Chinese leaders and individuals that have the greatest influence
on the lives and the futures of Tibetans. But there is less need to apol-
ogize for focusing on Western rather than Chinese political views than
one might at first expect, because both positions have much in common. The romanticism and exoticization, for example, that many
observers have found pervading Western writings about Tibet, is also
typical of much Chinese writing on this subject, and not only in the
descriptions of noble primitivism that constitute much of the work of
the "root-seeking" school of Chinese literature.[6] Official and semi-
official Chinese texts, especially those by scientists, refer routinely to
Tibet as the "Land of Snows" or the "Rooftop of the World"; there is
even fierce competition among officials in certain areas of China to
claim the title of being the original Shangri-la.[7] There is, however, a
more telling similarity between Western and Chinese representations of
Tibetans: Both tend to treat the Tibetans as objects in stories of heroic
achievement by outsiders, or as victims of abuse who are incapable of
agency. Perhaps this similarity should not surprise us overmuch, since
both the Western and the Chinese accounts arise within societies with
histories as invaders or would-be invaders of the Tibetan plateau—the
British in 1903, the Chinese in 1910 and 1950, and (to a limited extent)
the Americans in the guerilla campaign from 1956–73.[8] The history of
Western invasion and incursions into Tibet has, however, been missing
from Western political texts produced about Tibet since the 1980s, and
the possibility that Western intervention might have been as much a
cause as a solution in China's annexation of Tibet has not been aired
in this debate.[9] Instead, the emphasis in Western accounts has been on
Tibet as virgin territory untouched until the arrival of the PLA.

Violation and the Zone of Specialness

Western political discourse about Tibet, in the sense of formal statements by political bodies and representatives, was quiescent throughout the 1970s, once China had achieved its rapprochement with the
United States and been readmitted to the UN in 1971; until then
Tibet had been part of an anti-Chinese, Cold War agenda. In 1985

it re-emerged as an issue in the Western political domain when a group of ninety-one American Senators, probably organized by the exile leadership in Dharamsala, wrote to Li Xiannian, then president of the PRC.[10] That year the issue was raised by a nongovernmental organization in the UN, probably the first time the issue had been addressed there or in any major forum for some fifteen years.[11]

Since that time the dominant form in which Tibet has been put forward in Western and exile political discussions has involved the image of a zone of specialness, uniqueness, distinctiveness, or excellence that has been threatened, violated, or abused. The circulation of this image in recent political discussion seems to have stemmed largely from decisions made by the exile Tibetan leadership at a series of strategy meetings held between 1985 and 1987.[12] At these meetings, which followed the collapse of negotiations with the Chinese in 1984, the exile leaders for the first time asked the Dalai Lama to give political speeches abroad, and probably decided on the topics and images to be used in that campaign and in his speeches. In doing this they reverted to the policies of the 1940s, before the Chinese annexation, when a similar appeal to the West had been made: At that time too Tibetan leaders had used the notion of Tibetan uniqueness as a principal tool in their diplomacy.[13]

The representations of Tibet that emerged in Western discussions following the Dalai Lama's speeches in the late 1980s focused on the uniqueness and the violation of Tibet. In some more recent cases, as we shall see, the violation is seen as a result of advancing modernity or commercialization in general, a view that implicitly exonerates the state as a perpetrator of abuse. But usually this violation is identified with acts of violence, desecration, or intolerance that have been carried out by the Chinese authorities, whether these are seen as the Chinese Communist Party, the government, the military, or even individual citizens. In many cases this idea of violation seems to be linked to a perception of the place or the people as previously unimpaired, and now desecrated, as if for the first time. "The rape of Tibet is going on," a politician told a 1999 hearing of the U.S. Congress,[14] articulating an image that lies within much of the language of violation found in discussions of Tibet.[15] As in cases elsewhere of women depicted as victims of rape, such imagery tends to disempower its subjects by implying that they are either victims who are incapable of standing alone, or collaborators in the act of violation. This image thus risks being politically counter-productive: It carries within it a pervasive implication of Tibetan inno-cence and victimhood, suggesting that Tibetans are incapable of effective action or decision-making.

The imagery of sexual relations does not belong to only one side of the political spectrum: Many texts within Chinese political discourse also speak of Tibet as a sexual innocent.[16] There, however, the imagery involves marriage rather than violation, and the innocence is male, a result not of moral purity but of a lack of sophistication or moder-nity—in other words, an excess of barbarity. In this view, the newcomer in the liaison is not a male violator but a nonviolent female who brings knowledge and advanced culture. This is the paramount image in Chi-nese official and unofficial writing about Tibet's relationship with China and is found in its purest form in the frequently repeated accounts of the marriage of the seventh-century Tibetan ruler Songtsen Gampo with the Chinese princess Wencheng, who brings with her to Tibet ink, music, agriculture, geomancy, and other Tang dynasty tech-nologies.[17] Here, marriage is a metaphor for China's civilizing mission toward backward peoples; it is thus very similar to the Chinese view of their modernization project in Tibet in contemporary times, and very close to the romantic view in the 1980s "root-seeking" school of liter-ature of Tibetans as noble savages.

Such images of specialness, sexual union, or violation are used as broad, generalizing metaphors for the foreign encounter with a society, place or nation. They tend to rely on the application of a single char-acteristic to an entire culture or people, just as earlier writers who saw Tibet as a Shangri-la or as a feudal hell generalized their perceptions of spiritual accomplishment or social brutality. Thus in the Chinese case the language of socialist demonology is often mined for negative depic-tions to show Tibet as, for example, a barbarian needing civilizing.[18] At other times the terminology of social and national evolution is used to locate present-day Tibetans at a lower stage on the scale of evolution, and thus in need of assistance to progress to a more advanced stage: "Our overall purpose is to strive to construct a united, wealthy and civilized New Tibet!" as the Chinese reformer Hu Yaobang put it in

1980.[19] In Western depictions, terms such as peace, tolerance, and religion—probably borrowed from relevant texts of international norms—are reproduced in their adjectival forms in representations of Tibet, or Tibetans, to define them as peaceful, tolerant, or religious; in some cases the process is extended to superlatives, so that Tibetans are presented as the most advanced collective embodiment so far of this or that form of specialness.[20]

In each of the various forms in which this theme of violated specialness appears in Western political texts can be found a number of internal contradictions or weaknesses that diminish over time the effectiveness of that representation as discourse in the political arena. Indeed, one of these variations appears less and less often in political texts apparently because it is too vulnerable to contradiction—the view that Tibetans are intrinsically nonviolent. Although one British parliamentarian referred to it in 1999, "the Tibetans were a good and peaceful people—tending their gardens, growing vegetables and flowers, loving children and dogs," as she put it,[21] its use has diminished among professional politicians in the West during the 1990s; instead they have preferred more subtle, less essentialist phraseology about the "path of nonviolent resistance" pursued by the Tibetans, which suggests a choice rather than an inherent quality.[22] Even this phraseology has led to occasional embarrassment for less careful politicians who had suggested that nonviolence has been the Tibetans' sole strategy rather than a recent choice, since the history of recent Tibetan armed resistance, and some accounts of internal political violence,[23] are now well known.

Western politicians seem instead to have gravitated progressively toward three related versions of this representation: Tibet as a site of cultural, religious, or environmental specialness. "The world has witnessed the sad and almost total destruction of Tibet's unique culture and religion, and has done precious little to end the extraordinary repression," a U.S. Congressman said in 1999.[24] Language of this sort is apparently derived from the phrase "Tibet's unique culture," which has appeared in most of the political speeches given by the Dalai Lama after 1987, when he first began to speak on this subject abroad. Similar language can be found in resolutions put to parliaments, and in some cases passed by them, in Russia, France, Belgium, Germany, Australia, the United States, and other countries.[25] More extreme versions of this representation can also be found in speeches by individual parliamentarians, notably those who describe the Tibetans as a collective embodiment of religiosity or as the only society or state apart from the Vatican to be entirely religious. Again, parliamentary and government texts tend (at least explicitly) to avoid such absolute claims, instead referring only to the uniqueness or, more often, the distinctiveness of Tibetan religion or culture, and asserting that its survival is under threat from the Chinese authorities. It was this representation of Tibet as a violated religious zone that was the basis of the 1985 submission on Tibet in the UN,[26] the first since the admission of the PRC to that body in 1971 had halted the earlier efforts to raise the Tibet issue.

Although parliamentary initiatives in the late 1980s had talked about Tibet's unique culture and religion, by the early 1990s, perhaps stirred by the activism on the Tibet issue of Petra Kelly and the Green Party in Germany, parliamentary language about Tibet had started to include references to the environment, and sometimes to the idea that ecological deterioration in Tibet threatened South Asia and other regions. A European Parliament resolution was passed in 1992 "deploring the destruction wrought on the natural environment of Tibet by...the ruthless exploitation of the country's natural resources," which, it said, had "resulted in major deforestation around the upper reaches of Asia's greatest rivers, with catastrophic implications for the future of the region."[27] Much of this language also came from the Dalai Lama's own writing about a primordial Tibet:

> Prior to the Chinese invasion, Tibet was an unspoiled wilderness sanctuary in a unique natural environment. Sadly, in the past decades the wildlife and forests of Tibet have been almost totally destroyed by the Chinese.... What little is left in Tibet must be protected and efforts must be made to restore the environment to its balanced state.[28]

The environmental application of this model offers an insight into the basic character of the "specialness" representation: It is a view of Tibetans as an endangered species, or of Tibet as a threatened habitat.

As the American Buddhist scholar Robert Thurman described it, "the Tibetans are the baby seals of the human rights movement."[29] All the representations of Tibet as special share this sense of an unindividuated collectivity or zone that is unique and at risk. This is again important in a political analysis of these representations because it reproduces the colonializing type of relation between the writer and the subject that can be seen in literary texts of the romanticizing type and has disabling implications similar to those generated by the image of the rape victim.

It is also a reminder that in many ways the models presented by Chinese and Western political texts are very similar: the phrase "Tibet's unique natural environment," for example, is standard in Chinese official texts.[30] The models underlying this idea of specialness differ in the same ways as the choices of terminology and image—the Chinese official conception sees the uniqueness as backwardness that needs to be advanced or educated through the process of social evolution; the Western conception seems to view it as something quaint or special that needs to be preserved or returned to an earlier condition. At a basic level the differences between the Western and Chinese political representations are small, and, as we shall see, the two models are converging in both image and import, with all the indications of political rapprochement that this implies. The Chinese and Western views of Tibet as virginal and as special mainly differ, therefore, in whether the imagined inexperienced Tibet or Tibetan is regarded as a barbarian or as an innocent, as requiring civilizing or as needing protection and preservation.

But there is a point when representations have to be judged not morally by their closeness to some perceived reality or to a code of ethics or principles, but by the political message they are designed to convey and by the benefits they offer to those who buy into their imagery. One of the difficulties in the Western representations of Tibet as a victim is that if they were ever actualized, the offer they hold for their adherents is the restoration of pride, support for a nationalist ideal, and a return to a *status quo ante;* since these are essentially symbolic or psychological conditions, the sustainers of these representations do not have the power to enforce or actualize their texts. The offer implicit in China's representation of Tibet is that China will provide the material accouterments of what it defines as civilization or modernity, a promise that it has the ability to carry out; to some extent it has already done so. Intellectually and politically this representation seems therefore to be more practicable and, in real-world terms, more coherent than the Western offer. Nevertheless, as we shall see, some Tibetans have chosen to encourage the Western offer, apparently because they see it as useful in their efforts to realize their own visions of a desirable future.

Human Rights

There is nothing inherent or inevitable about the decision to view Tibet as a zone of violated specialness or virginity. The Western alliance that repossessed Kuwait in 1990 never felt it necessary, for example, to argue that the Kuwaiti sheikh was a man of extraordinary virtue, or that Kuwaiti culture was of exemplary quality; in fact, it was often noted that the Kuwaiti regime was implicated in quite extensive human rights abuses. In theory, Western politicians could have described Tibet as an invaded independent state, as they did with Kuwait, but although many activists and some individual politicians in the West believe that Tibet was independent when the Chinese troops arrived, that representation rarely appears in parliamentary statements (and certainly in no governmental statements) in the last twenty years, apart from the U.S. Congressional Resolution of May 1991 and its various restatements in the U.S. Congress;[31] even the Indonesian concession of independence to East Timor in 1999 provoked few comparisons with Tibet. Of course, this reticence is partly the result of realpolitik considerations by the politicians: Few would want to provoke a serious confrontation with China. But it may also be significant that the representation of Tibet as an invaded nation lacks the cachet of uniqueness offered by the model of violated specialness: Since some 180 other political entities are independent nation-states, there is nothing unique about being one. Neither can this notion be easily phrased so as to represent a condition of violated virginity, unless one were to ignore (as is usually done) the fact that Tibet had been invaded several times in the past, by the Chinese, British, Nepalese, and Ladakhis. An invaded Tibet might merit sympathy in that a universal principle of international law has been abused, but it might not serve so many years after the event to command public attention and interest.

The same observation could be made about the decision not to represent Tibet as a colony entitled to decolonization.[32] If such a model had been developed, it would also have been based on the violation of a universally accepted legal principle, but its appeal would have been through its collegiality with other colonized peoples rather than through its uniqueness. This representation has been in effect abandoned or ignored by Western politicians as far as Tibet is concerned, despite recent efforts by Tibetan leaders to introduce it.[33] This suggests that the perception of politics itself had changed among those Tibetan leaders and others who at least in the 1980s promoted the imagery of violated specialness: Instead of seeing politics as the effort to attract support from political institutions and their leaders by using the specialist vocabulary of that alliance to argue common purpose and mutual interest, they handled their international relations politics as a form of public relations—that is, as an endeavor to attract popular support through emotions such as sympathy or outrage.[34] These exile leaders, having realized in the mid-1980s that foreign governments had no strategic or political interest in raising the Tibet issue, decided instead to pressurize them by mobilizing popular support among their constituents. The colonial concept, however, offered none of the easily communicable attractiveness of the vivid imaginary worlds conjured up by the models of specialness and violation. In any case the prominent use of white intermediaries by Tibetans to present their case would have been regarded by many Third World politicians as in itself a form of colonialism and as contradicting any claim made on that basis. The Tibetan exiles instead turned for support to former colonizers rather than to the formerly colonized and chose public relations rather than political alliance as its form of politics. As I suggested earlier, the Tibet issue in the international domain is thus not really a political debate, since it does not address the political interests of other social forces; it is more an attempt to achieve political effects by engaging people in a shared image or representation.

The presentation of Tibet as violated specialness involved another choice: To which body of primordial principles should it appeal in order to locate or legitimize its perception of these incidents as violations? The Chinese authorities, who also saw Tibet as a site of violation, had appealed to various sets of general principles—to notions of statehood and territory when deploring imperialist interference in Chinese territory before 1950, to the unvarying precedents of history when dismissing claims to independence, to Marxist laws when defining the traditional Tibetan system of governance as a form of class oppression, and to the principles of social evolution or advancing civilization when explaining the need for Chinese intervention in Tibetan social structure. Increasingly—and this may be the most significant challenge to Tibetan political strategies in the West—Western politicians are starting to use this last model as their basis also for constructing an image of the situation in Tibet. But the dominant appeal in Western political rhetoric about Tibet remains that to the principles of human rights. It is in this choice that, perhaps, the influence of the exile Tibetan leadership can be seen most clearly.

The rhetoric of human rights has a long history, but as an active tool of policy in international relations it is a fairly recent device. There was a period after the First World War when Wilsonian assertions about the right of self-determination led eventually to the wide acceptance of the collective right to decolonization, but individual human rights did not emerge as a policy instrument until the Carter presidency, when they were used to attack the Soviet Union by focusing on its treatment of Jewish dissidents. However, even before the end of the Cold War the principle was being widely applied in the media and by politicians to other situations, and in early 1987 Roberta Cohen, formerly Carter's adviser on human rights, called for the principle to be applied to relations with the PRC.[35] At about the same time, the exile leaders in Dharamsala completed their plans for the Dalai Lama to give political speeches abroad in order to place international pressure on the Chinese to end abuses in Tibet.

There was a major representational aspect to this decision: Choices had to be made, consciously or not, about what was to be understood not just by the terms "violation" or "abuse," but also by much more loaded words: "international," "Chinese," "Tibet," "people" and "rights." As I understand it, it was at this time that it was decided that the main principle to which the Dalai Lama would appeal in his foreign speeches would be the principle of human rights; if so, the Tibetans could be seen as ahead of, rather than responding to, Western representations of Tibet, for whom the human rights model became dominant after the October 1987 demonstrations in Lhasa. The exile leadership also decided, as much through practical limitations as through considered strategy, that the notion "international" was to be understood as contiguous with Western. That mis/representation of the international community was to have extensive implications for the effectiveness of this strategy, since it meant that the Tibet issue would be identified with Western interests, and would attract little support from developing countries.[36] Whatever the reasons, in the summer of 1987 the Dalai Lama began a series of speeches, mainly in Western countries, in which he invoked the language of threatened and violated specialness and called for support for Tibet on the grounds of human rights.

Weaknesses in the Human Rights Approach: The Problem of Evidence

Many of the assertions behind these presentations of the Tibetan situation are problematic, even in the restrained forms in which they appeared in most parliamentary resolutions and yet more so in governmental statements. Claims that Tibetan resistance to the Chinese has always been nonviolent, for example, have been undermined by the publication of accounts of the guerilla movement. The idea that Tibet has a unique culture overlooks the Tibetan cultural world beyond political Tibet, wherever that is located, as well as a widely held view that culture is hybrid and constantly evolving; the notion of a wholly Buddhist society ignores its Bon and Muslim elements, as well as a probable atheist-Communist sector. The contradictions within the environmental view have been exposed by Toni Huber in his work.[37]

Nevertheless in some ways the claims to specialness provided an extraordinarily effective and sustained political vehicle for the Tibetan leadership: Over a dozen or so years the Dalai Lama was able to visit

forty countries on some 170 occasions, always amid extensive publicity, and often, despite strong Chinese objections and Western reluctance, meeting the political leaders of those countries as well. The
human rights approach has also shown evident advantages, particularly in that it has attracted wide media attention and public sympathy,
and in that it allowed access to the UN through its Commission on
Human Rights: For the planners in Dharamsala the deployment of this
approach was a strategic success of a high order. But it also included
gradual disadvantages that were not at first apparent. Some of these can
be seen by examining the role of evidence in appeals to principles of
human rights.

The notion of human rights being quasi legal, arguments to this
principle tend to require nourishment by evidence of one kind or
another. The evidence presented by the Chinese side—unquestionable
facts of history, statistics, and statements by officials—relied on its
claims to authoritativeness. The Tibetan notion of evidence seems to
have depended on a sense that the Chinese claims could be over-
whelmed by appealing to authenticity, as demonstrated by the experienced truthfulness of eyewitness reports, especially those given by
ordinary, previously unknown Tibetans.[38] The focus of the exile Tibetan
effort turned from the exile community as a site of enduring "Tibetanness" to the internal community in Tibet as enduring victims of abuse,
and newly arrived refugees who, from the late 1980s were crossing the
mountains into Nepal at the rate of two thousand or more a year, were
called upon to present testimonies of their personal experiences at
international forums. Much of the force of Tibetan exile presentations
during this period derived from the idea that the authentic voice of
ordinary Tibetans was being heard.[39]

The task of collecting evidence of violations in Tibet was taken up
by a number of organizations and individuals, some with connections
to the exile government or to the support movement, and others with
commitments to journalism or human rights research.[40] A permanent
post was established by the Tibetan exile government on the margins
of the UN Commission on Human Rights in Geneva, full time debrief-
ing operations were set up either by the exiles or by Western monitor-
ing groups at reception centers for refugees arriving in Kathmandu and

Dharamsala, and numerous organizations and individuals traveled to conduct their own interviews with these witnesses, or to visit Tibet to authenticate their own perceptions. All of this mirrored to some extent the process that the Tibetans had pursued in 1959 with their presentations to the International Commission of Jurists (ICJ), a process that had been deeply tarnished by the ICJ's involvement in the Cold War politics of the time.[41] This time, however, the appeal was to the supposedly ideology-free canon of human rights, rather than to a discredited principle of opposing Communism.

Another difference from earlier efforts was that this time the main vehicle for propagating the information was the liberal media: Tibet had become a cross-party or centrist issue in Western Europe and North America and was no longer confined to the conservative end of the political spectrum. Furthermore, much of the evidence this time was coming from Westerners, many of them journalists, who had been allowed into Tibet when it was opened to tourism after 1979, and there is no doubt that Western governments and the media were more ready to give credence to information gathered by Westerners than to the same information gathered by refugees.

A number of difficulties emerged with the spread of this human rights evidentiary approach. Firstly, the evidence was presented by some politicians or activists in ways that went beyond the normal conventions of quasi-legal evidence, particularly in the case of generalizations based on necessarily partial data. Mainstream journalists and human rights organizations rely on what one might call a notion of reasonable extrapolation, whereby a piece of evidence or testimony is cited as indicative of a number of similar but thus far undocumented incidents only if it can survive various tests of probability. These include such questions as whether the incident was feasible in practical terms, whether it could have achieved any reasonable purpose for the alleged perpetrators, whether the government in its published materials had ever indicated it even abstrusely, whether the evidence was first- rather than secondhand, whether the language of the evidence was neutral or emotive, and so on. In theory, evidence of abuses should be cited as indicative of a policy of human rights abuses only if it meets these criteria.

What happened in a number of cases, however, was that certain kinds of evidence—those with particular emotive or ideological appeal to some sectors of the political spectrum—were represented as indicating a far wider extent of abuse than could "reasonably" be claimed. This form of representation (or re-representation), which I call "totalization," attempts to maximize rhetorical effect by applying partial observation or information to an entire group or situation.

This totalizing tendency appeared most prominently in discussions of the issue of forced abortions among Tibetan women, where occasional or unclear reports of the practice were presented as if the incidents were rampant throughout Tibet.[42] This in turn led to the re-emergence in some Tibet-related political discourse in the West of the term "genocide," apparently on the assumption that the birth control policy was intended to wipe out Tibetans.[43] The allegation was unsustainable, since evidence of a forced sterilization policy in Tibet was still inconclusive, since such a policy would not have eradicated the Tibetan people (the abortions or sterilizations took place only after a certain number of births), and since the much stricter policy applied to the Chinese people has come nowhere near wiping them out. Claims of genocide could hardly be sustained by pointing to other forms of killings, since after 1990 the Chinese authorities had ended the shoot-to-kill policy applied to demonstrators in the streets from 1987–89 (though it has continued for prison protests), and since 1989, apart from within prisons, no deaths or executions for political actions had been reported from Tibet at all.[44] The term therefore disappeared in general from serious Western and exile discourse, to be replaced by the more measured but rather unclear term preferred by the Dalai Lama, namely "cultural genocide," a notion that retained the drama of the earlier phrase without the gross inaccuracy. This term was then in turn applied in a totalized way[45] with the result that in his speeches the Dalai Lama soon found it necessary to qualify even this phrase by the remark "whether intentional or not," since there was no evidence of a deliberate policy to wipe out Tibetan culture (though there was powerful evidence of restrictions placed on it). But it was too late: The term had become in its unqualified form a stable element of Western political discourse about Tibet, especially in more conservative political circles.

The forced abortion claims, in the totalized form that they assumed in some quarters, had another inherent weakness: They provoked independent scholars, obliged by academic conventions to contest evident inaccuracies, to disprove the claims. This was childishly easy to do when campaigners had described abuses as occurring systematically throughout Tibet. Thus when two leading scholars published data on increasing family sizes in the community where they had worked in Central Tibet, allegations of forced birth control became unsustainable in their overstated form, and even more measured claims were seen as suspect.[46]

The totalization trend had another consequence: It encouraged politicians with more extreme views to take up the Tibet issue. Thus, for example, the Tibet issue became rapidly more prominent on the agenda of politicians with ideological commitments to ending birth control. A similar process occurred with the religious issue: It was taken up by conservative politicians with a commitment to oppose religious suppression, particularly as it related to attacks on Christian evangelism. Chinese officials had significantly increased controls and harassment of religious practitioners in Tibet after 1994, but even so, suppression of religion was selective and specific to certain locations and practices. Thus, inflated accounts of religious suppression could easily be refuted by a casual visitor to Tibet on the grounds that they had seen pilgrims at prayer in prominent temples.[47] The decision to represent Tibet in terms of its "specialness," a choice made in part because the image was ideologically mild and intangible, yet imaginatively vivid and dramatic, had thus led to a drift toward the right and toward easy refutation.

This was problematic for the Tibetan exiles and the Tibet lobby groups, especially because it coincided with the re-emergence of strong, socially conservative political parties in Europe and in the United States, heightened by the disintegration of the Soviet bloc after 1989. It was an important strategic principle for the exile Tibetan leadership to try to prevent the Tibet issue from being isolated at one extreme of the political spectrum if it was to avoid a repeat of the collapse suffered by the Tibet question in the late 1960s, when its perception as an anticommunist movement had led to the discrediting of the evidentiary claims made by Tibetans,[48] as well as to the collapse of governmental support after the rapprochement that followed the meeting between Nixon and Mao in 1971. It had been difficult, therefore, for exile Tibetan leaders to capture a broad base of support in the West.

There had been Tibet support groups of a kind in Europe and elsewhere since 1959, but these had been conservative in character and strategy, working within political elites, and gradually becoming organizations focused on refugee relief work as they lost active support after 1971 from governments and even from right wing politicians. The great achievement, therefore, of the exiles' 1987 initiative was that, perhaps for the first time, the Tibetan issue became acceptable to center-leftists as well as to more conservative political sectors that had traditionally given it their support. The groups founded in 1987 or afterward represented the involvement in the issue of young, politically astute people from the liberal areas of the political spectrum, usually from the professional classes, who had a natural alliance with the media as well as with some sectors of the "New Age" movements in the West, which until then had been largely resistant to any political mobilization. The romantic representation of Tibet as a site of religious excellence or as a bastion of anticommunist resistance had been deeply alienating to this professionalized, left-of-center sector of Western society, just as it was to most professional politicians of that era and, most significantly, to the media. It was the representation of Tibet as a "specialized" site of human rights violations that seems to have made the issue palatable to a broad, cross-party community.[49]

In particular, the exiles' strategy of asking the Dalai Lama to travel abroad and speak on political issues had a perhaps unexpected bonus: It led to the reluctance or rumored refusal of Western governments to allow entry to the Dalai Lama on his round of tours. This created a mobilizing issue for those to whom the notion of universal human rights was of growing importance, and for whom the idea of a Western democratic government accepting Chinese dictates about whom it should meet was unacceptable.[50] Reports of such refusals and the controversies they provoked appeared not on the foreign pages but on the more influential domestic news pages of Western newspapers and involved opposition parties as well as lobby groups in accusing a sitting government of complicity with Chinese intolerance—a representation that was hard for any democratic government to refute so long as it refused access to the Tibetan leader. Thus the Tibetans' 1987 initiative had created a cross-party support base and had also moved the Tibet issue from the foreign agenda to the much more potent domestic agenda of many Western countries.[51] The Dalai Lama's presence at the fringes of the UN conferences in Brazil and Vienna in 1992 and 1993 lifted these issues of Western complicity onto a world stage.

This achievement in the late 1980s was put at risk by the drift of the human rights representation of Tibet toward overstatement, its attractiveness to far right conservatives, and its vulnerability to apparent contradiction. Thus, when a public dispute emerged in Australia in 1999 over a typical allegation about violations in Tibet, it was no longer a marginal pro-Chinese politician who was defending Beijing's record in Tibet but a senior member of the ruling party.[52] The tendency to representational distortion within the Tibet issue had, it seemed, alienated even centrist politicians.

Totalitarianism and Double Orientalism

An additional problem with the representation of Tibet as a site of human rights abuses was that in many cases it tended to become vulnerable because of what we might call "double orientalism"—the tendency to view the Chinese system of governance and society as deeply alien because it is "Eastern" or Asian, coupled with the tendency to view it as deeply alien because it is Communist and totalitarian. Essentialist constructions of this kind rendered ineffective some of the evidence that was integral to the human rights case made about Tibet from the 1980s onward. For example, a Westerner who imagines "the Chinese," "the Chinese Communists" or "totalitarianism," as ruthlessly efficient or monolithic in thought and operation, tends to assume that implementation of a policy will be uniform and comprehensive. However, because in China the press is controlled by the government, and because significant challenges to the state's authority are not allowed, a wide range of views, compliance, and policy implementation is tolerated in areas that are considered insignificant or that the state does not have the resources to control—exactly the opposite of what might be envisaged as characteristic of a totalitarian system. Another, perhaps (to outsiders) unexpected consequence of this system is that written orders and instructions are almost always vague and ambiguous, because no official wants to be held responsible in the event of a later reversal or reinterpretation of the policy. One therefore finds within China and Tibet extremely wide variations, from township to township, of the extent and form in which any policy is implemented and very little explicit written evidence that the policy exists. Thus even a reasonable claim that a certain policy has been implemented in Tibet or China is readily susceptible to contradiction by any visitor or researcher, since it might well have been implemented in one village but not in another. Claims of human rights abuses are thus frequently refuted because of the structural inadequacies within the conception they assume of the Chinese state.

There was another cluster of problems within the notion of human rights itself. That notion implied primordiality—the presumption that human rights principles have existed since an unspecified time in the remote past. In fact, a body of written, internationally accepted legislation on human rights has emerged only in the last century, but the notion, at least when used to mobilize popular support, is often presented in terms of "natural law," implying that these rights are immanent and preexisting, although strictly speaking they are imaginary or conventional. When the most powerful proponents of this view—usually Western governments—insist on the absolute correctness of their interpretations, it provokes other parties to see these absolutist readings of what is a recent, multi-authored text as a challenge to their political authority. The debates over "Asian values" and "noninterference in internal affairs" were partly responses to this conflict, but they were rapidly discarded by the Chinese (to the discomfort of their less adaptive allies)[53] and replaced by the accusation that Western powers were using human rights to bully developing countries. The use by the West of the human rights model for Tibet thus enabled China, Malaysia, India, and other countries to present the Tibet issue as a device to promote Western political domination. The evident fact that the Dalai Lama's team had directed all his efforts toward Western countries gave the Chinese authorities greater opportunity to represent the Tibet issue in this light. The human rights version of the Tibet issue was thus rapidly locked into larger debates of this kind, and to some extent became marginalized as post–Cold War tension increased during the 1990s between developing countries and Western powers.[54]

In early 1994 the United States reversed its position on China's trading status and ended attempts to link that status to human rights conditions, and essentially the role of human rights as a tool of leverage in international relations collapsed, at least in relation to China. It was replaced by the notion of "constructive engagement," which meant that countries met in private once or twice a year to discuss human rights issues, a practice that has not been shown to yield practical results.[55] At least at a superficial view, the human rights strategy pursued by the Tibetan exiles since 1987 had been neutralized and required adaptation.

Two further complications arose from the choice of the human rights–related representation in the political domain. One of these is related to the fact that this approach is ideologically indistinct—all parties in the political process, including those in China, since the 1980s express support for the principle of human rights, which is why it had seemed a good choice as a basis for a representation of Tibet's political conditions and needs. However, this absence of ideological precision renders the human rights approach relatively impotent as a political tool. It can define perpetrators in particular instances of abuse, and even in patterns of abuse, but it cannot invoke a politically coherent description of a state's policies, especially since almost all states posture to occupy the same ground within this discourse. Concepts like dictatorship, colonial power, and empire describe actual forms of the exercise of power rather than vaguely defined moral improprieties; as tools of criticism they address the structural bases of a wide swath of policies and outcomes, and invoke deep-seated responses among political activists and leaders as a result. The human rights approach, by contrast, addresses moral aberrations and ends up "policing" them rather than "struggling" for a cause. This approach leads to a further difficulty: As a largely moral strategy, it lends itself to a blurring of distinctions between word and deed. This is reflected in a typical confusion about the distinction between arms of government in the Western system.

Both legislative and executive arms of Western governments have expressed support for the human rights principles invoked in Tibetan cases since 1987, but most of these statements were legislative, not executive, and thus were rarely binding on governments; executive statements were naturally much weaker.[56] In general, the spate of statements about the importance of ending human rights abuses in Tibet that emerged from parliaments and governments during the late 1980s and the 1990s gave the impression that much was being accomplished in the political domain, while in fact the activity was almost entirely rhetorical in nature.

It is in fact a particular complication of human rights discourse that, since governments and politicians will interpret and implement their support for human rights principles in very different ways, it becomes very difficult to distinguish verbal from actual support. The "imaginary" character of the notion of human rights in itself encourages this scope for variant interpretations, and this becomes especially apparent in terms of the mechanisms that are offered as remedies. Essentially, putting aside the option of economic sanctions, which the exile Tibetan leaders themselves decided should not be called for, human rights remedies are rhetorical—they lack any realistic possibility of enforcement and are limited basically to a government, parliamentary, UN, or NGO official writing to the Chinese authorities and requesting, proposing, or demanding a remedy. The basic stratagem, therefore, is one of threatening to cause embarrassment. Before 1994 there was an implication of real economic and political consequences if the abuses were not corrected, mainly because of America's threats until that year to withhold the renewal of China's trading privileges. Indeed, until that time these threats were to some extent effective.[57] But the larger problem, apart from the effectiveness, was that it became rapidly impossible to tell if a Western government or politician was threatening to embarrass China in order to impress his or her domestic constituency, while indicating to China or assuming that the threat of embarrassment would be understood by Beijing as empty rhetoric.[58]

The other, and perhaps the most serious, complication that arose as a result of this approach was that the success of the human rights model appears to have been achieved at the expense of concerns much more central for the Tibetans, such as the question of Tibet's status. Western governments reluctant to antagonize Beijing expressed support for human rights while at that same time, as a quid pro quo to mollify Beijing, they scaled down or discarded their support for more substantive issues like Tibetan political or territorial claims.[59] These complications were not ignored by the Tibetan exiles and their advisers, who later made rather strenuous efforts to replace them with another, more suitable representation.[60]

Western governments, seeking the form of representation that would least antagonize China, had found that the models of specialness offered by pro-Tibet politicians were so lacking in political definition and specificity that they could be easily appropriated by governments to suit their own purposes—in other words, they offered a language that could be used ambiguously so that the domestic audience would see it as criticizing China while Chinese officials might be persuaded that the criticisms were sufficiently mild so as not to be threatening to fundamental concerns. They thus began from the early 1990s to invest strongly in a diluted version of the representation of Tibet as a special but imperiled culture, and to refer to "distinctive cultural, religious and ethnic" features of "the Tibetan people" that were at risk, often mentioning environmental issues as well. They avoided terms referring to total destruction, nationhood, territory, or status.

Although the language used resembles the model of "violated specialness" found in Tibetan, journalistic, and some parliamentary statements, the underlying model to which governmental statements about endangered forms of Tibetanness are referring is not necessarily one of a unique or special civilization that must be defended: It is equally likely to be a model of community relations such as pertains within most Western countries when they consider their domestic minorities or indigenous peoples. The words used in both models—protecting cultural, religious, and ethnic identity, and so on—may be indistinguishable, but the contexts may indicate very different connotations. The underlying model emerging in government statements—of perceiving Tibetans as having a "community" identity rather than a "national" identity—had been openly expressed by writers such as Neville Maxwell, who had argued strongly during the 1980s for the concept of "the multi-national

state," which defined countries like China or India as postcolonial and plu-
ralist variants of the nation-state and asserted that friction between ethnic groups within these states was normal and of purely local concern.
Some U.S. scholars have similarly presented the Tibetan situation as analogous to the condition of the black community in the United States and
noted that racial tension continues in the United States even after many
decades of attempts to resolve it. In these representations the Tibetan
nation is being reconstructed as a community or as an ethnic group.

These approaches, which denationalize and deterritorialize the issue,
offer governments a nonconfrontational way of dealing with the Tibet
issue.[61] Since China had represented itself from about 1993 as a state
that fully accepted the universality of human rights—apparently
because it had become clear that Western governments no longer
intended to use human rights as a tool of policy rather than rhetoric—
and since, as we have seen, it anyway regarded Tibetan and other
minority cultures as distinctive and in need of assistance for their preservation, the gap between Chinese and Western governmental positions
was narrowing. The community relations model and the theory of
social evolution have much in common, and it was no coincidence that
at about this time in China the word "ethnic" began to be widely used
instead of "nationality" in official translations of the term *minzu* to
describe Tibetans and other minority groups.

The success of the human rights violation model might thus be said
to have been something of a mixed blessing for the Tibetan exile leaders who had planned it. However, it is clear now that they and their
advisers had always envisaged a gradualist approach in which they
would use this model to engage wide, cross-party Western support, and
would then progress to other, more complex political issues or models.
But they were caught unawares by the speed with which the human
rights representation became successful and firmly established: they
underestimated the power of the construction.[62] In practice, they were
partially trapped by the success of the initial representation they generated, which was far more attractive to their most influential audience than other, more politicized, models to which they might have
wanted to progress. In fact, given that the essence of a representation
is that its force derives not from logic but from a kind of primordial

shared conviction, supplemented by evidence of various kinds, it could be argued that it would always have been very difficult to shift people from one effective shared representation to another. This is, however, easy to say with the advantage of hindsight and may have been unimaginable in meetings in Dharamsala before there were any signs of significant Western interest in the Tibetan political project.

"Misrepresentation Representations" and Other Models

The human rights model was not the only way in which the Tibet issue was represented in the international community. In India especially there was much interest in the representation of Tibet as a site of regional military threat, because of the reported placing of nuclear missiles on the Tibetan plateau, and because of recollections of the 1962 Sino-Indian war and the 1987 military clash over the siting of the Indo-Tibetan border, an issue still not resolved.[63] The preeminent Tibetan political scientist Dawa Norbu wrote that only if this representation were taken up would the Tibet issue ever be capable of resolution,[64] but despite attempts to introduce it elsewhere,[65] this approach appears in public political discourse mainly in India, where it appears to be confined chiefly to sections of the military and supporters of the Bharatiya Janata Party (the BJP). Briefly, in 1997, just after the BJP came to rule and declared India a nuclear power, this representation of Tibet as a zone of major strategic concern shifted dramatically from the legislative and media sectors to the government, when George Fernandes, then India's Minister of Defense, made a statement that China was India's main source of threat,[66] the first time in recent years that the Indian Government had taken a proactive position on the Tibet-China issue. The statement led to an immediate downturn in relations with China and had to be withdrawn; but the incident showed the potential force of representing Tibet as a zone of military or geo-strategic significance.

Since the early 1990s two other, interlinked representations have emerged that have been effective in public discourse, particularly in Western cultures, and that have come to dominate foreign journalistic discussions of Tibet so that in time they are likely to influence foreign political accounts also. One of these is the depiction of Tibet as a site of misrepresentation. The idea that Tibet is not really a mystical or romantic place reemerged as the standard journalistic comment on Tibet in the early 1990s not long after the publication of Peter Bishop's book, *The Myth of Shangri-la*. His description of Western fabulating about Tibet was not entirely new, since even in the 1970s, if not earlier, scholars had criticized mystical depictions of Tibet.[67] But it led in the last decade to a great proportion of foreign journalistic reports about Tibet being based on the revelation that Tibet was not utopia. "Clinton to Find no Shangri-la on Tibet," Reuters had announced in June 1998; "The Shangri-la That Never Was," declared a headline in the *New York Times* the following week.[68]

Such comments are in fact more a rhetorical device than a discussion about Tibet. They rely on the expression of surprise at something already known to be untrue, rather like publishing an exposé revealing that Camelot never existed, and depend on the unproven supposition that there exists a large and significant cohort of readers who conceptualize Tibet as a paradise; they are linked usually to the presumption that the writer has superior knowledge, acquired typically by visiting Tibet. Both these forms of "revelatory" device—one of exposing the truth to an illiterate or misreading audience, and the other of exposing the truth as a result of empirical knowledge—are found in academic writing about Tibet as well as in statements by journalists and politicians.[69]

This "misrepresentation representation" thus depends on writers claiming the authority to reveal their higher knowledge, and, accordingly, tends to communicate the perceptiveness of the author rather than a perception of a place or a people. There is no political specificity about the representation of Tibet as a site of misrepresentations: Writers at either end of the political spectrum find this model equally appropriate to their needs and can use it as part of their own projects.

A second category of texts within this "misrepresentation" group challenged not only the Shangri-la view of Tibet, but also the notion of violation. These writers also tended to rely on the authority they acquired from the performance of a visit, as a result of which they reported that there was little significant evidence of major human rights violations or of popular discontent,[70] although in some cases the abuses they refuted had been alleged only in totalizing discourse and, never having been defined with any precision, had had only a ghostlike presence in the debate. Out of this dialectical negotiation of misrepresentations there has emerged a growing and important body of writing. When writers of this school do describe a Tibet, rather than a debate, the model that is most often used is that of the spreading of modernity—a society changing under the influence of technology, modernization, communications, and globalized culture (in fact, the Tibet that is described by this model is almost entirely urban, as if the 88 percent of Tibetans who live in the countryside inhabit some other place). Again, this is a perception that writers of both political wings find themselves able to use: Since the 1979 reforms, and especially since Deng Xiaoping called for a commitment to rapid marketization of the economy in 1992, the principal Chinese rhetoric about Tibet has also become a rhetoric about modernity:

> We are engaged in the great undertaking of bringing a new, prosperous socialist Tibet into a glorious twenty-first century.... A modernization blueprint of unequalled magnificence will unfold before 2.3 million people of all ethnic groups.[71]

The proposition that Chinese rule provides modernization has now replaced liberation from feudal oppression as the central legitimation device for the Chinese state and the Communist Party in Tibet; the new theme recurs in almost all political texts that explain the Chinese role in Tibetan lives and futures. This means, of course, that there are two or more interpretations of the same modernization, of the same fax machines, mobile phones, metalled roads, computer links and multistoried asymmetrical office blocks with tinted glass and chrome exteriors that line the streets of Tibetan towns: To the Chinese state, these facets of modernization represent progress, while to some foreign writers and observers they represent modernization as encroachment, depravity, or the erosion of distinctiveness and tradition. Some of these writers raised the question as to how modernization should be considered, and recognized that interpreting this process was problematic.[72]

In more popular writings, however, it is often portrayed unquestion-
ingly as a threat to cultural survival:

> Li Wong stretches her legs invitingly towards the tourists.
> "Hello, come in," whispers the Chinese prostitute who works in
> one of the street brothels of Lhasa that surround the Potala
> palace, once the seat of the Dalai Lama and one of the holiest
> places of Tibetan Buddhism[73]

reported a German Press Agency in 1994. To writers of this school,
modernization is represented as an attack on Tibetan innocence by Chinese predators, in what appears to be another variation on the notion
of Tibet as sexually violated.[74]

Another version of this view, perhaps the most pervasive, describes
immigrant entrepreneurs—usually envisaged primarily as Chinese men
rather than Chinese prostitutes—as the new form of threat to the vulnerable culture; this view is central to the picture presented by the Dalai
Lama and his officials and has wide currency in the political as well as
the journalistic domains, where it is often linked directly to threats to
wipe out Tibetan culture.[75] It is particularly important because it is
often adopted by Western governments as well as parliamentarians,
albeit in more restrained terms. Thus the 1996 report of the U.S.
Department of State on human rights noted that

> ethnic Han and Hui immigrants from other parts of China,
> encouraged by government policies and new opportunities are
> competing with—and in some cases displacing—Tibetan enter-
> prises and labor...rapid and ecologically inappropriate growth
> has also disrupted traditional living patterns and thereby threat-
> ened traditional Tibetan culture. [76]

Modernization, therefore, is a theme that, like other representations, can be appropriated for almost any political need with very little change of language, even more readily than human rights
discourse. Thus the spectrum of foreign readings of modernization is
wide—it includes interpreting it as a Chinese extermination plot, as

a developmental consequence of globalization that exists irrespective of "the Chinese" and their policies, and as the process of beneficial social evolution. It therefore has the inherent ambiguity of an image, in that it can be proposed with one meaning while it is used politically in another, allowing a government to present a model of Tibet intended to be read by its domestic audience as concern for the threat to traditional culture, and by Chinese diplomats as sympathy for the difficulties of bringing a backward society into the modern world.

It is, in fact, inaccurate to consider the modernization process in Tibet as a value-neutral device by Chinese policymakers designed to advance living standards. Wang Lixiong, for example, although sometimes regarded as a critic of Chinese state policy, describes it quite openly in his influential paper on Tibet as a policy mechanism for countering religion and nationalism in Tibet:

> A market economy has certainly helped to clear up the religion problem, particularly among the urban Tibetans who have gotten more deeply involved in market actions, where the religious mind set is being steadily downplayed, and the people are starting to take an interest in worldly enjoyment.[77]

The modernization theme is therefore problematic for the Tibetan exile project: It neither accentuates the specialness of Tibet nor provides a language that identifies the policy objectives of Western governments and politicians if and when they take up this approach. Like human rights discourse, representations developed around this theme can be evocative as rallying calls within the "public relations" mode of political discourse (for example, by saying that the survival of Tibetan culture is threatened) but ambiguous and deceptive as builders of practical political positions and collective interests beyond the superficial level. It offers a shared linguistic framework within which Chinese and non-Chinese political forces can conceal their differences and, by exploiting its ambiguities, find themselves within what is in effect an alliance in diminishing or neutralizing the claims of Tibetan nationalists.

The Dalai Lama As Tibet

There have been a number of attempts to circulate counter-representations within the contemporary discussion of Tibet, most of them attacks on the personal credibility of the Dalai Lama. In 1995 the Chinese authorities sought to link him both to the Asahara cult in Japan[78] and, following revelations concerning Heinrich Harrer's past, to the Nazi Party.[79] Chinese writers also accused the Dalai Lama or his advisers of planning assassinations, bombings, and sabotage in Tibet,[80] as well as alleging that he wished to restore the "feudal-theocratic system." Western counterrepresentations focused more on the notion that the Dalai Lama's authority was in doubt because of his association with film stars,[81] disputes among Tibetans over the use of armed resistance,[82] or his ban of the sectarian protector-deity Dorje Shugden.[83] These negative images did not make any significant impact on the political texts produced by Western nations, or from countries with special connections to Tibet like India, Mongolia, Taiwan, and Japan, but in the rest of the world, where one finds little reference to the idea of Tibet as special or of the Dalai Lama as worthy of respect, these counter-representations are more influential, a reminder that foreign support for the Tibet issue is highly localized. But the persistent Chinese representation of the Dalai Lama as an unreliable negotiating partner, whether it was believed or not, has nevertheless come to dominate the consideration of the Tibet issue for Western policymakers. This can be seen from the famous remark that the U.S. president Bill Clinton found himself having to make to Jiang Zemin at the end of their press conference in Beijing in June 1998: "I have spent time with the Dalai Lama. I believe him to be an honest man and I believe that, if he has a conversation with President Jiang, they will like each other very much."[84] Clinton made no mention in this conversation of Tibet as such, or of its status, its political condition, popular demands, or even of the human rights situation there. In the Western political perception, judging by this crucial example, the Chinese representation of the issue had been rejected in content but accepted in form—the Sino-Tibetan conflict had come to revolve around the interpretation of the Dalai Lama as an individual.[85]

The inordinate success of the exiles' human rights initiative had thus led to the Dalai Lama rather than Tibet being placed on the international agenda, an outcome that the exile leader and his government had expressly sought to avoid. Tibet itself as an imagined community of some kind did assume a profile in the international press and in political statements, as we have seen, but by the end of the 1990s most political and governmental statements had come to focus largely on the role of the Dalai Lama as an object of negotiation.[86] I use the word "object" here because in these texts he is often referred to as someone with whom the Chinese should "converse," to use Clinton's word: There is little mention in foreign political and journalistic texts of what he or the Chinese should be talking about, or what the criteria for an acceptable resolution might be.[87] The notions of "dialogue" and "negotiation" have acquired in this discourse a kind of virtual quality, as if the act of a Chinese official speaking with the Dalai Lama would be a ritual performance that would constitute in itself a solution to the conflict.

In the political domain, especially in governmental documents, the dominant representation of the Tibetan issue in the late 1990s has thus become this representation of Tibet as the Dalai Lama. The elision of the leader with the nation runs deep within Tibetan tradition, as the Dalai Lama himself noted in his 1962 autobiography:

> I am a mortal being…but [the Tibetans] believed the Dalai Lama represented Tibet and the Tibetan way of life, something dearer to them than anything else. They were convinced that if my body perished at the hands of the Chinese, the life of Tibet would also come to an end. [88]

It is no mean achievement to have exported this perception of Tibet and the Dalai Lama as one into foreign discourse, because there is a constant tension between his role as a traveling teacher representing spirituality in general and his role as a representative of a country in crisis.[89] However, the Western version of this personification has taken a more literal form. Just as his words are taken as those of the Tibetan people, so his personal history is seen as the story of an exiled, religious people,[90] even though 97 percent of Tibetans remain in Tibet and many may not be religious. Journalistic accounts of meetings with him tend to find meanings in the details of his body or attire, seeing his laugh as symbolic of the collective cheerfulness of the Tibetan race and his robes as representing their religiosity and modesty.[91] The dangers of this kind of emblematic reading can be seen with the Dalai Lama's shoes. Many accounts had written of the sturdiness of his "well-worn leather Oxfords"—they are read as indicating the modesty of the Tibetan character—until 1997, when the *Denver Post* noted that the Lama had changed to a more modern brand. The story was picked up by the Associated Press [92] and led two years later to a statement by the most powerful media figure of all, the news magnate Rupert Murdoch. Murdoch had no problem in regarding the Dalai Lama's footwear as politically significant: "I have heard cynics who say he's a very political old monk shuffling around in Gucci shoes," said Murdoch of the Tibetan leader, "[Tibet] was a pretty terrible old autocratic society out of the Middle Ages.... it was an authoritarian, medieval society without any basic services," he added.[93] In the hands of the man whom many would regard as the most influential user of political representations, the new shoes had been deployed to represent cunning and feudal restorationism.

The perception of the Dalai Lama as Tibet remains rooted and accepted, despite the insistence by Western governments (as opposed to parliaments) that he is the spiritual rather than the political leader of Tibet. But although for Tibetans religion and politics are, traditionally, combined, it is not clear that for Western readers the Tibet he embodies is a political Tibet; as I have suggested, he has been imported into a discourse that is more about an idea of specialness than about people with varying interests and demands, which I take to be a determining aspect of politics. There is clearly a political dimension to the perception of the Dalai Lama in Western political discourse; even the Chinese, rather helpfully from this perspective, call him a "political tramp." He is refused visas regularly in Asian and African countries because of what he represents politically. He is cited in all Western governmental appeals to the Chinese authorities concerning Tibet as the person with whom they should negotiate with regard to the future of Tibet. But it is not clear that this Tibet that he represents and whose future he should negotiate is a political Tibet with a defined territory and customs, or a highly complex society in transition with a wide range of sectors and interests, and a rapidly changing social environment. Does he represent perhaps the Tibetan people wherever they find themselves, including those in the eastern areas that Lhasa rarely ruled?[94] Or all the followers of Tibetan Buddhism, or perhaps those who constitute "Tibetan culture"? If so, are Tibetan Buddhists in Ladakh or Sikkim, Tibetan Christians in Leh, or Tibetan Muslims now living in Kuwait or the Middle East included in this notion?

These are the typical questions posed by representational analysts. But even if they are resolved, there is another weakness within this representation: It fails to convey through its imagery a sense of the process by which the Dalai Lama comes to represent his constituents. There is no allowance in this image for the existence of multiple voices, or for the mechanisms by which the Dalai Lama distills disparate interests and views, processes that are central to the modern concept of a representative leader.[95] The absence of hybridity in this image is thus, in terms of political credibility, a source of weakness. The trope of personification by which the Dalai Lama comes to represent a country and a people conveys for a Western audience a sense of mystery, theocracy, and nondemocracy, which are principles he expressly rejects.

This tension is reflected in criticism within the exile community. "It is unfortunate but equally true that the Dalai Lama in exile has tended to discourage the emergence of alternative leaders, unless officially approved by him," Dawa Norbu has written. "However, both in exile and inside Tibet, one observes the emergence of a modern educated class that is independent of Communist or lamaist domination. It is tragic that the Dalai Lama sees no role for such modern educated Tibetans in his vision of a future Tibet in association with China."[96] This statement could be contested—in what was one of the most interesting of all his political initiatives, the Dalai Lama had announced in 1992 that existing cadres in Tibet would retain their positions should he return[97]—but it conveys something of the local, internal cost of a collective representation that might be appealing to outsiders but in which leading members of that collectivity cannot perceive significant inclusion of their role.

The political weakness of the Western view of the Dalai Lama is reflected in foreign attitudes toward ministers of the Tibetan exile government. The Dalai Lama told *Time* magazine in 1997 that he would "love to delegate some responsibilities to his deputies" but "even if some of my Cabinet ministers wanted to give public talks, nobody would come."[98] Logically speaking, if the Dalai Lama is genuinely thought of as a political institution representing the interests of Tibetans, then his elected and appointed ministers would be treated as if they also represented those interests and in principle would be worth meeting, much as the delegation of Tibetan government ministers had been when they visited England in 1948—they were given an official, red-carpet welcome at Victoria Station and then driven to Buckingham Palace, despite strong Chinese objections. The current failure of Tibetan ministers to acquire representative significance in Western perceptions is due in part to the fact that their government is now in exile, but the political imagery now applied to the Dalai Lama anyway depicts him as a personal rather than a political construction, and it has failed to develop imagery inferring a process by which his status, knowledge, or power can be delegated or transferred. For this or some similar reason, he seems to be disempowered in his dealings with Western politicians, as if he were a symbol rather than an agent. The writer Pico Iyer describes a telling remark made by the Dalai Lama in 1997, which perhaps reflects this liminal world to which he has been consigned, within the political domain but not truly of it:

> The single most difficult thing in his life, he admits, is "meeting with politicians. Realistically speaking, it's just symbolic. They cannot do much."[99]

In other words, it could be said that the Dalai Lama is seen as representing the Tibetan people not in a political but in a literary sense, in much the same way that some romanticists saw the Himalayan landscape as representing the Tibetan people. Thus the Tibet he personifies in these political texts seems to be a visionary Tibet rather than a political, shifting, composite, and hybrid Tibet constituted by disparate voices, which is how most "real" nations are conceived. In the final analysis, it would seem, the political imagery deployed in the effort to describe Tibet conspires against its admission into the community of nations.

Conclusion

Thus it seems that the difference between the literary and political envisionings of Tibet may, therefore, be very little. The various representations of Tibet in the political realm—as a site of brutalized innocence, as violated specialness, as an imperiled culture, or as a notion embodied in the person of the Dalai Lama—are all in a sense literary creations, sometimes noble, sometimes highly motivated, but all uniform imaginaries that are often devoid of a sense of political process or complexity, and without a space in which other, nonuniform voices may be heard and easily included.

They thus share with those various literary views of Tibet as a paradise, or of Tibet as a hell, a relation to their supposed subjects that is one that either omits most of them in the interest of uniformity, or deprives them of agency and treats them in the colonializing manner, as lesser, quaint, or predictable, or as victims or embodiments of an idea. As Rinchen Lhamo had pointed out some seventy-five years earlier, these disempowering images that originated from "a conventional statement about us put into vogue by travellers" in any case usually contradicted themselves. The current images, by depicting Tibetans in general as without agency, thus tend to weaken the strength of the claim that they are often invoked to support, the right of Tibetans to self-determination or independence. The appeal to human rights tends to drift toward overstatements that further deny variations and distinctions within the Tibetan situation, or it engenders in political statements an inability to distinguish between rhetorical and practical commitment: These are the typical inherent weaknesses of these models as political devices.

There is, however, a crucial difference from the view that Rinchen Lhamo proposed. The deployment of images of Tibet in Western political discourse since the mid-1980s does not appear to be derived purely from intervention by foreigners: They represent to a significant degree the agency of the Tibetan leadership in Dharamsala, as well as that of other Tibetans, and indicate its strategic use of certain traditionally based conceptual models of Tibet for political or media-related objectives that it regarded as vital to Tibetan interests. In this respect it has been outstandingly successful, even though, as the leaders were probably aware at the time, the models perpetuated in-built implications of political incapacity. If, as now seems probable, exile Tibetan politicians believed that the limitations of the initial images they encouraged in the Western political domain would be offset by their ability in due course to replace them with more sophisticated models, events suggest that they may still be proven right. In other words, it appears that the Tibetan leadership perceived political representation in the West if not elsewhere as a process of continuous adaptation and negotiation in which Tibetans, both in the elite and in other social groups, attempt to adapt and reshape the models that best express their needs or interests at the time. And indeed, within the two months since the first draft of this paper was prepared, two major changes have already taken place in Dharamsala, the seat of the exile government: In February 2000 the Dalai Lama was re-enthroned as the leader of Tibet in a ceremony that, by restaging the 1940 "*gser khri mnga' gsol*," (literally, the "enthronement on the golden throne"), reconstructed before the television cameras of the world the authority of the Dalai Lama as not merely spiritual or personal in its origin but as representing the Tibetan state.[100] In this model his virtue is secondary to the institutional authority invested in him by his office and his subjects: His personal attributes—his shoes, his smile, his beliefs—become less significant than his role as leader.

At the same time, by welcoming the arrival of the seventeenth Karmapa, the fourteen-year-old head of the Karma Kagyu school of Tibetan Buddhism who in January 2000 escaped to India from Tibet, the Dalai Lama initiated a discussion among Tibetans about a political decision that foreign experts and journalists had said was impossible because of the rigidity of Tibetan history, tradition, and sectarianism: the possibility that the Dalai Lama's role could be passed on not by reincarnation as it has been since the seventeenth century, but by consensus or appointment to the head of another religious school. That discussion, even if still tentative and premature, is the most sophisticated response yet by Tibetans to the Chinese strategy of isolating the debate over Tibet to the person of the Dalai Lama, and to the tendency among Western politicians to do the same: It means to Tibetans that even if the Dalai Lama died, their community and their interests could still be represented and embodied without the risk of an interregnum, a phenomenon that had so plagued the earlier system, and on which China appears to have relied since the early 1990s. We can see from such glimpses the quiet, traditionally rooted ways in which the Tibetan community is able to make difficult but creative, and sometimes rapid, shifts in its forms of self-imagining, just as it had done in the 1980s decision to seek international support, as it seeks to shape and adapt the institutional and national representations that its members wish to see held by both their own and other communities.

NOTES

1 A version of this paper was presented at the conference "Representing Tibet" held at the University of Boulder, Colorado, in January 2000. I am grateful to the participants for their contributions to this paper, to Jeanne-Marie Gilbert for assistance with the editing, and to the East Asian Institute at Columbia University. My efforts in this paper are in some ways complementary to Meg McLagan's studies of the representation of Tibet in contemporary political movements in the West, where she too notes "how Tibetans engage Western discourses about Tibetanness in the process of constituting themselves in exile" (McLagan, 1997: 89).

2 Rinchen Lhamo, 1926: 95–96, cited in Tsering, 1996: 3.

3 Jamyang Norbu has written widely on the role of representation. "For years, the only way Tibetans could get a hearing in the world's capitals was to emphasize our spirituality and helplessness ...Tibetans who pick up rifles don't fit that romantic image we've built up in Westerners' heads" (cited in Salopek, 1997). See also Norbu, 1989 and Shakya, 1991, 1993).

4 Donald Lopez describes the Western presentation of the Tibet issue as "a prison, in which Tibetan lamas in exile and their students are at once the inmates and the guards." He placed his discussion of Tibetan exile agency within a concept of mimesis or a "process of doubling," suggesting that the "Tibet that Tibetans in exile have come to appropriate and deploy in an effort to gain standing in exile" was to be seen "only as it was reflected in the elaborately framed mirror of Western fantasies about Tibet" (Lopez, 1998: 11, 13, 200). A discussion of Lopez's argument, with contributions by Germano,

Shakya, Thurman, and Lopez, has been published in *Journal of the American Academy of Religion,* volume 69, issue 1, in March 2001. Vincanne Adams questioned contemporary Tibetans' "authenticity," describing many of them as "engaging in scripted simulations, becoming the sort of Tibetans desired by Chinese and Westerners by reproducing and enunciating the scripts of authentic Tibetanness produced by outsiders." Adams, 1996b: 536.

5 This is perhaps indicated by the sacralization of this notion in official Chinese texts: "We are interested in preserving China's unity as a state. This is a holy good that every nation has to cultivate" (Mei Zhaorong, PRC ambassador to Germany [1996]). The term "sacred territory" is standard in PRC discussions of its territoriality.

6 "As described by the literary critic Huang Ziping, Root-Seeking Literature celebrated 'the aesthetic situation, the atmosphere, the cultural sedimentation,... the unrefined, wild and basic beauty in the crude, primitive mode of [Chinese] life.]'" Richard J. Smith, "Contemporary Chinese Literature And Art," Rice University website. Tian Zhuangzhuan's film *The Horse Thief* (1986) and Joan Chen's *Xiu xiu—the Sent Down Girl* (1999) apply similar notions to Tibetan nomads. Ma Jian's infamous story *Stick Out Your Furry Tongue, or Fuck-all* extended the approach of this school to depicting the supposed sexual profligacy of the elemental Tibetan (see Barmé and Minford, 1988: 413ff.).

7 The current front-runners in this competition are the leaders of Dechen Tibet Autonomous Prefecture in Yunnan, where the claim is connected to tourism development and the construction of a new airport (see *China Daily,* [1998a]). See also Xinhua (1997a), plus the commentary by Korski (1997a).

8 The CIA decision to support the Tibet operation was made in summer 1956, and the last payment was received in 1973 (see Knaus, 1999: 139 and 373, note 10).

9 Lopez notes that Western representations have damaged Tibetan political aspirations—"those fantasies are ultimately a threat to the realization of that goal" (Lopez, 1998: 11)—but the impact of historical British intervention has not been greatly explored.

10 See Goldstein, 1995, note 47.

11 The text of this statement can be found in "Oral intervention by Rene Wadlow of the International Fellowship of Reconciliation to the UN Commission on Human Rights, 1985" concerning Implementation of the Declaration on the Elimination of All Forms of Intolerance and of Discrimination Based on Religion or Belief."

12 Melvyn Goldstein refers to these meetings in his 1995 essay at note 45. The exile government in 1986 commissioned a brief on Tibet's legal status from the U.S. legal firm Wilder, Cutler and Pickering, which formed the basis of Michael van Walt van Praag's 1987 book *The Status of Tibet* and provided much of the legal rationale for the Strasbourg Proposal; it discusses the role

of human rights briefly but significantly in its conclusion (p. 203). Tsering Shakya and other observers have noted that this internationalization initiative coincided with an increase in political tension between India and China. Van Walt himself writes that the meetings began in 1985 (van Walt, 1996), not 1986 as Goldstein has it.

13 There is a long history of Tibetan political perceptions of their state as unique. The Tibetan National Assembly issued a communiqué addressed to Chiang Kaishek in 1946, copied to the British mission in Lhasa, which relies on this theme: "There are many great nations on this earth who have achieved unprecedented wealth and might, but there is only one nation which is dedicated to the well-being of humanity in the world and that is the religious land of Tibet which cherishes a joint spiritual and temporal system" (cited in Goldstein, 1989: 542). Shakya notes a similar rationale by Tibetan government officials in their reasons for not applying to enter the League of Nations in the 1920s (Shakya, 1985).

14 U.S. Congressman Chris Smith, R-NJ, chairman of the House International Relations Committee's human rights panel (House hearing on U.S.-Chinese relations, cited in Raum, 1999). See also Levin, 1994a, b.

15 Apart from two cases cited in Mary Craig (1992) and TIN (Tibet Information Network, 1999b) reports of physical rapes by officials or police in Tibet since 1980 seem to be rather rare, despite unspecified allegations in the press (for example, Yuthok [1994] and *The Philadelphia Inquirer* [1996]). However, the sexual brutalization of nuns in prison, which was frequent in the period 1988–90, has been extensively documented; some of these cases are described in the *Philadelphia Inquirer* article.

16 Other versions of the eroticization of "peripheral" peoples in state discourse in China are discussed in Harrell, 1995: 10–12, and Gladney, 1996: 103ff.

17 Israel Epstein writes of the knowledge brought by Wencheng as "warmly remembered" in Tibet (Epstein, 1983: 16), and Stuart Gelder describes a performance of the play *Princess Wencheng* during his 1962 visit to Lhasa, which showed the princess bringing luxury goods to Tibet (Gelder and Gelder, 1964: 151). The Tibetan account of a *srin-mo* or demoness lying across the country and tied down by the temples, famously elaborated in the *Mani bka' 'bum* in about the twelfth century, appears to depict the civilizing of Tibet as the restraining of an elemental feminine force. The Tibetan writers credit this image to external sources—in this case geomantic analyses provided by Princess Wencheng—in a way similar to the use of foreign models to promote political objectives that I suggest in this paper. On the supine demoness myth, see Aris, 1979, Sørensen, 1994, Gyatso, 1989, and Kapstein, 1992.

18 See, for example, this extract from an article published in the official Chinese press by an American working as a teacher in Xiamen University, Fujian Province: "The mystical but fictional Shangri-La, the land where time stood still, has nothing to do with Tibet! Tibetans are real people, with no inten-

tion of either stopping the clock or turning it back—because today they have a future free from inhumane feudalism" (Brown, 1997).

19 See TIN, 1999a. Hu's phrase about civilizing Tibet is still one of the main slogans used by the local government.

20 "The compassionate struggle of the Tibetan people...is the clearest example of brutality against compassion in the world today" (statement of Adam Yauch, June 1996). Other such cases have been noted in Lopez, 1998: 7–9.

21 Baroness Strange, debate on Tibet at the House of Lords (the upper house of the British Parliament), 10 May 1999. This view is also found in exile writings, such as those of Thubten Jigme Norbu and Tsipon Shakabpa.

22 "For the last 47 years, the Tibetan people have maintained a peaceful, non-violent resistance to the Chinese government's policy of cultural genocide; but time is running out for the Tibetans and the power to stop this is in our hands" ("BOYCOTT ALL CHINESE PRODUCTS," Press Statement, Milarepa Fund [San Francisco], 30 April 1996).

23 For example, three monks were murdered in Dharamsala on 4 February 1997 by Tibetan followers of the banned Shugden sect, according to the Indian police (see Clifton, 1997). A Tibetan exile official was murdered in India for his association with Taiwan in the 1970s, and between 1987 and 1990 Alu Choenjor, an exile who had returned to Tibet, and Jamyang Norbu, a writer in Dharamsala, were both severely beaten in Dharamsala by conservative Tibetans for expressing dissident or radical views. Another example of strategic violence could be found in the seven known bombings that took place in Tibet between 1995 and 1997, at least one of them placed by a Tibetan monk (see TIN, 1996b).

24 Benjamin Gilman, 1999.

25 For example, on 21 June 1996, the Liechtenstein Parliament passed a "Resolution to Welcome Dalai Lama" referring to "the endangered cultural identity of the Tibetan People" and calling for "a stop to be put to the obstruction of the cultural identity of the Tibetan People." See ICLT (1997) for other examples. Governments in the West repeated similar concerns in more muted terms—a European Union mission reported "the authorities in the TAR exercise extremely tight control over the principal elements of Tibetan religion and culture [but it] did not believe that this was derived from hostility to religion and culture per se" (European Union, 1998). A U.S. government report noted that "repressive social and political controls continue to limit the fundamental freedoms of ethnic Tibetans" (U.S. Department of State, 1997).

26 This was Rene Wadlow's 1985 submission on behalf of the International Fellowship of Reconciliation (see note 11 above).

27 The European Parliament resolution was passed on 15 December 1992. In May 1993, a conference of European Parliamentarians in London expressed "deep concern at the degradation of the Tibetan environment and exploitation of its natural resources for the benefit of China alone" (*Tibetan Bulletin*, 1993).

28 Cited in Lehman and Barnett, 1998. The fourth item in the Dalai Lama's Five Point Peace Plan of 1987 was "the restoration and protection of Tibet's natural environment." Toni Huber discusses this phenomenon in detail in Huber, 1997.

29 Cited in DeVoss, 1997. Richard Bernstein (1997) gives some helpful context to Professor Thurman's remark: "The image is apt, suggesting the innocent, pacific and largely defenseless Tibetans being clubbed by giant, powerful, merciless China. Given the harshness of the Chinese occupation, Tibet is a legitimate and compelling cause." Thurman has been seen as a champion of the romantic approach within Tibetan activism and religion in the United States, and has responded that literary and romantic presentations do not impact on policy decisions, since these remain, he argues, almost entirely driven by political pragmatism (see Thurman, 2001).

30 Chinese official discourse refers frequently to the uniqueness of Tibetan culture as well, but focuses on what are seen as its nonreligious aspects, such as the medical system or the *Gesar* folk epics.

31 "Resolved by the Senate (the House of Representatives concurring), That it is the sense of the Congress that Tibet, including those areas incorporated into the Chinese provinces of Sichuan, Yunnan, Gansu, and Qinghai, is an occupied country under the established principles of international law whose true representatives are the Dalai Lama and the Tibetan Government in exile as recognized by the Tibetan people" (ICLT, 1997).

32 One attempt to raise this model was made in August 1997 when the Unrepresented Nations and Peoples Organization (UNPO), a Dutch-based NGO, published the report of an unofficial fact-finding mission it had sent to Tibet that concluded that Tibet is a de facto colony of China (UNPO, 1997).

33 Lodi Gyari, the special envoy of the Dalai Lama in Washington, who was closely involved in forming the 1987 Dharamsala policy initiative, has made several efforts to reintroduce conceptions of colonialism in his presentations to Congress. See note 66 below.

34 I am using the term "popular" here in its loosest sense, since I do not mean to suggest that the notion of "popular support" has been used by supporters of Tibet in the sense of mass or proletarian mobilization: The targeted support community has been within middle-class or elite sectors of Western society, and there has been little attempt to approach working-class or peasant communities, as far as I know. The Dalai Lama has, however, been much keener than many of his Western advisers about appearing on populist television shows or mass circulation newspapers (notably the Terry Wogan show in the United Kingdom), but I think these are isolated incidents.

35 See Cohen, 1988.

36 Tibetan ministers in the Kashag (the exile Cabinet) involved in this decision pointed out to me shortly afterward that they had practical reasons for focusing on Western countries for support—namely, they had no contacts else-

where, and the financing for such trips could be obtained only from Western supporters. Lodi Gyari, the Dalai Lama's representative in Washington, has also pointed out to me that by the late 1980s the rhetoric of colonization and the appeal to a political alliance among colonized nations was already outmoded and regarded as specifically leftist or *passé* rhetoric, and replaced by *realpolitik* considerations.

37 See Toni Huber in this volume.

38 The testimony of foreign eyewitnesses was also important to Tibetans—above all, those who had been in Tibet before 1950. See "Eyewitnesses to History," *Tibetan Bulletin* (1994) for foreigners' written statements (including Robert Ford, Fosco Maraini, Kazi Sonam Topgyal, and Heinrich Harrer), plus a text by Hugh Richardson.

39 This seems to have acted as a kind of substitute within "specialness" discourse for the role played by the notion of representativeness in leftist or statist political discourse. For a study of testimonies in such forums, see McLagan (1996), chapter 3.

40 Human Rights Watch in New York published its first reports dedicated to Tibet in 1988 (AsiaWatch 1988a, b); Amnesty International followed soon after. The Tibet Information Network was officially constituted in London in 1988 as a nonpolitical research body. Dharamsala set up a Human Rights Desk within its Department of Information and International Relations, which was replaced in 1996 by the Tibetan Center for Human Rights and Democracy.

41 The alleged indirect CIA funding of the ICJ "casts grave doubts on the impartiality of the findings," wrote Chris Mullin in Greene and Mullin, 1978. Mullin gives the original source for the accusation of CIA funding as *New York Times,* 19 February 1967, p. 30, col.1, and *New York Times,* 17 August 1965, p. 33, col.3. See also Grunfeld, 1987.

42 Accounts of Westerner-obtained evidence of a campaign of forced sterilizations being carried out across Tibet were based initially on a single encounter between a Western activist and two monks in which, as far as I know, all the parties to the encounter were male, they had no common language, and the site of the incident alleged by the monks was not known. See Kerr, 1993 for details of his efforts to publicize this issue (discussed in McLagan, 1996: chapter 7, pp. 316ff.). There was and is important evidence of forced abortions, and in some cases of forced sterilizations as well, in parts of Eastern Tibet in the early to mid-1980s, and of "pilot" campaigns in certain areas in Central Tibet in the 1990s, but it is still not clear how widely these excesses took place, or that these policies were widely implemented beyond the pilot schemes. In Central Tibet birth control policies applied only to urban areas and government employees from 1985 in principle and 1992 in practice; there were pilot projects in some rural areas, but the scope of these remains unclear. See TIN (1992, 2000) and Barnett (1994a, b) for detailed studies of birth control policies in Tibet.

43 The term had been in use shortly after the 1959 Uprising, when the ICJ

famously reported that it had found "prima facie evidence" of genocide, a reference to evidence it had collected of mass killings in Tibet. See ICJ, 1959, 1960.

44 The executions of two prisoners in Lhasa, Migmar Tashi and Dawa, on 18 May 1990 were political although the authorities declared at the time that the two men were guilty of trying to escape from prison. (see Tibet Information Network Doc. 32[YY], pt. 2, 17 May 1990). Reports of prison deaths, on the other hand, remain quite frequent, and up to eleven prisoners are said to have died as a direct or indirect result of police actions at Drapchi prison in Lhasa during or after protests on 1 and 4 May 1998.

45 The idea of total cultural and demographic extinction was described, for example, by a U.S. Congressman after visiting Tibet as a tourist: "The clock is ticking for Tibet. If nothing is done, a country, its people, religion and culture will continue to grow fainter and fainter and could one day disappear" (Wolf, 1997).

46 See Goldstein and Beall, 1991. Another example of the disintegration of totalized representations can be seen in reports on the 1996 ban on Dalai Lama photographs. The ban was on the display, not the possession, of such photographs and it applied to public, not private, places (see *Xizang Ribao*, 5 April 1996, p. 1, or TIN, 1996a) but these distinctions were not always noted by politicians (see Wolf, 1997, and Jessie Helms, 1997). Although arrests for possession or distribution of texts, tapes, or books by the Dalai Lama are frequent, there are few reports of arrests for possession or display of a Dalai Lama photograph, apart from the case of Lobsang Sherab at Kirti Monastery in Ngaba (see TIN, 1999a). After 1996, sightings by Western visitors of a Dalai Lama photograph spotted in a monk's cell or private house were reported in several articles as evidence that the ban had been proven false, or that it had been rapidly relaxed.

47 See for example the statements of Australian MP Gary Nehl, deputy speaker of the House of Representatives, who "found no evidence of religious oppression, noting that he saw monks in the Potala freely engaging in normal religious rituals."(Xinhua, 1999). Stefan Baron, editor of the German magazine *Wirtschaftswoche* ("Economic Weekly"), after being taken to Lhasa wrote that the Potala Palace was proof that "the propaganda by the West about the destruction of the Tibetan culture is totally inaccurate" (Xinhua, 1997b).

48 Chris Mullin (in his writings before 1988) and A. Tom Grunfeld presented the CIA's involvement with the Tibetan resistance movement as evidence discrediting the political credibility of the Dalai Lama and the exiles (see Grunfeld, 1987, Mullin, 1975 and Mullin and Wangyal, 1983). Mullin later changed his position on this issue, notably in a speech at the Bonn Hearing on Tibet organized by Petra Kelly, April 1989. See Kelly et al., 1991.

49 In terms of publications, the most notable work of this kind was John Avedon's book *In Exile from the Land of Snows* (1984).

50 In the United Kingdom, for example, a Tibet Support Group—the first in the

world to have that name, later used in other countries—was formed in 1988 primarily because the U.K. government was rumored to have refused to issue a visa for the Dalai Lama. See McLagan, 1996 for an analysis of the emergence of the global Tibet Movement.

51 I owe this perception to Goldstein's remarks about the domestication of the issue in the United States (see the section "The United States and the Tibet Question" in Goldstein, 1995).

52 "I see more policemen [and] soldiers with guns on the streets where I live in Melbourne than were in Tibet in Lhasa," Peter Nugent, a Liberal MP and head of the parliamentary human rights subcommittee, told ABC radio in August 1999 (Nicholson, 1999).

53 From the time of the Vienna Conference in 1993, if not earlier, Chinese diplomats dropped the use of the term "Asian values" and asserted that it accepted that human rights were universal but subject to local variations in interpretation. This strategy prevented China from being sidelined or regionalized in international discussions of human rights. China had since at least the early 1980s accepted the right of interference in internal affairs in terms of some but not all human rights abuses, presumably to justify action on the issues of apartheid and Israel/Palestine.

54 The Chinese government was able to use the argument that country-specific human rights criticisms were a concealed form of Western "bullying" to defeat attempts to raise the Tibet or China issues in the UN.

55 Reports of human rights abuses in China increased markedly from November 1998 with the widespread arrests and sentencing of members of the Chinese Democracy Party and in 1999 with the banning of the Falungong sect.

56 See Barnett, 1991.

57 It is clear that the decision not to execute the Tibet University student activist Lobsang Tenzin in March 1990 was due in part to international pressure, since Amnesty International was named in an official press article at the time; in Chinese law there was no reason to commute his death sentence. Most other cases in this category related to sentences being shortened by a small amount (see, for example, UPI [1994]), but arbitrary killings definitely decreased.

58 The debate over this phenomenon arose principally over U.S. performance at the annual session of the UN Commission on Human Rights, when it would typically announce its support for a resolution criticizing Chinese human rights practices too late for other, smaller nations to receive appropriate voting instructions from their home capitals and so too late for the resolution to have a realistic chance of success.

59 I discuss this in more detail in Lehman and Barnett, 1998.

60 "The Tibetan problem is not simply a problem of continuing human rights violations against the people of Tibet, nor should it be dealt with as such.... Fundamentally, the issue of Tibet is an issue of colonial rule" (Lodi Gyari,

1997). As Michael van Walt told a conference of Tibet support groups in 1996: "Human rights is a useful tool but it can be dangerous if it continues to remain by itself. I say that because...China...has grown immune to it" (van Walt van Praag, 1996: 100).

61 Visits to the United Staets by officials from the TAR (Tibetan Autonomous Region) Government, which have been carried out since 1991 under the aegis of the U.S. Information Agency, include showing the visiting officials examples of interethnic relations in the United States so that the visitors can "learn more about the contribution of racial and ethnic minorities to American culture... [and] about Native American culture, including the relationship of tribes to federal, state and local government" (internal USIA documentation citing a Chinese source, 1999).

62 Personal information from one of the devisers of the plan, December 1998.

63 See the collection of newspaper articles and editorials surrounding the December 1996 visit of Jiang Zemin to India published by TPPRC (Tibetan Parliamentary and Policy Research Center) in 1997. This issue is also prominent in current Chinese political commentary: "For China to lose such a vast barrier...would expose our fatal "underbelly," [and] would be unacceptable from a national security perspective. Preparing for a possible future conflict with India is the bottom line as to why the Central Government cannot allow Tibetan independence" (Wang Lixiong, 1999).

64 Dawa Norbu, 1997: 336–37.

65 In the U.S. Congress there were also attempts to introduce this model, especially after the Indian nuclear tests of 1998 (see Gilman, 1999).

66 "China is potential threat number one," the defense minister [Fernandes] told the private Home TV network. "China has its nuclear weapons stockpiled in Tibet right along India's borders." (AFP, 1998).

67 See, for example, Agehananda Bharati's 1974 article, cited in Miller, 1988.

68 See Reuters, 1998, and Crossette, 1998.

69 The idea that a brief visit to Tibet constitutes superior knowledge coincides with the Chinese official slogan that "seeing is believing" and its long-standing practice of inviting foreign politicians and others to Lhasa. See Tsan-Kuo Chang, 1999 for the use of this argument by the Chinese in the 1960s to discredit American journalists who were then not allowed to enter China; for an academic example, see Adams, 1996.

70 See, for example, A. Tom Grunfeld in *The Guardian,* 10 December 1988; Macartney, 1996, and Lane, 1994.

71 *Xizang Ribao,* 1996. The sentence following this quotation illustrates how the advent of modernity and wealth is used to justify social and political control: "Translating this blueprint into reality requires...a stable social environment."

72 "After 30 years as an 'autonomous region,' Tibet is once again suffering a Chinese invasion. But this time the forces of the market, not Marx, are responsible" (Poole, 1995; see also, for example, Macartney, 1996). For a discussion of the immigration issue, see Hessler, 1999. The Dalai Lama acknowledged that there is a problem of interpretation, but focuses on Sinicization of culture as a threat: "I recognize that in all these years, the Chinese have modernized Tibet in certain ways. They have built schools, hospitals, roads, houses. But at the same time, they are introducing political education in schools and this is based on Chinese culture. The risk is of the extinction of our culture" (Reuters, 1997).

73 Krurup, 1994. A similar article about "Himalayan Bangkok" had appeared the previous month in London (see Dempsey, 1996). Tibetan and Chinese reports of the increase in sexual commerce are documented in *Social Evils: Prostitution and Pornography in Lhasa,* TIN, 1999.

74 In fact, brothels have been reported as commonplace around the Potala since at least the seventeenth century; the difference is that now the prostitutes and procurers are predominantly Chinese. Some depictions of modernity focused on karaoke bars and pop videos (see Gunness, 1994).

75 "The PRC has undertaken a program of mass infusion of Chinese people who probably now outnumber Tibetans in their own country...the inescapable conclusion is that China is swallowing Tibet. Stores, hotels, bazaars, businesses and tradesmen are largely Chinese. Driving out from Lhasa, one encounters as many Chinese villagers, shepherds, farmers, construction workers and travelers as Tibetan. In short, Tibet is disappearing... America and the rest of the free world must do more to urge China to back off from its clear goal to plunder Tibet" (Wolf, 1997). This is, however, the only report of Chinese shepherds or villagers in the TAR. I have discussed the issue of perceptions of immigration in some detail in Barnett, 1993. See also the *Special Envoy for Tibet Act of 1994,* U.S. Senate and Congress, 1994.

76 U.S. Department of State, 1997.

77 Wang Lixiong, 1999. Official texts also group modernization with the campaign against the independence movement, or describe one as the basis of the other: "Of course, the success or failure of the anti-splittist struggle depends on whether we can further promote reform and open policy in Tibet and its modernization construction" (Tenzin, 1993). Chinese public official texts since 1994 regularly say that the Dalai Lama's aim is to stop modernization (see Chen Kuiyuan, 1996).

78 Reuters, 1995. The story was developed in Germany by the magazine *Focus,* Munich, on 18 September 1995. The exile government replied in a press statement (Liaison Office of His Holiness the Dalai Lama for Japan, 1995). The Chinese took up the Asahara issue, paraphrasing the *Focus* story in *Guangming Ribao,* 9 October 1995 and in *Xizang Ribao,* 1995. It reappeared in *China's Tibet,* March 1996, summarized in Xinhua, 1996.

79 For Western reports of the Harrer connection, see Hellen, 1996, *Stern*, 1997, and Ferguson, 1997. For the Nazi allegations in Chinese media, see Li Jianhua, 1997: 6, and *China Daily*, 1998b. For a summary of the *Beijing Review* version, see Korski, 1997b.

80 See Li Bing, 1995.

81 The strongest attack in the Western media on the Dalai Lama was probably Christopher Hitchens (1998) in *Salon Magazine*: "Far from his holier-than-all image, the Dalai Lama supports such questionable causes as India's nuclear testing, sex with prostitutes and accepting donations from a Japanese terrorist cult."

82 In fact the Dalai Lama and his advisers had strategically encouraged Tibetan youth movements to express diverse opinions, because an image of increasing extremism among Tibetans was thought to make him look more conciliatory, and thus to encourage Beijing to come to the negotiating table. Personal informant in exile administration, 1989.

83 The press campaign by followers of this sect, in the form of leaflets sent by fax to the international media, began in England in May 1996 and led to a number of articles, for example Nanda, 1996. The Tibetan Government in Exile responded to the campaign on 14 May 1996—see Kashag, 1996. British papers later published articles discrediting the sect's English organization and followers (see Bunting, 1996 and Brown, 1996).

84 See Clinton, 1998.

85 The Dalai Lama and the exile government had expressly sought to avoid that outcome during and after the talks with Beijing that collapsed in 1985. See the Dalai Lama's letter to Jiang Zemin (Dalai Lama, 1993b) and Dawa Norbu, 1997: 325.

86 See, for example, the U.S. position that "the Administration has consistently urged the Chinese government to increase respect for human rights and to engage in a substantive dialogue with the Dalai Lama" (Taft, 1999).

87 In fact one parliamentary resolution does specify a criterion for the outcome of negotiations: The European Parliament resolved in 1997 that China should reach "an agreement which satisfies the legitimate requests of the Tibetan people" (European Parliament, 1997).

88 Cited in Moynihan, 1997.

89 Lopez, 1998: 206.

90 See Freeman, 1997.

91 See, for example, Gluckman, 1996.

92 For the "Oxfords" see Plommer, 1995, Gluckman, 1996, and AFP, 1988. The new version arose from a single sentence: "A 61-year-old claret-robed monk who wears Rockport shoes and a wristwatch, the Dalai Lama arrived from New York on a United Airlines flight" (Finley, 1997). This appeared in

AP as: "The Dalai Lama, who won the Nobel Peace Prize in 1989 for his non-violent efforts to resolve the Tibetan conflict, arrived at Denver International Airport in a claret-red robe, wearing designer walking shoes and a wrist watch" (AP, 1997).

93 Interview with *Vanity Fair,* cited in Broughton, 1999.

94 For an argument putting the case against Lhasa's political claim to Eastern areas, see Goldstein, 1994.

95 The Dalai Lama does of course receive hundreds of letters, appeals, petitions, and visits from Tibetans inside Tibet, so his support base and popularity are not in doubt.

96 Dawa Norbu, 1997: 337. Some commentators have said that this was due to popular resistance to pluralism, not to the Dalai Lama, who had to use his personal authority to force a draft constitution on the Exile Assembly which gave the Assembly the right to impeach him.

97 Dalai Lama, 1993a.

98 Pico Iyer, 1997.

99 Ibid.

100 This ceremony had the added advantage for the Tibetan exile leaders that it was one of the few major state events of that time that the Chinese authorities could not easily claim provides evidence of Chinese sovereignty over Tibet, because the Chinese claim to have officiated at this event was explicitly rejected by Ngapo Ngawang Jigme, former Chairman of the TAR, in 1989: "At the time of the enthronement of the present Dalai Lama Wu Zhongxin of the KMT came, but not to enthrone the Dalai Lama.... He just came to convey greetings" (tape recording of Ngapo Ngawang Jigme's speech [undated but probably 1989], held as TIN Doc. T1[XZ] and T2[XZ]. Ngapo published similar statements in an article in *Xizang Ribao,* 11 August 1989, cited in Cao Changqing, 1994. Other sources say the article was published on 31 August 1989.

"Orientalism" and Aspects of Violence in the Tibetan Tradition[1]

Elliot Sperling

THE DRAGON YEAR OF 1640–41, as described by the Fifth Dalai Lama in his autobiography, was marked by some rather unsettling events. Problems the Gelugpa *(dGe lugs pa)* sect had been experiencing in the Tsang *(gTsang)* region were ominous in view of the fact that the sect's political position was still not fully secure. The Dalai Lama noted that in the Tiger Year (1638–39) the regions' ruler, the Tsangpa Desi *(gTsang pa sde srid)*, had instigated a variety of problems for the monastery of Tashilhunpo *(bKra shis lhun po)*. People reported seeing a tired, worn-out Panchen Lama, the monastery's chief hierarch, bemoaning the state of affairs. All sorts of talk about the situation had arisen; people traveling to the Tsongon *(mTsho sngon)* region in the northeastern reaches of the Tibetan Plateau reported what they had seen and heard of all this to the leader of the Qošot Mongols, Gušri Qan, who was also the most powerful among the patrons and supporters of the Dalai Lama and the Gelugpa. Gušri Qan was incensed. Suddenly, the Dalai Lama records, word came that he was en route to Central Tibet but had taken a route via Beri *(Bi ri)*, in Kham *(Khams)*, where the Gelugpa were also opposed by the local ruler.[2] A military response to the travails of the Gelugpa was clearly imminent.

In the summer a number of Mongols from Khams began arriving in the Lhasa area. Šidi Batur, one of Gušri Qan's officers, brought a letter from the Mongol king and spoke with the Dalai Lama, who noted in his autobiography:

For our part, [I stated,] "Relying on that particular virtue which encompasses the bodhisattva—i.e., thinking of oneself and others in an equal manner—has not held back strife. Thus, though we might [continue] to act in accord with this sort of pretense, nothing other than shame before others would come of it."[3]

Furthermore, in relation to the actions of the Tsangpa, he said "Though we might take revenge, I, the last of those of Chongye *(Phyongs rgyas)*, the cleric occupying the seat of the omniscient ones, would not appear as a disobedient monk."[4] The Dalai Lama then ordered that Beri should be destroyed and that strife (that is, opposition) would not be tolerated.

Another incident throws further light on the Fifth Dalai Lama's thinking with regard to the use of military force to protect the interests of his government and his sect. In early 1660 he was confronted with a situation that he himself described as one of chaotic strife rooted in a rebellion in Tsang. Asserting that he was acting for the sake of beings in the area of Nyangme *(Nyang smad),* he sent out instructions that were direct and clear:

[Of those in] the band of enemies who have despoiled the duties
    entrusted to them:
Make the male lines like trees that have had their roots cut;
Make the female lines like brooks that have dried up in winter;
Make the children and grandchildren like eggs smashed against
    rocks;
Make the servants and followers like heaps of grass consumed
    by fire;
Make their dominion like a lamp whose oil has been exhausted;
In short, annihilate any traces of them, even their names.[5]

With his own pen the Fifth Dalai Lama made clear his role in the events just described. With regard to the first of these, he was explicit about authorizing the activities of Gušri Qan, through warfare, which made Ganden Phodrang *(Dga' ldan pho brang)* the unquestioned center of authority in Tibet. With regard to the second, his instructions evince a clear determination to unleash severe military retribution against those who had risen against his authority. One may say with some confidence that the Fifth Dalai Lama does not fit the standard image that many people today have of a Dalai Lama, particularly the image of a Nobel Peace Prize laureate.

I have purposely couched these remarks in provocative terms in order to emphasize the point that we cannot simplistically mix the actions and standards of different eras. This would seem to be obvious, yet it happens all the time. For partisan reasons one often finds discussions of historical figures from centuries ago framed around arguments relating to human rights values, democracy, and so forth, which were not part of the intellectual atmosphere of the period at issue.[6] While this is often done with a harshly critical goal in mind, the opposite also occurs, whereby polemical needs lead people into various lines of argumentation in order to prove that such and such a figure, institution, or state organization from earlier times in fact accorded with the standards of our own time and place (with the implication often being that the standards and values in question are positive and admirable ones). Thus my comment juxtaposing the actions of the Fifth Dalai Lama and the image of the Nobel Laureate; for we can in fact find modern writers projecting current ideas concerning the nonviolence associated with the present Dalai Lama back onto previous Dalai Lamas. This in turn makes it seem as if nonviolence of the Gandhian sort were one of the basic hallmarks of Tibetan Buddhism in general, not only in the religious and philosophical sphere, but in the political sphere as well.[7]

I should not be misunderstood here; kindness and compassion toward sentient beings are a significant part of Tibetan Buddhism, as is, of course, the idea of working for the benefit of sentient beings. These are not, however, identical with Gandhian *ahimsa;* nor are they all there is to Tibetan Buddhism in practice; among those ideas that have played a role in the political history of Tibet are notions about protecting the doctrine. These ideas and the methods for realizing them have, in fact, been of crucial significance in making Tibetan Buddhism a vehicle for power in the arena of world history, first for Tangut emperors, then for Mongol, Chinese, and Manchu rulers: Tibetan Buddhism, from this perspective, was a means toward the attainment of power—in defense of and for the spread of the doctrine, to be sure. It was clearly used by Zhang Rinpoche (1123/24–1193/94), whose disciples made war on his behalf and are said to have experienced religious visions in the midst of battle.[8] Yuan-dynasty Chinese writers recorded that when the armies of Qubilai swept into southern China, above them in the sky could be seen Mahākāla, a result of the propitiation rites performed by the Sakyapa *(Sa skya pa)* cleric sGa A-gnyan dam-pa.[9]

In spite of this, however, we can easily find descriptions of Tibetan Buddhism that take the present Dalai Lama's views on nonviolence—phrased, significantly, with the Gandhian term *ahimsa*—and make of them a Buddhist value that has dominated Tibetan political history and the institution of the Dalai Lama for centuries. Thus we come up with simplistic accounts that describe the Mongol adoption of Tibetan Buddhism in the thirteenth century solely in terms of the moral attraction that Buddhism held for the Mongol emperors. This is not to say that morality is not a part of Tibetan Buddhism, but the account we are often given of the conversion of the Mongols is a rather skewed reading of what actually transpired. The Fifth Dalai Lama has been described as having brought about the pacification of the Mongols four centuries later through his charismatic teaching of Buddhism. Lost in such descriptions is the fact that militant Mongol imperial ambitions were only quashed through the bloody extirpation of the Junγar Mongols in the mid–eighteenth century by the armies of Qianlong, who was revered by Tibetans in his own lifetime as an emanation of Mañjuśrī.[10] Such nonviolent readings of Tibetan history seem designed to create a historical tradition for the present Dalai Lama's views on the primacy of *ahimsa*.[11]

Why is there a need to create this sort of tradition? Given contemporary ideas and expectations, it's easy to see the utility of presenting Tibetan Buddhism to the present-day world as an eternal store of teachings on nonviolence and peace. Nevertheless, Tibetan Buddhism and the Dalai Lama are in and of the world, and (along with our perception of them) have to a certain degree been influenced by general currents in thought in the last decades of this century. They have not stood apart from or above all other things. The present Dalai Lama's views on nonviolence, laudable as they may be, cannot simply be ascribed to a largely unchanged, centuries-old tradition.

To clarify this it is necessary to digress a bit. In the late 1970s Edward Said created a small sensation in a variety of disciplines with his now well-known book *Orientalism*. Said maintained that the West had constructed an "Orient," a largely imagined and stereotyped realm whose construction as a violent, sensual, objectified "other" was meant to accord with and justify the entire colonial enterprise. Said argued that the seemingly "objective" construction of the Orient was, in fact, the product of the specific context from which it had been viewed:

> No one has ever devised a method of detaching the scholar from the circumstances of life, from the fact of his involvement (conscious or unconscious) with a class, a set of beliefs, a social position, or from the mere activity of being a member of a society.... I doubt that it is controversial, for example, to say that an Englishman in India or Egypt in the later nineteenth century took an interest in those countries that was never far from their status as British colonies. To say this may seem quite different from saying that all academic knowledge about India and Egypt is somehow tinged and impressed with, violated by, gross political fact —and yet *that is what I am saying* in this study of Orientalism. For if it is true that no production of knowledge in the human sciences can ever ignore or disclaim its author's involvement as a human subject in his own circumstances, then it must also be true that for a European or American studying the Orient there can be no disclaiming the main circumstances of *his* actuality: that he comes up against the Orient as a European or American first, as an individual second. And to be a European or an American in such a situation is by no means an inert fact. It meant and means being aware, however dimly, that one belongs to a power with definite interests in the Orient, and more important, that one belongs to a part of the earth with a definite history of involvement in the Orient since almost the time of Homer.[12]

Found guilty in this Orientalist enterprise were not only novelists and colonial officials but just about everyone else remotely involved, including philologists and archeologists.

Said's argument was scathingly parodied by Simon Leys in a critique in which he conceded the point that everyone is influenced in some degree by his or her environment:

> Edward Said's main contention is that "no production of knowledge in the human sciences can ever ignore or disclaim the author's involvement as a human subject in his own circumstances." Translated into plain English, this would seem to mean simply that no scholar can escape his original condition: his own national, cultural, political, and social prejudices are bound to be reflected in his work. Such a commonsense statement hardly warrants any debate. Actually, Said's own book is an excellent case in point; *Orientalism* could obviously have been written by no one but a Palestinian scholar with a huge chip on his shoulder and a very dim understanding of the European academic tradition (here perceived through the distorted prism of a certain type of American university with its brutish hyperspeculization, nonhumanistic approach, and close, unhealthy links with government).[13]

The point, of course, is that although one is subject to influences, these can still be understood in a variety of (often contradictory) ways and may or may not have the meaning Said finds overriding on the *individual* level. There is no doubt that there are biases and stereotypes (both positive and negative) that operate among people. However, the manner in which these might be manifested in a given individual cannot simply be reduced to a function of that individual's class, nation, and so forth. As a result, the critique of stereotypical images of Asia that has been spawned by *Orientalism* is in many instances the product of a large-scale decontextualization: The non-Western precedents for these stereotypes—including those of Tibet itself—are wholly ignored.[14] Most people are familiar with one or another of the Chinese stereotypes of Tibetans and other Inner Asians as "barbarians." An interesting stereotype about tea and its power over Tibetans and Mongols evolved in Ming and Qing times, on the basis of which the directors of Chinese statecraft proposed controlling them by cutting off their imports of

Chinese tea.[15] This idea carried over into foreign policy dealings with the British "other" during the late eighteenth century, when it was maintained that the British would find their lives endangered were they to go for a few days without Chinese tea and rhubarb.[16] Might we term this "Occidentalism"?

As it grew, the anti-Orientalist argument came to encompass critiques and attacks on alleged purveyors of both negative stereotypes of the Orient and its inhabitants (dirty, violent, poor, dishonest, etc.) and positive ones (spiritual, hard-working, noble, close to nature, ecological, etc.). These latter images, of course, present the romanticized version of the Orient, and although considered positive stereotypes, are nevertheless still held to be a construction based primarily on Western psychological needs. For a number of years this basic outline of the anti-Orientalist argument has held: The "Orient" is a Western construct meant to further imperial or Western psychological needs. It has even entered into the Western view of Tibet.[17]

In an interesting article that appeared in 1993 Amartya Sen, writing about India, pointed out that:

> [U]nless one chooses to focus on the evolution of specific conceptual tradition…"internal consistency" [which Said found underlying "Orientalist" images] is precisely what is hard to find in the variety of Western conceptions of, in this instance, India. For there are several fundamentally contrary ideas and images of India, and they have quite distinct roles in the Western understanding of the country, and also in influencing the manner in which Indians see themselves.[18]

It is self-evident that there are any number of stereotypes about the East that are part of our environment; however, their variety and roles cannot be simplified and apportioned as the "anti-Orientalists" would have it. As Sen makes clear, both positive and negative stereotypes have been at work in creating modern notions about India among Westerners and non-Westerners alike, as well as Indians. And in fact it has become increasingly recognized that ostensibly "Western" stereotypes and images of Asia are more universal than was previously acknowledged. The issue is not whether these stereotypical ideas exist as such, or whether they exert an influence on one peoples' view of another or on a peoples' self-image; the issue is whether they need to be understood in the reductionist, deterministic manner that is in evidence in much that has been written about them.

Which brings us back now to our original subject, the notion of the Dalai Lamas as almost uniquely men of peace, love, and compassion. It goes without saying that there are a variety of stereotypical notions associated with Tibet. But as with India, it is no longer possible to dismiss these simply as Western constructs. They have come to play a significant role in the Tibetan presentation of Tibet, particularly among Tibetans in exile. This is perhaps a natural development out of Tibetan participation in intellectual, political, and other facets of modern international life. It is, so to speak, an assimilation of viewpoints that have currency and legitimacy in the modern world, viewpoints that very much want to see a cloistered realm far away where people devote themselves *uniquely* to spiritual pursuits and not to the aspects of life that breed strife and discord. But these sorts of stereotypical images are not (with due respect to the anti-Orientalists) singularly Western— or even singularly modern. Starting, say, with the *Taohuayuan ji* of Tao Yuanming, one can make a respectable list of non-Western expressions of comparable yearnings for hidden realms of peace.

In its popular presentation to much of the modern world, the complex mix of ideas and doctrines in Tibetan Buddhism is often reduced (of late, by the Tibetan exile community) to an essential emphasis on love and compassion. As a result, a more balanced picture of the role of Tibetan Buddhism in the political world over the centuries has been lost to large numbers of people along the way. One might almost imagine that Tibetan Buddhism is a rather suicidal sort of faith, one whose adherents would rather see it perish than lift a hand in violence. That, frankly, has not been the case in Tibetan history. It was not the position of the Fifth Dalai Lama, who supported the use of military force in defense of Gelugpa interests. (And we may note that during his time the survival of Tibetan Buddhism in general was not at issue, just the welfare and authority of Ganden Phodrang). It was certainly not the position of the Thirteenth Dalai Lama, who actively sanctioned armed

Tibetan attacks on the Qing forces in Lhasa that were attempting to assert Qing rule in Tibet just before the dynasty's collapse.[19] Ultimately the reduction of Tibetan Buddhism, as far as its modern, international image is concerned, to a doctrine of nonviolence of the absolutist sort must be seen in light of the Tibetan exile assimilation of common images about the East, in much the same way as was the case with the generation of Gandhi and Nehru.

A fairly clear clue to this is found in the two versions of the Four-teenth Dalai Lama's autobiography *My Land and My People* (1962) and *Freedom in Exile* (1990). In both works the Dalai Lama writes of the influence he felt from Gandhi's life and philosophy when he visited the Rajghat. In the later version he specifically notes that the visit left him convinced that nonviolence was the only path for political action. While in the earlier one he states that he was determined never to asso-ciate himself with acts of violence, what "associate" means in this con-text must be tempered by further remarks in both versions of his autobiography. In the second the Dalai Lama tells of his escape and of the protection afforded him by armed guerillas—freedom fighters, he calls them—including at least two CIA-trained fighters. However, in the first he is more specific about his interests and concern for these Tibetan soldiers:

> In spite of my beliefs, I very much admired their courage and their determination to carry on the grim battle they had started for our freedom, culture, and religion. I thanked them for their strength and bravery, and also, more personally, for the protec-tion they had given me.... By then I could not in honesty advise them to avoid violence. In order to fight they had sacrificed their homes and all the comforts and benefits of a peaceful life. Now they could see no alternative but to go on fighting, and I had none to offer.[20]

While the mention of Gandhi in both versions reveals the influence of a general, modern attitude to the Indian leader prevalent throughout the world at the time of the Dalai Lama's visit to the Rajghat, the quote from the earlier autobiography reveals a sentiment largely in line with more traditional Tibetan (and even Tibetan Buddhist) attitudes on political violence. The influences that have led the Dalai Lama to threaten to resign his leadership role if Tibetans act violently toward Chinese in Tibet were not yet there;[21] indeed, one can hardly imagine the Dalai Lama making such a statement to the soldiers who guided him to safety in 1959.

Frankly, the adoption of *ahimsa* as an overriding principle represented a significant change in attitude from that of previous Dalai Lamas and from the policies of Ganden Phodrang. Most likely, the Dalai Lama came to adhere to it in a gradual manner. Only in India, in a milieu in which stereotypical ideas about the Orient and India were part of the intellectual environment, did it take on the centrality that people now associate with it. The Dalai Lama, as a human being in the world, certainly was influenced by this new environment that postulated nonviolence as one of the primary virtues—if not the highest of them—that an "Oriental" sage could espouse.

This is not necessarily to imply anything cynical or manipulative about the Dalai Lama's adoption of nonviolence as a leading principle. This is simply to place the Dalai Lama in history as a human being and as a party to intellectual and other currents that flow through the modern world. It is the assimilation of images and stereotypes espoused by Westerners and non-Westerners (including Tibetan exiles) that has placed the Dalai Lama within a constructed myth of eternal holy men practicing eternal virtues and eternal verities.

Kindness, compassion, nonviolence: All these have their place in Tibetan life and Tibetan Buddhist doctrine. But prior to the last three or more decades their centrality was nothing like what one sees now. Dalai Lamas have certainly counseled against violence and bloodshed in the past. But they have also found it necessary to sanction force to protect their perceived interests. There are instances in which Tibetan Buddhists have historically sanctioned force in the protection and advancement of the doctrine. This aspect of Tibetan Buddhist doctrine, including the empowerment of worldly monarchs who act to protect and advance the doctrine, is part of the political history of Tibet and of Tibet's relations with neighboring peoples. It is important to remember that Tibetan Buddhism has not always been opposed to the use of violent force under any circumstances. What one sees in recent years, a Dalai Lama threatening to abandon his leadership position if Tibetans use any violence against Chinese, is unprecedented. The extent to which this is so can be appreciated by the fact that it is generally acknowledged that the period since Tibet's annexation by the PRC has constituted a grave crisis for Tibet and Tibetan civilization, far greater than the threats occasioned by the Tsangpa rulers and their allies in the seventeenth century or even by Zhao Erfeng's occupation force in Lhasa in 1910–12, at which times both the Fifth and Thirteenth Dalai Lamas saw force as necessary.

A further interesting fact that I might add at this point relates to the Thirteenth Dalai Lama's reaction to a letter from Gandhi in which the Indian leader—mistakenly making a typical "Orientalist" assumption!—had expressed the hope that the Tibetans would diligently practice the Buddha's teaching of *ahimsa*. The Dalai Lama replied that he had no idea about what the word *ahimsa* meant as either an English or mantra term and that he needed further clarification of the term. Knowing of Gandhi's activities in general, though, he did tell him about Buddhism's concept of saving people from suffering.[22] If one takes his actions as a guide, however, it is obvious that the Thirteenth Dalai Lama did not consider the use of violent force to be at odds with this idea. Clearly, one can assume that he felt the use of force was sometimes necessary to prevent greater suffering. The corollary to this would then be that refraining from violence under such circumstances can actually engender even greater agonies.

Gandhian *ahimsa* as a primary Tibetan Buddhist tenet is a new phenomenon. Certainly we cannot speak of it as the overriding principle of political action for all previous Dalai Lamas. If we are to understand the institution of the Dalai Lama, we must accept that values and policies practiced by the Dalai Lamas cannot be wholly separated from their contemporary and historical milieu—though it must be emphasized again that we need not adopt a reductionist or ideological approach in order to understand or perceive the workings of such influences. The notion of the Dalai Lamas and the Tibetan Buddhist faith remaining untouched by the currents of time and history, with the former preaching peace and nonviolence to all peoples at all times, is part of a fanciful image of Tibet that unfortunately persists. The historical record contradicts it rather clearly; continuing attempts to present it as historical reality can only impede our understanding of Tibetan history, past and present.

NOTES

1 A longer version of this paper was originally presented in a lecture at the Amnye Machen Institute in Dharamsala in 1994. It will be published in the near future in *Lungta*.

2 Ngag-dbang blo-bzang rgya-mtsho, *Za-hor-gyi ban-de Ngag-dbang blo-bzang rgya-mtsho'i 'di snang-'khrul-ba'i rol-rtsed rtogs-brjod-kyi tshul-du bkod-pa du-kū-la'i gos-bzang,* vol. 1 (Lhasa: 1989), p. 192.

3 Ibid, p. 193: *rang-ngos-kyi cha bdag-gzhan mnyam-brje'i byang-chub-kyi sems dang ldan-pa'i yon-tan khyad-par-can-la brten-nas bde-gzar bshol-ba min-pas de-'dra'i o-zob byas-kyang gzhan khrel-ba-las mi-yong/.*

4 Ibid, pp. 193–94: *gal-te dgra-sha blangs-kyang nga 'Phyongs-rgyas-pa'i mi-mjug* [194] *thams-cad mkhyen-pa'i gdan-sar bsdad-pa'i btsun-pa zhig ban-log-pa mi-'char.*

5 rGyal-dbang lnga-pa, *Rgya-Bod-Hor-Sog-gi mchog-dman bar-pa-rnams-la 'phrin-yig snyan-ngag-tu bkod-pa rab-snyan rgyud-mang* (Xining, 1993), p. 225: *gnyer-du gtad-pa'i dam-nyams dgra-tshogs-kyi/ pho-brgyud shing-sdong rtsa-ba bcad-ltar thong/ mo-brgyud dgun-gyi chu-phran skems-ltar thong/ bu-tsha sgo-nga brag-la brdabs-ltar thong/ g.yog-'khor rtsa-phung me-yis bsregs-ltar thong/ mnga'-thang snum-zad mar-me bzhin-du thong/ mdor-na ming dang rjes-tsam med-par mdzod/* (the full text of the letter is on pp. 223–25).

6 E.g., some (but not all) of the polemics surrounding the five-hundredth anniversary of Columbus' 1492 Atlantic crossing typify this. Cf. Sale, 1990, and its review by Wills, 1990.

7 The most recent expression of these views is given by Thurman, 1995: 38–40, where the Fifth Dalai Lama is credited with having created in Tibet a "unilaterally disarmed society."

8 dPa'-bo gtsug-lag phreng-ba, *Dam-pa'i chos-kyi 'khor-lo bsgyur-ba-rnams-kyi byung-ba gsal-byed-pa mkhas-pa'i dga'-ston* (Beijing: 1986), p. 808: "[T]here were many among his disciples in whom Mahāmudrā insight was born on the battle lines. The officer Dar-ma gzhon-nu had a vision of Samvara (bDe-mchog) on the battle lines." Cf. Martin, 1990: 7.

9 See Franke, 1984: 161–62.

10 On the Junγar campaign, particularly the war of extermination in 1757, see Courant, 1912: 106–12. Note the reference, p. 108, to monks taking part in the fighting on the side of the Junγars. See too the reference to the campaigns in Thu'u-bkwan Blo-bzang chos-kyi nyi-ma, *lCang-skya Rol-pa'i rdo-rje'i rnam-thar* [*Khyab-bdag rdo-rje sems-dpa'i ngo-bo dpal-ldan bla-ma dam-pa ye-shes bstan-pa'i sgron-me dpal bzang-po'i rnam-par thar-pa mdo-tsam brjod-pa dge-ldan bstan-pa'i mdzes-rgyan*] (Lanzhou, 1989: 363–64). See also the positive comments and reactions of Thu'u-bkwan and lCang-skya Rol-pa'i rdo-rje to the rather bloody Manchu conquest of rGyal-rong in the 1770s, taken from the same work and cited by Martin, 1990a: 8–12.

11 Again, for the most recent expression of these views, see Thurman, 1995: 36–38.

12 Said, 1979: 10–11.

13 Leys, 1985: 95–96.

14 The best-known whipping boy in this context, the Western notion of Tibet as Shangri-la, is a good example, with antecedents going back several centuries. In the thirteenth century already we find an Arabic description of Tibet that notes: "In the country of Tibet are special properties in respect of their air and water, their mountains and plains. A man there laughs and rejoices continually." See the translation from the *Mu'jam al-Buldān* in Dunlop, 1973: 313.

15 For a modern version of this belief, see Gu Daquan, 1982: 49. An early Ming formulation of this idea can be found in Gu Zucheng et al., 1982: 107–8.

16 Peyrefitte, 1992: 526.

17 See, for example, the formulation of Bishop, 1989, particularly pp. 191–239.

18 Sen, 1993: 27–28.

19 Cf. Bell, 1987: 140–42.

20 Dalai Lama, 1964: 190.

21 See "Dalai Lama Interviewed," AFP report in FBIS-CHI-89-047, March 13, 1989, pp. 24–25: "If the militant types become more influential and go out of my control and won't listen to my ideas, then my alternative is I withdraw. I oppose violence."

22 See Tsering, 1984: 11–12.

TIBETAN CULTURE AS A MODEL
OF ECOLOGICAL SUSTAINABILITY

Helena Norberg-Hodge

SEEKING GREATER RESPECT FOR, and understanding of, non-Western cultures is today something of a thankless task. Accusations of "noble savage" romanticism await all who dare to make the attempt. We are, after all, living in a post–Cold War age in which history is commonly presumed to have ended with the triumph of Western democracy over all competing forms of social arrangement. As British political commentator Hugo Young wrote some years ago: "Argument about the substance of politics is almost at an end. The essential contest now lies between different claimants to superior management of the status quo" (quoted in *New Statesman,* 20 September 1991). The air of triumph, even arrogance, is clear—Western industrial society really *has* found the best way forward; all else is deluded idealism destined for the trash can of history.

There is irony in this dogma for someone like me who has spent more than twenty-one years seeking to understand a non-Western culture that fails utterly to conform to the ideals of the "new world order." The irony lies in the fact that the old world order, at least as represented by the traditional Tibetan culture of Ladakh, was patently far more rooted in the "real world," and therefore far more environmentally sustainable, than its Western counterpart. Indeed, it is clear to me that our unwillingness to learn from our nonindustrialized predecessors is, itself, a kind of soft-headed romanticism. It is the Western mainstream, purveyor of all things "realistic" and "commonsensical," that is guilty of clinging fanatically to the delusion that Western-style "progress" leads anywhere other than to an environmental abyss. This nihilism is rooted in an industrial ethic hell-bent on the annihilation of the majority of species and environments for the "benefit" of human beings. What has long been taken to be the "practical," "unsentimental" approach has led to nothing less than the dismantling of the planetary life-support systems on which the "winners" depend for their survival.

During my time in Ladakh, it became clear to me that this traditional, nature-based society was far more sustainable, both socially and environmentally, than Western society. The Ladakhi system was the result of a continuing dialogue between human beings and their surroundings, in which, over a two-thousand-year period of trial and error, the culture kept changing—co-evolving with its natural environment. The traditional Buddhist worldview emphasized change, but change within a framework of compassion and a profound understanding of the interconnectedness of all phenomena.

The traditional Ladakhi culture reflected fundamental human needs while respecting natural limits. And it worked. It worked for nature, and it worked for people. The various relationships in the traditional system were mutually reinforcing, encouraging harmony and stability. Most importantly for our doubting society searching for an alternative model of development, I am convinced that Ladakhis were significantly happier before the arrival of Western development in the mid-1970s than they are today. And what criteria for judging a society could be more important than, in social terms, the well-being of people and, in environmental terms, sustainability?

Since the mid-1970s, as Ladakh has become increasingly affected by the spread of Western culture, it has begun to score very poorly when judged by these criteria. Of course, for most Westerners, ignorance, disease, and constant drudgery were the rule for preindustrial societies. At first sight, the poverty, disease, and starvation we see in the Third World, and the chaos we see in modern Ladakh, might appear to substantiate this assumption. The fact is, however, that many, if not most, Third World problems today are the consequence of colonialism and misguided development imposed on cultures often powerless to resist. Over a period of some twenty years I have had the opportunity of observing how Ladakhi culture and society, finely tuned to the realities of environment and human needs, has been replaced by a Westernized hybrid that is producing an array of environmental and social problems that if unchecked will lead to irreversible decline.

It is true that, the overwhelming power of the West notwithstanding, the average Ladakhi did not go altogether unwillingly into this Westernized chaos. Young Ladakhis were seduced by the power of the great dream factories of Western media and advertising. Having been made to feel poor, stupid, and backward, they developed a desire for the neon-lit Western "good life" (as they were denied any depiction of the darker side that goes with it). In which case, some might ask, what have we to learn from a culture that was, at least to some extent, willingly abandoned by its own people? But the ability of a culture to resist power does not detract from the good qualities that such a culture may have incorporated over many thousands of years. We do not judge the virtue of an individual primarily by his or her ability to resist attack by an immensely powerful neighbor.

Over the centuries, the Ladakhis succeeded in creating an ecologically benign society out of an extremely demanding environment. Scorched by the sun in summer, the Tibetan plateau freezes solid for eight months in winter, when temperatures drop as low as minus forty degrees. This is the fiercest of climates: Winds whip up tornadoes along the empty corridors of desert; rain is so rare that it is easy to forget that there is such a thing as rain.

The vast majority of Ladakhis were self-supporting farmers, living in small, scattered settlements in the high desert; the principal crop was barley; natural resources were scarce and hard to obtain. Soon after I arrived in Ladakh I began to learn how this hardy people managed to survive. I began, for example, to learn the meaning of the word frugality. In the West, frugality conjures up images of old aunts and padlocked pantries. But in Ladakh frugality was fundamental to the people's prosperity and involved the careful use of limited resources in a way that had nothing to do with miserliness; this was frugality as intended by its original meaning of "fruitfulness": getting more out of little.

Where Westerners would consider something completely worn out, exhausted of all possible worth, and would throw it away, Ladakhis would find some further use for it. Nothing whatever was just discarded. What could not be eaten by people could be eaten by animals; what could not be eaten by animals could be used as fuel, or to fertilize the land.

Conservation and recycling had been developed into fine arts. Ladakhis patched their homespun robes until they could be patched no more. When winter demanded that they wear two or three on top of each other, they put the best one on the inside to keep it in good condition for special occasions. When no amount of stitching could sustain a worn-out robe, it was packed with mud into a weak part of an irrigation channel to help prevent leakage.

Virtually all the plants, shrubs, and bushes that grow wild, either around the edges of irrigated land or in the mountains—what we would call "weeds"—were gathered and served some useful purpose. The soil in the stables was dug up to be used as fertilizer, thus recycling precious animal urine. Dung was collected not only from the stables and pens, but also from the pastures. Even human excrement was not wasted. Each house had composting latrines consisting of a small room with a hole in the floor built above a vertical chute, usually one floor high. Earth and ash from the kitchen stove were added, thus aiding chemical decomposition, producing better fertilizer, and eliminating smells. Once a year the latrine was emptied at ground level and the contents used on the fields.

In such ways the Ladakhis traditionally recycled everything. There was literally no waste. Even with only scarce resources at their disposal, farmers managed to attain almost complete self-sufficiency, dependent on the outside world only for salt, tea, and a few metals for cooking utensils and tools.

With these few tools Ladakhis spent a long time accomplishing each task. Producing wool for clothes involved the time-consuming work of looking after the sheep while they grazed, shearing them with hand tools, and working the wool from beginning to end—cleaning, spinning, and finally weaving it. Food production, from the sowing of the seed until the food was served on the table, was similarly labor intensive. Despite the lack of labor-saving devices, I nevertheless found that the Ladakhis had an amazing abundance of time. They worked at a gentle pace and had an amount of leisure unknown to most working people in the West. Remarkably, Ladakhis did productive work for only four months of the year. In the eight winter months they of course had to cook, feed the animals, and carry water, but this work was minimal. Indeed, most of the winter was spent at festivals and parties. Even during the summer, hardly a week passed without a major festival or celebration of one sort or another. The myth of a life of preindustrial drudgery and never-ending work was therefore revealed as a product of centuries of Western infatuation with technological progress.

This leisured society in the midst of scarcity was a far cry from our own stressed society in the midst of plenty. In a recent self-completion survey of 11,095 readers of the *Guardian* newspaper, just over 50 percent of professors and lecturers—what one might think would be among our society's more interesting and glamorous career options—report that their job causes them stress all or most of the time. On a scale of one (low) to seven (high), nearly three-quarters rate the morale of their institution at three or less. Describing their mood in the previous two weeks, 36 percent recorded having felt depressed or very unhappy, and 59 percent said "no" when asked if they had felt "that things are going your way" (Kingston, 1996).

Can it be purely coincidental that the society created by the Ladakhis was as gentle on the people themselves as on the environment of which they were a part?

Ladakhi society was deeply rooted in, and committed to, the Buddhist devotion to compassion and the understanding that all is essentially one. There is a world of difference between the Western notion that compassion aids those who suffer, and the Ladakhi understanding that compassion aids the compassionate as well as those who suffer. In which case, why not be as compassionate and kind as often as possible with as many people as possible? In which case, when the well-being of one is clearly dependent on the well-being of all, why not be compassionate to all the fellow creatures with whom we share our environment? The Buddhist notion of karma had long taught Ladakhis that unkindness, the wanton destruction of other people and animals out of greed, anger, and ignorance, was sure to result in disaster for the destroyer. It is a lesson our culture seems destined to learn the hard way, as the effects of our institutionalized cruelty and greed build up in our warming atmosphere, in our diseased cattle, in the lungs of our children, and in the polluted and despoiled regions of the earth more generally.

An important factor in the environmental balance in Ladakh was undoubtedly the fact that people belonged to their place on earth. They were bonded to that place through intimate daily contact, through knowledge about their immediate environment with its changing seasons, needs, and limitations. For them the "environment" was not some alien, problematic sphere of human concern; it was where they were. They were aware of the living context in which they found themselves. The movement of the stars, the sun, and moon were familiar rhythms that influenced their daily activities.

The understanding that was gained through a life rooted in the natural world seemed to create a sense of kinship with plants and animals, which nurtured a profound respect for the humble creatures that shared the world of the Ladakhis. Children and adults who witnessed the birth, rearing, mating, and death of the animals around them were unable to view those animals as merely a "natural resource" to be plundered.

No one could deny the value of this kind of authentic education of the young—one that promotes the widening and enrichment of knowledge—in the development of an ecologically sustainable society. And yet, with the exception of religious training in the monasteries, the traditional culture had no separate process called "education." Education was the product of an intimate relationship between the community and its environment. Children learned from grandparents, family, and friends. Helping with the sowing, for instance, they would learn that on one side of the village it was a little warmer, on the other side a little colder. From their own experience children would come to distinguish between different strains of barley and the specific growing conditions each strain preferred. They learned to recognize even the tiniest wild plant and how to use it, and how to pick out a particular animal on a faraway mountain slope. They learned about connections, process, and change, about the intricate web of fluctuating relationships in the natural world around them.

For generation after generation, Ladakhis grew up learning how to provide themselves with clothing and shelter, how to make shoes out of yak skin and robes from the wool of sheep, how to build houses out of mud and stone. Education was location specific and nurtured an intimate relationship with the living world. It gave children an intuitive awareness that allowed them, as they grew older, to use resources in an effective and sustainable way.

As a model for an ecologically sustainable society, however, many individual aspects of the traditional culture were without doubt far from ideal: There was a lack of what we would consider basic comforts, like heating in the freezing winter temperatures. Communication with the outside world was limited. Illiteracy rates were high. Infant mortality was higher and life expectancy lower than in the West. All of these are serious problems that I do not mean to trivialize or deny. But they are not quite as they appear when viewed from an outside perspective. Traditional Ladakhis did not consider it a hardship, as we would, to fetch water every day from a stream or to cook their food on a dung fire. Nor did they feel the cold to the same extent that we do. On the other hand, there are plenty of hardships that we consider tolerable in the West—breathing poisoned air in our cities, working under great stress for eleven months of the year, being all but completely isolated from our neighbors, having next to no say in how our communities and workplaces are organized—that would be insufferable to the Ladakhis. So, despite the very real problems in the traditional society and the equally real improvements brought about by development, things look different when one examines the important relationships: to the land, to one another, and to oneself. Viewed from this broader perspective, the differences between the old and the new become stark and disturbing.

It is deeply tragic that our mainstream culture, led by government and industry, moves relentlessly toward continued economic growth and technological development. This path is fueled by the belief that satisfying selfish needs will somehow lead to increased prosperity and "progress." Meanwhile real human needs and the needs of a collapsing environmental order are all but ignored. I have become convinced that we need to decentralize our political and economic structures and broaden our approach to knowledge if we are to find our way to a more balanced and sane society. Changes in lifestyle are clearly required in order to reverse these trends. These changes, which would actually enrich our lives, are often viewed as sacrifices, even within the environmental movement. The emphasis is on giving things up and making do with less, rather than on recognizing how much we stand to gain. We forget that the price for never-ending economic growth and material prosperity has been spiritual and social impoverishment, psychological insecurity, and the loss of cultural vitality. We think of ourselves as "having everything," and are surprised when young people turn to drugs or gurus to fill what is actually a terrible emptiness in their lives.

Might has an unerring capacity to make us believe, not only that it is right, but also that it is inevitable. Today, many people take it for granted that Western-style economic development and the global consumer culture evolving out of it are the manifest destiny of planet earth. In reality, it only has to be this way because power is so good at persuading us to take seriously what is actually absurd. The notion that it is possible to structure society in a way that is both more ecologically and socially desirable than the global consumer culture works against the tiny minority of those who benefit from so-called growth.

In Ladakh I saw how human-scale structures nurtured intimate bonds with the earth and an active and participatory democracy, while supporting strong and vital communities, healthy families, and a greater balance between male and female. These structures in turn provided the security needed for individual well-being and, paradoxically, for a sense of freedom. It is high time that we had the courage and vision to rethink our assumptions about "progress" and in so doing recognize the lessons in sustainability we can draw from ancient cultures like Ladakh.

Tradition, Modernity, and Environmental Change in Tibet

Graham E. Clarke

Myth As Illusion and Symbol

WRITINGS ON ENVIRONMENTAL ISSUES in Tibet tend to follow a moral debate, and to be put forward in polar, politicized forms. One the one side, the Chinese state extends a vision of industrial modernity and material progress, and sees its efforts as held back only by harsh circumstance, native backwardness, and outside obstruction. On the other side, Western environmental and Tibet support groups accuse China of the planned destruction of a unique fauna and flora.

In China itself, notions of progress other than those propounding "market socialism," that is, equitable material growth based on commodity exchange and political stability, are rarely aired. Open debate is not a feature of public Chinese culture, and in a century that has seen massive economic and social upheaval into modernity, the implications of the idea that the traditional way was better than the modern are almost unthinkable. In the West, the problems of Tibet are rarely viewed as those inherent in administering an economically modernizing state with an unusual, high altitude ecology; instead they are laid directly at the door of China and contrasted with idealized images of a historical Tibet and Tibetan Buddhism. The socioeconomic contradictions of that historical Tibet, the general problems of economic development, or of any possible modernity in balancing present demands against future needs, receive scant attention.

Seemingly impressive facts are produced to support both sets of views. For the obvious reason that it is they who administer the area,

Chinese quantitative material tends to be more detailed and potentially more informative; but all statistics require clarification and interpretation.[1] Arguments on the Tibetan environment tend to use snapshot images of particular phenomena at particular moments and places, selected on the grounds that their outlines are clear in form. Combined with statistics, these "black and white" outlines come to stand in for general facts. In their turn, these allegedly general facts come to be given explanations that derive from cultural presupposition and political ideology, rather than neutral analyses of processes and circumstances on the ground. Instead of debate, idealized arguments pass each other by like ships crossing over in opposite directions in the night, each focusing steadfastly on its own passage and ignoring details of the other's course.

In the West, traditional Tibet at times is almost beatified, and becomes a spiritual emblem of all that is lost to industrial civilization. In idealized form, traditional Tibet comes to stand as an absolute symbol of a moral good, without the ambiguities and shades of gray that come with social or historical context. For green environmental movements, a statement of Buddhist pacifism and respect for life is taken to imply directly the idea of natural conservation, without account of the intermediary economic and social context that would direct the same, without an empirical view of how Tibetan villagers, pastoralists, monks, and officials lived either historically or today. Ideal is taken for practice.

And so myths—that is, myths in the sense of coherent but fictional accounts of what Tibet once was and of changes taking place currently—come to the fore in accounts of the Tibetan environment. Such a discourse is mythical in the everyday sense of a story that is a fiction—falsehood rather than fact. The word "myth" also has the sense of a story that embodies a popular idea about some significant historical event. In this second sense myths, much like epic sagas and legends, come to be analyzed technically in folklore and anthropology. As story, in sequential form, they come to explain why things have come to be as they are; the new is reinterpreted in terms of a history already well understood. Considered out of time, the overall configuration of such stories reflects underlying cultural values, that is, symbolism and meaning.[2]

Various factors may lead to Western thinking on Tibet in these terms. One is that the lack of readily comprehensible data fuels extremes of speculation. Another is that Tibetan Buddhism has taken root in the Western world as a refugee culture: Besides serving the needs of its own small diaspora of Tibetans for whom historical Tibet is a real memory, Tibetan culture has also come to fill an exotic religious "niche" in highly developed Western urban centers, and becomes reinterpreted and redefined in relation to that host society. Here, unlike historical Tibet where being Buddhist was part of the normal order of things, the Tibetan Buddhist cultural identity is a minority calling, a part-culture in relation to a wider Western cultural whole rather than a phenomenon in its own right. Popular support for Tibet in the West fixes mainly on values according to the norms of the West now—projections of the political ideals and individual needs of relatively well-educated, wealthy, and emancipated populations, without much consideration of social and historical context in its own terms. Hence the idealization of historical Tibet in the eyes of Westerners from those highly developed urban centers.[3] And here it would be as well to draw attention to a few points of social and historical context about Tibet, so as better to appreciate idealizations of the past as a bygone "golden age."

To a wide Western public Tibet symbolizes an isolated, peaceful, timeless Buddhist state. Yet, though it may have remained largely closed to the modern Western world until the early twentieth century (1904), within Asia Tibet was not closed to its neighbors India and China, and its political history is far from peaceful. The history of the central Tibetan state is a record of factional intrigue and internecine warfare worthy of a Shakespearean drama: From the eighteenth to the twentieth centuries (1706 until 1895), scarcely one Dalai Lama, that is, from the sixth through to the twelfth, survived long enough to attain power in adult maturity.[4] There is a checkered history of direct political contact between Tibet and China for more than twelve centuries, with almost continual trade and major cultural influences between literate centers in both directions. Few Westerners let alone Han Chinese know that Tibet sacked the Chinese capital of Changan (now part of Gansu) in the eighth century (763), and that the subsequent (albeit short-lived) Tibetan administration passed edicts that enforced local Han Chinese to cut their pigtails, wear Tibetan national dress, and celebrate Buddhist calendrical festivals.[5] Few Westerners dwell on the fact that a Chinese army occupied Lhasa in 1720, removed the city walls, and left a garrison of over three thousand men in place; or that subsequent Qing armies came to the defense of Tibetan territory against Nepal twice, in the late eighteenth and mid–nineteenth century (1791 and 1850); or that at the turn of the twentieth century the Central Tibetan court often used ceremonial Chinese clothing and food.

I do not hold that such facts in and of themselves may or may not legitimate a separate nationalist agenda; they can only be tactical points of evidence in a political argument that ultimately rests on current mass sentiment in a particular region or area. Intellectual debates on the legitimacy of any one nation-state leave begging the question of logical and historically prior alternatives. Looking out through the prism of modern nationalism may hinder an understanding of past historical forms of interlinkage, whether "nephew/uncle" or "priest/patron" or other again. That stated, the widespread institutionalization of Buddhist religious ideology may well differentiate Tibet from China; in that form Buddhism may act against the keeping of standing state armies or a policy of imperial expansion. However, the long period and density of connections is such that to emphasize a static image of a peaceful Buddhist state, invaded for the first time by China in the twentieth century, is misleading.

A second part of this image of Tibet is as an open, egalitarian society in which all were motivated toward religious attainment. Tibet was probably more open and had greater general literacy than most traditional Asian civilizations. A degree of literacy is suggested by a number of facts: The more socially concerned Mahāyāna form of Buddhism took hold in Tibet; recruitment to public/religious office was to a degree meritocratic, that is, rather than *solely* based on birth or economic class; and even today in the remaining outposts of Tibetan civilization scattered across the Himalayas, one finds a certain level of Tibetan-language literacy in "middle-class" landholding and trading families, especially of male heads of households. The actual level and content of this literacy is another matter. In some remote locations literacy has historically undergone a decline, and in others a renaissance.[6] However, that literacy is generally high relative to other nonindustrial societies does not make it comparable to modern society in terms of degree of literacy and mass emancipation. The hierarchical network of small urban settlements that led back to a larger sacred center was concerned on a day-to-day basis with looking after the produce of the land and maintenance of order, to which purpose religion was harnessed; but religion could provide significant opportunity for personal enlightenment and the rational pursuit of knowledge only to a few. And as is implicit in almost any empirical study of a Buddhist society, a publicly avowed religious ethic of compassion for all beings does not automatically translate into human behavior. Only in rare cases—as with the so-termed Sherpa peoples to the south of Mount Everest in the twentieth century—does this become similar to a modern civil society, that is, a rational, democratic, and egalitarian social order in which individual self-betterment and the pursuit of knowledge if not happiness come to be seen as popular rights.

Tibetan Buddhism had a number of different possible expressions, and the wider social order was hierarchic and differentiated into various parts and levels. The virtuoso path, whether in discourses of ethics and philosophy (sūtra) or through works for yoga practice (tantra), was not for all but for an elite, and only in part meritocratic. Faith and the following of simpler vows and precepts appropriate to a position as a householder were more common.

The agrarian central and southern regions of Tibet were more fixed and stable, and hierarchic, than outlying pastoral areas. For example, southeast Tibet has always been peopled by pastoral, seminomadic groups, who, much like many other pastoral and mountain peoples, were independent and competitive. They may have supported temples and yogis, but lived differently from them, as herdsmen who also carried out raids on travelers' caravans rather than as representatives of Buddhist compassion.[7] The large central monasteries existed as land-holding, bureaucratized wings of a theocratic state, with grades of monks who carried out manual work; in the late nineteenth century at Sera Monastery monks were organized as an armed police force *(ldob ldob)* notorious for their disorder.[8] Not all monks and householders were peaceful.[9]

In all societies there have been a few people who have risen above the conditions of their birth; but in nearly all pre-industrial civilizations, whether in feudal Europe, Russia, or parts of present-day Asia, most people formed an agrarian economic base in which peasant agriculture and minor trade were the main occupations. In pre-industrial civilizations social mobility was relatively low compared to modern society, and knowledge was usually the prerogative of an elite. It is only in technologically modern societies that there has been a more general emancipation, with literacy and education being made available to the masses, and ideals of self-betterment being applied generally (albeit that self-betterment has been understood publicly as material gain). Historically, Tibet was organized much like other premodern Asian states, with a small and in part urban-based hierarchy ruling over a far larger and separate agrarian base. Overall, the model of access to education and higher culture in traditional Tibet was close to that of urban guilds and monasteries in pre-industrial Europe.

The above points should not surprise us, given that traditional Tibet was a pre-industrial society. They do not detract from the attainment of Tibetan Buddhism. However, the emergence of Tibetan civilization depended on the control of the economic surplus from the land produced by most of the peasantry. Such conditions in the Western world fed the emergence of the Enlightenment, a rational and liberating intellectual movement, and the industrial revolution, which in principle provided humankind the ability to transcend those very physical and social conditions.

It may well be significant that people from the Western societies, which have gained most from the changes put in sway by the industrial revolution, have also been at the vanguard of modern environmental movements. It is one thing to argue for a simpler way of life from the secure, technologically advanced context of late twentieth-century Bonn, Geneva, London, or Los Angeles; it would be another altogether to argue for a simpler way of life from a materially frugal, pre-industrial economic base.

This account of myths of the environment in Tibet should clarify two further points. First, it is the absence of the use of modern, renewable energy resources developed by Western technology, not their imposition, that stands behind environmental problems in a Tibet that will inevitably modernize in an economic sense. Second, the mixed impact of such modernity cannot be understood in terms of simple dichotomies between good "environmental Tibetans" and bad "materialist Chinese." No universal humanist philosophy, whether Buddhist or socialist, will allow essential differences between peoples to be posited on grounds of ethnic origin, and Tibetans in Tibet may not be any more willing to renounce the global materialist mainstream than their refugee compatriots in the New World.

The next section is a qualitative outline of patterns and processes of change of the natural environment in Tibet that indicates the complex links between economic, physical, and social features that will act as counterpoint to simplistic fictions. The succeeding section is a summary exploration of the ideal of material progress that underlies China's economic program; it suggests that China's modern history is not too dissimilar to that of the Western world in the nineteenth century. However, here we have to make a distinction: History can explain and help us understand; but this does not absolve us of current political and moral responsibilities, or legitimate present injustices.

An Overview of Environmental Change in Tibet

Since 1982, when economic growth was initiated by administrative reform, there have been changes in the intensification of farming in both pastoral and rural areas, which have a potential environmental impact. In brief, there have been some increases in crop production in irrigated areas, in particular in grain and fodder production, and these are both economically viable and environmentally sustainable. There have also been increases in numbers of livestock on pasture, especially near towns, which, while profitable in the short term, may not be environmentally sustainable in that they call on nonrenewable resources. There have been other increases in rural wealth that have relied on direct and indirect cash subsidy from the state; these may not be economically viable, and may also be encouraging consumption of nonrenewable natural resources.[10]

For grain-producing areas, growth has come mainly from increased availability of capital, fertilizer, and mechanical equipment via the state, and is also linked to diversification into trade and town-based construction. For pastoralism, growth has come mainly from increased sales of livestock through towns and trade. In part, this economic growth is a general rebound from the earlier commune period after 1978. That repressed economy was so inefficient that *any* change was likely to be economically beneficial; moreover, the move to a *household* responsibility system was a reversion to the traditional Tibetan social unit, one well adapted for agriculture and livestock production.

Another related factor is growth in the transport sector. Since 1982 there has been spectacular growth in private trucking, largely by small-scale farmers/entrepreneurs, many of whom are Tibetan. This network links rural and urban areas and also allows for external trade. The result has been greatly increased peri-urban linkages, with the integration of markets in areas close to roads and towns and increased commodity-based trading beyond. This has been an important factor in increased livestock production and timber felling and collection, for market sale. This growth in long-distance trade can in one sense be seen as a renaissance of the traditional yak caravan trade; however, it differs from the traditional yak caravans that linked grain-producing and livestock areas both in being on a far larger scale, and in bringing about rural-urban rather than rural-rural trade.

Overall, the investment and the encouragement of market exchange have resulted in diversification and monetization of the economy: Growth has also resulted from increased demand from the towns, associated with both increased per capita demand and increased central urban population from internal growth and internal and external migration since the 1982 reforms.[11]

What is the effect of these market-based changes on the natural environment? First, we have to look at the vectors of impact. Growth in the modern and the traditional economies has been based largely on the use of natural biological resources, for energy and for food production—there is a notable lack of development in modern sources of energy. Much of the increase in production in the dominant agricultural and pastoral sectors is the response to market opportunity of local

producers who traditionally carried out small-scale, agricultural production. They have direct access to such local biomass resources. A
further point is the demand for energy and construction materials in the
towns, again supplied locally. Though there has been some use of
renewable power generated from thermal springs, this has fallen well
short of demand even in urban areas; the energy and material needs
associated with increased agricultural production and urban construction have derived largely from the use of local biomass, in particular,
forest and pasture products.

Second, we have to look at the capacity of the Tibetan ecology to
absorb this intensification of demand for biomass. As is partly true of all
semi-arid ecosystems, Tibet's high altitude and the extremes of climate
associated with it mean that primary forests and pasture do not always
act as renewable natural resources, and if used beyond a certain point,
will not regenerate. Such high-altitude agricultural ecologies tend to be
less rugged as production systems than their low-altitude, temperate-cli-
mate counterparts, and stable only within narrower physical limits—a
point an ecologist would term fragility, an economist a lack of elasticity.

There is a further characteristic of high-altitude and semi-arid and
arid systems, namely, a low population density and large distances,
which in economic terms makes for high transaction/access costs, and
decreases the capacity of the state to control the area directly.

The traditional direct rural-rural trade between pastoral communities on the plateau and grain-producing villages, because dispersed,
produced little in the way of localized environmental pressure. However, the modern system in which many products now pass in and out
of nodes at the towns does give rise to just such localized environmental pressure points. The spatial concentration results in high rates of utilization of natural resources in the areas surrounding towns and new
roads to which there is now access. Where this spatial pattern overlaps
with a fragile ecological system, such as rough grazing for livestock
along roads, severe and (for all practical purposes) irreversible land
degradation takes place.

The average pressures over the country as a whole are not so much
indicative as *localized* pressures. There are also other economic factors; but this interrelation between increased transport and market

demand, urban concentration along spatial patterns of exchange, and high-altitude ecological fragility creates a set of factors leading to non-sustainable use of natural resources. This is true not only for Tibet but also generally for elsewhere in Central Asia and other areas liable to desertification.

Changes rarely have an even distribution, and there is a variation of topography across the country from the lower, monsoonal, southeast to the higher and drier northwest. There are critical differences between the plateau and the relatively lower river valleys to the south; there are also differences between these areas and the southern slopes of the Himalayas in the southeast,[12] which, in marked contrast to the more northerly valleys and the plateau itself, have a highly variegated local "mosaic" topography. While there is a loose correlation between topography and land use, the environmental impact needs to be considered for each separate area, according to whether it is pastoral, grain producing, or forested. The interrelations between the different types of ecosystems and sectoral implications of market forces also have to be examined on a case-by-case basis.

Forestry

The conservation of primary forest is a key issue in the West's concern for Tibet, and rightly so, just as it is for other regions such as the Amazon and Indonesia. In Tibet the problem is serious: Areas such as Aba *(rNga ba)*, to the east of present-day Sichuan, experienced severe and in many cases irreversible deforestation from clear-felling even before the economic reforms of 1978.[13] The Nyinche *(Nying khri)* area north of Arunachal Pradesh in India is still well forested at least in part;[14] Lhokha further to the west, south of Lhasa and bordering on Bhutan, may currently be experiencing deforestation.

In the past state-led industrial forestry has been a key problem. It still continues to be in as far as it is not based on sustainable principles and long-term investment. Forests have no economic value when they stand, and only acquire it by being felled and sold. Hence any cutting down of trees, even a wasteful prime lumber extraction based on clear-felling, represents economic growth. While local features such as market reform can make for extra pressure, the basic problem is more general than Tibet or China, and has a lot to do with the application of industrial forms that originated in the West to the misuse of global natural resources.

Large-scale industry is not the only direct cause of deforestation, as it is also perpetrated by local people. In central and eastern Tibet, Tibetans collect timber for sale in towns; grazing by local pastoral groups on freshly felled areas also prevents long-term regeneration of the pasture.

Grain-Producing Areas

Demand for additional grain from the towns is not likely to cause environmental problems in traditional grain-producing areas in southern and central Tibet, such as at Panam *(Pas snam)* and Gyantse *(rGyal tse)*, which are located on the bottom of wide valleys with deep deposits of fertile alluvial soils and good irrigation.[15] There are environmental problems in these "grain-producing" counties, not in the lower valleys, but on the hillsides above, which are used as rough grazing by livestock and which constitute perhaps over 80 percent of the total land cover.

However, rough grazing is not valued in the local accounts for counties classified as grain producing. In these areas planning emphasizes agricultural investment in crop production and related conservation measures such as planting tree shelter-belts to protect valuable arable land in the valley bottoms, which constitute perhaps less than 5 percent of the land cover. Yet the rough grazing is critical to the large private pastoral sector that has grown up in these counties, and is the main area at risk from erosion.

Pastoralism

The settling down of pastoral groups close to roads puts greater pressure on nonrenewable timber and shrubs, and on the pasture itself for use both as grazing and fuel. The focus for settlement tends to be areas along the road, and households from distant settlements also bring their livestock through these nodal locations to market, or place them with relatives to fatten on the land before their final journey to market.

The problem is compounded by increased absolute numbers of livestock. This can be economically rational for individual household terms with "open access" resources (as in the confusingly termed, well-known "Tragedy of the Commons" scenario). Traditional use of livestock as vehicles of public cultural display may not be economically efficient, as such a herd will have greater numbers of old livestock than one reared for slaughter at the optimal age for market sale. Tibetan pastoralists, in part as Buddhists, have qualms about routine production of livestock for slaughter at market and prefer to keep some animals into old age. Animals also tend to be kept alive beyond optimal age because sheer numbers of livestock themselves are an expression of status and wealth. However, this may not give rise to the most critical environmental problems, for the reason that culture change occurs near centers of trade and communication, while traditional ideologies tend to be maintained in remote areas.

The numbers of livestock on peri-urban grazing areas being brought in for sale is the key problem. The main problem areas for pasture are, as indicated above, the dryland hill areas, and generally peri-urban areas by roads where there is a greater density of incoming livestock traffic, up to the highland plateau itself. The effects can be seen even on the hillsides to the north of Lhasa. The soils are thin glacial deposits of loess and are prone to erosion.[16]

Overgrazing has a number of follow-on effects: First, it lessens cover and makes land more vulnerable to erosion; second, the quality of the grasses decreases as close grazing of the nutritious grasses leads to an invasion of the non-nutritious grasses;[17] third, the overuse of available brush and greater numbers of people lead to the increased collection of animal dung for use as fuel, so removing it from the traditional "virtuous cycle" of use as fertilizer on the grassland. While dung was always used for fuel, in the past, however, there would only have been as many people present in pasture lands as were required to look after the livestock, so demands for dung as fuel remained low, ensuring sufficient amounts left over for fertilizer. In addition, pressure from overgrazing was temporary since groups moved around according to the seasons, allowing a fallow period for the land to recover.

In the past, pasture was cut up by nomads for use in forming a base for tent construction, and as fuel. Again, traditionally this was carried out in a transhumant pattern, which allowed for pasture recovery and did not lead to cumulative damage, but now the fixed infrastructure around road networks means a more localized impact; in addition, in locations where there is easy truck access, turf is now being cut up and removed not just for domestic use but for market sale as fuel.[18]

Some measures are in place to combat pasture degradation, such as reseeding and replanting, pest control, herbicides, fencing, and re-education campaigns on stocking. Together with measures for growing fodder to combat winter grazing shortages, these measures could be effective, but they work well only if combined with reduced stocking levels.

In peri-urban areas, there can be a progressive downward spiral of the condition of the pasture and rough grazing. In these same areas, there is also increased demand for timber or shrubs for construction and firewood, as well as for grazing. This increased demand for energy removes biomass directly from early parts of the input cycle to the land in a "nonvirtuous" cycle that accelerates the process of pasture degradation in areas that can be reached by road.

On the one hand, that this problem occurs in areas close to roads and towns implies that it is not widespread. In terms of the grassland as a whole the problem may not be significant, as such locations constitute less than 5 percent of the total grassland in Tibet; similarly there is no lack of rough hill land in Tibet, much of which in any case is semidesert and subject to erosion. On the other hand, the very intensity of the problem in these areas makes the process unsustainable and leads to land degradation in highly visible locations close by fixed economic infrastructure, some of which is in all likelihood irreversible. Land degradation as a result of human activity is occurring in the very peri-urban and road areas where it needs to be conserved as a resource for the livestock industry. Furthermore, the extent of this land degradation is likely to increase progressively rather than stabilize, both as more land has to be accessed to substitute for degraded grazing land, and as a function of growth of the road network.

Ecologists would describe this process as a "mining operation" in which one uses up a resource and moves on, rather than as sustainable development. Here, the problem is brought on not by industry, but by local groups and community. It is due not to poor planning, but to the lack thereof under market reform.

Urban Pollution

Lhasa has urban pollution problems. Urban growth in the capital has not been accompanied by construction of proper urban services, such as sewerage and sanitation, garbage or solid waste disposal, or hygienic abattoirs. In part this absence of infrastructure stems from a shortage of energy and technical service facilities for the cost-effective operation of machinery; it also has something to do with values and ideology. By and large popular attitudes—whether Han Chinese or Tibetan, whether traditional attitudes applied to a new setting or the replacement of traditional attitudes by commodity consumption—are not attuned or applied to modern problems of urban pollution.

There is a discrepancy between religious ideals and actual day-to-day life. Direct prohibitions on the taking of animal life are one thing, but traditionally there have always been livestock slaughter grounds in Lhasa run by Muslim Tibetans. (The myths of "Buddhist eggs" sold as allegedly laid cracked and thus unable to give life, and recipes for "vegetarian momos" are products of the reinterpretation of Tibetan culture for Western consumption in north India and Nepal, and not reflections of the domestic food habits of a meat-eating, pastoral society.)

The lifestyle of Tibetans who rear livestock for slaughter depends on a legalistic interpretation of the Buddhist prohibition of killing animals that draws a fine line between the moral responsibilities associated with agency and inaction. Tibetans who raise livestock sidestep this issue by tethering calves away from their mothers: Deprived of milk, the calves die. There is also the institutionalized slaughtering of cattle by separate itinerant castes of butchers, a role still performed by Muslims in Lhasa.

At large regional conferences in Lhasa, party members and religious figures have discussed whether Buddhism has helped or hindered economic development. Traditional Tibetan Buddhism, in ideology more than actual practice, continues to play some role in Tibet in promoting ideals of cooperation and community to people at large. In 1991 there were well-attended, monthly lay meetings at Drepung and other monasteries at which senior religious figures gave teachings on the implications of their Buddhism for everyday living to groups of over one thousand lay people.

Overall, Tibetan Buddhist values, when not sidestepped, can be of help in introducing popular conservation initiatives; but in other cases they are not helpful, and each has to be assessed as it comes. One cannot use ideological principles such as the Buddhist precepts on concern for life per se to come to any conclusion on the impact of Buddhism on the behavior of Tibetan Buddhists in rural, let alone the more complex urban, environments.

A new emphasis on consumption is creating an economic demand, and the supply for this relies on modern industrial production for which there are insufficient resources. Increased volumes of commodity sales and the localization of trade and supply through regional hubs with greater population densities introduce fresh public administration problems. Running a growing city with modern consumer values using preindustrial technology generates imports and pollution. For example, a combination of a lack of proper abattoirs, cut up meat carcasses for sale on the streets, and flies and dogs in the hot summer sun makes for a public health risk. In 1990 the number of dogs scavenging on the streets of Lhasa city was estimated by municipality officials to have increased to over fifteen thousand.

In 1991 garbage was dumped anywhere in Lhasa. This included the usual modern, nondisposable detritus of modern civilization: plastic wrappings, tin cans, batteries, other packaging, and bottles. When first introduced, these items had some status value in traditional society; now the volume is such that they are no longer collected but disposed of; the breaking of bottles after finishing their contents is the norm in Tibet, and broken glass litters not just waste piles but appears endemic to picnic sites anywhere close to roads in central Tibet.

Attitudes traditional and modern are one aspect of the problem; but attitudes notwithstanding, certain economic tactics could be used to create a system of incentives to maintain the "public good" of the environment. For example, in the case of bottles and glass, at present there is no deposit to collect on bottles, and hence no incentive to collect and return them whole. Second, due to the lack of energy and industry there is no rebottling plant in Lhasa; to be re-used the bottles would have to be trucked out again to lowland China, which, due to high transport costs, is not seen as financially viable.

Tibet has specific cultural forms and practices, to which changes can and will occur in its transformation from a traditional to modern society—changes that have occurred in other societies; what is particular to the situation here is Tibet's high-altitude ecology. The key social problem stems from the move away from traditional forms of incentive and control, which have not been replaced by effective modern institutional controls. With pasture as with forests, these ecological issues are not Tibet's alone. Similar problems with the conversion of forest into arable land by local communities are found in the Amazon, where local groups take up production for market sale. One key problem in Tibet appears to be the absence of clear property rights to rough grazing, which, as an "open access" resource, is ill treated. Fencing and policing by the state is not a cost-effective option in an area with such low population densities. Current theory in environmental economics would recommend the legal provision of securing long-term property rights, either to private individuals or as "common-property" to industry or local communities, as a critical step in bringing about sustainable long-term rates of timber and pasture use.[19]

In Tibet, investment planning has been led by a policy of import subsidy and market-led growth. There is nothing markedly unusual about such a program for economic investment by centrally planned states. The subsidized distribution of goods often creates a disposable, consumption-oriented, and dependent culture; a lack of profitability due to shielding from open-market forces and problems in investment is not unusual for physical-based planning systems.[20]

Behind the processes of market-led intervention, the key factor responsible for environmental damage has been increased localized demand for energy, both for immediate consumption and for production from local sources for market sale, which has resulted in increased pressure on biomass. In general terms, the problem stems from the reliance on nonrenewable natural resources to help enter an open-market economy. Traditionally, the rate of utilization of biomass was determined by the demands of a relatively stable population of people and livestock, with the overall pressure equalized across the area by an extensive nomadic cycle of grazing and settlement in the course of the year: This nomadic cycle allowed for fallow periods, kept back a reserve, and was sustainable. And here, principled Western opposition to the development of hydropower in Central Tibet on religious grounds would appear to be misplaced on environmental grounds, in that hydropower is a renewable natural resource.

Major changes in the use of natural resources that bring about irreversible environmental, social, and cultural changes are, unhappily, all too common side effects of the history of Western industrial economic development in the name of progress. What is unusual in the case of Tibet is the high-altitude ecosystem and the fact that some aspects of the traditional society were clearly adapted to it.

Of course, pointing to these wider continuities does not remove moral and political responsibility for what is taking place today. However, the simple polarized picture that contrasts Tibetans as naturally environment loving versus Chinese as environmentally destructive is a fiction. Historically, market forces have been introduced by China, but these market forces are not specifically Chinese—they go hand in hand with modern capital and technology. There is nothing intrinsically "Chinese" or "Tibetan" about these changes other than the combination of physical and historical conditions. Tibetans as well as Chinese take part in economic changes that are part of a wider global order, the ideas for which are mainstream to Western intellectual history.

NOTES

1 See Clarke, 1992: 217–40.

2 In anthropology, the work of the nineteenth-century comparative scholar James Frazer stressed the substantive interpretation and classification of myths (Frazer, 1890); that of more recent structuralist anthropology stresses more the contrasting aspects of symbolic form, myths being presumed to

reflect the application of various logical operations on similar universal underlying structures (Lévi-Strauss, 1962).

3   As any ethnographer of the High Himalaya knows, the reverse is also true: Images of Hollywood also function as heavenly idealizations for Tibetan Buddhists in the Himalayas today.

4   See Richardson, 1984: 308.

5   Cuguevskii, 1981: 1–56.

6   On this historical process, see Clarke, 1983: 21–37.

7   See, for example, in Guibaut, 1947 of the account of the shooting in east Tibet of Louis Victor Liotard.

8   See, for example, Tucci, 1988: 139.

9   See Sperling in this volume.

10 Goldstein and Beall, 1990 give a useful illustration of changes in one pastoral area. Quantitative data can be found in Clarke and Osmaston, Rong Ma, Schwartz, together with case studies by Gelek, Levine, and Manderscheid in Clarke, 1998.

11 See Clarke, 1994: 221–57.

12 Metog and part of Zayu *(rDza yul)* Counties are located on this southern chain.

13 See Winkler, 1998.

14 European Commission, 1995.

15 In 1996 the European Commission agreed on an agriculture/irrigation sector-based project with China in this area.

16 Osmaston, 1998.

17 See ibid.

18 For example, the pass above Gyantse to Rinbu *(Rin spungs)*.

19 See Pearce, 1995.

20 There are three important aspects of continued protection and dependency: first, there is reliance on subsidy for imports and transport from the national level in Beijing, which would be removed under a standard IMF economic "structural adjustment policy"; second, post-1979 foreign trade and investment is mediated through national-level agencies in Beijing; third, post-1994 development investment is to be led by twinning with lowland provinces of China.

Shangri-la in Exile

REPRESENTATIONS OF TIBETAN IDENTITY
AND TRANSNATIONAL CULTURE

Toni Huber

Introduction

IN MANY PUBLICATIONS and press releases issuing from the Tibetan exile community during the 1980s and 1990s, one encounters a set of claims about the fundamental identity of Tibetans and the character of their traditional society and culture. These claims include statements such as: "Tibetans are an essentially peaceful and nonviolent people, who never developed an army of their own," and "Environmentalism is an innate aspect of Tibetan culture," and "Women in traditional Tibet enjoyed a higher degree of equality than in other Asian societies." While seemingly innocent and perhaps even seductive, such images and their supporting texts often have little or nothing to do with so-called tradition and its continuity in the postdiaspora period.

Indeed, these types of reflexive, politicized notions of Tibetan culture and identity are unprecedented and distinctly modern. They should be understood as the products of a complex transnational politics of identity within which populations such as the Tibetan exiles, the Sherpas, and the Bhutanese are increasingly representing themselves and being represented by others.[1] They are also very recent, first appearing as an aspect of Tibetan exile self-representation during the mid-1980s. It is also important to note that such identity statements are a specific product of the small Tibetan exile milieu, being a response to the experience of exile rather than the experience of colonization. Thus, although such images circulate in the exile community and are now globally disseminated, they are also limited: They enjoy virtually no currency among the more than 95 percent of ethnic Tibetans living within the present claimed boundaries of political China.

I will not discuss the validity of recent Tibetan exile identity statements and claims herein, although it is certainly appropriate that they be scrutinized by both Tibetans and non-Tibetans alike, and contested if found wanting. Rather, I am primarily concerned with the representational style and agenda of this new type of Tibetan exile self-image. I will outline the social and historical context of their appearance and will consider the manner of their deployment by the exile community.

I will discuss four main points below:

(i) Tibetan exiles have reinvented a kind of modern, liberal Shangri-la image of themselves, which has its precedents in two different sets of discourses, the first of which is the product of the three powerful "-isms" of early modernity: colonialism, orientalism, and nationalism. The second set derives from liberal social and protest movements that originated mainly in the industrialized West, but which are now transnational in scope and appeal: environmentalism, pacifism, human rights, and feminism.

(ii) These new identity images were not spontaneously born out of a groundswell of changes in the general consciousness of the majority of the Tibetan exile population. Rather, they share the same general type of parentage as most identity images in emergent nationalisms throughout the developing world. In this case they are largely the creation of a political and intellectual elite in exile. This small group of educated and cosmopolitan Tibetans has learned and skillfully adapted a repertoire of modern representational styles and strategies during the course of their enforced and prolonged contact with the modern world.[2]

(iii) The experience of the diaspora provided the initial stimulus for modern Tibetan identity production. However, the Tibetan exile elite synthesized these new self-images only after they gained access to and began to draw heavily upon the globalized production and flow of cultural resources and institutions offered by the contemporary transnational cultural environment.[3]

(iv) The "myth of Tibet" was historically a Western enterprise. However, new Tibetan exile identity claims represent, at least in part, an appropriation of Western discourse by the objectified Tibetan "Other" and its creative reflection back to the West. Exile identity claims are often so appealing to, and uncritically accepted by, many Westerners precisely because of such feedback.

As my primary example, I will focus on the construction of an environmentalist Tibetan identity, because this was one of the first forms of exile identity to appear publicly, and it has since been articulated in the greatest detail.[4] It should be noted, however, that the same social forces at work here can also be seen in exile community projections of a non-violent or pacifist or gender-equal Tibet as well. Let us analyze some specific expressions of these identities.

Style and Content: The Example of Environmentalist Tibetans

The style and agenda of new Tibetan identity statements are complex, to say the least. This complexity in part reflects the variety of discourses that these new identities have drawn upon. It also derives from the intentions of the exile political and intellectual elite to create a distinct community of sentiment to direct at a liberal Western and non-Tibetan audience of potential supporters in lobbying for the cause of Tibetan independence from Chinese colonialism.

Invoking an environmentalist Tibetan identity has become an almost obligatory aspect of publicly presenting the issue of Tibet in the 1990s. We find such images in pro-Tibetan political literature, especially in a range of increasingly sophisticated texts issued by the Tibetan government-in-exile in Dharamsala, India. From these sources such images have become globally disseminated into popular world media. An article published in a leading German daily newspaper in 1995, and quoting a Tibetan exile spokesperson, provides a typical example:

[In Tibet] Buddhist faith dominated everyday life.... Plants, animals and "inanimate" nature were as important and valuable as human beings to the Tibetans. The Tibetans always tried to preserve the ecological balance upon which they felt they depended.... Since we [Tibetans] have lived like that for many centuries it has become difficult for us to distinguish between religious practice and concern for the environment.[5]

This excerpt is typical of statements of environmentalist Tibetan identity.[6] They stress the innateness of a certain type of traditional worldview or values and behavior, which are always described in terms of completely modern concepts and language, such as "ecological balance" and "preservation." Also Buddhism, the newly erected central pillar of contemporary Tibetan nationalism, takes center stage, as though this religion were the mainspring of the claimed identity.

Other exile statements boldly claim the global preeminence in space and time of this environmentalist Tibetan identity. For instance:

The Tibetan traditional heritage, which is known to be over three thousand years old, can be distinguished as one of [the] foremost traditions of the world in which...humankind and its natural environment have persistently remained in perfect harmony.[7]

The flip side of establishing the antiquity and tradition of this environmentalist identity is that its contemporary validity must also be simultaneously demonstrated. Thus, it is often stated that "there is a specific connection between the customs of ancient Tibet and contemporary environmental protection."[8] More specifically, Tibetans are said to have the same sort of systematic and reflexive "ecological" consciousness as that developed recently in Western scientific thought. Furthermore, this consciousness is claimed to be one that they have long applied to large-scale regional ecosystems:

[W]e Tibetans have always been aware of the interdependent nature of this world. We know that...[f]or most of Asia, Tibet's environment has always been of crucial importance. And so for centuries Tibet's ecosystem was kept in balance and alive out of a common concern for all humanity.[9]

While such texts are distinctly anachronistic, according to exile Tibetans, the key for understanding this contemporary validity of ancient traditions is Buddhism. We find many statements such as: "Both science and the teachings of the Buddha tell us of the fundamental unity of all things. This understanding is crucial if we are to take positive and decisive action on the pressing global concern with the environment."[10]

Expressions like "interdependence" and "fundamental unity of all things" are frequently used in exile appeals for the scientific validity of Tibetan culture and Buddhism, whether it be modern ecological science, subatomic physics, cosmology, or psychology under discussion.

Contact with the West and Its Legacy

It is tempting to view this style of representation in terms of the popular catchwords of the New Age movement, and therefore locate the agency for these representations in the West.[11] This would be partly correct, as Western countercultural movements have had a continuing impact on Tibetan exile intellectuals since the 1960s, especially in the exile "capital" of Dharamsala. However, for Tibetan exiles as a modern South Asian Buddhist community, there are much older genealogies to be traced out here. Such identity construction has its roots in nearly a century of what Heinz Bechert so aptly described as "Buddhist Modernism," some of whose salient features he described as: the reinterpretation of Buddhism as an essentially rational religion; the idea that Buddhism is a natural vehicle for various kinds of social reform; and the close connection between Buddhism and emergent South Asian anti-colonialism and nationalism.[12]

The colonial encounter between South Asian Buddhists and Westerners resulted in the interpretation of Buddhism as a so-called world religion. Central to this new interpretation was the notion of Buddhism as a rational and undogmatic system, more akin than, for example, Christianity to modern scientific rationalism. This involved rejecting as corruptions or distortions almost all the "superstitions" and traditional ritual elements found in the actual popular religious practices of

Asian Buddhist societies. Thus, both the Orientalists and modern Asian Buddhists claimed philosophy, psychology, and meditation as constituting the "authentic" or "original" Buddhism. This formed the basis for the connection between the apparently rational character of Buddhism and the outlook of modern science in the minds of modern Buddhists.

Since the 1970s in particular, the Dharamsala elite, heavily dominated by the Gelugpa *(dGe lugs pa)* sect of Tibetan Buddhism, has consistently projected a sanitized Buddhist modernist–style representation of Tibetan Buddhism to the rest of the world. It has also attempted to legitimize Tibetan Buddhism's modern validity by exploring its similarities to science, among other things. Such an interpretation was absolutely unthinkable in the reactionary, antimodernist Tibetan religious and political environment of less than half a century ago. The brutal reception given in mid-twentieth-century Lhasa to those such as Gendun Chophel *(dGe 'dun chos 'phel)*, who were inspired by Buddhist modernism to reform the Tibetan tradition, is ample testimony of this fact. Yet following colonization and diaspora, Tibetan exiles began learning the Buddhist modernist style via contact with the forums of international Buddhism, in which articulate South Asian Buddhist modernists of long standing, such as Theravādins from Sri Lanka, often made the link between Buddhism and science.[13] Thus, when environmentalism appeared on the exile agenda in the 1980s, it was easy to phrase claims about an environmentalist tradition and identity with terms lifted from the vocabulary of scientific ecology.

This is not all that the newly exiled Tibetans learned about identity construction from Buddhist modernism and international Buddhism, since their South Asian neighbors had already made Buddhism emblematic of the nation, of struggles against colonial oppression, and of social reform.

New international Buddhist groups, such as the World Fellowship of Buddhists (founded in 1950) and the World Buddhist Sangha Council (founded in 1966), began forming around the time of the Chinese colonization of Tibet and the subsequent diaspora. The Tibetans began participating in some of their activities. These international organizations understood their mission "as a contribution towards a solution of the problems of the world today."[14] The World Buddhist Sangha Council, in particular, felt its obligation was "to oppose war and to contribute towards achieving world peace 'by spreading the Buddha's message of compassion and wisdom against violence and materialist thinking devoid of moral values.'"[15] Various forums of Buddhists for world peace were later staged as a result, and Tibetan exile leaders such as the Dalai Lama participated in them. It does not take much familiarity with the 1980s and 1990s Tibetan exile discourse on world peace and the projection of an essential nonviolent Tibetan national identity to see their direct derivation from precedents set by international Buddhism in previous decades. Here there is pointed irony in a fact recently noted by certain exile intellectuals: The widespread, nationalistic, and violent resistance movement by eastern Tibetans against Chinese occupation actually styled itself the Volunteer Army to Defend Buddhism.[16] I mention this here in relation to recent nonviolent Tibetan identity claims because it demonstrates how quickly and effectively the exile elite has been able to transform the Tibetan Buddhist image. I will have more to say about the mechanisms of such transformations below.

Dynamics of Orientalism

Buddhist Modernism is but one of the foundations for the style and content of new exile identity images. There are also certain dynamics of Orientalist discourse in play by which the "myth of Tibet" has come full circle in various ways. One aspect of what some scholars label the "postcolonial predicament"[17] is the way in which the Oriental Other has also been the creative agent for essentialist constructions, and moreover an agent who reflects, refracts, and recycles Orientalist discourse back to what is held to be the dominant objectifying group. Such a process has often been fostered by the common experience of exile under colonialism, during which such discourses as the Romantic Orientalism of the nineteenth century were imbibed by elite natives from their readings of European sources. A well-known example of this is, of course, Gandhi, who first read the *Bhagavad Gita* in English. More recently, such an experience has not been uncommon among exiled Tibetans. Many younger refugees with no adult experience of life in Tibet, educated in postcolonial India or growing up even more remotely in Switzerland,

Canada, or the United States without their native language, have read of Tibet in the English-language accounts of an earlier generation of European writers including Bell, David-Néel, Harrer, Tucci, and Waddell.

An interesting example of the dynamics of imbibed Orientalist discourse, and one that has been demonstrably influential upon Tibetans, is Gandhian anticolonial rhetoric. The "Gandhian appeal to the greater spirituality of a Hindu India, compared with the materialism and violence of the West"[18] is well known. Gandhi, who had good examples like Vivekananda to follow, accepted the essentialist terms of nineteenth-century Romantic Orientalist constructions of an innately "spiritual" India versus an inherently rational and materialist West. Such formulations have also frequently appeared in Tibetan exile identity claims. The Dalai Lama has often credited the great influence of Gandhi upon his thinking, and Gandhi's biography became widely accessible to exile intellectuals when it was translated into Tibetan in the 1970s.[19] Taking a leaf directly out of the Gandhian book, and influenced as well by the same types of earlier Romantic Orientalist constructions of Tibet, exile identity statements frequently appeal to innate Tibetan spirituality or unique religious orientation. They simultaneously construct a negative Other, in particular the soulless materialism and moral bankruptcy of Communist China or the greed and spiritual impoverishment of the industrialized Western world. For example, in an environmentalist Tibetan identity an innate and superior Tibetan religiosity is directly linked to the Tibetan's apparent satisfaction with material simplicity, disinterest in material consumption, and even such things as the poor development of mining.[20] In opposition to this is posited the essential environmentally destructive Chinese or industrialized Western Other. The appearance of a negative Western Other here is of interest since China is the logical opposite for these Tibetan reverse-Orientalist appeals, because as dominant colonizer it so heavily devalued Tibetan religious life. Yet the modern, Westernized world system also becomes a negative Other of modern exile identity not only via Gandhi but through the borrowed Western cultural critique implicit in modern environmentalism, romantic ethnography, and travel writing.

Another aspect of Orientalist discourse appearing in Tibetan identity claims is derived from what Tsering Shakya has called the "travelogue" interpretation of Tibet found in many Western texts. Shakya has noted a central strategy of this style that developed around the image and role of the "harsh and splendored" landscape in these accounts. For Western travelogue writers, he states, "This landscape they saw reflected in the essential nature of the Tibetan character and philosophy."[21] Herein lay the basis for environmental determinist portrayals of Tibetan society that are an essentializing strategy of long-standing in the contact history of European societies and their native Other. The Dalai Lama and other exile advocates often espouse exactly this form of environmental determinism. In their texts, innate Tibetan environmentalist culture and religiosity is specifically seen as a product of the "unique" natural world of the Tibetan plateau in which they live.[22] Appeals to "primitivism" are yet another commonly borrowed style of the so-called Green Orientalism of Western writers now found in these Tibetan identity claims.[23]

Cultural Identity and Transnational Institutions

The genealogies of essentialism in anticolonial writings, travelogues, and current Tibetan exile self-images have to be appreciated within a much larger and more complex frame of reference: the long history of contact between post-enlightenment Europeans and the rest of the world. The rise and development of Western notions of "culture" and their influence upon non-Western peoples in the contact process is of central importance. All modern Tibetan identity construction is related to this point—there is nothing about the process of forming new Tibetan self-images that cannot be seen to be operating in a myriad of other preceding contact situations between the West and its (variously conceived of) "Other." In the twentieth century the culture concept lies at the heart of postcontact identity representations for both parties, and various ideas of "culture" are a key feature in the construction and fixing of difference.

It is instructive here to think about nativistic movements as discussed by Ralph Linton in the 1940s. Nativism can be seen in terms of "conscious, organized" attempts to perpetuate selected aspects of culture. This can only occur when one is aware of one's culture as being unique—that is, in the contact situation. Nativistic movements seem to arise only in response to certain conditions, but particularly when a group finds itself politically and economically dominated or suppressed.[24] Such is the case of modern Tibetans. From the contact situation imposed by exile, Tibetans have learned to express coherently particular concepts of "culture" and have collected a whole range of representational styles and strategies during the process. It took some time before customs, practices, habits, and laws long taken for granted became selected and then eloquently objectified as their "unique culture." But, by the mid-1980s, the more sophisticated fruits of this process began to appear in the form of a modern, liberal, reinvented Shangri-la identity image.

As I have already suggested, the timing of the appearance of new exile identities is also closely linked to Tibetan participation within organized international institutional frameworks. Relating specific ideas of a unique Tibetan culture with identity took place only after this participation, upon gaining access to the resources it made available. It is at these points that specific reflexive, politicized identities started being forged: When nonviolent, pacifist Tibetan identity grew out of international Buddhists for world peace, an eco-friendly Tibetan identity arose out of the new environmental consciousness of world religions, and a gender-equal Tibet came forth from feminist critique.

Once again we can look briefly to the well developed environmentalist Tibetan identity projection for a good insight into this process. Building on increasing links between the ecology movement and world religions in the 1960s and 1970s, a new discourse came into existence that forcefully linked religion with environmentalism. This has been called the "religious environmentalist paradigm,"[25] and was made accessible to many groups like exile Tibetans via the founding of a transnational institutional network. Tibetans lagged behind other oppressed or colonized peoples in reflexively representing themselves as ecologically sensitive. Yet from 1985 onward, as soon as the Dharamsala elite began to participate in the growing transnational institutions of the religious environmentalist network, things changed rapidly. In just two years Dharamsala had joined in the Global Forum of Spiritual and Parliamentary Leaders on Human Survival, the World Wildlife

Fund–sponsored Buddhist Perception of Nature project, World Environment Day, and the Assisi Interfaith Ceremony on World Religions and the Environment. Immediately after this the first essential environmentalist Tibetan identities went into print.[26]

One major irony of the institutionalized mainstreaming of new identity images is that by appealing to the most commonplace of contemporary, liberal representations, the very uniqueness they persistently claim is negated. For example, since the invention of the first "ecological [North American] Indian" by the ecology movement in the late 1960s,[27] scores of in-harmony-with-nature identities have appeared. Joining other nonindustrialized populations of Amazon forest peoples, Polynesians, Australian Aborigines, native North Americans, and so on, Tibetans have added themselves to the growing list, which now also includes local and transnational commercial or industrial groups, political parties and politicians, world religions, and many other social movements. In turn, the purpose of promoting oneself with such liberal identities is now becoming transparent to all observers. They are no longer just a signal of commitment to the environment, nonviolence, equality, and so on—they are a specific form of self-marketing. They have much to do with strategic positioning for social, economic, and political advantages and resources within the contemporary world system. Not surprisingly, many such identities are now frequently contested.

There is much more to say on this topic, about which I have been able to give only the briefest introduction herein. A related issue of great interest concerns the way these new Tibetan identity images get encoded into all sorts of larger texts and how they are then spread into local and global media and information networks. I have suggested elsewhere that the Department of Information and International Relations of the Tibetan government-in-exile is nowadays the prime site for this type of activity.[28] It is certainly a telling point that many of these identity images first appeared in multiple English texts, before they appeared in Tibetan versions.[29] This gives a pretty clear indication of their initial target audience and purpose: as a self-marketing device aimed at the West and a weapon in an ongoing propaganda battle waged against the colonial Chinese state.

Tibetans and the Modern, Liberal Shangri-la

In conclusion, I would like to offer some thoughts about the meaning of these new identities for Tibetan exiles. Tibetan refugees were
themselves initially not the intended consumers of these identities. Yet,
they have increasingly become exposed to them as they now appear
more frequently in the government-in-exile-controlled Tibetan-language
media. It is my personal impression that in general they have so far
made little impact outside of a very small circle of mostly younger, educated, and articulate cosmopolitan Tibetans, the type of persons with
whom Westerners have the most frequent contact. The majority of ordinary refugees—the carpet weavers, farm workers, sweater sellers, small
traders, motor mechanics, and the many illiterate or semiliterate
Tibetan exiles throughout India and Nepal—have, in my experience, little knowledge of or interest in these new identities emanating out of
Dharamsala. In terms of identity, these persons are still often enmeshed
in the tenacious internal politics of regionalism and sectarianism. They
are far more accustomed to comparing themselves to their Indian or
Nepali neighbors with whom they must interact everyday than to projecting a politically correct liberal image to the rest of the world. This
situation may slowly change over time, however, if the exile elite keeps
environmentalist, peace-loving, and gender-equal Tibetan identities in
circulation within the Tibetan exile community, and if the majority of
exiles become increasingly mobile and cosmopolitan.

In many instances, new Tibetan exile identity images appear to be
just another means by which the exile government can continue to sidestep critical historiography into the future. Heather Stoddard recently
observed that "[a] considerable number of new books written in
Tibetan...have been censored or banned from publication [by the exile
government] because they do not conform to the desired image of traditional Tibetan society. Any serious discussion of history and of possible shortcomings in the society before 1959 is taboo."[30] This type of
censorship is fully operational in all new identity image-making. For
example, in a recent article I have outlined how elite exile text writers
depend upon historical distortion and the editing out of negative evidence to construct environmentalist Tibetan identity images.[31] In relation

to new pacifist Tibetan images, Jamyang Norbu has described how a lack of exile inquiry and scholarship about the Tibetan resistance movement of the 1950s has enabled the government-in-exile to, as he puts it, "successfully rewrite history...fostering the fiction that the popular resistance was nonviolent. Though unhesitatingly subscribed to by many friends of Tibet, this story is patently untrue."[32] Norbu's clear-minded comments on this matter sum up my own observations about the politics of Dharamsala's identity industry perfectly: "Tibetan officials, Buddhist followers, Western supporters and intellectuals... regard the resistance movement as an embarrassment...because it somehow detracts from the preferred peace-loving image of Tibet as a Shangri-La."[33]

Just how long the image of Tibet as a Shangri-la will serve the purposes of the present Tibetan exile elite we cannot say. The French philosopher Antoine Cournot once remarked that "we do not resolve difficulties, we merely displace them." As all elites who, like the Tibetan government-in-exile, work at nation-building seem to discover, the skeletons they have displaced to the closet of unwanted identity and history come back sooner or later to haunt them.

Acknowledgments

My thanks are due to P. Hansen, D. Lopez, and P. Pedersen for useful comments they made on earlier versions of this paper. I also wish to thank several unknown persons attending the conference Mythos Tibet who also made valuable suggestions when the paper was first publicly presented at Bonn in May 1996.

NOTES

1 See, for example, Adams' interesting study of representations of the Sherpas of Nepal (1996a).

2 The result of contacts with the modern West has likely been an active although, prior to the diaspora, limited aspect of Tibetan identity representation since the turn of the century, when British colonial diplomats and others began courting the Tibetan political and religious elite in Central Tibet itself.

How outsiders' representations of Tibet might have influenced Tibetan self-representations in the past remains a question for investigation, cf. Lopez (1995b, 1996) and Hansen (in this volume).

3 See Appaduri, 1991.

4 For a detailed assessment of new environmentalist Tibetan exile images, see Huber, 1997.

5 Anon., 1995: 3; my translation from the German.

6 For a range of alternative versions in both English and Tibetan, cf. the relevant passages in Anon., 1994: 7, Atisha, 1991, 1994, Department of Information and International Relations, 1992: section 1.9, Namgyal, 1994: 29, Rowell, 1990: 11, Vigoda, 1989, Yeshi, 1991, and Yuthok, 1992.

7 Yuthok, 1992: 1.

8 Editor's introduction, 1994; my translation from the Tibetan.

9 Atisha, 1991: 9.

10 Dalai Lama, 1990b: 81; cf. also fig. 16 and caption in Adams (1996a: 162) for a link between these types of statements and those made by Westerners but deployed by contemporary Tibetans.

11 On the New Age movement and Tibet, see Lopez, 1994.

12 Bechert, 1984: 275–77.

13 See Harris, 1991: 110–11, and on intellectual interest in Buddhism and nature in the 1970s, see Samartha and de Silva, 1979.

14 Bechert, 1984: 284.

15 Ibid., 285.

16 Norbu, 1994: 193.

17 Breckenridge and van der Veer, 1993.

18 Abu Lugod, 1991: 144.

19 Stoddard, 1994: 154. Gandhi's works were of course very influential in many movements. For example, on Gandhi in relation to the links between Buddhism and environmentalism, see Kantowsky, 1980, Macy, 1985, and also Ariyaratne and Macy, 1992 on the Sarvodaya movement in Sri Lanka and Kvaloy, 1987.

20 See, for example, Dalai Lama, 1990b: 80 and 1983: 224.

21 Shakya, 1994: 4, cf. Bishop, 1989.

22 See Dalai Lama, 1990: 87; cf. Rowell, 1990: 11.

23 See Lohmann, 1993 and Huber, 1997; cf. Ellen, 1986 and Sackett, 1991.

24 See Linton, 1943.

25 Pedersen, 1995.

26 For details, see Huber, 1997.

27 See Martin, 1978: 157; cf. Vecsey, 1980.

28 For details, see Huber, 1997.

29 Cf. Stoddard, 1994: 150, 153, on the Tibetan exile preference for English.

30 Stoddard, 1994: 152. The recurring problems associated with developing a Tibetan exile "free press" as an alternative voice to the government-controlled print media is a further indication of this ongoing intolerance and censorship. The recent independent Dharamsala-based Tibetan-language newspaper *Mangtso (dMang gtso)* ceased production in early 1996 just at the point where it was growing widely in popularity. In an open letter to its Western subscribers explaining the closure, *Mangtso* editors explicitly identified negative pressure and harassment from elements within the government-in-exile as being instrumental.

31 Huber, 1997.

32 Norbu, 1994: 188.

33 Ibid., 195–96.

Behind the Lost Horizon

DEMYSTIFYING TIBET

Jamyang Norbu

FIVE YEARS AGO there was a completely unprecedented spate of Israeli tourists in Dharamsala. Being a resident of this small Indian hill-station, which is the Dalai Lama's seat in exile, and never having encountered an Israeli tourist before, I was somewhat intrigued by this sudden invasion of Israeli youth. I asked a visiting Jewish scholar from the States if he knew of any reason for this novel phenomenon. He told me that Lobsang Rampa's books had recently been published in Hebrew.

My scholar friend was probably being facetious, but thinking about it now, his was as plausible an explanation as any. Lobsang Rampa, actually an English plumber Cyril Hoskin, is probably the most widely read author on Tibet, and though his works belong, properly, in the category of fiction (Hoskin claimed they are based on recollections of his former life in Tibet), they were regarded till fairly recently by quite a few people in the West as the authentic testimonies of a Tibetan spiritual master.

One would presume that these days with the opening up of Tibet to tourism and with the Dalai Lama himself being completely accessible to Westerners—what with his many visits to and lectures in the West, and his Kālacakra initiations in the United States, Switzerland, and Australia—that the "Rampaesque" fantasies of Tibet would have been replaced by a more down-to-earth appreciation of the country and its problems. But an examination of the many new travel books on Tibet and the New Age works on Tibetan religion and "culture" (most with introductions by the Dalai Lama) leaves one with the uncomfortable feeling that nothing substantial has changed in the West's perception of Tibet since the days when books such as James Hilton's *Lost Horizon* and Lobsang Rampa's *The Third Eye* constituted the bulk of available literature on Tibet.

One indicator of this is the quality of the attention and sympathy Tibetans receive internationally, which, though considerable at present, somehow never quite translates into hard political support for the Tibetan cause. Often it seems that the very reason Tibet attracts so many people in the first place is what makes this attention so inconsequential. Tibet's appeal to the West stems primarily from some variation or the other of the Shangri-la story—of the kingdom of ancient learning and wisdom hidden deep in the heart of Asia, whose powerful mythic elements interject a dreamlike quality into Western awareness of the Tibetan situation, making it appear less immediate, real, and consequential than other conflicts and crises around the globe. The discomforting realization of China's immense size and power—especially economic power—could also be an unconscious factor in the reluctance of many to see Tibet in its reality.

The Shangri-la fantasy has primarily to do with the psychological needs of certain people in the West. It should therefore come as no surprise that in nearly all works of imagination about Tibet, the country and people come across merely as the mise en scène for the personal drama of white people. In the archetypal work of fiction on Tibet, James Hilton's *Lost Horizon*, the protagonist, Conway, is English. The head lama is European, as are most of the top brass of Shangri-la. The Tibetans are essentially superstitious peasants and laborers, hewers of wood and drawers of water—coolies—for the white elite of Shangri-la. The intermediary between the white elite and the native Tibetans is, appropriately enough, a Chinese who acts as the major-domo of the Shangri-la monastery.

I am not going to enter into a discussion here on the role of Tibet in Western fiction, but it must be said that in the literature and film I have had the opportunity to examine, Tibet and its people and culture serve only as a background or foil to the more important business of the white protagonist. Tibetans themselves do not seem to consider such condescending characterizations of their country and culture objectionable. In fact, although they may not be accurate or altogether flattering, Tibetans consider these depictions good publicity for the Tibetan cause. In a limited sense they are, but the underlying premise is that Tibet is only relevant if it serves the needs of the West.

Conrad's novel *Heart of Darkness* can be read as an attack on Belgian colonial exploitation and subjugation of the Congo. Yet Chinua Achebe, the distinguished Nigerian novelist, assailed *Heart of Darkness* as racist. In *Culture and Imperialism,* Edward Said tells us that Achebe believes that *Heart of Darkness* is an example of the Western habit of setting up Africa "as a foil to Europe, a place of negations…in comparison with which Europe's own state of spiritual grace will be manifest." Obsessed with the black skin of Africans, Conrad's real purpose was to comfort Europeans in their sense of superiority. *Heart of Darkness* projects the image of Africa as "the other world," the antithesis of Europe and therefore of civilization, a place where man's vaunted intelligence and refinement are finally mocked by triumphant bestiality.

Tibet is seen as the "antithesis" of the West not so much in the sense of a "darker" civilization, but rather in the matter of corporeality. The West, whatever its failings, is real; Tibet, however wonderful, is a dream; whether of a long-lost golden age or millenarian fantasy, it is still merely a dream.

It is this dreamlike, "Shangri-la" quality of Tibet, most observed in the medieval flavor of its society and culture and in its strange, esoteric religion, that Westerners find most attractive. From tourists to academics, this is the feature of Tibet that is focused on, to the exclusion of other aspects of Tibetan life or culture, no matter how important they may be to the Tibetans themselves.

The desire to maintain the cultural purity of such Shangri-la-like societies as Tibet and Ladakh or certain Amazon Indian tribes seems to necessitate cocooning them against the realities of the outside world, especially politics, commerce, and technology. Development for such societies is only deemed appropriate when it is nonmilitary, nonindustrial, and environmentally friendly in nature. Such considerations are probably well meant and sincere, but very often ignore that society's own changing history, its role, however humble, in geopolitical strategies, and even the desires of its people, who may be seeking change, for whatever reasons of their own. For instance, in a controversial article "The Dragon and the Snowlion: The Tibetan Question in the Twentieth Century," the anthropologist and professor Melvyn Goldstein (1991) advocated a solution to the Tibetan question whereby the Chinese would retain political, military, and economic control over Tibetans, but would allow the Tibetans to exist within "cultural reservations." The suggestion may have been well intended but it is difficult to see anyone seriously advocating such a solution to the Palestinian question, or the problems in Northern Ireland or Bosnia, or anywhere else in the real world for that matter.

When Claude Lévi-Strauss said that anthropology is the handmaiden of colonialism, he was probably not envisioning the kind of "New Age" colonialism that the few surviving ancient cultures in this world have to put up with, but the connection to anthropology he postulated still seems to hold good.

In her book *Ancient Futures* Helena Norberg-Hodge (1991) celebrates the traditional Ladakhi way of life and excoriates the tourism and development that she feels is destroying the ecological balance and social harmony of this "Little Tibet." What such advocacy conveniently ignores is the harsh geopolitical climate in which such an essentially frail society exists. It is not the strength of traditional Ladakhi culture but rather the Indian army, the progressive political system of the Indian Republic, and probably even exposure to Western tourism that have allowed Ladakh to retain its identity and a considerable part of its old way of life. Just across the border, inside Tibet, a culture unprotected by a modern army and antagonistic to change and progress has suffered near extinction.

Calling on people in underdeveloped societies to live passive, traditional, and ecologically correct lifestyles—and not emulate the wasteful lifestyles of people in Western consumer societies—is no doubt laudable, but does not sit too well coming from someone who may own a car or who has running hot and cold water in his or her home. Slavenka Drakulic, the Eastern European feminist writer, puts a political spin on this New Age attitude in her book *How We Survived Communism and Even Laughed.* After seeing Castro on TV talking about how he was promoting environmentally sound policies by denying Cubans access to things like cars, Drakulic realized the frightening totalitarian idea in ecology. "Asking for post-consumer eco consciousness in a poor pre-consumer society was nothing but the act of the totalitarian mind."

Though the Shangri-la stereotype is a Western creation, Tibetans, especially Tibetan refugees, are gradually succumbing to a similarly fantastic idea of their lost country. This shift in perspective is somewhat self-conscious in those aware of the fantasy's strong selling point in the West, but in ordinary refugee society the change is more subtle as life in exile takes on the routines of permanence and the collective goal of returning to Tibet becomes an increasingly distant dream.

The promotion of the image of pre-1959 Tibet as a land of peace, harmony, and spirituality is one of the main tasks of the Tibetan leadership in exile. Among other things this endeavor has unfortunately required a certain amount of rewriting of Tibetan history, especially its modern history. One such revision is in the playing down of the role of the armed revolt against the Chinese since 1956 and the fostering of the fiction that the popular resistance against the Chinese was nonviolent and was led, Gandhian style, by the Dalai Lama. (See Norbu, 1994.)

The Western viewpoint before which the Tibetan leadership strives to maintain a positive image is essentially a New Age one, and many policy decisions made by the Tibetan government-in-exile in the last decade reflect this. The national struggle for an independent Tibet has been replaced by an amorphous agenda of environmental, pacifistic, spiritual, and "universal" concerns that often has little to do with Tibet's real problems. The Dalai Lama's recent statements that achieving Tibetan independence is not as important as the task of preserving Tibetan Buddhist culture reflects not just His Holiness' frustration at Beijing's intransigence on the Tibetan issue but also the influence of his Western followers for whom the problems of Tibet as the nation of the Tibetans is nowhere near as relevant or important as that of Tibet as the repository of the secret wisdom necessary to save a materialistic and self-destructive West.

The propagation of the Shangri-la myth of Tibet, whether by the West or by the Tibetans themselves, has not gone entirely unchallenged. The following articles and lectures serve as interesting examples: Tsering Shakya's "The Myth of Shangri-la" in *Lungta* (special issue on Tibetan writers, 1991); Donald S. Lopez, Jr.'s "New Age Orientalism: The Case of Tibet" in *Tricycle: The Buddhist Review* (spring 1994); and two lectures titled "Orientalism and the Dalai Lamas" and "Ethno-Nationalism and the Tibetan Issue" delivered by Professor Elliot Spering at the Amnye Machen Institute on October 13, 1994 and at the Library of Tibetan Works and Archives on January 31, 1995, respectively.

In the conclusion of his article Donald Lopez contends that for Westerners to indulge in the Shangri-la fantasy of Tibet is "to deny Tibet its history, to exclude Tibet from a real world of which it has always been a part, and to deny Tibetans their role as agents participating in the creation of a contested quotidian reality."

However hopeless their cause or marginal their survival, Tibetans are better off living their own reality than being typecast in ethereal roles in the fantasies of the West.

Buddhism in the West and the Image of Tibet[1]

Dagyab Kyabgön Rinpoche

I WOULD LIKE TO INVESTIGATE the genesis of the Western image of Tibet by first employing a historical sketch. Principally, we perceive the other in two fundamentally different ways: How is the other different from us, and how is the other similar to us? In each case, the other is subject to a value judgment. Europeans usually see in Tibet that which seems familiar to them—such as the apparent similarities between the religious customs of Tibet and the Catholic Church. On the other hand, Europeans judge the uniqueness of Tibet to lie either in its backwardness or in its manifestation of that which the West has lost. Until recently, Tibet's geographical isolation meant that only small amounts of information about its culture reached Europe. Its seclusion lent the country an aura of mystery and magic. For this reason, Tibet offered itself as a screen upon which Western fantasies could be projected. The essential elements of the Western image of Tibet were already fully developed in the eighteenth century. In what follows, I would like to show that these stereotypes have been reiterated without change up to the present day. For example, the comparisons between Tibetan Buddhism and Catholicism and the fascination with the role of lamas in Tibetan society remain unchanged. The only thing that has changed is the associated value judgment.

The image of Tibet is embedded in a dualism of Asia and Europe. Europe defines itself as rational, enlightened, discursive, scientific, active, and democratic. In contrast, Asia is perceived as irrational, unenlightened, contemplative, and passive. Asia is emotional, and tolerant of paradox; it appears as a culture that has deteriorated into pantheism and mysticism. Politically, Asia is despotic; its sovereigns are absolute and its subjects without rights. Thus, the "rule of priests" in Tibet, embodied in the unique role of the lama within his own society, appears to Europeans as a medieval relic. Asians also appear to Europeans as ageless and withdrawn. This notion may cause anxiety in Europeans, who fear the disintegration of individual personality into an undifferentiated mass. This very dissolution into undifferentiated unity is, at the same time, a temptation, in that it often evokes a yearning for liberation from one's own ego and for the lifting of the separation of the human and the divine, or of man and nature. The paradox that lies between defensiveness and yearning has subliminally determined the European image of Asia up to the present. So writes the German author Paul Cohen-Portheim in 1920:

> The European ideal is one of action, individuation, and intellectualization. The West senses that man is separate from nature and is diametrically opposed to her.... The spirit of the West is active, since it seeks out power.... Passivity, universality, and intuition distinguish the East. There man does not feel himself separated from nature but instead feels himself as a part of nature.... He does not seek power but rather harmony with all that lives. He wants to enter into nature, to offer himself to her, to become one with her. Hence I call the Easterner passive, and individualism strives against him.[2]

Very early testimony to the Western image of Tibet are the entries for "Tibet" and "lama" in Zeidler's *Universal Lexicon* of 1744. This gigantic lexicon was the most important reference work in Germany until 1800. The information in these particular entries is based on the travel reports of the seventeenth century, when Western missionaries first arrived in Tibet. Among those missionaries were the Austrian Johannes Grueber (1660), several Italian Capuchins in the years 1707-33, and the Jesuit Ippolito Desideri (1716). As missionaries they all see Tibet primarily in terms of religion. In their reports we see clearly that they understood Tibetan religion only inasmuch as it was similar to their own Catholicism. Tibetans are thus said to believe in a trinity, in heaven and hell, and in exorcisms. Their believers employ rosaries, and their clergy rule the laity. The European missionaries see Tibetan religion not as something separate, but rather as a distortion of their own "culture."

Europeans saw the worship of lamas, especially of the "great lama" (that is, the Dalai Lama) as idolatry. They considered the *tulku* system a fraud and believed the discovery of new incarnations a deception meant to ensure the lamas' power. In the section about the Dalai Lama, Zeidler claimed:

He is called the "great lama." In order to cause the people to believe that he lives forever, the other priests set another in his place as soon as he dies, and thus continue the deception. The priests babble to the people that the lama has lived for more than seven hundred years and will continue to live eternally.[3]

To enlightened Europeans of the eighteenth century, Tibetans were unenlightened barbarians. Johann Gottfried Herder called Tibetans a rough mountain people, whose religion is both inhumane and intransigent. At the same time, he saw Tibetan culture as the curious fruit of climate and history. For Herder, Buddhism was a delusion. As a fruit of the Eastern spirit, however, it was a step in the direction of humanism nonetheless, even if Europeans had already reached this stage in their own development. Buddhism, then, had the merit of having humanized the wild Tibetans and having lifted them onto a higher cultural plateau.[4]

Immanuel Kant's image of Tibet is much more negative than Herder's. His remarks created the paradigmatic European understanding of the self against Asian conceptions. For Kant, Tibetan religion is the religion of mystics, pantheists, and fanatics. In other words, Tibetan religion is the irrational religion *par excellence*. Instead of engaging in reason, Asians sit in dark rooms, stare at walls, and brood—as Kant says in an essay called "Über das Ende aller Dinge."[5] However, in his treatise "Zum Ewigen Frieden," Kant asked if certain aspects of Greek mysticism grew from what he thought were similar Tibetan notions.

Kant proposed an ancient link between Tibet and the West. Although his attempt seems absurd in this case, it was not without its own significance, for Kant was trying to trace a part of European culture to an Asian origin. Here, Tibet appears as the origin of the wisdom that the West has lost. Perhaps that which the West forgot was preserved in Tibet. This idea that Tibet is a mythical place of origin proved quite successful. Later European authors also looked to Tibet as an Aryan homeland or the origin of Hungarian culture. Similar ideas lay the foundation for the positive myth of Tibet that emerged in the nineteenth and twentieth centuries.

In the nineteenth century, Europe conquered the world—both politically and scientifically. The philological study of Buddhism and the geographical acquisition of the last "blank spaces" on the map of the world went hand in hand with this colonial expansion. Tibet was one of these "blank spaces," and attempts to penetrate its core were not merely in the interests of science. After the journeys of Bogle (1775) and Turner (1783), the British attempted to open Tibet for trade. These attempts ultimately led to Younghusband's violent march to Lhasa in 1903–4. The Catholic missionaries Huc and Gabet were the sole Europeans with religious designs on Tibet. In their journals, however, Tibet is portrayed as a backward, archaic country. Compare these with the journals of Bogle and Turner, who in 1775 and 1783 met with the Third and Fourth Panchen Lamas. They are not particularly interested in religious questions, although they do wonder about the similarities between Catholicism and so-called lamaism. They are interested rather in Tibetan politics and trade relations. They remark that the administration of the country is healthy, and seem quite impressed by the lamas, especially the Panchen Lama.

In the course of the nineteenth century, however, the image of Tibet became increasingly negative. The mid- to late-nineteenth-century study of Buddhism led to the deprecation of Tibetan Buddhism. The question as to which form of Buddhism was most authentic was answered by the Western researchers chronologically: Naturally, the oldest form of Buddhism was most authentic. Consequently, "pure" Buddhism was to be found in the Pali canon and the Theravāda school. In contrast, all later developments were "degenerations," among which tantric Buddhism was the worst. Scholars characterized Tibetan Buddhism as "lamaism," a term with unquestionably negative connotations. Unfortunately, these prejudices have continued unchanged in select publications up to the present day. This view of Buddhism was obviously influenced by nineteenth-century Protestant theology and its historico-critical method. The Mahāyāna generally, and Tibetan Buddhism especially, appear to these authors as a type of popery in which the priesthood manipulates the people's superstitions in order to keep them dependent. For Western authors, the prayer wheel *(ma ni 'khor lo)* was the symbolic embodiment of such superstitions.

For Austin Waddell, writing in 1895, tantric Buddhism was little more than "devil-worship" and "sorcery":

> The bulk of the lamaist cults comprise much deep-rooted devil-worship and sorcery... Lamaism is only thinly and imperfectly varnished over with Buddhist symbolism, beneath which the sinister growth of poly-demonist superstition darkly appears.[6]

Meyer's *Konversations-Lexikon* epitomizes this supposedly "scientific" image of Tibet. Written in 1889, it says:

> Cringing servility towards the powerful and arrogance towards the low mark the character of the Tibetan.... The population organizes itself socially into clergy and laity; unfortunately, the secular and religious hierarchies of both sexes (!) do not positively influence the people's morality.... The monks are quite uneducated, and thus have loose morals. Their religious habits support superstition, well known is the use of the prayer wheel.... For the evocation of spirits, [Tibetans] need Lamas, who manifest their skills of deception at every opportunity. The only real worship, occurring through pageantry, music, and incense, is confusing to the spirit.[7]

Thus, religion has made the Tibetans passive and weak, and they are themselves to blame when foreign powers invaded their country. Francis Younghusband justified his violent expedition of 1904 in this manner.

However, Tibet exerted an especially strong pull on Western researchers and adventurers after 1880. The race to see who could first penetrate the "forbidden city" of Lhasa was highly contested. At this time, Tibet became an embodiment of the hidden and unknown. Many successful writers, such as Rudyard Kipling, contributed to the popularization of this image. A travelogue of the American William Rockhill introduced the "yeti" to the West. The myth of Tibet also came into vogue among Western esoteric thinkers around 1880. For such men and women, Tibet was a mysterious land in which ancient "esoteric" knowledge had survived. Helena Petrovna Blavatsky, the founder of Theosophy, claimed as much when she maintained that her secret doctrines had originated with the mahatmas, who lived in Tibet. Tibetan monasteries supposedly preserved an ancient *Book of Dzyan,* which was the source for all other holy books. Blavatsky also claimed to have been in Tibet for three years, albeit only in her "astral body." One of her closest colleagues, the German Theosophist Franz Hartmann, writes in 1898, "Blavatsky actually lay for days in a deathly sleep. Upon awakening, she beamed to her friends that she had been in Tibet, her 'home.'" The teachings of the Theosophists actually had little to do with Tibetan Buddhism. Theosophy was rather one of the first syntheses of Western esotericism and Hinduism. It was the first attempt to integrate Eastern religions into Western culture. Suffice it to state that the importance of Theosophy for the reception of Buddhism in the West has never really been studied.

In this realm saturated with esotericism, "Tibet" was not a real nation but rather a symbol for an origin. "Tibet" embodied a mysterious tradition, with "spiritual masters" and "preceptors of mankind" directing the world's course behind the scenes. Not surprisingly, the lamas' reputation was quite enhanced—they accordingly embodied the archetype of the "old wise ones." They were the protectors of ancient traditions, and all lamas had supernatural powers. The results of this fantasy continue today. The appeal of "Tibet" and "Tibetan lamas" is most favored in esoteric circles to legitimate their own claims, most likely because such claims are so difficult to verify.

A modest modernization began in Tibet after the Younghusband expedition at the turn of the twentieth century. Young Tibetans were sent to India for schooling, and a telegraph line connected Lhasa to the outside world. In 1921, the Thirteenth Dalai Lama even had a telephone and two cars. In the Western literature dealing with Tibet, none of this was acknowledged, since the West was fascinated more with the magical and mystical aspects of Tibet. In the 1930s and 1940s, Western authors were interested in the search for Shambhala, the description of rare phenomena like the *lung gom pa* trance walkers and the so-called *Tibetan Book of the Dead*. For Westerners disillusioned with the world, Tibet became a utopia, a positive counterimage to their own culture. In James Hilton's bestseller *Lost Horizon* (1933), Tibet finally became Shangri-la, the last place of refuge for those fleeing an approaching catastrophe.

Tibetan lamas first arrived in the West with the occupation of Tibet by the Chinese in the 1950s and 1960s, and the West established direct contact with Tibetan culture and Buddhism. This should not distract us from the fact that the historic paradigm continues to have great influence: Westerners still see Tibet as either a reflection of themselves or as a symbol of their yearnings. This is especially true in mass media such as the press, film, and television. On the one hand, the negative image of Tibet persists: Leftist critics still accuse devotees of Tibetan Buddhism of practicing a species of Catholicism, wherein the Dalai Lama is worshiped as a "pope." On the other hand, the myth of Tibet that arose at the end of the previous century also persists: The Theosophists and James Hilton still count Tibet as the place where esoteric knowledge is preserved. The more the Chinese destroy authentic Tibetan culture, the more the West loves this myth of Tibet. Today, the cliché of the wise old lama thoroughly saturates the mass media. In 1995, the German illustrated magazine *Bunte* wrote about the American actor Richard Gere:

> When he went on a trip to the Himalayas, Richard Gere met the Dalai Lama, who is the Tibetan pope of Buddhism. The Tibetans are the preservers of the Buddhist tradition: the old, the wise, the high priests of a religion.

And so forth. Even here, Tibetan Buddhism and its lamas are again compared to the Catholic Church, here in a thoroughly positive sense. Tibet stands for the values of tradition, community, wisdom, religion, and modesty. The concept of "Tibet" becomes a symbol for all those qualities that Westerners feel lacking: *joie de vivre,* harmony, warmth, and spirituality. For many Westerners today, "Tibet" is the primordial, the actual, and the real. It is their real "home." Tibet thus becomes a utopia, and Tibetans become "noble savages." On the one hand, this description of Tibetans is wishful thinking. On the other, it allows Europeans to criticize their own culture.

How, then, have these images of Tibet, both positive and negative, effected the spread of Buddhism in the West? Since the late sixties, exiled Tibetan lamas have taught an authentic Tibetan Buddhism in both Europe and the United States. Numerous groups, organizations, and centers have arisen in the meantime. With all that, the myth of Tibet is a tangible reality for many Westerners. The "great wise ones" can be admired "live." One can engage them and even enter into a teacher-student relationship. Just imagine what fantasies are projected in these relationships!

After thirty years of dynamic propagation of Tibetan Buddhism in the West, we can see that the romantic image of Tibet still persists and only hesitantly is giving way to more realistic considerations. The persistence with which Westerners cling to the myth of Tibet only shows how urgently they need it to compensate for the inner necessities they lack. Such clinging says more about the condition of Western society than about Buddhism itself. We Tibetans are aware of some Western followers who believe that Tibetan lamas are enlightened buddhas and infallible gurus, despite their all-too-human deficiencies. It is disillusioned Westerners, who in the course of their lives have experienced the total collapse of their ideals, and who cling to the wishful image of a holy and healing Tibetan tradition. Wherever angst, insecurity, and despair are strong, there is a corresponding desire for something superior, and Westerners project fatherly power upon the lamas. A false understanding of Buddhist teachings, especially that of the Vajrayāna, has impelled these projections.

The myth of Tibet and the Western crisis of the senses thus work together to make a quick, but rather superficial, spread of Tibetan Buddhism possible. Tibetan Buddhism, however, has quite a bit more to offer than exotic symbolism and mystical sensations. It is a path that one must take seriously: Clear instructions and a disciplined, systematic practice are its foundation. Tibetan opinions diverge on the question of the capacity of Western believers to recognize the path that lies behind their images—and their capacity to walk that path. Two different approaches have emerged over the last ten years. The first approach, which stems from a conscious attempt to abandon the myth, leads to a more realistic and, ultimately, more authentic and spiritual attitude. It is only in this way that the culturally *neutral* message of Buddhism can be grasped gradually and transformed on the individual level, so that Tibet and its lamas no longer stand in the spotlight, but rather the believers themselves do. The second approach is marked by the persistent clinging to a romantic image of Tibet, and it leads, necessarily, to a neglect of reality. This in turn leads to superstition, sectarianism, and dogmatism, and perpetuates the negative aspects of the myth of Tibet among outside observers. Inner development, as Buddhism teaches, is impossible under these conditions, and stagnation, delusion, and defensive rigidity stand in their place.

We must admit, however, that both approaches have been encouraged, unfortunately, by Tibetan lamas themselves. The special conditions of exile have contributed to the lack of critical reflection among many. Perhaps they themselves have fallen prey to the seduction of the myth and are basking in the light of these projections. Perhaps they, too, are seeking to use the myth for questionable religious goals. Although one can assume that most exiled lamas show a sincere interest in preserving and spreading their religious culture, their integrity and credibility are still endangered when they try to play the "great wise ones." This makes their work easier—at least at first—and people can easily approach them. With time, however, an unhealthy and ultimately unavoidable dynamic is set in motion. In contrast, the Dalai Lama exemplifies the positive approach with his personal and ideological credibility, especially insofar as he refuses to project certain images.

Historically speaking, one could claim that the Tibetan people idealized and even worshiped lamas. But the Dalai Lama is trying to oppose just such religious and social degeneration with his reforms. Pious Tibetans often listened to a lama teach publicly for days—without understanding a word. They were satisfied with the blessings his presence afforded and practiced Buddhism according to their own level of understanding. Such people were devoted indeed, but also naive and superstitious. Such is unacceptable for long-term growth among Tibetans, much less Westerners. It is my opinion that a progressive, critical investigation of the myth of Tibet and its effects is necessary in order to prevent harmful developments of this sort. After thirty years, we can now see that the positive aspects of the traditional image of Tibet have had rather negative consequences for the long-term propagation of Buddhism, while the negative aspects of this image, at the very least, have stimulated Tibetan lamas and their students to evaluate themselves critically and, in the end, fruitfully.

Notes

1 Original Tibetan-German translation by Dr. Thomas Lautwein and Regine Leisner.

2 Cohen-Portheim, 1920: 29.

3 Paraphrased from Zeidler, 1745: 28–29.

4 Herder, 1909: 23.

5 Kant, 1983: 185.

6 Waddell, 1895: xi.

7 Meyer, 1889: 689.

PART FOUR
Final Considerations

Imagining Tibet: Between Shangri-la and Feudal Oppression

Attempting a Synthesis

Thierry Dodin and Heinz Räther

The Myth of Tibet through History

THOUGH ALREADY THE STUFF OF LEGEND, Tibet doesn't appear to have received special attention in accounts from classical antiquity.[1] Rather, as was the case for most areas along the borders of what was then the known world, legends and mythology seem to have usurped accuracy. This phenomenon was not exclusive to the classical Western world; early India and China, for example, had similar legendary accounts of the "outside world."[2]

With the first firsthand reports, however, we immediately enter into *medias res;* from the Middle Ages onward Christian emissaries to Mongol khans occasionally report on Tibet. Even though legendary elements still influence these accounts and make them only conditionally accurate, their focus on Tibetan religion is already remarkable. It is thus evident that from time immemorial Tibetan religion exerted a certain fascination on non-Tibetans. It is therefore no wonder that the realm of the legendary Prester John, a fabled Central Asian Christian diaspora, was said to be located in Tibet.[3]

One of the most important figures in this context has been the Venetian traveler Marco Polo,[4] whose travelogue remains the most widely read contemporary account. Though he mentions Tibet, he does so only in passing and without much accuracy, simply repeating the legends he had heard in China.

Religion remained a central issue in the first direct encounters of
Westerners with Tibetans, largely because the first Europeans to set
foot in Tibet were Christian missionaries like Andrade (1580–1643)
and Desideri (1684–1733).[5] Interestingly and surprisingly, despite their
evangelical zeal, these missionaries' image of Tibet was quite sophisticated. As Kaschewsky demonstrates in this volume, their approach
toward Tibetan Buddhism was remarkably objective and enlightened
for their time.[6] This encounter resulted in a genuine intercultural dialogue, the intellectual level of which remained unsurpassed well into the
twentieth century.

Unfortunately, when the information from these missionary
accounts was culled for European encyclopedias and travel compendi-
ums, the selection was biased, narrow, and unflattering. Bigotry, priestcraft, idolatry, and "devil-worship" were the leitmotifs that thus came
to dominate the image of Tibet. As several authors in the present volume show, these strongly biased excerpts of the missionaries' narratives laid the foundations for the image many Western intellectuals and
literati like Kant, Herder, Rousseau, and Balzac had of Tibet. Thus, the
pre-modern "myth of Tibet," as it circulated in the West, was predominantly negative.

The age of European colonialism gave rise to another close
encounter between the West and Asian cultures. In this phase extremely
divergent views about Tibet and its culture and religion emerged.

The first objective and comprehensive studies on Tibet were published by the Hungarian traveler-scholar Alexander Csoma de Körös
(1784–1842), who might rightfully be considered the founder of
Tibetology. Csoma took up Tibetan studies by pure accident: He was
trekking through Central Asia on a search for the origin of the Hungarian people and got stuck in Zangskar, the southwestern part of
Ladakh, where he spent several years studying Tibetan language and
religion. The colonial context of his work is noteworthy: His pioneering work, *The Dictionary of the Tibetan Language*,[7] was commissioned
by the British colonial government in India, which was keen to explore
Tibet as the "backyard" of its empire. Later, Csoma's work was continued by Indian agents of the colonial government. The most famous
of these so-called pandits was Sarat Chandra Das, who based his own

Fig. 1 The Dalai Lama as Magus Melchior (from: La Dépêche, Verneuil, 30.12.1989)

Tibetan dictionary on Csoma's labors.[8] Unlike Csoma, however, whose interests in Tibet were purely scientific, the Indian pandits sought specifically political, military, and economic information to meet the more practical needs of a colonial administration.

The nineteenth-century colonial context also provided a new opportunity for large-scale missionary endeavors in the wider Tibetan cultural area. But the missionaries of this age had little of the objectivity that characterized the sophisticated approach of their predecessors, and they showed limited interest in the regional culture or religion. Instead, their attitude reflected the European arrogance characteristic of the time: local culture was generally seen as backward and primitive compared to European superiority. Rare and remarkable exceptions to this rule were the Moravian missionaries who settled in Lahul and Ladakh in the westernmost part of the Tibetan cultural area. Their encounter with the Tibetan civilization was relatively constructive, and some Moravians even produced valuable scientific contributions to the study of Tibet.[9] This tolerant attitude was, however, part of their broader missionary strategy, which envisioned the establishment of local autonomous Christian communities as essential. Moreover, more than other contemporary Christian missionaries, they considered a sound knowledge of the culture and religion of those they sought to convert essential for their endeavors.

During the nineteenth century, Orientalists took up the scientific study of Buddhism and started to accept it as an important part of humanity's cultural heritage. The focus of their attention, however, was on early Indian schools of Buddhism. Tibetan Buddhism was openly dismissed as a degeneration steeped in magic and superstition since it contradicted in many ways the Western scholarly construction of a "pure" and "original" Buddhism. It is in this context that the term "Lamaism" was coined, epitomizing the scholarly reluctance to accept Tibetan Buddhism as Buddhism at all.

The Western academic interest in Tibet was mainly due to the preservation in Tibetan translation of a large number of Indian texts that had been lost in the original. These Tibetan texts were retranslated into Sanskrit and other Indian languages—a practice that has now come under heavy criticism in the scholarly community.

The first extensive account of the specific Tibetan form of Buddhism was L. A. Waddell's *The Buddhism of Tibet or Lamaism*, which bolstered the widespread negative images of Tibet with a "scientific" foundation. Waddell found the topic of his research so dubious that he even took to censoring some of its more "shocking" aspects.[10] Nevertheless, his book was used as a standard work in the academic world well into the second half of the twentieth century, with new editions being published as late as in the 1990s.

Even quite recently the scientific study of Tibet focused on religion, largely neglecting most other aspects of Tibetan culture. Until well into the 1960s there were only a handful of important Tibetological works focusing on nonreligious subjects.[11] Many books were little more than descriptions of monasteries and temples, leaving the reader to wonder about the economic basis of these monasteries, or their methods for recruiting new monks. The first detailed description of the Tibetan political system, Melvyn C. Goldstein's doctoral thesis *An Anthropological Study of the Tibetan Political System*, was published only in

1968, and general ethnographic accounts came even later: Martin Brauen's *Heinrich Harrers Impressionen aus Tibet* came out in 1974, and the edited volume *Der Weg zum Dach der Welt* in 1982 (Müller and Raunig, 1982).

Yet at least up to the 1970s even, the study of Tibetan religion was confined to the Indian-derived "high" Buddhism practiced in Tibet by a religious elite. Popular Tibetan religion was almost entirely neglected until much later, and even then was studied more by anthropologists than Tibetologists. The indigenous Bönpos and the small but socially important Muslim communities in the urban centers of Central and Eastern Tibet as well as in Ladakh were completely neglected as well.

The distanced, even largely disapproving, scholarly discourse on Tibet, particularly its religion, did not remain uncontested. As early as the nineteenth century, shortly after the emergence of Tibetology as a scholarly discipline of its own, the Theosophical movement built up Tibet into a spiritual El Dorado. Ignoring the then dominant critical Western discourse, Theosophical writings sensationalized Tibet as the spiritual center of the world. Isolated from modernity on "the roof of the world," Tibet was suddenly perceived as a repository of secret

Fig. 2 Guesthouse signboard in Dharamsala (photo by Dodin)

knowledge and sublime wisdom untarnished by the ages. The reasons
the Theosophists chose Tibet as a screen for the projection of their
dreams, longings, and fantasies are manifold and not yet fully understood. What seems certain is that other Central Asian people who stood
under the influence of Tibetan Buddhism, like the Mongols and the
Manchus had already developed similar notions about Tibet.[12]

In addition, the Theosophical image of Tibet echoes the Tibetan
eschatological myth of Śambhala.[13] Based on the texts of the Kālacakra
Tantra, this myth refers to a legendary land hidden behind impassa-
ble mountains, where wisdom and harmony prevail even as darkness
and chaos rule the outside world. Only when time ripens will the sun
of Shambhala dawn and give humanity its long-desired "golden age."
Even though the Tibetans never thought of their own country as the
fabulous Shambhala, the legend was a living, almost tangible, reality for them. Further research might determine whether the founders
of Theosophy were aware of this myth and ultimately projected it
onto Tibet. In any case, as Frank Korom and Poul Pedersen have
shown in this volume, Tibet's politically motivated isolation left a
blank though tangible space onto which Europeans could project their
fantasies and longings.

The Theosophists were a small group of mostly eccentric Europeans and North Americans. As such, their overall importance for
the West, then in the heyday of colonialism, was negligible. Their
influence upon the West's image of Tibet, however, was formidable.
The Theosophists were fascinated with ancient Egypt. This fascination spurred the first translation of the *Bardo Thödol,* a Tibetan ritual text intended to guide the dead to a higher rebirth. The translation
was entitled *The Tibetan Book of the Dead,* awakening slumbering
Western fantasies about ancient Egypt. Theosophy influenced many
key figures of the ensuing propagation of Tibetan Buddhism in the
West, like Anagarika Govinda, Marco Pallis, and Sangharakshita.[14]
The same was true of the Russian painter and mystic Nicholas Roerich,
who in the 1920s undertook a long expedition to central Asia and
Tibet to search for Shambhala.[15] Henry Wallace, then U.S. Secretary of
Agriculture and later a presidential candidate, helped finance this
expensive undertaking.[16]

Fig. 3 The Dalai Lama as a Hollywood star. (from: *Far Eastern Economic Review,* Hongkong 26.12.1996)

Caption: News Item: Hollywood celebrities oppose Beijing's "attempt to impose worldwide censorship" on films in or about China—including the Disney-distributed *Kundun.* Bun Heang Ung

The emergence of the Theosophical image of Tibet preceded and certainly influenced Tibet's appearance in Western literature, as with Rudyard Kipling's *Kim* (1898), Antonin Artaud's writings of the 1920s, and, most influentially, James Hilton's 1933 popular novel *Lost Horizon.*[17]

Even the odd ideas about Tibet prevalent among the German Nazis drew on notions spread by the Theosophists, although the Nazis replaced the generally open-minded (albeit slightly Eurocentric) attitude of the Theosophists toward Asia with a bizarre, racist ideology.[18]

The political image of Tibet proved mutable as well. Peter Hansen and Alex McKay have shown in this volume that British colonialists thought of Tibetans as either backward and barbaric or noble and charming. Interestingly, the partisans of the former category tended to perceive Tibet as a part of China's sphere of influence—even though they rarely specified exactly how—while those of the latter emphasized the obvious autonomy of Tibet in both the cultural and political spheres. It is also this latter group who demanded a greater involvement of Britain in Tibet. When British civil servants actually acquired a foothold in Tibet after the British military expedition of 1904, they promoted this view and painted a positive portrait of Tibet by carefully selecting and censoring their representations. Only a few explorers traveling in eastern Tibet or otherwise escaping British control, like William McGovern, Alexandra David-Néel, and—later on—Heinrich Harrer, could present an alternative image.[19] British administrators, who McKay terms the "Tibet cadre," tried to fit Tibet into Western political concepts and portrayed it as a unified political entity willing to enter the global community then dominated by the colonial powers. The seriousness and sobriety required in politics, however, prevented them from using any mystical, romantic Shangri-la-type images. The image of Tibet they promoted might have been one-sided, but it was not mere propaganda. Reflecting as it did the converging political concepts of the highest Tibetan political elite, including the Thirteenth Dalai Lama, and the British "Tibet cadre," it simply projected their anticipated vision of Tibet's future as present reality. This vision, however, was never realized since—as Goldstein has masterfully demonstrated[20]—the reforms of the Thirteenth Dalai Lama were sacrificed to the selfish interests of ultraconservative monasteries in and around Lhasa. British civil servants also failed to persuade their government to support their plans. Even then the main thrust of the British political agenda in this region was the preservation of good relations with China. Despite their Tibet cadre's sympathy and influence, Great Britain never had more than scant interest in Tibet. Both the national government in London and the colonial government in Delhi consistently refused to recognize Tibet as an independent state. The same kind of concern for *realpolitik* moved other Western powers to adopt this position as well.

Tibet did not make the international headlines again until 1950–51, when China invaded the country. The invasion raised much compassion in the West for a defenseless people devoured by an imperialist power, but this feeling never generated any substantial political support. Few countries supported resolutions in the United Nations that dealt with Tibet's plight, and those that did were minor political powers like Costa Rica and Ireland.

Fig. 4 Encounter with the myth of Tibet in daily life. A shoepolisher in Dharamsala, July 1991 (photo by Dodin)

The flight of the Dalai Lama and many other Tibetans into exile in 1959 resulted in the first relatively large-scale encounters between Westerners and Tibetans, especially high-ranking Buddhist clerics. For the first time Tibetan Buddhism had to be acknowledged as a living tradition, not just a petrified and distorted relic of vanished Indian and Chinese traditions. The danger that Tibetan Buddhism might be lost forever impelled scholars, especially younger ones, to study it with greater vigor than ever before. In the present volume, Per Kvaerne, Heather Stoddard, and Jeffrey Hopkins—as well as Donald Lopez in his "Foreigner at the Lama's Feet"[21]—clearly articulate the feelings of urgency and concern among young scholars of the time. Still, it would take another decade for this new view of Tibetan Buddhism as a living religion to reach the "established" scholarly community.

Soon Tibetan Buddhism started attracting many people outside the academic world. Most of these were youth searching for new forms of spirituality, who had come to know about the Tibetan tradition of

Buddhism through reports of the first "backpack tourists" in Asia, documentary films, conferences, and books like Arnaud Desjardin's *Le message des Tibétains*. Now they had the chance to acquire first-hand experience. In the United States, the one-time Harvard professor Timothy Leary and a group of young intellectuals gathered around him rewrote the *Tibetan Book of the Dead* as an allegory about mind expansion, thereby bringing Tibet to the attention of the LSD generation.[22]

In the 1970s Tibetan lamas, invited by their new American and European disciples, started traveling to the West and laying the foundation for what Stoddard calls in this volume the "globalization of Tibetan Buddhism." Far from becoming a mere continuation of what it had been in pre-1959 Tibet, Tibetan Buddhism in the West developed specific forms, the diversity of which need not be described in detail here. For our concern, it seems worth noticing though that the notions of Tibetan culture that prevailed (and to some extent still prevail) among Western converts have been thoroughly positive but largely uncritical. Very often a mixture of half-understood Buddhist doctrine and naive belief in magic and miracles obstructed the serious study of Tibetan Buddhism,[23] impeding the necessary adaptation of its culturally neutral doctrinal positions to Western needs and understanding. This might be the reason for an experienced teacher of Tibetan Buddhism in Europe, like Loden Sherab Dagyab, to establish in this volume:

> After thirty years of dynamic propagation of Tibetan Buddhism in the West, we can see that the romantic image of Tibet still persists and only hesitantly is giving way to more realistic considerations. The persistence with which Europeans cling to the myth of Tibet only shows how urgently they need it to compensate for the inner necessities they lack. Such clinging says more about the condition of Western society than about Buddhism itself.

Coming back to the field of politics, two opposing views emerged after Tibet lost its independence: Conservatives and other rightists who until then had tended to regard Tibet from a rather critical, Euro-centric perspective, echoing images coined in previous centuries, suddenly started criticizing the brutal oppression of a seemingly peace-loving people together with the large-scale destruction of its ancient and noble culture—a destruction that had actually started long before the onset of the cultural revolution. Tibet provided them with an opportunity to denounce the evils and destructive power of communism and decry the "red" and the "yellow" perils at the same time. This, however, proved little more than verbal support, and that, too, soon died. Although the CIA supported the guerrilla war of the Khampas with military training and a steady supply of weapons, these measures were intended more to irritate China than to liberate Tibet. The CIA doctrine of "low-level conflict" caused the Khampas' campaign to drag. Support for the Khampas' cause eventually ended with the diplomatic agreements between China and the United States under President Nixon. Now Tibet was completely erased from the political agenda, and the "orphans of the Cold War" were abandoned.[24] Clearly, little more lay behind the support for Tibetan liberation than thinly veiled anticommunism. This was but one more sad episode in the Cold War, with no real sympathy exhibited for the Tibetans and their fate.

In contrast to this, for the political left—especially the "New Left"—historic Tibet was a prime example of "Oriental despotism." The influential position of religion in a political entity under the leadership of an absolutist god-king, the monasteries' liberal share of national resources, and the people's alleged obedience and submission to the lamas in "pre-liberation" Tibet starkly confirmed the leftists' belief that religion was the "opiate of the masses." Official Chinese reports of "liberated" Tibet confirmed the leftists' position. Propaganda pictures of selfless barefoot doctors, liberated "serfs," and laughing farmers hand in hand with Chinese comrades in the middle of lush fields of grain promoted a utopian image and made the self-appointed Western "Red Guards" believe that at last the new era of mankind had arrived.[25] At the same time, centuries-old cultural artifacts of immeasurable worth were senselessly destroyed or sold to Western art dealers via Hong Kong. Those Tibetan intellectuals who did not make it into exile were exterminated, and a totally irrational rearrangement of grain production patterns caused the first severe famine in the recorded history of Tibet. We still do not know how many Tibetans perished as a result of starvation during this period.

Leftists dismissed these by now incontrovertible facts (which were available even then) as reactionary propaganda to discredit the "New China" that had supposedly liberated itself from colonial servitude and that they perceived as marching toward a gleaming, socialist future. They naively and pathetically celebrated "China's red sun over Lhasa,"[26] and listened to bizarre propaganda about human sacrifices in the name of religion and other crimes said to be committed by the "Dalai-regime." Like their political opponents, the leftists were not interested in Tibet itself—they were only attracted by images that supported their own preconceived notions and ideological positions.

Finally, around 1980, Chinese communism lost its threat potential for the rightists, just as the leftists' cultural hero Mao lost much of his magic. This led to another drastic change in the political images of Tibet. Conservatives recognized the economic potential of the human masses of the "sleeping giant" China (another face of the once perceived "yellow peril") and immediately stopped toying with Tibet. Afraid of hurting Chinese feelings and thereby obstructing profitable trade relations, they decided to accept Tibet as part of the "Chinese political family." At the same time leftists shed their Marxist ideology and acknowledged the Tibetan people's right of self-determination, which made many of them support far-reaching autonomy or even total independence for Tibet.

Between Shangri-la and Feudal Oppression

Looking at past and present images of Tibet, it seems obvious that a balanced approach has been the exception rather than the rule. This fact seems particularly obvious in consideration of the overwhelming attention paid to Tibetan religion and the almost total disregard of other aspects of Tibetan culture. This is not altogether unexpected, as the Tibetan concern for religion has been matched by few other people in the world. Moreover, after the collapse of their empire in the ninth century, it was through religion that the Tibetans themselves managed to maintain influence over vast sections of Central Asia and of China under the Mongol (Yuan) and Manchu (Qing) dynasties.[27] This, however, does not imply that Tibetan Buddhism and Tibetan culture are identical, or that the average Tibetans have known no other concern than religion, though such assumptions remain—at least tacitly—frequent. This overemphasis on religion, which more often than not was strengthened by foreign perceptions, came to supersede all other aspects of Tibetan culture, thus distorting the overall image of Tibet. Such unbalanced intercultural perceptions are frequent: patterns of norms and behavior, as well as the horizons of the experience of the observer, often lead to a selective emphasis on specific aspects of an alien culture under consideration—sometimes to the total neglect of other equally important aspects. Thus, certain traits of a culture are stressed in a way that cannot stand up to sober analysis.

A further peculiarity of the perception of Tibet by outsiders is the ambivalence between two extreme and mutually exclusive views. On the one hand, the land on the "roof of the world" evokes ideas of sublime wisdom and simple cheerfulness. On the other hand, it is associated with superstition and cruelty, as well as with a deeply reactionary and oppressive political regime. In both views, the resonance of religion remains remarkably ubiquitous. At times considered a bastion of wisdom, at times a dungeon of despair, a realm of light or one of darkness, Tibet appears to inspire both attraction and revulsion, giving rise to the diametrically opposed visions of a Shangri-la and a feudal hell, dividing those concerned with Tibet into Tibetophiles and Tibetophobes.

Indeed, traditional Tibet was a land of extremes and, considering the small size of its population, extraordinary diversity. Alongside highly centralized institutions, one could find stateless regions in which a strong individualism was subjected to nothing but local territorial or "tribal" loyalties.[28] Within the religious institutions, clear-cut rivalries existed between the various religious schools, between monasteries of the same school, and even between individual colleges of the same monastery.[29] In Tibet the normative ideals of peacefulness, harmony, and compassion can be found alongside a self-assertiveness that verges on violence, and intense religiosity can be found side by side with crass materialism. Creative Tibetan intellectuals time and again questioned an all-too-common intellectual rigidity, especially that of religious scholasticism, and were able to make a significant impact. Beyond these social and intellectual contrasts, even the natural environment of Tibet[30] is one of the most extreme ever inhabited by human beings. Bleak highlands and thick subtropical forests are found only a few kilometers apart, giving rise to an extraordinary socioeconomic diversity.

Given such diversity, the unambiguous nature of most images of Tibet, whether positive or negative, appears all the more astonishing and raises suspicion as to whether those who coined the images in question did not—consciously or unconsciously—suppress that part of the picture that did not match their global perceptions.

It is obvious that the different images of Tibet presented in detail in the papers collected in this volume and summarized in this essay generally reflect observers' longings, expectations, and moral or political discourses more than they depict Tibetan realities. Heberer's essay, for example, demonstrates this with exceptional clarity. Heberer describes how for centuries Chinese (Han) perceptions of Tibet reflect a xenophobic and ethnocentric attitude toward the "other" and yet illustrate a longing for an unencumbered *joie de vivre* and supposed (particularly sexual) freedom, sorely lacking in the observer's own cultural environment. By comparison, with a few notable exceptions, Western images of Tibet remained relatively vague until the nineteenth century, owing mainly to the geographical distance between Tibet and Europe. With the increase of direct, firsthand contacts in the colonial period, however, those bland, half-legendary stereotypes gave way to more clarity and precision. Objectivity, though, was still a long way off, since physical proximity also generated emotions that distorted perceptions, filtering data through the lens of the observer's personal background, agenda, and the *zeitgeist* of his lifetime.

Thus, in the late eighteenth century, when Tibet was still relatively accessible to foreigners, British officers such as Bogle, who had been sent to foster trade relationships, painted a very favorable image of Tibet. Certainly Bogle's personal curiosity and open-mindedness reflected the spirit of European enlightenment then still at its height. By contrast, during the period of more assertive colonialism in the nineteenth century, some British officers developed fantasies of filling the imperial treasury with the immense riches and huge natural resources that their poor knowledge and greedy imaginations made them

Fig. 5 Advertising the "Tibet-Winter collection 1994," C&A Fashion House, Bonn (photo by Dodin)

expect on the "roof of the world." Frustrated by the conservative monasteries' collusion with the hegemonial power of the Manchus to keep Tibet inaccessible, they consequently perceived the Tibetans as wildly barbaric xenophobes who obstinately refused to partake of the blessings of modernity. These civil servants' perceptions of Tibet were not unlike contemporary British ideas about Afghanistan, which also had obstinately turned its back on the empire.

Christian missionaries were not so concerned with such macro-political issues. Instead, their attention focused on the local conditions directly affecting their missionary work and how to deal with those while spreading the Gospel. But despite their great efforts, they never met with much success in their endeavor to convert the Tibetans. Accordingly, in resignation, most of them depicted Tibet as a land caught in the spell of dark superstitions. Its religion was perceived as based on the unconditional submission of its devotees to a tyrannical caste of priests consciously subjugating the people and on the mindless repetition of shallow cult practices. During the Victorian period the sexual customs of the Tibetans seemed especially lamentable: horrify-

Fig. 6 Advertising the "Tibet-Winter collection 1994," C&A Fashion House, Bonn
(photo by Dodin)

ing narratives of polyandry—an even more offensive vice than
polygamy—and of alleged secret sexual rituals exemplified the
Tibetans' apparent sexual depravity.[31]

Toward the end of the nineteenth century, as has been mentioned,
the Theosophists in their "revolt against positivism" challenged such
views by "discovering" Tibet as a sublime spiritual treasure house. This
"discovery," however, was in fact little more than a forgery. Their
highly fanciful depiction of Tibetan religion provides ample evidence of
the Theosophists' indulgence in projecting their own longings and fantasies. It is immediately conspicuous that their "Tibetan sages," bearing the Indian title of mahatma and Indian-sounding names, as well as
their reminiscences of Old Egypt cannot have anything to do with an
actual Tibet. What they labeled as "Tibetan wisdom" rather exposes
their almost complete ignorance of Tibet. Historically, the Theosophists
were thus the first Westerners to deliberately use Tibet as a glamorous
vessel for contents defined by alien scopes and concerns.[32]

In the same vein, as Bishop and Norbu have shown in this volume,
Tibetan-themed fictional literature produced since the late nineteenth

century has rarely made use of genuine Tibetan material. Instead, Tibet found itself being used as an exotic backdrop for Western heroes—a backdrop painted with both the well-established positive and negative stereotypes. Set in Shangri-la, Hilton's *Lost Horizon,* the archetypal novel about Tibet, depicts a society consisting of two distinct strata: monks who, strangely enough, have white skin and local (obviously Tibetan) "coolies" who work the fields and engage in other menial tasks. Here the archetypal positive (wisdom and sophistication) and negative (roughness, simplemindedness, and superstition) images of Tibet find themselves juxtaposed on one and the same place, but while the negative connotations apply to the locals, the positive ones happen to be reserved for the white elite. Compared to the Theosophists, some Western novelists thus went a step further in the process of appropriation by taking up positive symbols and leitmotifs associated with Tibet while depriving them of their Tibetanness. This, however, turned out to be only a momentary episode in the depiction of Tibet, since later the Shangri-la archetype was again applied to the Tibetans themselves.

Blending Bogle's favorable view with the heavy sense of duty of their predecessors during the golden age of colonialism, the British civil servants who gained a foothold in Tibet at the beginning of the twentieth century interpreted the Tibetan history and political system according to notions they were familiar with, such as "nation-state," "parliament," and "cabinet." When they found essential items such as a flag or a national anthem lacking, they did their best to create them. This episode, which McKay has dealt with at length in this volume, not only underlines once more that sympathy for Tibet depends on compatibility with the concerns of the observers, it is also the first historic attempt to actively gain sympathy for the tangible Tibet by deliberately staging such compatibility. At least in this case, the motivation was real concern for Tibet, and as has been mentioned, the idea of Tibet thus propagated won the basic consent and even active participation of parts of the Tibetan elite.

Compared to this, the naked anticommunism and anti-imperialism that marked the positions of the political Right and Left after the Chinese invasion of Tibet was of a completely different nature. Both sides avoided any proper analysis of Tibetan culture and history, and neither

showed much concern for the actual fate of the Tibetans. Instead, they
were satisfied with linking Tibet with the stereotypes they associated
with their respective political opponents, as the keywords and phrases
they used in their discourses demonstrate: "feudalism," "world communism," "liberation of the serfs from the yoke of religion," "reactionary propaganda," "imperialistic ambitions," and so forth. In such
an ideological discourse, Tibet itself played, if any, only a minor role.
The subject of debate could just as well have been somewhere in Africa.

Upon closer inspection, contemporary images of Tibet too seem
closely related to ideologies, worldviews, and agendas that are not necessarily linked with Tibet itself. This can be illustrated by the discussion
in this volume between Norberg-Hodge and Clarke of whether Tibetan
culture has an "ecological consciousness."[33] While both authors emphasize the successful adaptation of traditional culture to the extreme environmental conditions of Tibet, Norberg-Hodge links this to the altruistic
attitude promoted by Tibetan Buddhism. Clarke, however, detects here
little more than environmental determinism now superseded by modern
lifestyles. From what both of them write, it appears that the views
expressed reflect their positions within a broader Western political controversy in which Tibet plays a mere illustrative role. While Norberg-
Hodge demands a worldwide roll-back of industrialization and strictly
opposes the current trend toward deregulation of the world economy,
Clarke objects to the primacy of ecology over broader political concerns that he clearly associates with the presumed vain romanticism of
an affluent society. Clarke particularly questions the moral right of the
West to claim such a primacy on the global stage, since the West itself
initialized the very technology and economic systems that now endan-
ger the biosphere. Norberg-Hodge sees traditional Tibetan (or, as the
case may be, Ladakhi) society as a viable model for global change,[34] a
position far from being unanimously held by Ladakhis and Tibetans
themselves.[35] By contrast, Clarke thinks Tibetans past and present
destroyed the environment just as much as Chinese or Westerners have.

Thus, whatever perspective has been adopted throughout history, alien
concerns clearly dominated the perceptions of Tibet and accordingly
inspired the images propagated. Accuracy was, when of concern at all,
generally given secondary importance. While in the distant past dis-

tortions might have been generated by filling in gaps of knowledge in a highly imaginative manner, in more recent times increasingly available accurate information has been heavily interpreted to fit with the concerns of the observers.

Today's images of Tibet in the West are generally positive. Though this owes in part to the persistence of earlier spiritual images—especially those influenced by the Theosophists, which found themselves echoed here even in small details[36]—it is rather the emerging presence of Tibet in the mass media that has predominantly initiated this new development. Whereas fifteen or twenty years ago demonstrations in Tibet or campaigns of the Tibetan government-in-exile would have reached the public only rarely, they are now regularly seen on TV as well as in newspapers, magazines, and on the internet,[37] inspiring sympathy with Tibetans and solidarity with their struggle toward autonomy among a broad Western public.

Above all, in the person of the Fourteenth Dalai Lama, Tibet has a highly charismatic leader who gained popularity in the West even before receiving the Nobel Peace Prize in 1989. Hardly any other political or religious leader of our time has such a positive image, and this image is almost automatically transferred to Tibet as a whole—as are his liberal and pacifist political ideas.

What is most remarkable about this current positive Western image of Tibet is that it builds up the land itself into a metaphor of good, as the last refuge of spirituality amidst a materialistic and radically demythologized world that seems to have been deprived of all its magic. The influence of the pro-Tibet movement on public opinion in the West has been so formidable that it has almost completely eclipsed the previously widespread negative views of Tibet as a "feudal hell" that are also analyzed in detail in this volume.[38] A closer analysis of the images of Tibet thus generated will, however, reveal its often romantic and clearly glamorized nature, which, as was the case in the past with most other images of Tibet, rarely reflects a balanced picture of both past and present Tibet, its history and culture. As has been repeatedly established in this volume, Tibet support groups as well as members of the Tibetan exile community have made extensive use of such uncritical and undifferentiated images of Tibet.

It certainly goes without saying that the small Tibetan population can garner the attention and support of the global community only if it depicts itself as worthy of sympathy on a grand scale. Here, however, the question must be raised whether the use of such unbalanced and uncritical images of Tibet ultimately benefits the unquestionably justified struggle of the Dalai Lama and his people to regain agency over their country and culture. In other words, must one adopt such an idealized image of Tibet in order to support Tibet's right to self-determination?

Summarizing the current leitmotifs of the still-timid—though in the last couple of years progressing—discussion among exiled Tibetans, Tibet supporters, and scholars of Tibetan studies on this question,[39] Barnett demonstrated in this volume that the current discourse on Tibet remains problematic, since it is intrinsically apolitical, tending to (partly contradictory) overstatements and more involved in rhetorical proclamations than practical commitments. In a controversial work, Donald Lopez declared this current image of Tibet a mere product of the historical reception of Tibet in the West, which according to him reduced the Tibetans to hapless "prisoners of Shangri-la."[40] This view, however, seems to ignore the very active participation of the Tibetans in the emergence and continuing reiteration of the current image of their country and culture, as well as their remarkable skills in promoting it. As such, it has been refuted by Tsering Shakya[41] and by Germano, who points out Lopez's latent conservative interpretation of Tibetan culture and history and instead points to the dialectic of autochthonous creativity and inculturation of exogenous ideas so typical of Tibet's cultural history.[42] Like other scholars before,[43] Barnett also, although without referring to Lopez, points out the Tibetan agency in the current discourse on Tibet.

It is certainly important to notice that the current instrumentalization of an uncritical "myth of Tibet" has been extremely successful in gaining global sympathy for the Tibetan cause by making the Tibetans the "baby seals of the international human rights movement" as Robert Thurman has put it. The visibility that the Tibetans thus could gain for their cause is particularly obvious if one compares them with the Muslims of Xinjiang who suffer a fate similar to the Tibetans' but, though as worthy as them, never benefited from much international attention. Nevertheless, as far as the *realization* of the Tibetans' aspirations for autonomy is concerned, the scorecard of the movement, as all of us know, has remained rather poor. After more than forty years of exile and about twenty years of intensive mobilization of the world's public opinion along these lines, the Tibet question has remained noticeably absent from the agendas of world politics. It was only when a sober and matter-of-fact approach—instead of declamatory rhetoric and glamorizing strategies of representation—was at work that noticeable, though admittedly still modest, successes could be achieved. For example, accurate and dispassionate arguments of the Tibet Information Network (TIN) greatly helped stop the World Bank funding of the settlement of non-Tibetans in the Amdo region as planned by the People's Republic of China government in 2000. This seems to illustrate the primacy of critical and differentiated approaches over idealizing and emotional representations in the arena of world politics, where the treatment of the Tibet question without any doubt belongs.

Apart from matters of sustainability, the question must be raised as to the effects of idealized images of Tibet on Tibetan society itself, which, after all, is the intended beneficiary of a resolution of the Tibetan question. For if support for Tibet comes from uncritical followers who only extol its perceived past, Tibetan society runs the risk of getting trapped once more in a rigid conservatism, not to say cultural sedimentation. In order to develop and realize its goals, any society must critically evaluate itself and its history instead of capitalizing on an often misunderstood past, for, as Joseph Beuys has rightly said, "creativity is our real capital."

Indeed, the willingness among Tibetans and quite a few of their declared supporters to produce self-indulgent pictures of Tibet both past and present all too often prevents a sound analysis of Tibetan history and society. This is particularly true with regard to crucial questions, such as why in the first half of the twentieth century all attempts to modernize Tibet failed, or which internal conditions contributed to the loss of Tibet's hard-won independence and which changes are still necessary for Tibetan society to continue developing in the new millennium. As recent history has shown, by projecting expectations onto

the past instead of the future, such idealizing approaches seriously inter-
fere with the creative efforts of open-minded Tibetan personalities like
the president of the Tibetan parliament-in-exile, Samdhong Rinpoche,
the political scientist Dawa Norbu, the writer and political activist
Jamyang Norbu, and many other less-known Tibetans, in particular
gifted intellectuals and artists who often do not find the attention they
deserve in Tibetan society and finally choose to live outside of it, many
of them even settling abroad.[44] It also prevented progressive institutions, like the *Amnye Machen Institute* in Dharamsala, from developing a satisfying operation level, since their goals do not match the
preservation of an idealized cultural heritage and hence appear neither
worthy of attention for the Tibetan society itself nor worthy of funding for foreign sponsors. Last but not least, such approaches have often
obstructed or even prevented the realization of goals pursued by the
Dalai Lama himself.

Since time immemorial, a broad scope of attitudes and approaches
between charismatic creativity and institutional ultraconservatism has
been characteristic of Tibetan society and culture. Unfortunately, both
Westerners and Tibetans frequently ignore this and by glorifying the
former in effect promote the latter. Thanks to its multipolarity, old
Tibet benefited from a kind of de facto liberalism that without any
doubt was fundamentally different from the deliberate liberalism of
modern societies, implemented and administered by political structures
under the rule of law and the guaranteed autonomy of individuals and
institutions. Still, it seems to be the deep sense of local-rootedness and the
plurality of political structures, patrons, and religious institutions that
provided a social space within which a remarkable creativity as well as
locally inseminated external influences could germinate and give rise to
new forms. It seems those very worldly circumstances, rather than astral
Shangri-la–type fantasies, gave Tibet its attractiveness and allowed such
different and rich personalities like Thantong Gyalpo, Milarepa, the Sixth
Dalai Lama, Gendun Chophel, and Khunu Rinpoche to rise to prominence in Tibetan society, their traces still remaining for posterity to follow. Tradition, though, is passing on a fire, not worshiping its ashes.[45]

A legitimate sympathy for the plight of Tibetans aside, we must
again ask if myth-making is ultimately helpful. If one wishes to accept

Tibet as a real part of the global community instead of a dreamland on the "roof of the world," maybe allowing for some *dis*illusionment would be a more sensible approach and would help us appreciate the human face of Tibet in all its richness and vitality, rather than dreaming of a lost wonderland.[46] As stated earlier, the Tibetans' precarious situation forces them to turn to the outside world for as much support as possible in order to deflect the imminent threat of cultural extinction. And the modern world's need for a utopia does provide a potential balance to the dictates of "realpolitik" and "economic rationale." Visions, however, need not necessarily be based on glamorized images and indeed they should better be oriented toward the future, not the past. Every country and culture has brought forth its own myths and idealizations, and we certainly do not wish to promote any kind of cynical deconstructionism like those that have become fashionable in many academic ivory towers. With this in mind, Tibet has everything to win from a constructive and critical engagement with its past, present, and future. We believe it is this that the Dalai Lama means when he says, "In our fight for freedom, truth is the only weapon we have."

The essays presented in this volume have examined both truths and untruths about Tibet. Some of their claims may strike the reader as unjustified or excessive, some provided contradictory statements, but if this volume provides even a small contribution to the promotion of a constructive discussion about Tibet—and thus, as we believe, helps Tibetans realize their just goals—we will have fulfilled our own goals in examining the endeavor of "imagining Tibet."

NOTES

1 See Lindegger, 1979–93.

2 Compare Heberer in this volume.

3 See Schmidt and Lammers, 1960.

4 See Polo, 1978.

5 See Kaschewsky in this volume.

6 See Kaschewsky in this volume.

7   Csoma de Körös, 1980–82; See also Csoma de Körös, 1834.

8   Das, 1902 has remained a standard tool in Tibetan studies ever since his. His dictionary also relied upon Jäschke's work.

9   Most notable among them were H. A. Jäschke, who published, among other works, a Tibetan-English Dictionary (Jäschke, 1881), and A. H. Francke (see the extensive bibliography of Walravens and Taube, 1992).

10   See Stoddard's essay in this volume.

11   Among the most notable exceptions we find R. A. Stein's *La civilisation tibétaine* (1981 [1962]) and parts of Giuseppe Tucci's *Tibetan Painted Scrolls* (1949).

12   Already Marco Polo mentions the great esteem existing at Khubilai Khan's court for the Tibetan "magicians." The construction of the Potala replica at Jehol shows that awe and fascination for Tibet as a visual myth is not a child of the nineteenth and twentieth centuries only (Chayet, 1985).

13   See Grünwedel, 1915 and Bernbaum, 1980. It should be mentioned that the myth of Śambhala was also well-spread among the Mongols and Manchus. Among others the Japanese instrumentalized it in order to gain influence over the Mongols who came under their domination in the course of the Sino-Japanese war (Unkrig, 1926; Narangoa, 1926).

14   See Govinda, 1968, Pallis, 1939, Sangharakshita, 1971, etc.

15   For Nicholas Roerich, see Decter, 1989; for his expedition, see N. Roerich, 1929 and G. Roerich, 1933.

16   Wallace's political career was brought to an abrupt end during the 1948 presidential campaign when *Newsweek* published his correspondence with Roerich under the title "Guru Letters"; see Decter, 1989: 136.

17   See Bishop's and Norbu's essays in this volume, as well as Brauen, 2000.

18   For a discussion of the Nazis' image of Tibet, see Greve, 1995, as well as his article in *Mythos Tibet,* the original German edition of this volume (Greve, 1997). Later, Martin Brauen dealt in detail with the precursors of the Nazis' image of Tibet (Brauen, 2000.)

19   See McGovern, 1924; David-Néel, 1927; Harrer, 1952, 1984.

20   See Goldstein, 1989.

21   See Lopez, 1995b.

22   See Leary et al., 1964.

23   It seems we find here an updated version of the Theosophical Society's images of Tibet with a good dose of the superficial eclecticism typical of the "New Age" movement, which appropriated many of the Theosophists' ideas.

24   See Avedon, 1984; Knaus, 1999.

25   For a somewhat less extreme version of this view, see Grunfeld, 1987.

26 See Han Suyin, 1977 and Weggel, 1997.

27 See Sagaster, 1960, 1976 and Kämpfe, 1974.

28 For the enormous diversity of political structures in Tibet, see Samuel, 1993.

29 See for example Hopkins' essay in this volume.

30 For the perceived influence of nature on Tibet and its culture, compare Kvaerne's comments on the "nature-romantic school" in this volume.

31 See Bray in this volume.

32 A similar appropriation occurred in the past, when the Mongol (Yuan) and Manchu (Qing) dynasties used Tibetan Buddhism to stabilize their rule over the Central Asian dependencies of their empires. However, this utilization was of a different nature, as Tibetans actively participated in it, thus serving their own interests. Also, being followers of Tibetan Buddhism themselves, the Mongols and Manchus made use of Tibetan Buddhist institutions but did not alter their original teachings.

33 Compare Räther, 1994.

34 Compare the title of her book: *Ancient Futures: Learning from Ladakh* (Norberg-Hodge, 1991).

35 It is, however, Helena Norberg-Hodge's incontestable merit to have raised consciousness on ecological questions in Ladakh, and she therefore remains in high esteem among many locals.

36 See for instance our remarks above in note 22.

37 See Bray, 2000.

38 There are, however, a few dissenting voices who contest the dominance of the positive image of Tibet and, instead, continue to spread the old clichés of the "feudal-hell syndrome" via the internet and some scattered publications. But the heavily dogmatic character of these circles, their marginality and the poor quality of their arguments make them negligible (see for instance: Ditfurth and Goldner, 1996, Ditfurth, 1997, Goldner, 1999, and Trimondi, 1999).

39 See, among many others, the contributions of Toni Huber and Jamyang Norbu in this volume, as well as the very important recent book published by Tseten Norbu, *La reconquête du Tibet* (Norbu, 1999).

40 Lopez, 1998.

41 Shakya writes: "The Tibetan invocation of the language of popular political rhetoric is a strategic calculation rather than a transformation of the Tibetan value system." Shakya, 2001: 189.

42 See Germano, 2001. Beyond Tibet itself, it should be noted that people of Tibetan culture living within the borders of India and Nepal have recently undergone strikingly similar processes of creative adaptation of exogenous

forms while developing strategies for the survival of their own culture, though with mixed success. See Dodin, 1997, 2000, and Dodin (in press).

43 See among others Räther, 1994, and Toni Huber's essay in this volume.

44 Clare Harris provides some interesting insights into the difficulties faced by modern Tibetan painters both in Tibet itself and in exile (Harris, 1999).

45 This sentence is taken from the title of a movie by Austrian film director Gustav Deutsch ("Tradition ist die Weitergabe des Feuers und nicht die Anbetung der Asche").

46 How powerful the "human face of Tibet" can be is admirably demonstrated by Khyentse Norbu's movie *The Cup,* which abstains from the usual idealized images of Tibet and instead depicts the daily life of "normal" Tibetans in realistic environments. With its touching poetry and its sense of humanity, the film provides a direct and holistic insight into Tibetan culture while transmitting a clear political message.

Bibliography

Abramson, Marc (1998). "Mountains, Monks, and Mandalas: *Kundun* and *Seven Years in Tibet*." *Cineaste,* Vol. 23, No. 3, pp. 8–12.

Abu-Lughod, Lila (1991). "Writing against Culture." Fox, Richard G. (ed.). *Recapturing Anthropology: Working in the Present,* pp. 137–62. Santa Fe, NM: School of American Research Press.

Adams, P. (1995). "The Hitchhiker's Guide to the Infobahn." *21C3,* pp. 45–47.

Adams, Vincanne A. (1996a). *Tigers of the Snow and Other Virtual Sherpas: An Ethnography of Himalayan Encounters.* Princeton, NJ: Princeton University Press.

—— (1996b). "Karaoke As Modern Lhasa, Tibet." *Cultural Anthropology.* Vol. 11, No. 4, pp. 510–546.

AFP (1988). "Dalai Lama Cites Positive Chinese Signs but Makes No Concessions." AFP, Washington, November 7, 1988.

AFP (Agence France Presse) (1998). "China Bigger Threat to India than Pakistan: Defence Minister." AFP, New Delhi, May 3, 1998.

Ahmad, Aijaz (1992). "Orientalism and After: Ambivalence and Metropolitan Location in the Work of Edward Said." Ahmad, Aijaz: *In Theory: Classes, Nations, Literatures.* London: Verso.

Algeo, John (1995). "Review Essay: K. Paul Johnson's *The Masters Revealed.*" *Theosophical History,* Vol. 5, No. 7, pp. 232–47.

Almond, Philip C. (1988). *The British Discovery of Buddhism.* Cambridge: Cambridge University Press.

Amundsen, Edward (1910). *In the Land of the Lamas: The Story of Trashi Lhamo, a Tibetan Lassie.* London/Edinburgh: Marshall Bros.

Anderson, Benedict and Richard O'Gorman (1992) [1981]. *Imagined Communities: Reflections on the Origin and Spread of Nationalism.* London: Verso.

Anon. (n.d.). "Tibet: A Reading List." Information sheet available from the Tibet Society, UK.

Anon. (1901). *Dictionnaire thibétain-latin-français, par les missionaires catholiques du Thibet*. Hong Kong: Imprimière de la Société des Missions Étrangères.

Anon. (1936). "James Huston Edgar. An Appreciation and Interpretation." *Journal of the West China Border Research Society,* Vol. 8, pp. 19–23.

Anon. (1965). *Tibet House Museum*. New Delhi.

Anon. (1974). *Tibet Heute*. Peking: Verlag für fremdsprachige Literatur.

Anon. (1988). *Tibet—A General Survey*. Peking: New World Press.

Anon. (1994). "Bod kyi khor yug gi gnas stangs ngo sprod." *Shes bya,* No. 1, pp. 7–11.

Anon. (1995). "Das Schatzhaus wird geplündert." *Der Tagesspiegel,* 6.7.1995, p. 3.

Antweiler, Christoph (1994). "Eigenbilder, Fremdbilder, Naturbilder. Anthropologischer Überblick und Auswahlbibliographie zur kognitiven Dimension interkulturellen Umganges." *Anthropos,* Vol. 89, No. 1–3, pp. 137–68.

AP (Associated Press) (1997). "Dalai Lama Brings Message of Hope to Youths in Denver." Associated Press, June 1, 1997.

Appaduri, Arjun (1991). "Global Ethnoscapes. Notes and Queries for Transnational Anthropology." Fox, Richard G. (ed.). *Recapturing Anthropology: Working in the Present,* pp. 191–210. Santa Fe, NM: School of American Research Press.

Aris, Michael (1979). *Bhutan, the Early History of a Himalayan Kingdom*. Warminster: Aris and Phillips.

—— (1994). *The Raven Crown: The Origins of Buddhist Monarchy in Bhutan*. London: Serindia.

—— (1995). *'Jigs-med-gling-pa's "Discourse on India" of 1789* (Studia Philologica Buddhica, Occasional Paper Series, 9). Tokyo: International Institute for Buddhist Studies of the International College for Advanced Buddhist Studies.

Ariyaratne, Ahangamage T,. and Macy, Joanna Rogers (1992). "The Island of Temple and Tank. Sarvodaya: Self-Help in Sri Lanka." Batchelor, Martine and Brown, Kerry (eds.). *Buddhism and Ecology,* pp. 78–86. London: Cassell.

Artaud, Antonin (1972). *Anthology*. San Francisco, CA: City Lights Books.

Aschoff, Jürgen C. (1989). *Tsaparang—Königsstadt in Westtibet. Die vollständigen Berichte des Jesuitenpaters António de Andrade und eine Beschreibung vom heutigen Zustand der Klöster*. Munich: MC-Verlag.

AsiaWatch (1988a). *Human Rights in Tibet*. New York, NY: AsiaWatch.

—— (1988b). *Evading Scrutiny*. New York, NY: AsiaWatch.

Atisha, Tenzin Phuntsok (1991). "The Tibetan Approach to Ecology." *Tibetan Review,* Vol. 26, No. 2, pp. 9–11, 14.

—— (ed.) (1994). *Bod kyi rang byung khor yug ngo sprod dang / da lta'i gnas stangs / srung skyob skor/.* Dharamsala: Central Tibetan Administration.

Avedon, John (1984). *In Exile from the Land of Snows.* New York, NY: Knopf.

Bachelard, Gaston (1971). *The Poetics of Reverie: Childhood, Language, and the Cosmos.* Boston, MA: Beacon Press.

Bai Bing (1996). "Das wahre Gesicht des Dalai Lama." *Beijing Rundschau,* Vol. 33, No. 19, May 7, 1996, pp. 26–27.

Bailey, Alice Ann (1968) [1957]. *The Externalisation of the Hierarchy.* New York, NY: Lucis Publications.

Balzac, Honoré de (1913) [1835]. *Old Goriot.* London: J. M. Dent and Sons.

Barborka, Geoffrey Avery (1973). *The Mahatmas and Their Letters.* Adyar: Theosophical Publishing House.

—— (1974) [1966]. *H. P Blavatsky, Tibet and Tulku.* Adyar: Theosophical Publishing House.

Barglow, Raymond (1994). *The Crisis of the Self in the Age of Information: Computers, Dolphins and Dreams.* London: Routledge.

Barker, Alfred Trevor (1962) [1923]. *The Mahatma Letters to A. P. Sinnett from the Mahatmas M. and K. H.* Adyar: Theosophical Publishing House.

Barker, Ralph (1975). *One Man's Jungle: A Biography of F. Spencer Chapman.* London: Chatto and Windus.

Barmé, Geremie and Minford, John (eds.) (1988). *Seeds of Fire: Chinese Voices of Conscience.* New York, NY: Hill and Wang.

Barnett, Robert (1991). "The Effectiveness of Parliamentary Initiatives on Tibet." Kelly, Petra, Bastian, Gerd and Aiello, Pat (eds.). *The Anguish of Tibet.* Berkeley, CA: Parallax Press.

—— (1993). *Tibetan Views of Immigration into Central Tibet, 1992–93: A Study of Reports from Tibet.* TIN Background Briefing Paper, London: Tibet Information Network.

—— (1994a). *Survey of Birth Control Policies in Tibet.* TIN Background Briefing Paper, London: Tibet Information Network.

—— (1994b). *Documents on Birth Control.* TIN Background Briefing Paper, London: Tibet Information Network.

Barrows, John Henry (ed.) (1893). *The World's Parliament of Religions.* Chicago, IL: Parliament Publications.

Bechert, Heinz (1966). *Buddhismus, Staat und Gesellschaft in den Ländern des Theravada-Buddhismus,* Vol. 1. Frankfurt a.M.: Alfred Metzner.

—— (1984). "Buddhist Revival in East and West." Bechert, Heinz and Gombrich, Richard (eds.). *The World of Buddhism,* pp. 273–85. London: Thames and Hudson.

Beck, Ulrich (1993). *Die Erfindung des Politischen*. Frankfurt a.M.: Suhrkamp.

Becker, Andrea (1976). *Eine chinesische Beschreibung von Tibet aus dem 18. Jahrhundert*. Ph.D. diss., University of Munich.

Beckwith, Christopher Irving (1977). "Tibet and the Early Medieval Florissance in Eurasia: A Preliminary Note on the Economic History of the Tibetan Empire." *Central Asiatic Journal,* Vol. 21, No. 2, pp. 89–104.

Béguin, Gilles (1977). *Dieux et démons de l'Himalaya*. Paris: Réunion des Musées Nationaux.

—— (1990). *Art ésoterique de l'Himalaya*. La donation Lionel Fournier, Paris: Réunion des Musées Nationaux.

Bell, Charles Alfred (1928). *The People of Tibet*. Oxford: Clarendon Press.

—— (1987) [1946]. *Portrait of a Dalai Lama*. London: Wisdom Publications.

—— (1992) [1924]. *Tibet Past and Present*. Delhi: Asian Educational Services.

Benavides, Gustavo (1995). "Giuseppe Tucci, or Buddhology in the Age of Fascism." Lopez, Donald S. (ed.). *Curators of the Buddha: The Study of Buddhism under Colonialism,* pp. 161–96. Chicago, IL: University of Chicago Press.

Berger, Peter L. and Luckmann, Thomas (1970). *Die gesellschaftliche Konstruktion der Wirklichkeit. Eine Theorie der Wissenssoziologie*. Frankfurt a.M.: Fischer.

Bernbaum, Edwin (1980). *The Way to Shambhala: A Search for the Mythical Kingdom beyond the Himalayas*. Garden City, NY: Anchor Books.

Bernstein, Richard (1997). "Behind U.S. Celebrities' Love Affair with Tibet." *New York Times,* March 19, 1997.

Bhabha, Homi (1984). "Of Mimicry and Man: The Ambivalence of Colonial Discourse." *October 28,* Spring, pp. 125–33.

Bharati, Agehananda (1974). "Fictitious Tibet: The Origin and Persistence of Rampaism." *Tibet Society Bulletin,* Vol. 7, pp. 1–11.

—— (1975). "The Future (if any) of Tantrism." In Fields, Rick (ed.). *Loka: A Journal from Naropa Institute,* pp. 126–30. Garden City, NY: Anchor Books.

Bishop, Peter (1984). "Jung, Eastern Religion, and the Language of Imagination." *The Eastern Buddhist,* N.S. Vol. 17, No. 1, pp. 42–56.

—— (1989). *The Myth of Shangri-La: Tibet, Travel Writing, and the Western Creation of Sacred Landscape*. Berkeley, CA: University of California Press.

—— (1993). *Dreams of Power: Tibetan Buddhism and the Western Imagination*. London: Athlone.

—— (1994). "Dialing Jung: Tibet, Vitamins and the Telephone." *Harvest,* Vol. 40, pp. 77–83.

Blavatsky, Helena Petrovna (1892). *The Theosophical Glossary*. London: Theosophical Publishing Society.

—— (1921) [1888]. *The Secret Doctrine: The Synthesis of Science, Religion, and Philosophy*. London: Theosophical Publishing House.

—— (1923) [1877]. *Isis Unveiled: A Master-Key to the Mysteries of Ancient and Modern Science and Theology*. London: Theosophical Publishing House.

Böckelmann, Frank (1996). "Blicke aufs Fremde." *Frankfurter Allgemeine Zeitung*. April 13, 1996.

Borges, Jorge Luis (1974). *The Book of Imaginary Beings*. Harmondsworth: Penguin.

Bourdieu, Pierre (1991). *Language and Symbolic Power*. Cambridge, MA: Harvard University Press.

Brauen, Martin (1974). *Heinrich Harrers Impressionen aus Tibet*. Innsbruck: Pinguin.

—— (2000). *Traumwelt Tibet: westliche Trugbilder*. Bern: Haupt.

Braun, Christina von (1994). "Ceci n'est pas une femme. Betrachten, Begehren, Berühren—von der Macht des Blicks." *Lettre*, No. 25, pp. 80–84.

Bray, John (1983). "The Moravian Church in Ladakh: The First Forty Years, 1885-1925." Kantowsky, Detlef and Sander, Reinhard (eds.). *Recent Research on Ladakh*, pp. 81–91. Munich: Weltforum.

—— (1991). "Language, Tradition and the Tibetan Bible." *The Tibet Journal*, Vol. 16, No. 4, pp. 28–58.

—— (1992):"Christian Missionaries on the Tibetan Border: The Moravian Church in Poo (Kinnaur), 1865–1924." Shoren, Ihara and Zuiho Yamaguchi (eds.). *Tibetan Studies*, pp. 369–75. Narita: Naritasan Shinshoji.

—— (1997a). "The Roman Catholic Mission in Ladakh, 1888–1898." Osmaston, Henry and Tsering, Nawang (eds.). *Recent Research on Ladakh 6*, pp. 29–42. New Delhi: Motilal Banarsidass.

—— (1997b). "French Catholic Missions and the Politics of China and Tibet 1846–1865." Krasser, Helmut, Much, Torsten Michael, Steinkellner, Ernst and Tauscher, Helmut (eds.). *Proceedings of the Seventh Symposium of the International Association of Tibetan Studies, Graz, June 1995*, Vol. 1, pp. 83–95. Vienna: Verlag der Österreichischen Akademie der Wissenschaften.

—— (1999). "August Hermann Francke's Letters from Ladakh 1896–1906: The Making of a Missionary Scholar." Eimer, Helmut, Hahn, Michael, Schetelich, Maria and Wyzlic, Peter (eds.). *Studia Tibetica et Mongolica. Festschrift für Professor Manfred Taube* (Indica et Tibetica 34), pp. 17–36. Swisttal-Odendorf: Indica et Tibetica Verlag.

—— (2000). "Tibet, Democracy and the Internet Bazaar." *Democratization*, Vol. 7, No. 1, pp. 157–173.

Breckenridge, Carol Appadurai and van der Veer, Peter (eds.) (1993). *Orientalism and the Postcolonial Predicament: Perspectives on South Asia*. Philadelphia: University of Pennsylvania Press.

Broughton, Philip Delves (1999). "Murdoch Launches 'Self-Serving' Attack on Dalai Lama." *The Daily Telegraph*, London, September 7, 1999 (citing *Vanity Fair*, September 1999).

Brown, Andrew (1996). "The Battle of the Buddhists." *The Independent*, London, July 15, 1996.

Brown, David (1994). *The State and Ethnic Politics in Southeast Asia*. London: Routledge.

Brown, William N. (1997). "Western History of Tibet a Deceit." In the series "CHINA through My Eyes." *China Daily*, September 17, 1997.

Bublitz, Hannelore (1992). "Geschlecht." Korte, Herrmann and Schäfers, Bernhard (eds.). *Einführung in die Hauptbegriffe der Soziologie*, pp. 59–78. Opladen: Leske and Budrich.

Buckley, Neil (1949). *Stuart in Tibet*. London: George Newnes.

Bunting, Madeleine (1996). "Special Report—Shadow Boxing on the Path to Nirvana." *The Guardian*, London, July 6, 1996.

Burnouf, Eugène (1844). *L'Introduction de l'histoire du buddhisme indien*. Paris: Imprimière Royale.

Burroughs, William Seward (1984). *Cities of the Red Night*. London: John Calder.

—— (1988). *The Western Lands*. London: Picador.

Byron, Robert (1933). *First Russia: Then Tibet*. London: Macmillan.

Cable, Mildred and French, Francesca (1925). *Despatches from North-West Kansu*. London: China Inland Mission.

Camp, Lyon Sprague de (1954). *Lost Continents: The Atlantis Theme in History, Science, and Literature*. New York, NY: Gnome Press.

Campbell, Bruce F. (1980). *Ancient Wisdom Received*. Berkeley, CA: University of California Press.

Cao Changqing (1994). "The Tibetan People's Rights: Independence—Research on the Theoretical Plane." *Beijing Spring*, New York, No. 18, pp. 30–36.

Cao Changqing and Seymour, James D. (ed.) (1998). *Tibet through Dissident Chinese Eyes: Essays on Self-Determination*. Armonk, NY: Sharpe.

Caplan, Lionel (1991). "'Bravest of the Brave': Representations of 'The Gurkha' in British Military Writings." *Modern Asian Studies*, Vol. 25, No. 3, pp. 571–98.

Caracostea, Daniel (1991). "Alexandra David-Néel's Early Acquaintances with Theosophy, Paris 1892." *Theosophical History*, July–October, pp. 209–13.

Carey, James J. (1968). *The College Drug Scene*. Englewood Cliffs, NJ: Prentice-Hall.

Carey, William (1902). *Travel and Adventure in Tibet*. London: Hodder and Stoughton.

Carlson, Maria (1993). *No Religion Higher than Truth: A History of Theosophical Movement in Russia, 1875–1922*. Princeton, NJ: Princeton University Press.

Carter, Paul A. (1971). *The Spiritual Crisis of the Gilded Age*. DeKalb: Northern Illinois University Press.

Certeau, Michel de (1986). *Heterologies: Discourse on the Other*. Minneapolis: University of Minnesota Press.

Chang, Tsan-Kuo (1999). "China from Here and There: More than Two Decades of Closed Borders and Narrowed Vision." *Media Studies Journal,* Winter 1999.

Chapman, Frederick Spencer (1937). "Tibetan Horizon." *Sight and Sound,* Vol. 6.

—— (1938a, 1992). *Lhasa, the Holy City*. London: Chatto and Windus.

—— (1938b). "A Kodachrome Film of Tibet." *Photographic Journal,* Vol. 78, pp. 262–66.

Chayet, Anne (1985). *Les temples de Jehol et leurs modèles tibétains*. Paris: Edition Recherches sur les Civilisations.

Chen Kuiyuan (1996). "On the Understanding of Several Questions Concerning Socialist Spiritual Civilization." *Xizang Ribao,* July 23, 1996 (Published in Translation as "Tibet Party Leader Chen Kuiyuan Discusses Spiritual Civilization." BBC SWB, September 9, 1996).

Child, Lydia Maria (1871). "The Intermingling of Religions." *The Atlantic Monthly,* Vol. 28, No. 168, pp. 25, 386–95.

China Daily (1998a). "New Airport." *China Daily,* January 5, 1998.

—— (1998b). Nazi Authors 'Seven Years in Tibet.'" *China Daily* (citing Xinhua), January 22, 1998.

Clarke, Arthur C. (1972). "The Nine Billion Names of God." Clarke, Arthur C. (ed.). *Of Time and Stars*. London: Victor Gollancz.

Clarke, Graham E. (1983). "The Great and Little Traditions in the Study of Yolmo, Nepal." Steinkellner, Ernst and Tauscher, Helmut (eds.). *Contributions on Tibetan Language, History and Culture* (Wiener Studien zur Tibetologie und Buddhismuskunde 10), pp. 21–37. Vienna: Arbeitskreis für Tibetische und Buddhistische Studien, Universität Wien.

—— (1992). "Research Design in the Use of China's Census and Survey Data for Rural Areas and Households." Vermeer, Eduard (ed.). *From Peasant to Entrepreneur* (Proceedings of the Second European Conference on Agriculture and Rural Development in China, Leiden, January 14–17, 1991), pp. 217–40. Wageningen: Pudoc.

—— (1994). "The Movement of Population to the West of China: Tibet and Qinghai." Foot, Rosemary and Brown, Judith M. (eds.). *Migration: The Asian Experience,* pp. 221–57. London: Macmillan.

—— (ed.) (1998). *Development, Society and Environment in Tibet: Papers Presented at a Panel of the Seventh Seminar of the International Association for Tibetan Studies, Graz 1995.* Schloss Seggau 1995, Vol. 5. Vienna: Verlag der Österreichischen Akademie der Wissenschaften.

Clift, Charmian and Johnston, George (1949). *High Valley.* Sydney: Angus and Robertson.

Clifton, Tony (1997). "Cult Mystery." *Newsweek,* April 28, 1997.

Clinton, William J. (1998). [Remarks at press conference broadcast live by Chinese Central TV], Chinese Central TV, June 27, 1998 (published by BBC SWB in "Chinese, U.S. Presidents Give Live News Conference," June 28, 1998).

Cohen, Roberta (1988). *People's Republic of China: The Human Rights Exception.* London: Parliamentary Human Rights Group.

Cohen-Portheim, Paul (1920). *Asien als Erzieher.* Leipzig: Klinkhardt and Biermann.

Coleman, William Emmette (1895). "The Sources of Madame Blavatsky's Writings." Solovyoff, Vsevolod Sergyeevi: *A Modern Priestess of Isis.* London: Longman's, Green.

Conan Doyle, Arthur (1980). *Sherlock Holmes: The Complete Short Stories.* London: John Murray.

Conze, Edward (1959) [1951]. *Buddhism: Its Essence and Development.* New York, NY: Harper and Bros.

—— (1979). *The Memoirs of a Modern Gnostic.* Sherborne: Samizdat.

Cosgrove, Denis. (1990). "Environmental Thought and Action: Premodern and Postmodern." *Transactions of the Institute of British Geographers,* N.S. Vol. 15, pp. 344–58.

Courant, Maurice (1912). *L'Asie centrale aux XVIIe et XVIIIe siècles,* Lyon: A. Rey.

Cox, Harvey (1977). *Turning East: Why Americans Look to the Orient for Spirituality—and What That Search Can Mean to the West.* New York, NY: Simon and Schuster.

Craig, Mary (1992). *Tears of Blood—A Cry for Tibet.* London: Harper Collins.

Cranston, Sylvia (1993). *HPB: The Extraordinary Life and Influence of Helena Blavatsky, Founder of the Modern Theosophical Movement.* New York, NY: Putnam's Sons.

Crossette, Barbara (1998). "The Shangri-la That Never Was." *New York Times,* July 5, 1998.

Csoma de Körös, Alexander (1834). *Grammar of the Tibetan Language, in English*. Calcutta: Baptist Mission Press.

—— (1980–82) [1834]. *Sanskrit-Tibetan-English Vocabulary, Parts 1–3* (Bibliotheca Indo-Buddhica 5–6). New Delhi: Sri Satguru Publications.

Cuguevskii, L. I. (1981). "Touen-Houang du VIII au X siècle." Soymié, Michel (ed.). *Nouvelles contributions aux etudes de Touen-Houang* (Centre de Recherche d'Histoire et de Philologie de la IV Section de l'École Pratique des Hautes-Études II, Hautes Études Orientales 17), pp. 1–56. Genève: Droz.

Cutler, Joshua W. C. (1995). "Foreword." Geshe Wangyal, *The Door of Liberation: Essential Teachings of the Tibetan Buddhist Tradition*, pp. xi–xxvii. Boston, MA: Wisdom Publications.

Cutting, Charles Suydam (1940). *The Fire Ox and Other Years*. New York, NY: C. Scribner's Sons.

Dabringhaus, Sabrine (1994). *Das Qing-Imperium als Vision und Wirklichkeit. Tibet in Laufbahn und Schriften des Song Yun (1752–1835)*. Stuttgart: Franz Steiner.

Dalai Lama (1964, 1983) [1962]. *My Land and My People*. New York: Potala Co.

—— (1990a). *Freedom in Exile: The Autobiography of His Holiness Dalai Lama of Tibet*. London: Hodder and Stoughton.

—— (1990b). *My Tibet*. Berkeley: University of California Press.

—— (1993a). "Guidelines for Future Tibet's Polity and the Basic Features of Its Constitution, Dharamsala." Undated but Circulated March 1993.

—— (1993b). Note accompanying His Holiness the Dalai Lama's letter to Mr. Deng Xiaoping and Mr. Jiang Zemin, general secretary of the Chinese Communist Party, September 11, 1992. *Tibetan Government in Exile: Statement by His Holiness the Dalai Lama*, Press Release, Dharamsala, September 4, 1993.

Danziger, Kurt (1991). *Constructing the Subject: Historical Origins of Psychological Research*. Cambridge: Cambridge University Press.

Das, Sarat Chandra (1902). *A Tibetan-English Dictionary with Sanskrit Synonyms*. Calcutta: Bengal Secretariat Book Depot.

Dasa, Pilangi (1887). *Swedenborg the Buddhist or the Higher Swedenborgianism: Its Secrets and Thibetan Origin*. Los Angeles, CA: The Buddhistic Swedenborgian Brotherhood.

David-Néel, Alexandra (1927). *Voyage d'une Parisienne à Lhassa*. Paris: Plon.

Davidson, Lionel (1964) [1962]. *The Rose of Tibet*. Harmondsworth: Penguin.

Decter, Jacqueline (1989). *Nicholas Roerich: The Life and Art of a Russian Master*. Rochester, VT: Park Street Press.

Dempsey, Mike (1996). "Chinese Pervert Tibet's Spiritual Power." *The Independent*, London, October 5, 1996.

Department of Information and International Relations (1992). *Environment and Development Issues 1992.* Dharamsala: Central Tibetan Administration.

Derrida, Jacques (1982). "White Mythology: Metaphor in the Text of Philosophy." *Margins of Philosophy.* Hemel Hempstead, Herts: Wheatsheaf.

Desgodins, C. H. (1885). *Le Thibet d'après la correspondence des missionaires.* Paris: Librairie Catholique de l'Oeuvre de St. Paul.

Desideri, Ippolito (1722). "Letter from 10 April 1716." *Lettres édifiantes et curieuses.* Vol. 15, pp. 183–209. Paris: Le Clerc.

—— (1752). "Letter from 13 February 1717." Zaccaria, Francesco A. (ed.). *Bibliotheca Pistoriensis.* Vol. 1, pp. 185ff. Torino: Typogr. Regia.

Desjardins, Arnaud (1966). *Le Message des tibétains. Le Vrai visage du tantrisme.* Paris: Table Ronde.

DeVoss, David (1997). "Tibet Makes the Big Time As the Dalai Lama Tours America." *Asia Times,* Los Angeles, June 11, 1997.

Didier, Hugues (1988–92). "António de Andrade à l'origine de la tibétophilie européenne." *Portugiesische Forschungen der Görresgesellschaft,* Vol. 20, pp. 43–114.

Dikötter, Frank (1992). *The Discourse of Race in Modern China.* London: Hurst.

—— (1996). "Culture, 'Race' and Nation: The Formation of National Identity in Twentieth Century China." *Journal of International Affairs,* No. 2, pp. 590–605.

Ditfurth, Jutta (1997). *Entspannt in die Barbarei. Esoterik, (Öko-)Faschismus und Biozentrismus.* Hamburg: Konkret Literatur Verlag.

Ditfurth, Jutta and Goldner, Colin (1996). "Ahnungslose Schwärmerei. Tibet Politik: Die Dalai Lama-Verehrung in Deutschland." *Die Tageszeitung,* February 17, 1996.

Dodin, Thierry (1997). "Transregional Buddhist Organisations in Himalaya." Stellrecht, Irmtraut and Winiger, Matthias (eds.). *Perspectives on History and Change in the Karakorum, Hindukush, and Himalaya* (Culture Area Karakorum Scientific Studies, 3), pp. 189–213. Cologne: Rüdiger Koppe.

—— (2000). "Buddhism in Post-Revolution Nepal: Between Revival and 'Communalism.'" Thapa, Ram Pratap and Baaden, Joachim (eds.): *Nepal: Myths and Realities. In Commemoration of the 75th Birthday of Dr. Wolf Donner,* pp. 394–409. Delhi: Book Faith India.

—— (in press). "The Ladakh Budh Vihar of Delhi. The Fate of a Ladakhi Outpost in the Indian Capital." Blezer, Henk (ed.): *Proceedings of the Ninth Seminar of the International Association for Tibetan Studies, Leiden, June 2000.*

Drakulic, Slavenka (1992). *How We Survived Communism and Even Laughed.* London: Hutchinson.

Duff, Douglas Valder (1950): *On the World's Roof*. London: Abbey Rewards.

Dunlop, D. M. (1973). "Arab Relations with Tibet in the Eighth and Early Ninth Centuries A.D." *Islam Tetkikleri Enstitüsü Dergisi*, Vol. 5, pp. 301–318.

Dye, Daniel Sheets (1936). "James Huston Edgar, Pioneer." *Journal of the West China Border Research Society*, Vol. 8, pp. 14–18.

Eberhard, Wolfram (1982). *China's Minorities: Yesterday and Today*. Belmont, CA: Wadsworth.

—— (1983). *Lexikon chinesischer Symbole*. Cologne: Diederichs.

Edgar, James Huston (1930/31). "The Great Open Lands." *Journal of the West China Border Research Society*, Vol. 4, pp. 20–31.

Editor's Introduction to Bya-dur bSod-nams bzang-po (1994). *Bod kyi gna' bo'i zhing 'brog lam lugs*. Dharamsala: Central Tibetan Administration.

Ekvall, Robert Brainerd (1938). *Gateway to Tibet. The Kansu-Tibetan Border*. Harrisburg, PA: Christian Publications.

—— (1939). *Cultural Relations on the Kansu-Tibetan Border*. Chicago, IL: University of Chicago Press.

—— (1954). *Tents against the Sky*. New York, NY: Farrar, Straus and Young.

—— (1964). *Religious Observations in Tibet: Pattern and Function*. Chicago, IL: University of Chicago Press.

—— (1968). *Fields on the Hoof*. New York, NY: Holt, Rinehart and Winston.

Eliade, Mircea (1969). *The Quest: History and Meaning in Religion*. Chicago, IL: University of Chicago Press.

—— (1973). *Fragments d'un journal*. Paris: Gallimard.

—— (ed.) (1987): *Encyclopedia of Religion*. New York, NY: Macmillan.

Ellen, Roy F. (1986). "What Black Elk Left Unsaid: On the Illusory Images of Green Primitivism." *Anthropology Today*, Vol. 2, No. 6, pp. 8–12.

Ellenberger, Henri F. (1970). *The Discovery of the Unconscious: The History and Evolution of Dynamic Psychiatry*. New York, NY: Basic Books.

Ellwood, Robert S. (1979). *Alternative Altars: Unconventional and Eastern Spirituality in America*. Chicago, IL: University of Chicago Press.

Emmons, Zette and Somi, Roy L. (1992–93). "This Side of Shangri-la: Showcasing Tibet." *Cinemaya*, Vol. 17/18, pp. 70–72.

Epstein, Israel (1983). *Tibet Transformed*. Beijing: New World Press.

Essen, Gerd-Wolfgang and Thingo, Tsering Tashi (1989). *Die Götter des Himalaya*. Munich: Prestel.

European Commission (1995). *Pre-Feasibility Study on High Mountain Ecological Engineering Project*. Brussels: European Framework Group.

European Parliament (1997). *Resolution on Human Rights in Tibet,* Strasbourg, March 14, 1997.

European Union (1998). *Report of the EU Troika Human Rights Mission to Tibet: 1–10 May 1998.* London: Foreign and Commonwealth Office, June 19, 1998.

Evans-Wentz, Walter Yeeling (1935). *Tibetan Yoga and Secret Doctrines.* London: Oxford University Press.

—— (1954). *The Tibetan Book of the Great Liberation.* Oxford: Oxford University Press.

—— (1957). *The Tibetan Book of the Dead.* Oxford: Oxford University Press.

Fabian, Johannes (1983). *Time and the Other: How Anthropology Makes Its Object.* New York, NY: Columbia University Press.

Fairbank, John K. (ed.) (1974) [1968]. *The Chinese World Order.* Cambridge, MA: Harvard University Press.

Farrell, John (1993). "Tibet Film Festival." *Film Ireland,* Vol. 35, pp. 29–30.

Ferguson, Julia (1997). "Dalai Lama's Austrian Tutor Says Was in Nazi Party." Reuters, Vienna, May 28, 1997.

Fields, Rick (1992) [1986]. *How the Swans Came to the Lake: A Narrative History of Buddhism in America.* Boulder, CO: Shambhala.

Finley, Bruce (1997). "Dalai Lama Greeted Warmly." *Denver Post,* May 31, 1997.

Fischer, Ernst (1963) [1959]. *The Necessity of Art: A Marxist Approach.* London: Penguin.

Forke, Alfred (1925). *The World-Conception of the Chinese.* London: Arthur Probsthain.

Foucault, Michel (1986). "Of Other Spaces." *Diacritics,* Vol. 16, pp. 22–27.

Francke, August Herrmann (1906). "Kleine archäologische Erträge einer Missionsreise nach Zangskar in Westtibet." *Zeitschrift der Deutschen Morgenländischen Gesellschaft,* Vol. 60, pp. 645–61.

—— (1907). *A History of Western Tibet.* London: S. W. Partridge.

Franke, Herbert (1984). "Tan-pa, a Tibetan Lama at the Court of the Great Khans." Sabattini, Mario (ed.). *Orientalia Venetiana,* No. 1, pp. 157–80.

Franke, Otto (1967). *Geschichte des chinesischen Reiches: eine Darstellung seiner Entstehung, seines Wesens und seiner Entwicklung bis zur neuesten Zeit.* Taipei: Ch'eng Wen Publishing Co.

Franke, Wolfgang (1962). *China und das Abendland.* Göttingen: Vandenhoeck and Ruprecht.

Frazer, James George (1890). *The Golden Bough.* London: Macmillan.

Freeman, Laurence (1997). "The Clan Which Embodies the Soul of a Nation." *The Tablet,* London, July 5, 1997.

Fremantle, Francesca and Trungpa, Chögyam (1975). *The Tibetan Book of the Dead.* Boulder, CO: Shambhala.

French, Patrick (1994). *Younghusband: The Last Great Imperial Adventurer.* London: HarperCollins.

Fromm, Erich (1987) [1960]. *Psychoanalysis and Zen Buddhism.* London: Unwin.

Fuller, Jean Overton (1988). *Blavatsky and Her Teachers: An Investigative Biography.* London: East-West Publications.

Gay, Peter (1984). *The Bourgeois Experience: Victoria to Freud,* Vol. 1: Education of the Senses. New York, NY: Oxford University Press.

Gelder, Stuart and Gelder, Roma (1964). *Timely Rain—Travels in New Tibet.* London: Hutchinson.

Germano, David F. (2001). "Encountering Tibet: The Ethics, Soteriology, and Creativity of Cross-Cultural Interpretation." *Journal of the American Academy of Religion,* Vol. 69, No. 1, pp. 165–182.

Gilman, Benjamin (1999). "Opening Statement of Chairman Benjamin A. Gilman." Full Committee Hearing on Tibet, March 11, 1999 (republished in WTN, March 19, 1999).

Giorgi, Antonio A. (1987) [1762/63]. *Alphabetum Tibetanum missionum apostolicarum commodo editum.* Unveränderter Nachdruck der Ausgabe Rom 1762–63. Mit einer Einleitung von Rudolf Kaschewsky. Cologne: Una Voce.

Gladney, Dru C. (1994). "Representing Nationality in China: Refiguring Majority/Minority Identities." *The Journal of Asian Studies,* Vol. 53, No. 1, pp. 92–123.

—— (1995). "Tian Zhuangzhuang, the Fifth Generation, and Minorities Film in China." *Public Culture,* Vol. 8, No. 1, pp. 161–76.

Gluckman, Ron: "The Private Life of the Dalai Lama." *Asiaweek,* May 10, 1996.

Godden, Rumer (1971) [1939]. *Black Narcissus.* London: Peter Davies.

Godwin, Joscelyn (1994). *The Theosophical Enlightenment.* Albany: State University of New York Press.

Goldner, Colin (1999). *Dalai Lama—Fall eines Gottkönigs.* Aschaffenburg: Alibri.

Goldstein, Melvyn C. (1968). *An Anthropological Study of the Tibetan Political System.* Ph.D. diss., University of Washington. Seattle, WA.

—— (1989). *A History of Modern Tibet, 1913–1951.* Berkeley: University of California Press.

—— (1991). "The Dragon and the Snow Lion: The Tibetan Question in the Twentieth Century." *Tibetan Review,* Vol. 26, No. 4, pp. 9–26.

——— (1994). "Change, Conflict and Continuity among a Community of Nomadic Pastoralists: A Case Study from Western Tibet, 1950–1990." Barnett, Robert and Akiner, Shirin (eds.). *Resistance and Reform in Tibet*, pp. 76–111. London: Hurst.

——— (1995). *Tibet, China and the United States: Reflections on the Tibet Question*. The Atlantic Council of The United States, Occasional Paper 1995.

Goldstein, Melvyn C. and Beall, Cynthia M. (1990). *Nomads of Western Tibet: The Survival of a Way of Life*. Berkeley: University of California Press.

——— (1991). "China's Birth Control Policy in the Tibet Autonomous Region: Myths and Realities." *Asian Survey*, Vol. 31, No. 3, pp. 285–303.

Goleman, Daniel (1976) "On the Significance of Buddhist Psychology for the West." *The Tibet Journal*, Vol. 1, No. 2, pp. 37–42.

Gombrich, Richard and Obeyesekere, Gananath (1988). *Buddhism Transformed: Religious Change in Sri Lanka*. Princeton, NJ: Princeton University Press.

Gómez, Luis O. (1995). "Oriental Wisdom and the Cure of Souls: Jung and the Indian East." Lopez, Donald S. (ed.). *Curators of the Buddha: The Study of Buddhism under Colonialism*, pp. 197–250. Chicago: University of Chicago Press.

Goodall, John A. (1979). *Heaven and Earth: 120 Album Leaves from a Ming Encyclopedia: San-Ts'ai Tiu-hui, 1610,* Selected and Annotated by John A. Goodall. Boulder, CO: Shambhala.

Gordon, R. (1995). *The Tibetan Book of the Dead*. An Opera to Be Performed at Rice University, Houston, May/June 1996.

Goré, Francis (1938). *Trente ans aux portes du Thibet interdit*. Hong Kong: Maison de Nazareth.

Gould, Basil (1957). *The Jewel in the Lotus: Recollections of an Indian Political Officer*. London: Chatto and Windus.

Govinda, Lama Anagarika [Hoffmann, Ernst] (1959). *Foundations of Tibetan Mysticism*. London: Rider.

——— (1968) [1956]. *The Way of the White Clouds: A Buddhist Pilgrimage in Tibet*. London: Hutchinson.

Graham, J. A. (1937). *Stray Thoughts upon the Possibility of a Universal Religion*. Kalimpong.

Gramsci, Antonio (1957). *The Modern Prince*. New York, NY: International Publishing Co.

Granet, Marcel (1985) [1934]. *Das chinesische Denken*. Frankfurt a.M.: Suhrkamp.

Gray, Berkeley (1941): *The Lost World of Everest*. London: The Children's Press.

Greene, Felix and Mullin, Chris (1978). "The Question of Tibet." *China Now,* London, No. 78.

Greene, Raymond (1936). "Introduction to Everest." *The Geographical Magazine,* Vol. 3, No. 1, pp. 17–43.

Greenfield, Robert (1975). *The Spiritual Supermarket.* New York, NY: E. P. Dutton & Co.

Grenard, Fernand (1904): *Tibet: The Country and Its Inhabitants.* London: Hutchinson.

Greve, Reinhard (1995). "Tibetforschung im SS-Ahnenerbe." Hauschild, Thomas (ed.). *Lebenslust und Fremdenfurcht. Ethnologie im Dritten Reich,* pp. 168–99. Frankfurt a.M.: Suhrkamp.

—— (1997). "Das Tibet-Bild der Nationalsozialisten." Dodin, Thierry and Räther, Heinz (eds.). *Mythos Tibet. Wahrnehmungen, Projektionen, Phantasien,* pp.104–13. Cologne: DuMont.

Groot, Jan J. M. de (1921). *Die Hunnen der vorchristlichen Zeit.* Berlin: de Gruyter.

Grunfeld, A. Tom (1987). *The Making of Modern Tibet.* London: Zed.

Grünwedel, Albert (1915). *Der Weg nach Shambhala (Shambhala'i lam yig) des dritten Gross-Lama von bKra shis lhun po Blo bzang dpal ldan ye shes.* Munich: Franz.

Gu Daquan (1982). "Songdai Sichuan tong Tufan deng zu de chama maoyi." *Xizang yanjiu,* No. 1.

Gu Zucheng et al. (1982). *Ming shilu Zangzu shiliao.* Lhasa.

Guangming Ribao (1995). [Title Unknown] October 9, 1995 (Published in translation in BBC SWB, October 16, 1995).

Guibaut, André (1947). *Tibetan Venture.* London: John Murray.

Gunness, Christopher (1994). "Buddhist Spirit Resists Yak-Burger Culture." *BBC Worldwide Magazine,* London, December 1994.

Gussner, R. E. and Berkowitz, Stephen D. (1988). "Scholars, Sects, and Sanghas, I: Recruitment to Asian-Based Meditation Groups in North America." *Sociological Analysis,* Vol. 49, pp. 136–70.

Gyari, Lodi G. (1997). "Testimony of Special Envoy of His Holiness the Dalai Lama." Washington: House Committee on International Relations Committee Hearing of the Status of Sino-Tibetan Negotiations, November 6, 1997.

Gyatso, Janet (1989). "Down with the Demoness: Reflections on a Feminine Ground in Tibet." Willis, Janice Dean (ed.). *Feminine Ground.* New York, NY: Snow Lion, pp. 33–56.

Hacking, Ian (1994). "Memoro-Politics, Trauma and the Soul." *History of the Human Sciences,* Vol. 7, No. 2, pp. 29–52.

Halbfass, Wilhelm (1988). *India and Europe: An Essay in Understanding.* Albany: State University of New York Press.

Han Suyin (1958). *The Mountain Is Young*. London: The Book Club.

—— (1977). *Lhasa, the Open City: A Journey to Tibet*. New York, NY: Putnam.

Hanlon, Henry (1892/93). "Journal of a Mission Journey to the Shayok and Nubra Valley." *St. Joseph's Foreign Missionary Advocate*, Vol. 2, pp. 312–19, 334–50.

Hansen, Peter H. (1996). "The Dancing Lamas of Everest: Cinema, Orientalism, and Anglo-Tibetan Relations in the 1920s." *American Historical Review*, Vol. 101, pp. 712–47.

Harrell, Stevan (ed.) (1995a). *Cultural Encounters on China's Ethnic Frontiers*. Seattle: University of Washington Press.

—— (1995b). "Introduction: Civilizing Projects and the Reaction to Them." Harrell, Stevan (ed.). *Cultural Encounters on China's Ethnic Frontiers*. Seattle: University of Washington Press.

Harrer, Heinrich (1952). *Sieben Jahre in Tibet*. Vienna: Ullstein.

—— (1953). *Seven Years in Tibet*. London: Hart-Davis.

—— (1984). *Return to Tibet*. London: Weidenfels and Nicolson.

Harris, Clare (1992). "Tibet: Paradise Lost?" *Bazaar,* Vol. 21, Summer, p. 19.

—— (1999). *In the Image of Tibet: Tibetan Painting after 1951*. London: Reaktion Books.

Harris, Ian (1991). "How Environmentalist Is Buddhism?" *Religion*, Vol. 21, No. 2, pp. 101–14.

Havnevik, Hanna (1989). *Tibetan Buddhist Nuns: History, Cultural Norms and Social Reality*. Oslo: Norwegian University Press.

—— (1995). *Combats des nonnes tibétaines*. St. Michel en l'Herm.

Hay, Stephen N. (1970). *Asian Ideas of East and West: Tagore and His Critics in Japan, China, and India*. Cambridge, MA: Harvard University Press.

Heber, A. Reeve and Heber, Katherine (1926). *In Himalayan Tibet*. London: Seeley and Co.

Hellen, Nicholas (1996). "The God-King and the Darling of the Nazis." *Sunday Times*, London, July 14, 1996.

Helms, Jesse (1997). "Opening Statement to Senate Foreign Relations Committee's Hearing on the Situation Facing Tibet and Its People, May 13, 1997." Published in World Tibet Network News, May 15, 1997.

Herder, Gottfried (1909). *Sämtliche Werke,* Vol. 14. Berlin: de Gruyter.

Hergé (1972). *Tin Tin in Tibet*. London: Methuen.

Hermanns, Matthias (1949). *Die Nomaden von Tibet*. Vienna: Herold.

—— (1959). *Die Familie der Amdo-Tibeter*. Freiburg: K. Alber.

—— (1965). *Das National-Epos der Tibeter. Gling König Kesar.* Regensburg: Habbel.

Herodotus (1959). *Historien (Histories apodeixis).* Stuttgart: Kröner.

Hessler, Peter (1999). "Tibet through Chinese Eyes." *The Atlantic Monthly,* February 1999.

Higham, Charles (1976). *The Adventures of Conan Doyle: The Life of the Creator of Sherlock Holmes.* London: Hamish Hamilton.

Hildebrand, Joachim (1987). *Das Ausländerbild in der Kunst Chinas als Spiegel kultureller Beziehungen: Han—Tang.* Stuttgart: Franz Steiner.

Hilton, Isabel (1999). *The Search for the Panchen Lama.* London: Viking.

Hilton, James (1933, 1947). *Lost Horizon.* London: Macmillan.

Hitchens, Christopher (1998). "His Material Highness." *Salon Magazine,* July 13, 1998.

Hoffmann, Helmut (1961) [1956]. *The Religions of Tibet.* London: Allen and Unwin.

Hopkins, P. Jeffrey (tr.) (1977). "The Wanderer." *Virginia Quarterly,* April.

—— (forthcoming in 2002). *Reflections on Reality.* Berkeley, CA: University of California Press.

Hopkinson, Arthur John (1950). "The Position of Tibet." *Journal of the Royal Central Asian Society,* Vol. 37, No. 3–4, pp. 228–39.

Hopkirk, Peter (1983). *Trespassers on the Roof of the World: The Race for Lhasa.* London: Oxford University Press.

Howell, Basil P. (ed.) (1925). *The Theosophical Society: The First Fifty Years.* London: Theosophical Publishing House.

Hsiao Kung-chuan (1979) [1930]. *A History of Chinese Political Thought.* Princeton, NJ: Princeton University Press.

Huber, Toni (1997). "Green Tibetans: A Brief Social History." Korom, Frank J. (ed.). *Tibetan Culture in the Diaspora: Papers Presented at a Panel of the Seventh Seminar of the International Association for Tibetan Studies, Graz 1995.* June 18–24, 1995, Schloss Seggau, Vol. 7, pp. 103–19. Vienna: Verlag der Österreichischen Akademie der Wissenschaften.

Huc, Evariste Regis (1928) [1850]. *Travels in Tartary, Tibet and China, 1844–46.* London: George Routledge and Sons.

Hughes, Henry Stuart (1974) [1958]. *Consciousness and Society: The Reorientation of European Social Thought 1890–1930.* Frogmore: Paladin.

ICJ (International Commission of Jurists) (1959). *Tibet: The Question of Tibet and the Rule of Law.* Geneva: ICJ.

—— (1960). *Tibet and the Chinese People's Republic,* Geneva: ICJ.

ICLT (International Committee of Lawyers for Tibet) (1997). *Legal Materials on Tibet*. Berkeley, CA: ICLT.

Inden, Ronald (1990). *Imagining India*. Oxford: Basil Blackwell.

Iyer, Pico (1997). "The God in Exile—a Visit with the Leader of Tibet, the Subject of a New Movie, but a Star without a Stage." *Time*, Vol. 150, No. 26, December 22, 1997.

Jack, Alex (1977). "Shambhala and the American Revolution." *East West Journal*, May, pp. 66–70.

Jackson, Carl T. (1981). *The Oriental Religions and American Thought*. Westport, CT: Greenwood Press.

Jackson, David Paul (1996). *A History of Tibetan Painting: The Great Tibetan Painters and Their Traditions*. Vienna: Verlag der Österreichischen Akademie der Wissenschaften.

Jackson, Paul (1968). "The Meeting of East and West: The Case of Paul Carus." *Journal of the History of Ideas*, Vol. 29, pp. 73–92.

Jagchid, Sechin and Symons, Van Jay (1989). *Peace, War, and Trade along the Great Wall: Nomadic-Chinese Interaction through Two Millennia*. Bloomington, IN: Indiana University Press.

Jan, Michel (ed.) (1992). *Le Voyage en Asie Centrale et au Tibet: Anthologie des voyageurs occidentaux du moyen age à la première moitié du XXe siècle*. Paris: Laffont.

Jäschke, Heinrich August (1881). *A Tibetan-English Dictionary with Special Reference to the Prevailing Dialects*. London: Routledge and Kegan Paul.

Ji Wen (1981). "Guanyu minzu lilun wenti de zhengming." *Minzu Yanjiu*, No. 1, pp. 74–79.

Johnson, Paul (1994). *The Masters Revealed: Madame Blavatsky and the Myth of the Great White Lodge*. Albany, NY: State University of New York Press.

—— (1995). "Response to John Algeo's Review of The Masters Revealed." *Theosophical History*, Vol. 5, No. 8, pp. 264–69.

Johnston, George (1947). *Journey through Tomorrow*. Melbourne: F.W. Cheshire.

Jones, Richard Hubert (1979). "Jung and Eastern Religious Traditions." *Religion*, Vol. 9, No. 2, pp. 141–56.

Jordens, Joseph T.F. (1978). *Dayananda Sarasvati: His Life and Ideas*. Delhi: Oxford University Press.

Jung, Carl Gustav (1968) [1954]. "A Psychological Commentary." Evans-Wentz, Walter Yeeling: *The Tibetan Book of the Great Liberation*. Princeton, NJ: Princeton University Press.

—— (1969) [1936]. "Yoga East and West." *Psychology and Religion: East and West*, Vol. 11. Princeton, N.J.: Princeton University Press.

—— (1978). *Psychology and the East*. Princeton, NJ: Princeton University Press.

—— (1995). *Jung on the East*. London: Routledge.

Kaminsky, Arnold P. (1986). *The India Office, 1880–1910* (Contributions in Comparative Colonial Studies, 20). New York, NY: Greenwood Press.

Kant, Immanuel (1970). *Werke*. Vol. 6. Darmstadt: Wissenschaftliche Buchgesellschaft.

—— (1983). *Werke* Vol. 9. Darmstadt: Wissenschaftliche Buchgesellschaft.

Kämpfe, Hans-Rainer (1974). *Die soziale Rolle des 2. Pekinger lCang skya qutuqtu Rol pa'i rdo rje (1717–1786). Beiträge zu einer Analyse anhand tibetischer und mongolischer Biographien*. Ph.D. Dissertation, University of Bonn.

Kantowsky, Detlef (1980). *Sarvodaya: The Other Development*. New Delhi: Vikas.

Kapstein, Matthew (1992). "Remarks on the Mani bKa'-'bum and the Cult of Avalokiteśvara in Tibet." Goodman, Stephen D. and Davidson, Ronald M. (eds.). *Tibetan Buddhism: Reason and Revelation*, pp. 79–93. Albany: State University of New York Press.

Kaschewsky, Rudolph (1983). "Ptolemäus und der kupferfarbene Berg des Padmasambhava." Sagaster, Klaus and Weiers, Michael (eds.). *Documenta Barbarorum. Festschrift für Walther Heissig* (Veröffentlichungen der Societas Uralo-Altaica, 18), pp. 218–24. Wiesbaden: Otto Harrassowitz.

Kashag, the (1996). "Statement from Kashag—the Cabinet of the Tibetan Government in Exile." Dharamsala, May 14, 1996.

Katz, Nathan (1977). "Anima and mKha'-'gro-ma: A Critical Comparative Study of Jung and Tibetan Buddhism." *The Tibet Journal*, Vol. 2, No. 3, pp. 13–43.

Kearney, Richard (1988). *The Wake of Imagination: Ideas of Creativity in Western Culture*. London: Hutchinson.

Kelly, Petra K., Bastian, Gert, and Aiello, Pat (eds.) (1991). *The Anguish of Tibet*. Berkeley, CA: Parallax Press.

Kerr, Blake (1993). *Sky Burial: An Eyewitness Account of China's Brutal Crackdown in Tibet*. Chicago: Noble Press.

Kingston, Peter (1996). "Powerful People." *The Guardian*, October 29, 1996.

Kipling, Rudyard (1963) [1898]. *Kim*. London: Macmillan.

Klein, A. Norman (1972). "Counterculture and Cultural Hegemony: Some Notes on the Youth Rebellion of the 1960s." Hymes, Dell (ed.). *Reinventing Anthropology*, pp. 312–34. New York, NY: Pantheon Books.

Klieger, P. Christiaan (1994). *Accomplishing Tibetan Identity: The Constitution of a National Consciousness*. Ph.D. diss., University of Hawaii, Honolulu.

—— (1997). "Shangri-la and Hyperreality: A Collision in Tibetan Refugee Expression." Korom, Frank J. (ed.). *Tibetan Culture in the Diaspora: Papers*

Presented at a Panel of the Seventh Seminar of the International Associa-tion for Tibetan Studies, Graz 1995. June 18–24, 1995, Schloss Seggau, Vol. 7, pp. 59–68. Vienna: Verlag der Österreichischen Akademie der Wis-senschaften.

Klimburg-Salter, Deborah (1982). *The Silk Route and the Diamond Path.* Los Angeles: University of California Los Angeles Art Council.

Knaus, John Kenneth (1999). *Orphans of the Cold War: America and the Tibetan Struggle for Survival.* New York, NY: Perseus Books.

Knight, William Henry (1863). *Diary of a Pedestrian in Cashmere and Thibet.* London: Richard Bentley.

Kohl, Karl-Heinz (1979). "Abwehr und Verlangen. Der Eurozentrismus in der Ethnologie." *Berliner Hefte,* No. 12, pp. 28–42.

Kojima, Sabine (1994). *Bilder und Zerrbilder des Fremden. Tibet in einer Erzäh-lung Ma Jians* (Chinathemen, 83). Bochum: Brockmeyer.

Korom, Frank J. (1987). "Conversion Narratives in Context."

——— (1992). "Of Navels and Mountains: A Further Inquiry into the History of an Idea." *Asian Folklore Studies,* Vol. 51, No. 1, pp. 103–26.

——— (ed.) (1997). *Tibetan Culture in the Diaspora: Papers Presented at a Panel of the Seventh Seminar of the International Association for Tibetan Studies, Graz 1995.* June 18-24, 1995, Schloss Seggau, Vol. 7. Vienna: Verlag der Österreichischen Akademie der Wissenschaften.

Korski, Tom (1997a). "Could This Be Utopia?" *South China Morning Post Sat-urday Review,* Hong Kong, November 29, 1997.

——— (1997b). "Dalai Lama a 'Nazi Dupe Who Succumbed to Hitler.'" *South China Morning Post,* Hong Kong, October 3, 1997.

Krurup, Bernward (1994). "Lhasa No Longer a Tibetan City As Flesh Trade Thrives around Potala." Deutsche Presse-Agentur, November 1, 1994.

Kuløy, Hallvard Kåre & Imaeda Yoshiro (1986). *A Bibliography of Tibetan Stud-ies.* Narita: Naritasan Shinshoji.

Kungfutse (1985). Gespräche, Lun Yü. Cologne: Diederichs. [Confucius. *The Analects of Confucius: A Literal Translation with an Introduction and Notes by Chichung Huang.* New York, NY: Oxford University Press, 1997].

Kværne, Per (1973). *A Norwegian Traveller in Tibet.* New Delhi: Manjusri Publishing House.

Kvaloy, Sigmund (1987). "Norwegian Ecophilosophy and Ecopolitics and Their Influence from Buddhism." Sandell, Klas (ed.). *Buddhist Perspectives on the Ecocrisis,* pp. 49–72. Kandy: Buddhist Publication Society.

Kychanov, Evgenij Ivanovich (1993). "The State of Great Xia (982–1227)." Piotrovsky, Mikhail (ed.). *Lost Empire of the Silk Road: Buddhist Art from Kharakhoto (Tenth–Thirteenth Century)*, pp. 49–58. Milano: Electa.

Lalou, Marcelle (1957). *Les Religions du Tibet* (Mythes et Religions, 35). Paris: Presse Universitaire de France.

Lamb, Alastair (1989). *Tibet, China and India, 1914–1950.* Hertingfordbury: Roxford.

Lambert, John C. (ed.) (1907). *The Romance of Missionary Heroism.* London: Seeley and Co.

Landon, Perceval (1988) [1905]. *Lhasa.* Delhi: Kailash.

Lane, Fred (1994). "The Warrior Tribes of Kham." *Asiaweek,* March 2, 1994.

Lash, John (1990). *The Seeker's Handbook: The Complete Guide to Spiritual Pathfinding.* New York, NY: Harmony Books.

Lawson, Annetta (1980). *The Lucky Yak.* Oakland, CA: Parnassus Press.

Learner, Frank Doggett (1934). *Rusty Hinges: A Story of Closed Doors Beginning to Open in North-East Tibet.* London: China Inland Mission.

Leary, Timothy, Ralph Metzner, and Richard Alpert (1964). *The Psychedelic Experience: A Manual Based on the Tibetan Book of the Dead.* New York: University Books.

Lehman, Steve and Barnett, Robert (1998). *The Tibetans—Struggle to Survive.* New York, NY: Umbrage.

Leichtman, Martin (1979). "Gestalt Theory and the Revolt against Positivism." Buss, Allan R. (ed.). *Psychology in Social Context,* pp. 47–76. New York, NY: Irvington.

Leiris, Michel (1979). *Die eigene und die fremde Kultur.* Frankfurt a.M.: Syndikat.

Lévi-Strauss, Claude (1962). *La pensée sauvage.* Paris: Plon. [*The Savage Mind.* Chicago, IL: Chicago University Press, 1966].

—— (1964). *Das Rohe und das Gekochte.* Frankfurt a.M.: Suhrkamp.[*The Raw and the Cooked.* Chicago, IL: Chicago University Press, 1983].

—— (1993). "Rasse und Kultur." Claude Lévi-Strauss: *Der Blick aus der Ferne.* Frankfurt a.M.: Fischer.

Levin, Bernard (1994a). "Behind Chinese Walls." *Times,* London, October 18, 1994.

—— (1994b). "The Seeds of Betrayal." *Times,* London, March 10, 1994.

Leys, Simon [Pierre Ryckmans] (1985). *The Burning Forest. Essays on Chinese Culture and Politics.* New York, NY: New Republic Books.

Lhamo, Rinchen (1926). *We Tibetans.* London: Seeley and Co.

Li Bing (1995). "Dalai Is a Tool of Hostile Forces in the West." *Xizang Ribao,* December 11, 1995 (Published in translation in SWB, January 8, 1996).

Li Ge (1992). *Ethnic Relations and Chinese State Policy.* M.A. thesis, University of Manitoba, Winnipeg.

Li Jianhua (1997). "Harrer, Dalai's Former 'Teacher,' Was a Nazi." *Renmin Ribao,* June 25, 1997, p. 6.

Li Zehou (1992). *Der Weg des Schönen. Wesen und Geschichte der chinesischen Kultur und Ästhetik.* Freiburg: Herder.

Liaison Office of His Holiness the Dalai Lama for Japan East-Asia (Tibetan Government in Exile) (1995). "A Total Bankruptcy of China's Criticism against the Dalai Lama." Tokyo, October 24, 1995.

Linck, Gudula (1995). "Die Menschen in den vier Himmelsrichtungen. Chinesische Fremdbilder." Schmidt-Glintzer, Helwig (ed.). *Das andere China. Festschrift für Wolfgang Bauer zum 65. Geburtstag,* pp. 257–90. Wiesbaden: Otto Harrassowitz.

Lincoln, Bruce (1994). *Authority: Construction and Corrosion.* Chicago, IL: University of Chicago Press.

Lindegger, Peter (1979, 1982, 1993). *Griechische und römische Quellen zum peripheren Tibet.* Teil 1–3 (Opuscula Tibetana 10, 14, 22). Rikon: Tibet Institut.

Linton, Ralph (1943). "Nativistic Movements." *American Anthropologist,* Vol. 45, pp. 230–40.

Lohmann, Larry (1993). "Green Orientalism." *The Ecologist,* Vol.23, No.6, pp. 202–4.

Loiskandl, Helmut (1966). *Edle Wilde, Heiden und Barbaren. Fremdheit als Bewertungskriterium zwischen Kulturen* (Sankt Gabrieler Studien, 21). Mödling bei Wien: St. Gabriel Verlag.

Loizos, Peter (1993). *Innovation in Ethnographic Film.* Chicago, IL: University of Chicago Press.

Lopez, Donald S. (1994). "New Age Orientalism: The Case of Tibet." *Tricycle,* Vol. 3, No. 3, pp. 36–43.

—— (1995a). "Introduction." Lopez, Donald S. (ed.). *Curators of the Buddha: The Study of Buddhism under Colonialism,* pp. 1–29. Chicago, IL: University of Chicago Press.

—— (1995b). "Foreigner at the Lama's Feet." Lopez, Donald S. (ed.). *Curators of the Buddha: The Study of Buddhism under Colonialism,* pp. 251–96. Chicago, IL: University of Chicago Press.

—— (ed.) (1995c). *Curators of the Buddha: The Study of Buddhism under Colonialism.* Chicago, IL: University of Chicago Press.

——— (1996). "'Lamaism' and the Disappearance of Tibet." *Comparative Studies in Society and History,* Vol. 38, No. 1, pp. 3–25.

——— (1998). *Prisoners of Shangri-la: Tibetan Buddhism and the West.* Chicago, IL: University of Chicago Press.

Low, Rachel (1971): *The History of the British Film, 1918–1929* (History of British Film, 4). London: Allen and Unwin.

Lowe, Stephen (1981). *Tibetan Inroads.* London: Eyre Methuen.

Ma Jian (1987). "Liangchu nide shetai huo kongkongdangdang." *Renmin Wenxü,* No. 1–2, pp. 98–116.

Macartney, Jane (1996). "Tibet Modernization Fraught with Controversy." Reuters, Lhasa, October 8, 1996.

MacCormack, Carol P. (1989). "Natur, Kultur und Geschlecht: Eine Kritik." Arbeitsgruppe Ethnologie Wien (ed.). *Von fremden Frauen. Frausein und Geschlechterbeziehungen in nichtindustriellen Gesellschaften,* pp. 68–99. Frankfurt a.M.: Suhrkamp.

Macdonald, David (1991) [1932]. *Twenty Years in Tibet.* Delhi: Vintage Books.

MacDougall, David (1998). *Transcultural Cinema.* Princeton, NJ: Princeton University Press.

Mackenzie, John M. (1986). *Propaganda and Empire: The Manipulation of British Opinion, 1880–1960.* Manchester: Manchester University Press.

Macy, Joanna Rogers (1985). *Dharma and Development: Religion As Resource in the Sarvodaya Self-Help Movement.* West Hartford: Kumarian Press.

Magill, Daniela (1989). *Literarische Reisen in die exotische Fremde: Topoi der Darstellung von Eigen und Fremdkultur.* Frankfurt a.M.: Lang.

Marcuse, Herbert (1964). *One Dimensional Man.* Boston, MA: Beacon Press.

Martin, Calvin (1978). *Keepers of the Game.* Berkeley: University of California Press.

Martin, Dan (1987). "On the Origin and Significance of the Prayer Wheel According to Two Nineteenth-Century Tibetan Literary Sources." *Journal of the Tibet Society,* Vol. 7, pp. 13–29.

——— (1990a). "Bonpo Canons and Jesuit Cannons: On Sectarian Factors Involved in the Ch'ien-lung Emperor's Second Goldstream Expedition of 1771–1776 Based Primarily on Some Tibetan Sources." *Tibet Journal,* Vol. 15, No. 2, pp. 3–28.

——— (1990b). "Zhang Rinpoche and the Emergence of Sectarian Polity in Twelfth-Century Tibet." Paper delivered at the Midwest Conference on Asian Affairs, Bloomington, IN, Nov. 1990.

Marx, Karl and Engels, Friedrich (1969). *Deutsche Ideologie.* Marx, Karl and Engels, Friedrich: *Werke,* Vol. 3. Berlin: Dietz.

Matthiessen, Peter (1980). *The Snow Leopard,* London: Picador.

McGovern, William Montgomery (1924). *To Lhasa in Disguise.* New York, NY: Century.

McKay, Alex C. (1992). "The Establishment of the British Trade Agencies in Tibet: A Survey." *The Journal of the Royal Asiatic Society,* 3d Series, Vol. 2, No. 3, pp. 399–421.

—— (1994). "The Other Great Game: Politics and Sport in Tibet, 1904–47." *The International Journal of the History of Sport.* Vol. 11, No. 3, pp. 372–86.

—— (1995). *Tibet and the British Raj, 1904–47: The Influence of the Indian Political Department Officers.* Ph.D. Dissertation, London University.

—— (1997). "Tibet 1924: A Very British Coup Attempt?" *Journal of the Royal Asiatic Society,* 3d Series, Vol. 7, No. 3, pp. 411–24.

McLagan, Meg (1996). *Mobilizing for Tibet: Transnational Politics and Diaspora Culture in the Post-Cold War Era.* Ph.D. diss., New York University.

—— (1997). "Mystical Visions in Manhattan: Developing Culture in the Year of Tibet." Korom, Frank J. (ed.). *Tibetan Culture in the Diaspora: Papers Presented at a Panel of the Seventh Seminar of the International Association for Tibetan Studies, Graz 1995.* June 18–24, 1995, Schloss Seggau, Vol. 7, pp. 69–89. Vienna: Verlag der Österreichischen Akademie der Wissenschaften.

Meade, Marion (1980). *Madame Blavatsky: The Woman Behind the Myth.* New York: G. P. Putnam's Sons.

Meckel, Daniel J. and Moore, Robert L. (1992). "Introduction: The Dialogue Between Jungian Psychoanalysis and Buddhist Spirituality." Meckel, Daniel J. and Moore, Robert L. (eds.). *Self and Liberation: The Jung-Buddhism Dialogue* pp. 1–10. New York, NY: Paulist Press.

Mehra, Parshottam Lal (1969). "The Mongol-Tibetan Treaty of January 11, 1913." *Journal of Asian History,* Vol. 3, No. 1, pp. 1–22.

Mehta, Bhupatray (1968). *Light of Theosophy: A Classified List of Inspiring Articles in* The Theosophist *Covering the Period 1910–1967.* Ahmedabad: Sarasija.

Mei Zhaorong (1996). "Now We Defend Ourselves." *Die Zeit* (Published in translation as "PRC Envoy Criticizes FRG Tibet Resolution." BBC SWB, June 22, 1996).

Meyer, J. (1853). *Meyer's Conversations-Lexicon für die gebildeten Stände,* Vol. 12. Hildburghausen: Bibliographisches Institut.

—— (1889). *Meyers Konversations-Lexicon.* Leipzig: Bibliographisches Institut.

Miller, Beatrice D. (1988). "American Popular Perceptions of Tibet from 1858–1938." *Tibet Journal,* Vol. 13, No. 3, pp. 3–19.

Miller, Roy Andrew (1963). "Notes on the Relazione of Ippolito Desideri, S. J." *Monumenta Serica,* Vol. 22, No. 1, pp. 446–69.

Minto, James R. (1974). *Graham of Kalimpong.* Edinburgh: William Blackwood.

Morreale, Don (ed.) (1988). *Buddhist America: Centers, Retreats, Practices.* Santa Fe, NM: John Muir.

Moynihan, Maura (1997). "What China Fears." *The Washington Post,* April 30, 1997.

Müller, Claudius C. (1980). "Die Herausbildung der Gegensätze: Chinesen und Barbaren in der frühen Zeit." Bauer, Wolfgang (ed.). *China und die Fremden. 3000 Jahre Auseinandersetzung in Krieg und Frieden,* pp. 43–76. Munich: Beck.

Müller, Claudius C. and Raunig, Walter (eds.) (1982). *Der Weg zum Dach der Welt.* Innsbruck: Pinguin.

Mullin, Chris (1975). *Far Eastern Economic Review,* Hong Kong, September 5, 1975.

Mullin, Chris and Wangyal, Phuntsog (1983). *The Tibetans. Two Perspectives on Tibetan-Chinese Relations.* (Report No. 49.) London: Minority Rights Group.

Namgyal, Damdul (1994). "Buddhist Ecology—Its Theoretical Base." *Tibet Environment and Development News,* No. 1, pp. 27–30. Dharamsala: Department of Information and International Relations.

Nanda, Prakash (1996). "Dalai Lama Is Oppressing Buddhist Sect." *Times of India,* June 27, 1996.

Narangoa, Li (1998). *Japanische Religionspolitik in der Mongolei, 1932-1945: Reformbestrebung und Dialog zwischen japanischen und mongolischen Buddhismus.* Wiesbaden: Harrassowitz.

Nebesky-Wojkowitz, René de (1956). *Oracles and Demons of Tibet.* s'Gravenhage: Mouton and Co.

Neff, Mary K. (1937). *Personal Memoirs of H. P. Blavatsky.* New York, NY: E. P. Dutton.

Nichols, Bill (1991). *Representing Reality: Issues and Concepts in Documentary.* Bloomington, IN: Indiana University Press.

Nicholson, Brendan (1999). "MPs Trip on Road to Tibet." *The Age,* September 25, 1999.

Nicolazzi, Michael Albrecht (1995). *Mönche, Geister und Schamanen. Die Bön-Religion Tibets.* Solothurn: Walter.

Noll, Richard (1994). *The Jung Cult: Origins of a Charismatic Movement.* Princeton, NJ: Princeton University Press.

Norberg-Hodge, Helena (1991). *Ancient Futures: Learning From Ladakh.* San Francisco, CA: Sierra Club Books.

Norbu, Dawa (1997). *Tibet: The Road Ahead*. London: Rider.

Norbu, Jamyang (1989). *Illusion and Reality*. Dharamsala: Tibet Youth Congress.

—— (1994). "The Tibetan Resistance Movement and the Role of the CIA." Barnett, Robbie and Akiner, Shirin (eds.). *Resistance and Reform in Tibet*, pp. 186–96. London: Hurst and Co.

—— (1998). "Dances with Yaks: Tibet in Film, Fiction and Fantasy of the West." *Tibetan Review*, Vol. 33, No. 1, pp. 18–23.

Norbu, Tseten (1999). *La Reconquête du Tibet* (Indigène esprit, 5). Montpellier: Indigène.

Norwick, Braham (1985). "The First Tsha-tsha Published in Europe." Aziz, Barbara Nimri and Kapstein, Matthew (eds.). *Soundings in Tibetan Civilization*, pp. 73–85. New Delhi: Manohar.

O'Brian, Patrick (1976). *The Road to Samarcand*. London: White Lion.

O'Connor, William Frederick Travers (1937). "Tibet in the Modern World." *Geographical Magazine*, Vol. 6, No. 2, pp. 93–110.

Olcott, Henry Steel (1895). *Old Diary Leaves: America 1874–1878, First Series*. New York, NY: G. P. Putnam's Sons.

Oppenheim, Janet (1985). *The Other World: Spiritualism and Psychical Research in England, 1850–1914*. Cambridge: Cambridge University Press.

Oppitz, Michael (1974). "Shangri-la, le panneau de marque d'un flipper. Analyse sémiologique d'un mythe visuel." *L'Homme*, Vol. 14, No. 3–4, pp. 59–83.

Orr, J. Russell (1931). "The Use of the Kinema in the Guidance of Backward Races." *Journal of the African Society*, Vol. 30, pp. 238–44, 301–6.

Ortner, Sherry B. (1973). "On Key Symbols." *American Anthropologist*, Vol. 75, pp. 1338–46.

—— (1999). *Life and Death on Mount Everest*. Princeton, NJ: Princeton University Press.

Osmaston, Henry A. (1998). "Agriculture in the Main Lhasa Valley." Clarke, Graham E. (ed.). *Development, Society and Environment in Tibet: Papers Presented at a Panel of the Seventh Seminar of the International Association for Tibetan Studies, Graz 1995*. Schloss Seggau 1995, Vol. 5, pp. 121–52. Vienna: Verlag der Österreichischen Akademie der Wissenschaften.

Pacific Spirit (1995). *The Mystic Trader*. Forest Grove, OR: Pacific Spirit Corporation.

Pal, Pratapaditya (1990). *Art of Tibet*. Los Angeles, CA: Los Angeles County Museum of Art.

—— (1991). *Art of the Himalayas: Treasures from Nepal and Tibet*. New York, NY: Hudson Hills Press.

Pallis, Marco (1939). *Peaks and Lamas.* London: Cassell.

Parabola (1978). "Taming the Wild Horse: A Conversation with Lobsang Lhalungpa." *Parabola,* Vol. 2, No. 4, pp. 44–57.

Pascalis, Claude (1935). *La Collection tibétaine: Musée Louis Finot.* Hanoi: École Française d'Extrême-Orient.

Patterson, George Neilson (1954). *Tibetan Journey.* London: Faber.

—— (1990). *Requiem for Tibet.* London: Aurum.

Pearce, David W. (1995). *Blueprint 4: Capturing Global Environment Value.* London: Earthscan.

Pedersen, Poul (1995). "Nature, Religion and Cultural Identity: The Religious Environmentalist Paradigm." Bruun, Ole and Kalland, Arne (eds.). *Asian Perceptions of Nature: A Critical Approach,* pp. 258–76. London: Curzon Press.

Perrig, Alexander (1987). "Erdrandsiedler oder die schrecklichen Nachkommen Chams. Aspekte der mittelalterlichen Völkerkunde." Köbner, Thomas and Pickerodt, Gerhart (eds.). *Die andere Welt, Studien zum Exotismus,* pp. 31–87. Frankfurt a.M.: Athenäum.

Petech, Luciano (1954–56). *I Missionari italiani nel Tibet e nel Nepal.* Parte 5–7: Ippolito Desideri S. I. Rome: Instituto Poligrafico dello Stato.

Peyrefitte, Alain (1992) [1989]. *The Immobile Empire.* New York, NY: A. A. Knopf.

Philadelphia Inquirer (1996). "The *Philadelphia Inquirer* Documents Torture, Rape, Murder." PINewswire, Philadelphia, December 6, 1996 and December 8–15, 1996.

Pickerodt, Gerhart (1987). "Aufklärung und Exotismus." Köbner, Thomas and Pickerodt, Gerhart (eds.). *Die andere Welt, Studien zum Exotismus,* pp. 121–36. Frankfurt a.M.: Athenäum.

Plommer, Leslie (1995). "In Harmony and Diversity with the God-King." *The Guardian,* London, September 18, 1995.

Polo, Marco (1978) [1299]. *Le Livre de Marco Polo ou le Devisement du Monde.* Paris: Prodifu.

Poole, Teresa (1995). "Paying the Price of Progress." *The Independent on Sunday,* London, August 20, 1995.

Prebish, Charles S. (1979). *American Buddhism.* North Scituate, MA: Duxbury Press.

Prothero, Stephen (1996). *The White Buddhist: The Asian Odyssey of Henry Steel Olcott.* Bloomington, IN: Indiana University Press.

Ptolemaios, Klaudios (1971). *Geographie (Geografike hyphegesis).* Rome: IsMEO.

Puini, Carlo (1904). *Il Tibet (geografa, religione, costumi) secondo la relazione del viaggio del P. Ippolito Desideri* (Memorie della Società Geografica Italiana, 10). Rome: Società Geografica Italiana.

Rabinowitz, Paula (1994). *They Must Be Represented*. London: Verso.

Rampa, T. Lobsang [Hoskin, Cyril] (1964, 1970) [1956]. *The Third Eye: The Autobiography of a Tibetan Lama*. New York, NY: Ballantine.

—— (1968). *The Rampa Story*. New York, NY: Bantam Books.

—— (1990). *Doctor from Lhasa*. New Brunswick, NJ: Inner Light Publications.

Räther, Heinz (1994). "Views on Ecology among Tibetan Intellectuals." Kværne, Per (ed.). *Tibetan Studies. Proceedings of the Sixth Seminar of the International Association for Tibetan Studies, Fagernes 1992*, pp. 670–75. Oslo: Institute for Comparative Research in Human Culture.

Raum, Tom (1999) "House Condemns China over Rights." Associated Press, Washington, March 11, 1999.

Rechler, Theodor (1874). "The Moravian Mission in Tibet." *Periodical Accounts Pertaining to the Mission of the United Brethren*, Vol. 30, pp. 227–43.

Renov, Michael (ed.) (1993). *Theorizing Documentary*. New York, NY: Routledge.

Reuters (1995). "Dalai Lama Denies Japan Cult Guru Was Disciple." Reuters, Tokyo, April 6, 1995.

—— (1997). "Dalai Lama Prays China Congress Will Back Reforms." Reuters, Rome, September 8, 1997.

—— (1998). "Clinton to Find No Shangri-la on Tibet." Reuters, Beijing, June 22, 1998

Rhie, Marylin M. and Thurman, Robert A. F. (1991). *Wisdom and Compassion: The Sacred Art of Tibet*. New York, NY: Harry N. Abrams.

Ribbach, Samuel (1940). *Drogpa Namgyal. Ein Tibeterleben*. Munich-Planegg: O.W. Barth. [*Culture and Society in Ladakh*. New Delhi: Ess Ess Publications, 1986].

Richards, Thomas (1992). "Archive and Utopia." *Representations*, Vol. 37, pp. 102–33.

Richardson, Hugh E. (n.d.). "My Direct Experience of Independent Tibet." Information Sheet Available from the Tibet Society UK.

—— (1956). "Imaginary Tibet." *Daily Telegraph and Morning Post,* November 30, 1956.

—— (1984) [1962]. *Tibet and Its History*. Boston, MA: Shambhala.

Rider Haggard, Henry (1971) [1887]. *She*. London: Hodder.

Rijnhart, Susie (1902). *With the Tibetans in Tent and Temple*. Edinburgh: Oliphant, Anderson and Ferrier.

Ritvo, Harriet (1995). "Border Trouble: Shifting the Line between People and Other Animals." *Social Research,* No. 3, pp. 481–500.

Robson, Isabel Stuart (1910). *Two Lady Missionaries in Tibet*. London: S.W. Partridge.

Roerich, Georges de (1933). *Sur les pistes de l'Asie centrale*. Paris: P. Geuthner.

Roerich, Nicholas (1929). *Altai-Himalaya: A Travel Diary*. New York, NY: Stokes.

Rony, Fatimah Tobing (1996). *The Third Eye*. Durham, NC: Duke University Press.

Root, Deborah (1996). *Cannibal Culture: Art, Appropriation, and the Commodification of Difference*. Boulder, CO: Westview Press.

Roszak, Theodore (1969). *The Making of a Counterculture*. Garden City, NY: Anchor Books.

Rousseau, Jean-Jacques (1973) [1762]. *The Social Contract*. London: J.M. Dent and Sons.

Rowell, Galen (1990). "Introduction." Dalai Lama: *My Tibet*. Berkeley, CA: University of California Press.

Rudhyar, Dane (1975). *Occult Preparations for a New Age*. Wheaton, IL: Theosophical Publishing House.

Ruttledge, Hugh (1938). *Everest 1933*. London: Hodder and Stoughton.

Sackett, Lee (1991). "Promoting Primitivism: Conservationist Depictions of Aboriginal Austalians." *The Australian Journal of Anthropology*, Vol. 2, No. 2, pp. 233–46.

Sagaster, Klaus (1960). *Ngag dbang blo bzang chos ldan (1642–1714). Leben und historische Bedeutung des 1. (Pekinger) lCang skya khutukhtu. Dargestellt anhand seiner mongolischen Biographie Subud erike und anderer Quellen*. Ph.D. diss., University of Bonn.

—— (1976). *Die weisse Geschichte. Eine mongolische Quelle zur Lehre von den beiden Ordnungen Religion und Staat in Tibet und der Mongolei* (Asiatische Forschungen 41). Wiesbaden: Otto Harrassowitz.

Said, Edward William (1978, 1979, 1995). *Orientalism: Western Conceptions of the Orient*. London: Penguin.

—— (1993). *Culture and Imperialism*. London: Chatto and Windus.

Sale, Kirkpatrick (1990). *The Conquest of Paradise: Christopher Columbus and the Columbian Legacy*. New York, NY: Knopf.

Salopek, Paul (1997). "How the CIA Helped Tibet Fight Their Chinese Invaders." *Chicago Tribune*, January 25, 1997.

Samartha, Stanley J. and de Silva, Lynn (eds.) (1979). *Man in Nature: Guest or Engineer?* Colombo: The Ecumenical Institute for Study and Dialogue.

Samuel, Geoffrey (1993). *Civilized Shamans: Buddhism in Tibetan Societies*. Washington, D.C.: Smithsonian Institution Press.

Samuel, Raphael (1995). *Theatres of Memory*. London: Verso.

Sangharakshita (Dennis Lingwood) (1971). *The Three Jewels. An Introduction to Buddhism.* London: Rider.

Schell, Orville (2000). *Virtual Tibet: Searching for Shangri-la from the Himalayas to Hollywood.* New York, NY: Metropolitan Books.

Schiern, Frederik E.A. (1873). *Über den Ursprung der Sage von den gold-grabenden Ameisen.* Vortrag in der Sitzung der Kgl. Dänischen Gesellschaft der Wissenschaften vom 2. Dezember 1870. Copenhagen: Ursin.

Schmidt, Adolf and Lammers, Walther (eds.) (1960). *Otto von Freising: Chronik oder Die Geschichte der zwei Staaten (Chronica sive historia de duabus civitatibus).* Darmstadt: Wissenschaftliche Buchgesellschaft.

Schwab, Raymond (1984) [1950]. *The Oriental Renaissance. Europe's Rediscovery of India and the East, 1680–1880.* New York, NY: Columbia University Press.

Schwartz, Benjamin I. (1974). "The Chinese Perception of World Order, Past and Present." Fairbank, John K. (ed.). *The Chinese World Order: Traditional China's Foreign Relations,* pp. 276–88. Cambridge, MA: Harvard University Press.

Schwartz, Ronald D. (1994a). "Buddhism, Nationalist Protest, and the State in Tibet." Kværne, Per (ed.). *Tibetan Studies. Proceedings of the Sixth Seminar of the International Association for Tibetan Studies, Fagernes 1992,* pp. 728–38. Oslo: The Institute for Comparative Research in Human Culture.

—— (1994b). *Circle of Protest: Political Ritual in the Tibetan Uprising.* London: Hurst and Co.

Scofield, Aislinn (1993). "Tibet: Projections and Perceptions." *East-West Film Journal,* Vol. 7, pp. 106–36.

Seager, Richard Hughes (ed.) (1993). *The Dawn of Religious Pluralism: Voices from the World's Parliament of Religions, 1893.* La Salle, IL: Open Court.

—— (1995). *The World's Parliament of Religions: The East/West Encounter, Chicago, 1893.* Bloomington, IN: Indiana University Press.

Sen, Amartya (1993). "India and the West." *The New Republic,* June 7, 1993.

Shakya, Tsering (1985). "Tibet and the League of Nations." *Tibet Journal,* Vol. 10, No. 3, pp. 48–56.

—— (1991). "The Myth of Shangri-la: Tibet and the Occident." *Lungta,* Vol. 5, pp. 20–23.

—— (1992). "Tibet and the Occident: The Myth of Shangri-la." *Tibetan Review,* Vol. 27, No. 1, pp. 13–16.

—— (1993). "Whither the Tsampa Eaters?" *Himal,* Vol. 6, No. 5, pp. 8–11.

—— (1994). "Introduction: The Development of Modern Tibetan Studies." Barnett, Robbie and Akiner, Shirin (eds.). *Resistance and Reform in Tibet,* pp. 1–14. London: Hurst and Co.

—— (2001). "Who Are the Prisoners?" *Journal of the American Academy of Religion,* Vol. 69, No. 1, pp. 183–89.

Sharf, Robert H. (1995). "The Zen of Japanese Nationalism." Lopez, Donald S. (ed.). *Curators of the Buddha: The Study of Buddhism Under Colonialism,* pp. 107–60. Chicago, IL: Chicago University Press.

Sinnett, Alfred P. (1886). *Incidents in the Life of Madame Blavatsky.* London: George Redway.

Snell, Merwin-Marie (1888). "Parseeism and Buddhism." *Catholic World,* Vol. 46, pp. 415–57.

Somerset Maugham, William (1972) [1944]. *The Razor's Edge.* London: Heinemann.

Sørensen, Per K. (1994). *The Mirror Illuminating the Royal Genealogy.* Wiesbaden: Harrassowitz.

Sperling, Elliot H. (1994). "Orientalism and the Dalai Lamas." Paper read at the Library of Tibetan Works and Archives, Dharamsala, October 13, 1994.

—— (1995). "Ethno-Nationalism and the Tibetan Issue." Paper read at the Library of Tibetan Works and Archives, Dharamsala, January 31, 1995.

Spierenburg, Henk J. (1991). *The Buddhism of H. P. Blavatsky.* San Diego, CA: Point Lama Publications.

Stein, Rolf Alfred (1981) [1962]. *La civilisation tibétaine.* Paris: Le Sycomore. [*Tibetan Civilization.* London: Faber and Faber, 1972].

Stern (1997). "A Hero with a Nazi Stain." *Stern,* May 28, 1997.

Stoddard, Heather (1994). "Tibetan Publications and National Identity." Barnett, Robbie and Akiner, Shirin (eds.). *Resistance and Reform in Tibet,* pp. 121–56. London: Hurst and Co.

Stone, Donald (1978). "New Religious Consciousness and Personal Experience." *Sociological Analysis,* Vol. 39, No. 2, pp. 123–34.

Styles, Showell (1955). *The Lost Glacier.* London: Rupert Hart-Davis.

Taft, Julia V. (1999). "Prepared Statement by the Special Coordinator for Tibetan Issues before the House International Relations Committee." Washington: House International Relations Committee, March 11, 1999.

Tenzin (1993). "Speech by Comrade Tenzin." TAR Conference on External Propaganda Work Document No. 8, Regional Conference on External Propaganda Work, Beijing, March 11, 1993 (Internal Document). International Campaign for Tibet (ed.). *China's Public Relations Strategy on Tibet: Classified Documents from the Beijing Propaganda Conference.* Washington: International Campaign for Tibet.

Thevenet, Jacqueline (1980). *Le Lama d'occident.* Paris: Éditions Seghers.

Thomas Jr., Lowell (1950). *Out of This World.* New York, NY: Greystone Press.

Thurman, Robert A. F. (1985). "Tibet: Mystic Nation in Exile." *Parabola,* Vol. 10, No. 2, pp. 56–69.

—— (1995). *Essential Tibetan Buddhism.* San Francisco, CA: Harper.

—— (2001). "Critical Reflections on Donald Lopez's Prisoners of Shangri-la: Tibetan Buddhism and the West." *Journal of the American Academy of Religion,* Volume 69, No. 1, pp. 191–201.

Tibetan Bulletin *(1993).* "Statement Issued after a Meeting of European Parliamentarians in London, May 4, 1993." *Tibetan Bulletin,* July–August 1993.

—— (1994). "Eyewitnesses to History." *Tibetan Bulletin,* Dharamsala, November–December 1994.

TIN (Tibet Information Network) (1992). "Tibet Birth Control Regulations." *TIN News Update,* TIN, London, October 5, 1992.

—— (1996a) "Dalai Lama Photographs Banned from Monasteries—Dalai Lama 'No Longer a Religious Leader.'" *TIN News Update,* London, April 29, 1996.

—— (1996b). "Bombing in Sog County: 'Strike Hard' to Continue." *TIN News Update,* London, December 26, 1996.

—— (1999a). "Monks Arrested at Kirti after Major Protest." *TIN News Update,* London, January 18, 1999.

—— (1999b). "Tibetan Girls Raped by Police." *TIN News Update,* TIN, London, February 16, 1999.

—— (1999c). *Social Evils: Prostitution and Pornography in Lhasa.* TIN Briefing Paper. London: Tibet Information Network.

—— (2000). "Increased Restrictions on Birth of Children in Tibet." *TIN News Update,* London, February 9, 2000.

Toscano, Giuseppe (ed.) (1981ff.). *Opere tibetane di Ippolito Desideri S.J.* Rome: IsMEO.

TPPRC (Tibetan Parliamentary and Policy Research Center) (1997). *Indian Press on India-Tibet-China Relations: Selections from the Press.* New Delhi: TPPRC.

Trimondi, Victor and Trimondi, Victoria [Herbert and Mariana Röttgen] (1999). *Der Schatten des Dalai Lama.* Düsseldorf: Patmos.

Trungpa, Chögyam (1987) [1973]. *Cutting through Spiritual Materialism.* Boston, MA: Shambhala.

Tsering, Tashi (1984). "Gandhi: An Old Friend of Tibet." *Tibetan Review,* Vol. 19, No. 1, pp. 11–13, 23.

—— (1996). "How the Tibetans Have Regarded Themselves through the Ages." Dharamsala: Amnye Machen Institute.

Tucci, Giuseppe (1949). *Tibetan Painted Scrolls.* Rome: Libreria dello Stato.

—— (1956). *To Lhasa and Beyond.* Rome: Libreria dello Stato.

—— (1974). *Théorie et pratique du mandala*. Paris: Fayard.[*The Theory and Practice of the Mandala, with Special Reference to the Modern Psychology of the Subconscious*. London: Rider, 1961].

—— (1988). *The Religions of Tibet*. London: Routledge.

—— (1988–89). *Indo–Tibetica* (Śata-Piṭaka series 347–53). New Delhi: Aditya Prakashan.

Tung, Rosemarie Jones (1980). *A Portrait of Lost Tibet*. London: Thames and Hudson.

Tweed, Thomas A. (1992). *The American Encounter with Buddhism 1844–1912: Victorian Culture and the Limits of Dissent*. Bloomington: Indiana University Press.

Unkrig, W. A. (1926). "Aus den letzten Jahren des Lamaismus in Rußland." *Zeitschrift für Buddhismus*, München-Neubiberg: Benares Verlag.

UNPO (Unrepresented Nations and Peoples Organization) (1997). *China's Tibet: The World's Largest Remaining Colony*. The Hague: UNPO.

Unsworth, Walt (1991). *Everest*. London: Grafton Books.

UPI (United Press International) (1994). "China Releases Four Tibetan Prisoners." UPI, Beijing, November 6, 1994.

Uray, Gezay (1983). "Tibet's Connections with Nestorianism and Manicheism in the Eighth–Tenth Centuries." Steinkellner, Ernst and Tauscher, Helmut (eds.). *Contributions on Tibetan Language, History and Culture*, pp. 399–429. Vienna: Arbeitskreis für Tibetische und Buddhistische Studien, Universität Wien.

U.S. Department of State (1997). *China Country Report on Human Rights Practices for 1996*. Washington: Bureau of Democracy, Human Rights, and Labor.

U.S. Senate and Congress (1994). *Special Envoy for Tibet Act of 1994*. Washington: U.S. Senate and Congress.

van Walt van Praag, Michael (1987). *The Status of Tibet: History, Rights and Prospects in International Law*. Boulder, CO: Westview.

—— (1996). *Second International Conference of Tibet Support Groups*. Bonn: Friedrich Naumann Stiftung.

Vecsey, Christopher Thomas (1980). "American Indian Environmental Religions." Vecsey, Christopher Thomas and Venables, Robert W. (eds.). *American Indian Environments: Ecological Issues in Native American History*, pp. 1–37. Syracuse, NY: Syracuse University Press.

Vigoda, Marcy (1989). "Religious and Socio-Cultural Restraints on Environmental Degradation Among Tibetan Peoples—Myth or Reality?" *Tibet Journal*, Vol. 14, No. 4, pp. 17–44.

Waddell, L. Austine (1971) [1895]. *The Buddhism of Tibet, or Lamaism*. Cambridge: Heffer.

Waitz, Theodor (1859). *Anthropologie der Naturvölker.* Leipzig: Fleischer.

Waldenfels, Bernhard (1990). *Der Stachel des Fremden.* Frankfurt a.M.: Suhrkamp.

Walravens, Hartmut and Taube, Manfred (1992). *August Herrmann Francke und die Westhimalaya-Mission der Herrnhuter Brüdergemeine. Eine Bibliographie mit Standortnachweisen der tibetischen Drucke* (Verzeichnis der orientalischen Handschriften in Deutschland, Suppl. 34). Stuttgart: Franz Steiner.

Walzer, Michael (1996). *Lokale Kritik—globale Standards: Zwei Formen moralischer Auseinandersetzung.* Hamburg: Rotbuch Verlag. [*Thick and Thin: Moral Argument at Home and Abroad.* Notre Dame: University of Notre Dame Press, 1994].

Wang Lixiong (1999). "Tibet: PRC's Twenty-First Century Underbelly." *Beijing Zhanlue Yu Guanli,* pp. 21–33.

Washington, Peter (1993). *Madame Blavatsky's Baboon: Theosophy and the Emergence of the Western Guru.* London: Secker and Warburg.

Watts, Alan W. (1962). *The Joyous Cosmology: Adventures in the Chemistry of Consciousness.* New York, NY: Random House.

Webb, James (1974). *The Occult Underground.* La Salle, IL: Library Press/ Open Court.

—— (1976). *The Occult Establishment.* La Salle, IL: Library Press/Open Court.

—— (1988). "The Occult Establishment." Basil, Robert (ed.). *Not Necessarily the New Age: Critical Essays,* pp. 54–83. Buffalo, NY: Prometheus Books.

Weber, Max (1958). "The Sociology of the World Religions." Gerth, Hans H. and Mills, Charles Wright (eds. and trs.). *From Max Weber: Essays in Sociology.* New York, NY: Oxford University Press.

Weggel, Oskar (1982). "China und Tibet: wie Feuer und Holz." *China aktuell,* No. 12, pp. 744–60.

—— (1997). "Die politische Rechte und Linke im Meinungschaos um das Tibet-Problem." Dodin, Thierry and Räther, Heinz (eds.). *Mythos Tibet. Wahrnehmungen, Projektionen, Phantasien,* pp. 150–64. Cologne: DuMont.

Wei Jingsheng (1993). "Letters from Prison to Deng Xiaoping on the Tibetan Question." Translation, published by Tibet Press Watch, December 1993 (from the Internet).

Weigel, Sigrid (1987). "Die nahe Fremde—Das Territorium des 'Weiblichen' zum Verhältnis von 'Wilden' und 'Frauen' im Diskurs der Aufklärung." Köbner, Thomas and Pickerodt, Gerhart (eds.). *Die andere Welt, Studien zum Exotismus,* pp. 171–99. Frankfurt a.M.: Athenäum.

White, John Claude (1909). *Sikkim and Bhutan: Twenty-One Years on the North-East Frontier, 1887–1908*. London: Arnold.

Wickert, Erwin (1983). *Vom politischen Denken der Chinesen*. Wiesbaden: Steiner.

Wilby, Sorrel (1989). *Wombat and Emu Trekking in Tibet*. Melbourne: Macmillan.

Williamson, Margaret D. (1987). *Memoirs of a Political Officer's Wife in Tibet, Sikkim, and Bhutan*. London: Wisdom Publications.

Wills, Garry (1990). "Goodbye, Columbus." *New York Review of Books*, November 22, 1990, pp. 6–10.

Windshuttle, Keith (1994). *The Killing of History*. Sydney: Macleay Press.

Winkler, Daniel (1998). "Deforestation in Eastern Tibet." Clarke, Graham E. (ed.). *Development, Society and Environment in Tibet: Papers Presented at a Panel of the Seventh Seminar of the International Association for Tibetan Studies, Graz 1995*. Schloss Seggau 1995, Vol. 5, pp. 79–96. Vienna: Verlag der Österreichischen Akademie der Wissenschaften.

Winkler, Ken (1982, 1992). *Pilgrim of the Clear Light: The Biography of Dr. Walter Y. Evans-Wentz. Berkeley*, CA: Dawnfire Books.

—— (1990). *A Thousand Journeys: The Biography of Lama Anagarika Govinda*. Longmead: Element Books.

Witcombe, Rick Trader (1982). *The New Italian Cinema*. London: Seckler and Warburg.

Wolf, Frank (1997). "A Firsthand Look: Tibet—August 9–13, 1997: Statement by U.S. Representative Frank R. Wolf." Washington: International Campaign for Tibet (Published in *World Tibet Network News*, August 22, 1997).

Woodside, Lisa N. (1989). "New Age Spirituality: A Positive Contribution." Ferguson, Duncan S. (ed.). *New Age Spirituality: An Assessment*, pp. 145–68. Louisville, KY: Westminster/John Knox Press.

Wylie, Turrell (1959). "A Standard System of Tibetan Transcription." *Harvard Journal of Asiatic Studies*, Vol. 22, pp. 261–67.

Wyngaert, Anastasius van den (ed.) (1929). *Itinera et Relationes Fratrum Minorum Saeculi XIII et XIV* (Sinica Franciscana, 1). Firenze: Collegium S. Bonaventurae.

Xinhua (1996). "Chinese Magazine Article Accuses Dalai Lama of Supporting Leader of Aum Sect." March 8, 1996 (Summarizing an Article in *China's Tibet*, March 1996) (Published in translation in BBC SWB, FE/D2556/CNS 090396).

—— (1997a). "China to Develop Original Shangri-la into Tourist Spot." Kunming: Xinhua, September 15, 1997.

—— (1997b). "German Editor Says Dalai Lama's 'Propaganda' Is 'Untrue.'" Xinhua, Beijing, August 17, 1997.

—— (1999). "Australian Official 'Amazed' by Changes in Tibet." Xinhua, Beijing, September 17, 1999 (Published by BBC SWB, September 17, 1999).

Xizang Ribao (Tibet Daily) (1995). "What Does the Collusion between the Dalai and Asahara Shoko Show?" *Xizang Ribao,* November 14, 1995.

—— (1996). "No Mercy in 'Grim' Antiseparatist Struggle in Tibet." *Xizang Ribao,* Lhasa, May 10, 1996, p.1.

Ya Hanzhang (1991). *The Biographies of the Dalai Lamas.* Beijing: Foreign Languages Press.

Yauch, Adam (1996). "Testimony at Congressional Briefing on Human Rights in Tibet, June 24, 1996." Republished in *World Tibet Network News,* June 25, 1996.

Yeshi, Kim (1991). "The Tibetan View of the Environment." *Chö-Yang,* Vol. 4, pp. 264–69.

Yong Xuau and Dong Gao (n.d.) [1751]. *Huang Qing Zhigong tu,* Vol. 1.

Younghusband, Francis Edward (1985) [1910]. *India and Tibet.* Oxford: Oxford University Press.

Yuthok, Karma Gelek (1992). "The Tibetan Perception of the Environment." Paper presented at the Sixth Seminar of the International Association of Tibetan Studies, Fagernes, August 21–28, 1992.

Yuthok, Kunzang (1994). "Trickle-Down Human Rights Has Failed: It Is Time to Revoke China's MFN Status." *Seattle Post-Intelligencer,* March 16, 1994 (Published in *Canada Tibet News,* March 16, 1994).

Zeidler (1745). Universal-Lexicon, Vol. 44. Leipzig.

Zhou Bian (1996). "Wahrung der staatlichen Einheit—Grundlage der Dialoge." *Beijing Rundschau,* No. 35, p. 24.

Zirkoff, Boris de (ed.) (1950–91). *H. P. Blavatsky: Collected Writings.* Vols. 1–14. Wheaton, IL: Theosophical Publishing House.

LIST OF CONTRIBUTORS

ROBERT BARNETT (United Kingdom) is a resident scholar at Columbia University in New York and a founding director of the Tibet Information Network (TIN), London.

PETER BISHOP (Australia) is associate professor in the School of Communication, Information, and the New Media at the University of South Australia, Magill, where he teaches communication and cultural studies. He has been researching the Western engagement with Tibet and its religion for about twenty-five years and is currently interested in the changing notions of place in the contemporary era of technoculture. His publications include *The Myth of Shangri-la* (1989), *Dreams of Power* (1993), and numerous articles on the relationship between Tibet and Western media and popular culture.

JOHN BRAY (United Kingdom) is an independent scholar based in London. His research focuses on Ladakh, Bhutan, and Burma. His publications include *Bibliography of Ladakh* (1988), *Burma: The Politics of Constructive Engagement* (1995), and a series of essays on contemporary international politics and the history of Ladakh and the Tibetan border areas.

GRAHAM E. CLARKE (United Kingdom) (d. 1998) was coordinator of anthropology and development at Queen Elizabeth House in Oxford. A social anthropologist, he specialized in developmental issues, conducting field research in Nepal and Tibet. He was a member of the Panam Project Identification Mission of the European Community in Tibet.

LODEN SHERAB DAGYAB RINPOCHE (Germany) is a Geshe Lharampa and researcher at the Institute of Central Asian Studies at Bonn University. A reincarnate lama, he is spiritual and secular head of the province of Dagyab in Eastern Tibet. He fled to India in 1959, and has lived in Germany since 1963. His publications include *Bod brda tshig mdzod chen mo* (*Tibetan-Tibetan Dictionary*, 1966), *Tibetan Religious Art* (1977), and *Buddhist Symbols in Tibetan Buddhism* (1996). He is the spiritual director of several Buddhist centers in Germany.

THIERRY DODIN (Germany/France) is a researcher at the Institute of Central Asian Studies, Bonn University. His subjects of research are Tibetan popular culture, recent history and cultural change in the Himalayas, and the politics of the Tibetan cultural area. He is the author of a series of essays on these subjects and coeditor of *Recent Research on Ladakh VII* (1997). He is a member of both the Permanent Committee of the International Association for Ladakh Studies and of the board of the Tibet Information Network (TIN), London.

PETER H. HANSEN (United States), is associate professor of history in the Department of Humanities and Arts at Worcester Polytechnic Institute, Worcester, Massachusetts. He works on the history of mountaineering and the role of mass media in the colonial and postcolonial eras in Tibet.

THOMAS HEBERER (Germany) is professor of East Asian politics at the Institute of East Asian Studies at Gerhard-Mercator University at Duisburg, Germany. He worked as a lecturer and translator at the Foreign Language Press in Beijing and has conducted field research in China and Vietnam on issues of ethnic minorities and rural and social change. Author of many books and articles, his recent publications include *Entrepreneurs As Strategic Groups: On the Social and Political Function of Entrepreneurs in China and Vietnam* (2001) and *China's Rural Society under Transformation: Urbanization and Socioeconomic Change in the Countryside* (coauthor W. Taubmann, 1998). He is also author, coauthor, or editor of books on the issue of nationality in China, corruption in China, Chinese rock music, Mao Zedong, and the political participation of women in East Asia.

P. JEFFREY HOPKINS (United States) is professor of Tibetan and religious studies in the Department of Religious Studies at the University of Virginia, Charlottesville. He has written many books and essays on Tibetan philosophy and a textbook of Tibetan colloquial language and has translated several Tibetan religious works. He served as the Dalai Lama's translator for many years.

TONI HUBER (New Zealand) lectures on Tibetan studies in the Department of Religious Studies at Victoria University in Wellington. He is the author of several scholarly books and numerous articles about Tibetan society, culture, and history.

RUDOLF KASCHEWSKY (Germany) is a research fellow at the Institute of Central Asian Studies at Bonn University. His fields of study are Indology, Tibetan and Mongolian studies, theology, and Semitic languages. His publications include books on the life of Tsongkhapa, the Tibetan epics, and Tibetan Buddhist rituals, as well as essays on Tibetan grammar and Mongolian Buddhist terminology.

FRANK J. KOROM (United States) is assistant professor of religion and anthropology at Boston University. He is the author and editor of five books, including two volumes on Tibet, entitled *Tibetan Culture in the Diaspora* (1997) and *Constructing Tibetan Culture* (1997). He is also the editor of the *Religious Studies Review*. He is currently completing a manuscript entitled *Hosay Trinidad: Muharram Performances in Indo-Caribbean Diaspora*.

PER KVAERNE (Norway) is professor of history of religions and Tibetology in the Department of Culture Studies at the University of Oslo. He has written many books and essays on Tibetan studies, most notably on Bon religion. He is a member of the Norwegian Academy of Science and Letters, editor of the journal Acta Orientalia, and secretary of the International Association for Tibetan Studies.

DONALD S. LOPEZ, JR. (United States) is the Carl W. Belser Professor of Buddhist and Tibetan Studies in the Department of Asian Languages and Cultures at the University of Michigan, Ann Arbor. His recent publications include *Curators of the Buddha: The Study of Buddhism under Colonialism* (1995), *Buddhism in Practice* (1995), *Elaborations on Emptiness* (1996), *Religions of Tibet in Practice* (1997), *Prisoners of Shangri-La: Tibetan Buddhism and the West* (1998), and *The Story of Buddhism* (2001).

ALEX MCKAY (New Zealand) is a historian and a research fellow at the School of Oriental and African Studies, London. His publications include *Tibet and the British Raj: The Frontier Cadre, 1904–1947* (1997), and *Pilgrimage in Tibet* (1998).

HELENA NORBERG-HODGE (United Kingdom) is a freelance writer and head of both the Ladakh Project and the International Society for Ecology and Culture. She founded the Ladakh Ecological Development Group, for which she received the Alternative Nobel Prize. Her publications include *Ancient Futures: Learning from Ladakh* (1991) and a dictionary of the Ladakhi language.

JAMYANG NORBU (India/United States) is cofounder and codirector of the Amnye Machen Institute for the Study of Neglected Aspects of Tibetan Culture in Dharamsala, India. He is the cofounder of Tibetan Youth Congress, and former director of the Tibetan Institute of Performing Arts, Dharamsala. His publications include *Warriors of Tibet* (1987), *Sherlock Holmes the Missing Years* (2001), and numerous political essays. He was formerly co-editor of the Tibetan language newspaper *Mangtso,* and is currently the editor of the magazine *Lungta.*

POUL PEDERSEN (Denmark) is associate professor in the Department of Ethnography and Social Anthropology at Aarhus University in Denmark. An anthropologist, he conducts fieldwork in South India and Ladakh. His publications include (with Toni Huber) "Meteorological Knowledge and Environmental Ideas in Traditional and Modern Societies: The Case of Tibet" (*Journal of the Royal Anthropological Insti-*

tute 2, 1997) and *Ladakh: Culture, History and Development between Himalaya and Karakoram* (1999), which he coedited with K. B. Bertelsen and M. v. Beek.

HEINZ RÄTHER (Germany) is a research fellow at the Institute of Anthropology at Ulm University. Over the years he has studied Tibetology, comparative religion, and Indian art history. He is coeditor of *Recent Research on Ladakh VII* (1997). He currently works on Ladakhi pilgrimage, Tibetan art, cultural change in the Himalayas, and social and political issues in the Tibetan cultural area.

ELLIOT SPERLING (United States) is associate professor of Tibetan Studies in the Department of Central Eurasian Studies at the University of Indiana in Bloomington. A historian, he has written many essays on Tibetan history and Sino-Tibetan relations.

HEATHER STODDARD (France) is maitre de conference at the Institut National des Langues et Civilisations Orientales (INALCO), where she is responsible for the Tibetan section. She is maitre de recherche in the Department of Tibetan Language and Culture at the Centre National de la Recherche Scientifique (CNRS) in Paris. She has conducted extensive fieldwork in Tibet. Her publications include *Early Sino-Tibetan Art* (1975) and *Le Mendiant de l'Amdo* (1986). She is the founding director of the Shalu Association for Tibetan Cultural Heritage.

INDEX

ABOUT WISDOM

WISDOM PUBLICATIONS, a not-for-profit publisher, is dedicated to making available authentic Buddhist works from all the major traditions as well as related cultural studies. We publish translations of the sutras and tantras, commentaries and teachings of past and contemporary Buddhist masters, and original works by the world's leading Buddhist scholars.

To learn more about Wisdom, or to browse our books online, visit our website at wisdompubs.org.

If you'd like to receive our mail-order catalog, please write to:
Wisdom Publications
199 Elm Street, Somerville, Massachusetts 02144 USA
Telephone: (617) 776-7416 • Fax: (617) 776-7841
Email: sales@wisdompubs.org • www.wisdompubs.org

Wisdom Publications is a nonprofit, charitable 501(c)(3) organization and affiliated with the Foundation for the Preservation of the Mahayana Tradition (FPMT).